THE IMAGE OF THE ENEMY

THE
IMAGE
OF THE
ENEMY

INTELLIGENCE ANALYSIS OF ADVERSARIES SINCE 1945

PAUL MADDRELL
Editor

Georgetown University Press / Washington, DC

Library of Congress Cataloging-in-Publication Data

The image of the enemy : intelligence analysis of adversaries since 1945 / Paul Maddrell, editor.
    pages cm
  Includes bibliographical references and index.
  ISBN 978-1-62616-239-6 pb : alk. paper—ISBN 978-1-62616-238-9 hc : alk. paper—ISBN 978-1-62616-240-2 eb
  1. Intelligence service—Case studies.   I. Maddrell, Paul, editor.
JF1525.I6I43   2015
327.12—dc23

                                                           2015001488

16 15   9 8 7 6 5 4 3 2   First printing

Printed in the United States of America

Cover design by Beth Schlenoff
Cover image courtesy of the U.S. National Archives

*This book is dedicated to the memory
of the late Professor Ernest R. May,
an outstanding historian and pioneer
in the study of intelligence.*

CONTENTS

ABBREVIATIONS

BAFT: Bureau of Alcohol, Firearms, and Tobacco (United States)
BND: Bundesnachrichtendienst (West German Federal Intelligence Service)
BNE: Board of National Estimates (United States)
CBW: chemical/biological weapon
CDU/CSU: Christlich-Demokratische Union / Christlich-Soziale Union (Christian Democratic Union / Christian Social Union, West Germany)
CGA-OT: coordinator of government activities in the Occupied Territories (Israel)
CGS: Chief of the General Staff (Pakistan)
CIA: Central Intelligence Agency (United States)
CIMP: Commission of Inquiry on Missing Persons (Pakistan)
Comecon: Council for Mutual Economic Assistance
CPGB: Communist Party of Great Britain
CPSU: Communist Party of the Soviet Union
CSCE: Conference on Security and Cooperation in Europe
CTC: Counterterrorism Center (of the CIA's DO)
DCI: director of Central Intelligence (the director of the CIA who from 1947 to 2005 also presided over the entire US intelligence community and coordinated its work)
DG: Director-General
DGB: Deutscher Gewerkschaftsbund (German Trade Union Confederation, West Germany)
DI: Directorate of Intelligence (of the CIA)
DIA: Defense Intelligence Agency (United States)
DNI: director of National Intelligence (who since 2005 has presided over the entire US intelligence community and coordinated its work)
DO: Directorate of Operations (of the CIA)
EEC: European Economic Community (also known as the EC: European Community)
EIG: Egyptian Islamic Group
EIJ: Egyptian Islamic Jihad

EU: European Union
FBI: Federal Bureau of Investigation (United States)
FDP: Freie Demokratische Partei (Free Democratic Party, West Germany)
FRG: Federal Republic of Germany (otherwise known as West Germany)
FSF: Federal Security Force (Pakistan)
GDR: German Democratic Republic (otherwise known as East Germany)
Gestapo: Secret State Police (of Germany under Nazi rule)
GHQ: General Headquarters (Pakistan)
GRU: Main Intelligence Directorate (of the Soviet army)
GSOTG/GSFG: Group of Soviet Occupation Troops in Germany; later known
    as the Group of Soviet Forces in Germany
HM: Hizb-ul Mujahideen (Party of Holy Warriors, Pakistan and Kashmir)
HUMINT: human intelligence
HVA: Hauptverwaltung Aufklärung (Main Intelligence Directorate, Ministry
    for State Security, East Germany)
IB: Intelligence Bureau (Pakistan)
IC: US intelligence community
ICBM: intercontinental ballistic missile
IDF: Israel Defense Forces
IMF: International Monetary Fund
IMINT: imagery intelligence
INLA: Irish National Liberation Army (United Kingdom)
INR: Bureau of Intelligence (of the State Department of the United States)
IRTPA: Intelligence Reform and Terrorism Prevention Act (United States)
ISI: Inter-Services Intelligence Directorate (Pakistan)
JEM: Jaish-e Mohamed (The Army of Mohammed, Pakistan and Kashmir)
JIC: Joint Intelligence Committee (United Kingdom)
KGB: Komitet Gosudarstvennoi Bezopastnosti (Committee for State Security,
    Soviet Union)
KIT: Key Intelligence Topics (Israel)
LeT: Lashkar-e Toiba (The Army of the Righteous, Pakistan and Kashmir)
LOC: Line of Control (between India and Pakistan)
MAD: mutually assured destruction
MfS/Stasi: Ministerium für Staatssicherheit (Ministry for State Security, East
    Germany)
M/H: Memorandum for Holders (United States)
MI: Directorate for Military Intelligence (Pakistan)
MID/AMAN: Military Intelligence Directorate (Israel)
MIRV: multiple independently targetable reentry vehicle
Mossad: Institute for Intelligence and Special Duties (Israeli foreign intelligence
    service)
MQM: Muhajir Qaumi Mahaz (Muhajir Qaumi Movement, Pakistan)

NACTA: National Counter Terrorism Authority (Pakistan)
NATO: North Atlantic Treaty Organization
NCTC: National Counterterrorism Center (United States)
  ESA: Office of Near East and South Asian Analysis (of the CIA)
NFIB: National Foreign Intelligence Board (United States)
NCO: Noncommissioned Officers
NGO: nongovernmental organization
NIC: National Intelligence Council (United States)
NIE: National Intelligence Estimate (United States)
NIO: national intelligence officer (United States)
NSA: National Security Agency (United States)
NSC: National Security Council (United States; also Pakistan)
NVA: Nationale Volksarmee (National People's Army, East Germany)
OECD: Organization for Economic Cooperation and Development
ONE: Office of National Estimates (United States)
Org.: Gehlen Organization (West Germany)
OTA: Office of Terrorism Analysis (of the CIA's CTC)
PA: Palestinian Authority
PDB: President's Daily Brief (United States)
PFIAB: President's Foreign Intelligence Advisory Board (United States)
PGU: First Chief Directorate (of the KGB)
PHOTINT: photographic intelligence
PIRA: Provisional Irish Republican Army (United Kingdom)
PLO: Palestine Liberation Organization
PPP: Pakistan People's Party
RAF: Red Army Faction (West Germany)
RAW: Research and Analysis Wing (India)
RSHA: Reichssicherheitshauptamt (Reich Security Main Office, Nazi
    Germany)
RUC: Royal Ulster Constabulary (United Kingdom)
RYaN/VRYaN: Nuclear-Missile Attack / Surprise Nuclear-Missile Attack
SALT I: Interim Agreement and Protocol on Limitation of Strategic Offensive
    Weapons
SALT II: Treaty on the Limitation of Strategic Offensive Arms
SAPMO-BA: Stiftung Archiv der Parteien und Massenorganisationen der
    DDR im Bundesarchiv (Foundation Archive of the Parties and Mass
    Organizations of the GDR in the Federal Archive, Germany)
SBZ: Sowjetische Besatzungszone (Soviet Occupation Zone of Germany)
SD: Sicherheitsdienst (Security Service, of the SS, Nazi Germany)
SDI: Strategic Defense Initiative
SED: Sozialistische Einheitspartei Deutschlands (Socialist Unity Party, East
    Germany)

SEIB: Senior Executive Intelligence Brief (United States)
Shabak / Shin Bet: General Security Service (Israel)
SHAPE: Supreme Headquarters Allied Powers Europe
SIGINT: signals intelligence
SIS: Secret Intelligence Service (United Kingdom)
SNIE: Special National Intelligence Estimate (United States)
SOVA: Office of Soviet Analysis (of the CIA)
SPD: Sozialdemokratische Partei Deutschlands (Social Democratic Party, West
    Germany)
SS: Schutz Staffel (Protection Staff, Nazi Germany)
SVR: Foreign Intelligence Service (Russia)
S&TI: scientific and technological intelligence
TECHINT: technical intelligence
ULFA: United Liberation Front of Assam (India)
USSR: Union of Soviet Socialist Republics
WB: World Bank
WMD: weapon of mass destruction
ZAIG: Zentrale Auswertungs- und Informationsgruppe (Central Evaluation
    and Information Group, Ministry for State Security, East Germany)

Introduction

Achieving Objective, Policy-Relevant Intelligence

PAUL MADDRELL

THIRTY YEARS HAVE PASSED since Ernest May published his influential collection *Knowing One's Enemies*, which examined how well intelligence services and policymakers assessed intelligence on their adversaries before the outbreak of the two world wars. Since the Second World War all the Great Powers have understood the importance of intelligence to their security. During the Cold War immense intelligence communities in both East and West, spending unprecedented sums of money, collected vast quantities of intelligence and reported on it to their political leaderships. *Knowing One's Enemies* was published when the Cold War was still being waged; indeed, the editor's aim was to draw lessons from history that might help prevent a third world war.[1] Since the waging of the Cold War relied so heavily on intelligence, the time has come to consider how well this intelligence was analyzed by analysts and understood by policymakers.

Moreover, international relations since 1945 have been plagued both by interstate conflicts and by terrorist challenges to the state. The Cold War was only one instance—though one global in its reach—of a bitter interstate conflict that presented policymakers and intelligence analysts with the difficult problem of both understanding and fighting their foe. Understanding one's enemy calls for a cooler head and a more objective point of view than fighting spirit allows. Pakistan's military rulers and Israel's political leaders—both natural fighters— have often been more aggressive than was reasonable in the light of the intelligence available to them, as this book demonstrates.

The world over, terrorist foes have proved to be a particularly persistent threat to state security. The State of Israel was born as the Cold War was beginning, yet Israel has still not defeated its terrorist enemies and has anticipated terrorist attacks better than it has foreseen the development of Palestinian opinion. The independent states of Pakistan and India were also born as the Cold War was starting, but the conflict between them, particularly over Kashmir, continues to this day. It fuses nuclear, conventional military, political, and terrorist dangers in a way reminiscent of the Cold War. This collection shows that Pakistan's rulers and intelligence agencies have often displayed a poor understanding of India. The grievances of Northern Ireland's republican movement against the United Kingdom predated the Cold War and gave rise to a decades-long campaign of terrorist violence that is still not quite over. The grievances of Salafi jihadist terrorists against the United States are of more recent date but will evidently threaten the United States and Americans throughout the world for a long time to come.

The intelligence dimension of the Cold War was an example of a broader phenomenon of interstate hostility; its lessons apply to many other cases. Today's terrorist threats present challenges different from interstate rivalry with which policymakers and intelligence agencies will continue to struggle—chiefly terrorism's propensity to develop very quickly, the obscurity of both the intentions and capabilities of terrorist networks (powerful states' capabilities are not so obscure), the networks' changing relationship with a wider community, their appeal to young people capable of rapid and often undetectable radicalization, and the fact that policymakers rarely have direct dealings with them.[2]

Two Key Issues: Analytical Error and the Reception of Intelligence by Policymakers

As far as analysts are concerned, the key issue that persistently arises is how to prevent analytical error and so maintain policymakers' confidence in the analysts' reports. The efforts of the US intelligence community (IC) to avoid mistakes long predated May's book. The end of the Cold War spurred a further wave of reform. The collapse of the Soviet Union and Soviet Bloc in 1989–91, confounding expectations of only a few years previously, and analysts' discovery after the Gulf War of 1991 of their underestimation of Saddam Hussein's project to develop an Iraqi atomic bomb encouraged the Central Intelligence Agency (CIA) in 1993–94 to review the analytical methods of its Directorate of Intelligence (DI). Analysts tried to make their analyses more convincing and transparent. Misjudgments in the late 1990s, such as the DI's failure to warn of India's nuclear tests in 1998, increased concern that US intelligence analysts made avoidable mistakes and were too unimaginative. They made false assumptions, relied too much on slender evidence, failed to consider sufficiently alternative interpretations of the conduct and intentions of foreign states, and often assumed that they would behave as the United States did. The attention that analyses receive from the congressional oversight committees and, when leaks occur, from the media as well may also encourage excessive caution.[3]

Al-Qaeda's attacks on the World Trade Center and the Pentagon in September 2001 and the IC's gross overestimation of Iraq's weapon of mass destruction (WMD) capabilities in 2002–3 led to further reform of intelligence analysis. The attacks heightened awareness of how easily and naturally misjudgment arises from human beings' cognitive shortcomings and encouraged the use of analytical techniques designed to compensate for them. The 9/11 Commission was critical of a lack of imagination on the part of analysts and poor sharing of intelligence among agencies.[4] Proper analytical standards were set out in the Intelligence Reform and Terrorism Prevention Act of 2004 (IRTPA). The IC now stresses even more than before that analysis is a task that should be performed collaboratively, so that alternatives to a leading hypothesis are considered. Analysis is structured, thoroughly footnoted, and made transparent so that it is open to criticism.[5] Collaborative analysis is intended to guard against "groupthink" by ensuring that alternative interpretations are thoroughly considered.[6] All this may amount to no more than a heightened emphasis on cooperation and the need to consider alternatives. It is open to the objection that, faced with a mass of ambiguous and often contradictory information, every analyst needs a mental model to make sense of it.[7] Attempting to undermine these mental models may either be impossible or may lead to analyses too indecisive to be useful. Moreover, collaboration depends on groups and so may encourage, rather than undermine, groupthink.

There has been much research into the causes of mistakes in analysis. Richards Heuer's *Psychology of Intelligence Analysis*, published in 1999, has proved influential in prompting efforts to develop better analytical methods. Heuer's findings, which chiefly concern intelligence analysts and rely heavily on cognitive psychology, confirm those of May, which relate to both policymakers and analysts and are based on the historical record. The two men stress the same flaws in human beings' cognitive processes: the tendency to make evidence more coherent and rational than it is; the tendency to overestimate one's enemy, considering him to be more rational than he is; and the tendency of the human mind to look more for evidence that confirms existing beliefs than evidence that conflicts with them. Both men regard the chief cause of misjudgment to be the application of inappropriate mindsets, or mental models, to the evidence (May uses the term "presumptions").[8] Both men stress the need to keep presumptions under review. Both point to the consistent failure, on the part of both policymakers and analysts, to see a situation as the target state sees it.[9] Robert Jervis reached the same conclusions about policymakers in his book *Perception and Misperception in International Politics*.[10]

Another persistent issue is the failure of policymakers to understand or make use of intelligence. The present collection addresses this issue as well. Richard

Betts has argued that the main instances of surprise result from the failure of policymakers, not analysts, to understand intelligence. "Intelligence failure is political and psychological more often than organizational," he wrote in a famous article in 1978.[11] However, he did not in that article examine instances of this, nor has anyone yet undertaken a thorough study of the Cold War looking to see how well policymakers understood intelligence. This collection does that and finds much support for Betts's argument.

Raymond Garthoff, opening the collection, shows how Soviet leaders during the Cold War were more swayed by their ideological convictions about the United States, their contacts with American presidents, pressure from bureaucratic interests, and their own traits of character than by intelligence. Indeed, the Soviet political system discouraged any proper analysis of the United States. Turning to the United States, Ben Fischer demonstrates that the authors of National Intelligence Estimates, in the last twenty years of the Cold War, set themselves high standards of objectivity in their analysis of the Soviet Union's international behavior but lacked much-needed information and tended to "mirror-image" Soviet policy in ways that reflected American policy.

The division of Germany contributed to the outbreak of the Cold War; the country's reunification helped to end it. How well the leaderships of the two German states understood intelligence on one another is, therefore, an important theme of Cold War history. Paul Maddrell examines both the analysis—or, more accurately, the communist substitute for it, which was mere reporting—of intelligence on West Germany by the East German Stasi's foreign intelligence service, the Main Intelligence Directorate (Hauptverwaltung Aufklärung, or HVA), and the reception of that intelligence by East Germany's communist leaders.[12] Matthias Uhl then studies analysis of intelligence on the German Democratic Republic (GDR) and the Soviet Bloc by the West German Federal Intelligence Service (Bundesnachrichtendienst, or BND) in four key Cold War crises. All four chapters rely on important new sources, chiefly declassified records.

Alongside the Cold War ran bitter regional conflicts in Israel-Palestine, the Indian subcontinent, and Northern Ireland. Two of these continue to this day; the communal strife in Northern Ireland also continues, though in less grave a form. The time has also come to consider how well these threats—chiefly terrorist ones—have been understood. Eunan O'Halpin analyzes the attitudes of British policymakers to the Troubles in Northern Ireland in their early years, including their attitude toward intelligence. Tamir Libel and Shlomo Shpiro consider both the Israeli intelligence community's understanding of Palestinian terrorism since 1948 and Israeli leaders' reception of intelligence. Julian Richards concentrates on policymakers, examining the mentality of Pakistan's military rulers and the Inter-Services Intelligence Directorate since the state's foundation in 1947. Finally, Mark Stout turns attention back to intelligence analysis as he studies the understanding of Al-Qaeda and jihadist terrorism that has developed in the US intelligence community since 1989.

The present collection is timely because historians have much better access to the records of many intelligence services than they did thirty years ago, though they still have no access to the archives of others.[13] The collection exploits important sources that have become available only since the Cold War ended. It breaks new ground in the case studies it employs, many of which are very difficult to research into and are little discussed in the academic literature. The need for a study of intelligence analysis since 1945 is great, since leading writers on intelligence bemoan how small the academic literature on analysis is.[14] The existing literature also concentrates, as far as the Cold War is concerned, on case studies of analytical error, the outstanding ones being American analysts' failure to warn of the deployment of Soviet nuclear missiles in Cuba in 1962 and various instances of surprise attack, such as North Korea's invasion of South Korea in June 1950 and the outbreak of the Yom Kippur War in October 1973.[15] The present collection also answers calls for a comparative study of the performance of the intelligence communities of East and West.[16]

The collection goes beyond the works of Jervis, May, and Heuer in stressing the role of ideology in generating misperceptions of other states (Jervis and Heuer were concerned with the influence of cognitive psychology on perceptions, while ideology was a minor theme of May's book). While histories of the Cold War abound with discussions of the influence of ideology on the decision making of the two sides' leaders, its interaction with intelligence is a neglected topic.[17] Owing to the size of the subjects they consider and sometimes severe restrictions on access to government records, all nine authors in this collection have been selective in their approach to their chosen topics.

"Politicization"

Intelligence estimates have to consider both an enemy's capabilities and his intentions (or "proclivities," as Ernest May more generally described them). May suggested three tests of an intelligence estimate's quality. First, in relation to both matters it should ask the right questions, which he defined as "the questions, right answers to which could be useful guides to action." The most important estimates needed to ask the big questions, on which key presumptions depended. Second, estimates should be accurate. Third, they should reach conclusions acceptable to policymakers since they would be useless if they could not influence their readers.[18]

The main point the collection makes is that since 1945, most of the intelligence agencies discussed here—though not all—have tried to produce assessments that meet all three of these criteria. The intelligence services of communist states did not ask the right questions because they were not allowed to.

The collection makes clear time and again that the character of a government inevitably affects the nature and quality of its intelligence agencies' reporting. It is necessary to distinguish here between intelligence analysis in most Western states, where analysts are expected to be objective, and communist states, whose intelligence agencies were not permitted to report objectively.

In the former, a mild form of "politicization" is natural since analysts have to make their information acceptable to policymakers. To do so, they have to show that their conclusions are significant for policymaking. The more significant their analyses become the more they will be seen as "politicized" by groups within the decision-making process. The simple fact of significance for policy can cause an analysis to be seen as "politicized." As this collection shows, analysts are also influenced to some extent by the views, policies, and military doctrines of the decision makers they serve, as well as by the interests of the government of which they are a part. Seeing relations with the target state from the policymakers' viewpoint, analysts can come to share their mindset (or part of it). Lawrence Freedman calls this a shared "adversary image," which he defines as "a set of coherent views over what can reasonably be expected" from an adversary.[19] He made the point about the relationship between the US government and its intelligence analysts, but it also applies to the communist regimes. Teamwork tends naturally toward groupthink. It may be a subconscious process. Since the military prizes teamwork and hierarchy so much, the pressure toward groupthink is particularly strong in military intelligence organizations. Analysts, whether civilian or military, do not want to present intelligence that policymakers will reject out of hand because it conflicts with the rationale for existing policies. This collection demonstrates that policymakers have a persistent tendency to discount intelligence they receive. They do so because it conflicts with fixed assumptions about their enemies, personal experience, or the rationale for policy. They also do so because they regard the intelligence analyses as reflecting bureaucratic self-interest or as ways of influencing them to pursue particular policies.

Analysts are also prone to the same cognitive errors as policymakers. The most important of these, as writers such as May, Jervis, and Heuer have explained, are the tendency to regard one's enemy as more rational and centralized than he is and a tendency to overestimate rather than underestimate him.

In these circumstances, "politicization" is a misnomer. "Governmentalization" might be a better term. What really takes place is that policy and the government's thinking color intelligence as the latter seeks to make itself relevant to the former. This can occur without the analysts' objectivity being compromised.[20] It falls far short of deliberate distortion of intelligence so that it supports a particular policy. The most strident allegations of politicization have been made about analyses that related to political issues of the highest importance, such as Soviet strategic objectives (in the mid-1970s) and whether Iraq, in 2001–3, represented a threat to the United States.[21]

More was unacceptable to communist leaders than to those of democratic states. Their intelligence agencies could therefore not report objectively; politicization became severe. Communist leaders had difficulty tolerating information that criticized their policies or challenged their legitimacy. Criticism could not be constructive; it was deeply subversive since it implied that Marxism-Leninism was wrong and not as "scientific" as it claimed to be. They could not even tolerate independent thinking. Consequently, analysis was degraded to mere reporting of intelligence. The communist intelligence services did not achieve the independent thinking expected of American analysts. Raymond Garthoff demonstrates that the reporting of the principal Soviet foreign intelligence service, the First Chief Directorate of the KGB (Komitet Gosudarstvennoi Bezopastnosti, or Committee for State Security), was deliberately cautious and intended to give no support for policy change. Information that the Soviet leader would not like was withheld from him. As léader, Leonid Brezhnev was supplied with flattering exaggerations of the impact of his speeches. The intelligence provided served the interests of the intelligence agencies concerned and of their ally, the military-industrial complex. The military intelligence supplied consistently made the case for further weapons development and high defense spending. Mikhail Gorbachev was so incensed by this biased and self-serving intelligence that he rebuked his intelligence chiefs for submitting it to him and discounted their reports.

Paul Maddrell shows that, in the GDR's case, the HVA was more willing than the KGB to supply unpalatable information to the regime's leaders. However, this information was reported as having been spoken by West German politicians or contained in West German government reports; the HVA refrained from providing its own analysis of foreign developments. The information it supplied was largely factual in character, and the leaders were left free to disregard it or impose their own analysis. They usually did one or the other. The HVA made no attempt to challenge their misperceptions, which were often severely deluded. Indeed, the HVA's own reporting on foreign economic developments was distorted by a crude, mistaken Marxist understanding of economics that can only have encouraged the leaders' belief that the Western economies had profound problems and communism would ultimately triumph.

Intelligence "analysts" in communist states were not analysts at all but newsmen. They did not try to achieve an understanding of foreign events independent of that of the communist regimes they served. Nor, as a rule, did they make forecasts or prepare long-term analyses of trends. Instead, they summarized incoming information. In American terminology, they provided current intelligence (even though they were well-suited to providing estimative intelligence since they obtained numerous policy documents from ministries and international organizations). As a rule, they only supplied an analysis of a long-term trend or a forecast if one were contained in the information they were summarizing. They passed on news rather than understanding.

Intelligence performed better in the democratic states than the communist ones. One reason for this was that analysts were expected to think for themselves. This automatically gave them more weight in government: The government leaders were presented with ideas with which they had to engage. Most is known about the performance of intelligence in the United States. The US intelligence community tried harder than the communist intelligence services to turn intelligence into a usable understanding of foreign developments. The principal Soviet foreign intelligence service had a very small intelligence assessment staff during Josef Stalin's rule; its main task was to pass on information. As Raymond Garthoff shows, for intelligence assessment the Soviet leadership relied heavily throughout the Cold War on bodies outside the intelligence community, particularly the Party Central Committee, the Foreign and Defense Ministries, and academic institutions. These academic institutions in the Union of Soviet Socialist Republics (USSR) were, in practice, emanations of the Communist Party. The fact that the party played such a prominent role in assessment guaranteed ideologically biased conclusions. Yuri Andropov expanded the KGB's intelligence assessment staff in the 1970s partly to exert influence over Soviet policy. However, in the 1970s and 1980s the ratio of analysts to operations officers in the KGB was 1:10, whereas in the CIA it was 1:1.

American intelligence analysts also had a wider responsibility than their communist counterparts. First, they considered the significance of new developments for national policy and pointed out opportunities for action. Second, they gave warning of attack and of dangerous situations. Lastly, they prepared longer-term analyses of important political, economic, scientific, and military trends.[22] As Ben Fischer emphasizes, their job was very much to forecast Soviet international behavior. They followed Sherman Kent's prescription that the job of intelligence was to "perceive the statics, the dynamics, and the potentials of other countries; . . . [to] perceive the established things, the presently going-on things, and probable things of the future."[23] They were scholars who tried to convey understanding.

Consequently, intelligence analysis in the United States was far more sophisticated than in the Soviet Bloc. May, Heuer, and Jervis all agree that a common cause of misperception in international affairs is the tendency of political leaders to see what they expect to see and to interpret information consistently with beliefs they already hold. They argue that the job of intelligence agencies is to present policymakers with alternative interpretations. During the Cold War, the US intelligence agencies did this far better than their communist counterparts. They frequently presented policymakers with viewpoints with which they disagreed. For example, the Nixon administration thought CIA assessments of the aims of Soviet antiballistic missile development too moderate. The Carter administration considered CIA analyses of Soviet policy toward Poland and Afghanistan too alarmist.[24]

Moreover, in the United States an effort was made to reconcile conflicting perceptions and form them into an agreed view. That is what National Intelligence Estimates represented. By contrast, in the communist states perceptions and practices were confused and contradictory. The West's ("imperialism's") capabilities were both over- and underestimated. It was seen as the cause of all dissent in the communist world; its subversive capability was greatly overestimated. However, its economic vitality was underestimated because capitalism's tendency toward self-destructive crisis was exaggerated. Despite the appeal of the West German lifestyle for East Germans, Hermann Axen, the Central Committee secretary responsible for international relations, insisted in the 1980s that the GDR wielded more influence over the Federal Republic than the latter did over it. The US intelligence community achieved both more diversity of view and more agreement.

Overall, intelligence assessment was better in the democracies. National Intelligence Estimates may have had no effect on policy, but at least they asked the right questions, pointed out opportunities for action, and gave policymakers the assurance of an agreed view.[25] They reflected thinking shared between policymakers and intelligence officials about what they should be thinking about. Moreover, they were only one intelligence product; there were many others. Richard Kerr, a former deputy director for intelligence at the CIA, thinks that US intelligence has "provided American presidents and their foreign affairs teams with the broadest and most comprehensive information of any government on the planet." Successes have greatly outnumbered failures. His firm belief is that "what the record shows is that CIA's analysis has helped to reduce the inherent uncertainty surrounding many foreign events, raise the level of understanding of the policy debates conducted by national security teams, and alert decision makers to many critical issues that they would otherwise have missed or judged unimportant."[26]

The US intelligence community avoided the mistake made by the communists: It did not maintain that every development that conflicted with US interests was the work of the USSR. Both the KGB and the Stasi had this tendency. KGB officers knew that their assessments would be acceptable to decision makers if problems and reverses were simply blamed on the "Main Adversary."[27] Conspiracy theory prevailed over any proper analysis of intelligence. At the root of this were the expectations of the Communist Party, the regime's insistence on the "scientific" nature of Marxism-Leninism, and the KGB's terrible fear and suspicion of their adversary in the bipolar context of the Cold War. The psychological tendency to overestimate one's opponent affected the communists, but the KGB's obsession with a Western conspiracy against them was more ideological invention than psychological exaggeration. It was imposed on them by the Communist Party and followed naturally from the Marxist-Leninist belief that the world was divided into two camps, the one progressive and the other reactionary, and that the former was destined to prevail over the latter.[28] As Raymond Garthoff relates, where the KGB embellished Marxism-Leninism was in believing that this conspiracy was directed by the Western secret services. The Stasi's leaders also believed this; they regarded the Western intelligence services as inspiring all the opposition to communism in the Soviet Bloc.[29] In part this was an extreme example of the psychological tendency to overestimate an adversary; the reason for it was fierce competition with the US intelligence community. In part it reflected the projection of their own character onto their enemy. Conspirators themselves, they judged their enemy by the people they knew best—themselves.[30] Ideology underlay both psychological tendencies.

American statesmen had their own ideological beliefs, of course, but these were vaguer and less prescriptive, amounting to little more than the wish that the world become more "free."[31] Consequently, they were less at odds with reality. In the American case, the cognitive barriers to acceptance of intelligence were psychological rather than ideological.[32]

US intelligence analysts understood the Soviet Union's military capabilities better than its military or political intentions. This was natural since most intelligence was collected on military capabilities as the principal threat to the United States. Furthermore, intentions are, by nature, more obscure. They therefore tended to be inferred from capabilities. The expansion and modernization of the USSR's nuclear-missile force were assessed "reasonably well."[33] Ben Fischer's chapter provides much evidence of the discrepancy. The Soviet Union's formidable military power long attracted too much of analysts' attention. Alongside a good understanding of it ran a weaker understanding of political change in the Soviet Union. In the mid-1980s, entrenched views about the Soviet political system made analysts skeptical of the view that Gorbachev offered real change.

The CIA's assessments of Soviet economic performance relied chiefly on sophisticated recalculations of official Soviet economic statistics. Its estimates of the USSR's economic growth were good and have consistently found favor with economists.[34] From the mid-1970s it increasingly brought attention to the USSR's economic malaise.

Richard Kerr and Roger George argue that what US analysts did worst was give warning of imminent danger. They failed to warn of the Soviet deployment of nuclear missiles in Cuba in 1962, the Yom Kippur War of 1973, and the Soviet invasion of Afghanistan in 1979. They thought that they understood the situations concerned and discounted evidence that did not fit this understanding.[35] As Raymond Garthoff shows, the Soviet decisions were made by a tiny number of leaders and without asking the KGB to report on the likely US reaction. Expected Soviet awareness of the likely US reaction was one reason why American analysts considered aggressive moves by the USSR unlikely in 1962 and 1979. As Ben Fischer demonstrates, analysts did not understand the Soviet leaders well enough, did not understand the Soviet foreign policymaking process, and relied too heavily on presumptions about Soviet international behavior. They assumed that the Soviet leaders calculated the harm that aggressive action would do to the USSR's interests better than they in fact did. This accords perfectly with the conclusion of May, Jervis, and Heuer that analysts and policymakers overestimate their foes because they are loath to underestimate them. Consequently, they perform badly when they try to put themselves in their enemies' shoes. Richard Kerr's view is that analysts' understanding of the USSR's leaders and politics was always poorer than its understanding of military capability or the economy.[36]

How politicized was US intelligence during the Cold War? Its politicization was far milder than was intelligence reporting in the Communist Bloc. Politicization is a "complicated phenomenon," as Richard Betts has rightly observed.[37] Gregory Treverton argues that there are five forms. The first is pressure on analysts from policymakers to reach conclusions that support particular policies. An example is the pressure put by the Nixon administration on US intelligence analysts in 1969 to present the Soviet Union as seeking a first-strike nuclear-missile capability, as this would provide justification for the administration's policy of developing antiballistic missiles.[38] Tamir Libel and Shlomo Shpiro, in this collection, provide another good example of this, showing that Israeli analysts have told policymakers in intelligence briefings what they wanted to hear and have sought to protect themselves from criticism by keeping reports with more sensible conclusions on file should the matter be the subject of an official investigation.[39] The second is a "house view" within an analytical group that causes other views to be suppressed or ignored. (The Iraqi WMD affair provides a good example of this: Analysts were reluctant to underestimate Iraq's WMD programs a second time, having done so prior to the Gulf War.) The third is "cherry-picking" by policy officials (or intelligence officials) of preferred views from a range of analyses. (Iraq's WMD programs again provide a good example: The George W. Bush administration had decided for several reasons on war with Iraq and favored intelligence estimates that concluded Iraq had, and was continuing to develop, WMDs.) The fourth is the asking of questions that steer analysis toward particular answers. (A good example is the repeated questioning of the IC by the Bush administration in 2001–3 over whether Saddam Hussein's regime was in cahoots with Al-Qaeda since, as the IC advised, there was inadequate evidence of collaboration to justify such relentless questioning.) The last is "mindsets" or presumptions that policymakers and intelligence analysts share and that strongly influence their attitude toward incoming information on the subjects concerned. (Both the underestimation of Al-Qaeda prior to September 2001 and the overestimation of Saddam's WMD programs in the years prior to the Iraq War of 2003 are good examples of this.) As Treverton observes, the case of "mindsets" is a borderline one for such politicization as does take place is imposed by the analysts on themselves.[40]

While the American experience demonstrates other forms of politicization at work during the Cold War, the main problem, certainly as far as assessments of the Soviet Union were concerned, was that of shared mindsets. Ben Fischer demonstrates that for most of the 1970s, both analysts and policymakers held views of Soviet conduct that represented severe mirror-imaging of Soviet policy; this mirror-imaging underpinned both the US government's policy of détente with the USSR and analysts' favorable assessments of détente. Such mirror-imaging was possible owing to the lack of high-grade intelligence on the Soviet leadership's thinking. Heavy reliance on technical intelligence, chiefly on the USSR's military capabilities, meant that analysts tended to infer Soviet intentions from it. Nuclear capabilities were inevitably very menacing; this led to menacing assessments. The "Team A / Team B" dispute in 1976 between intelligence community analysts and outside experts over Soviet strategic objectives shows how much all involved relied on inference.[41]

Analysts presented the Soviet leadership as reassured by the USSR's achievement of strategic nuclear parity with the United States, as likely to moderate its international behavior in consequence, as pursuing "rough parity" rather than superiority in strategic missile forces, and as vulnerable to American pressure to stay within reasonable limits if they were minded to act aggressively. These presumptions made a policy of détente easier to pursue. They were undercut by what were seen as aggressive Soviet moves, beginning with the USSR's expansion and modernization of its strategic missile force and its support for national liberation movements and Marxist regimes in the third world. This Soviet course culminated in the invasion of Afghanistan in 1979. By the early 1980s, when the Carter administration gave way to the Reagan administration, a new shared mindset prevailed in both Washington and Langley. Intelligence analyses now stressed the threat posed to American interests by Soviet interventions in the third world and argued that American support for allies and resistance movements was containing Soviet expansion.

By contrast, all five forms of politicization severely distorted the intelligence reporting of the intelligence services of the Communist Bloc. The very concepts of a malign "imperialist" conspiracy and of a Main Adversary represented pressure on intelligence reporters to keep their reporting factual and to pass on intelligence that supported these ideas. Raymond Garthoff shows that there was a "house view" within the KGB's assessment staff in the 1970s: The analysts believed in the regime's anti-Western conspiracy theory, and their analyses contained views more anti-American than those of the Communist Party's leaders. The leading KGB officers were among the most anti-American elements in the entire regime. During the crisis over the Prague Spring in Czechoslovakia in

1968, the KGB chairman, Yuri Andropov, deliberately supplied the Politburo with biased intelligence assessments that supported the case for military intervention. He also withheld from the Politburo evidence that undermined his argument that the West was trying to stage a coup in Czechoslovakia. The KGB's Washington station (its "residency," in Soviet parlance) had obtained US government documents showing that the US government neither had anticipated the reform movement nor was controlling it; Andropov had them destroyed.[42] This represents cherry-picking of intelligence. It was part of a general practice: As Garthoff demonstrates, in the 1970s and 1980s much intelligence was sent daily by Soviet intelligence agencies to the Central Committee General Department, but it forwarded only a small fraction on to the leadership. It withheld information the Soviet leader would not like. Tellingly, the HVA and the KGB were not given specific questions to answer; rather, they were required to collect intelligence that presupposed a grave Western threat. Their mindset was as hostile to the West as that of their regimes.

On the present state of the evidence, neither the communist intelligence agencies nor their political masters were able adequately to comprehend or exploit either political or economic intelligence on the Western world. As John Lewis Gaddis and Vojtech Mastny have both argued, despite plentiful intelligence on the West, Soviet diplomacy under Stalin, Nikita Khrushchev, and Brezhnev was remarkable for its clumsiness; the Soviet leaders repeatedly took initiatives that either harmed their relations with the West or even played into the West's hands.[43] Intelligence on political and economic developments was ignored more often than was the case in the United States. The only information that seems to have benefited the USSR was military intelligence and scientific and technological intelligence (S&TI). The military intelligence would have greatly benefited it in war.[44] The S&TI enabled it to develop weapons that were broadly comparable in quality with those of the United States and the other powers of the North Atlantic Treaty Organization (NATO). However, the barriers the communist command economies put in the way of innovation and greater productivity prevented the communists from exploiting S&TI to revive their sclerotic civilian economies. Indeed, so bad was the information the communist leaders received on their own economies that they believed late in the Cold War that the free-market economies had greater problems than their own. Even Mikhail Gorbachev, when he spoke to the Twenty-Seventh Congress of the Soviet Communist Party in 1986 on the need for "new thinking" in foreign policy, maintained that the crisis of capitalism was continuing to get worse.[45]

For the most part, the intelligence cycle worked better in the democracies than in the communist states. The major steps in it are tasking, collection, analysis and production, and dissemination. Analysis has already been discussed. Both sides were proficient at collection (though the Soviet human intelligence collection was better than that of the United States, and the Americans' technical intelligence collection better than the Soviets'). As regards tasking and dissemination, the democratic states were, again, clearly superior.

The communist regimes did not ask the right questions. Such was the party leadership's power that it tasked the intelligence services as it wished. In the Soviet case, tasking depended very much on the leader himself. The Soviet leader often did not bother to task his foreign intelligence services to consider and report on the probable Western reaction to key initiatives. He judged the likely reaction himself—and severely misjudged it. The Berlin Crisis of 1958–62, the Cuban Missile Crisis of 1962, Soviet support for national liberation movements and Marxist regimes in the third world in the 1970s, the invasion of Afghanistan in 1979, and the Reykjavík summit of 1986 are all examples. Stalin probably did not request, either, an intelligence assessment of the likely reaction of the United States to his decision to give his consent to North Korea's invasion of South Korea in 1950.[46] By contrast, a fundamental principle of American policymaking during the Cold War was that policymakers needed analysts' advice on the likely Soviet reaction to their initiatives.[47]

The same weakness is visible in the case of the GDR. There the Soviets had the last word on the tasking of the foreign intelligence service. They consistently gave preference to their own interests. The HVA's tasking in the 1970s and 1980s was too military in character; this did not suit the GDR, which fell to a popular revolution, not a military attack.[48]

The East German communist leadership also had a large say in the Stasi's tasking. It also tasked it badly. Like all faiths, Marxism-Leninism was hostile to unbelief and disliked whatever encouraged it. In the late 1950s, the GDR's leaders, chief among them party leader Walter Ulbricht, disliked the intelligence reports they received on the situation in East Germany because they passed on public criticism of the regime. The leadership laid down rules for the reporting of the Stasi and its foreign intelligence service with the aim of making it less critical. Thenceforth, the Stasi's reporting was principally on the outside world, not on the GDR. In addition, the Stasi's reporters provided information only on particular matters of interest. They could not ask themselves whatever questions they wanted, and they did not ask the right ones. They consistently reported on "hostile activity" (*Feindtätigkeit*), which assumed that particular forms of political activity were meant to be hostile to the GDR and that they, rather than the communists' own illegitimacy and misrule, were the main cause of popular dissatisfaction. The Stasi's reports could not be too critical. They were short information reports. They never examined a subject comprehensively.

Dissemination of intelligence within the US intelligence community has been criticized in recent years. Poor dissemination of intelligence between intelligence agencies contributed to the success of Al-Qaeda's surprise attack on the United States in September 2001.[49] However, a more important matter is the dissemination of intelligence to policymakers. They cannot respond to perspectives that are not presented to them or act on information they do not have. Intelligence was very poorly shared and discussed in communist states. This was partly because it was very sensitive, partly because the regimes were extremely centralized. Little intelligence was supplied to most members of the Soviet Communist Party's Politburo. As Raymond Garthoff stresses, most of them knew little about the Western world. They received no more information about it than was printed in the party's newspaper, *Pravda*. Even the top leaders received little. The GDR's Politburo could not discuss intelligence, first because it was secret and second because there was no intelligence report, akin to the US Senior Executive Intelligence Brief, that was sent to all Politburo members. People received intelligence reports on particular subjects according to their expertise. Only the general secretary knew the full list of recipients of the *Parteiinformationen*. Once the recipients had read the reports, they had to give them back and could not discuss them. Thus the reports did not serve as a basis for collective decision making.[50]

The only respect in which the communist states were clearly superior to the democracies was security. Strict communist security influenced the intelligence collection of the Western intelligence agencies and thus affected their understanding of the Soviet Union and its bloc. There was very little high-grade political intelligence. Well-placed human sources could have provided it but, as the Commission on the Intelligence Capabilities of the United States Regarding Weapons of Mass Destruction conceded ten years ago, decades of effort by the CIA and other services to recruit human agents yielded only a few good sources reporting on the Soviet Union.[51] American successes in decrypting high-grade Soviet ciphers were evidently rare. The only known successes are the decryption of cables sent to Moscow during the Second World War by Soviet intelligence offices in the United States (codenamed "Venona") and, in the late 1970s, the decryption, thanks to the advent of the supercomputer, of high-level Soviet political, diplomatic, and military communications.[52]

The secrecy of military, economic, and scientific developments in the Soviet Union was severely diminished by the advent of American satellite reconnaissance of the Communist Bloc in 1960. Thereafter, both sides had greater security against surprise attack. Each also had a good understanding of the other's military capabilities, though the United States' National Intelligence Estimates tended to overestimate the future capability of the Soviet armed forces (Soviet intelligence analysts may well have done the same).[53] The tendency to produce "worst-case" estimates inevitably fueled the arms race. Nevertheless, from the early 1960s on, no Soviet weapon system took the United States by surprise. It was thanks to confidence in satellite reconnaissance that the arms limitation treaties of the 1970s were signed and Cold War tension moderated.[54]

Nevertheless, there remained serious gaps in understanding of the Soviet Union's military capability. For example, knowledge of its nuclear weapon production complex, though good, was not complete.[55] Another is Soviet missile technology. Some of the most serious disagreements between Team A and Team B arose from uncertainties over the accuracy of Soviet intercontinental ballistic missiles (ICBMs). Team B assumed that Soviet missile technology and engineering were as good as American, which Team A criticized as unjustifiable mirror-imaging. Team B therefore exaggerated the threat to the US ICBM force (its "counterforce" capability).[56]

Good security also harmed the West German government's understanding of the GDR. The poor quality of the BND's analyses undermined its government's confidence in them. Matthias Uhl's chapter in this collection indicates that the service's successes against the GDR were small ones. It was able to monitor the popular uprising in East Germany in June 1953 and gave the government some forewarning of the Berlin border closure of August 1961 and the Warsaw Pact's invasion of Czechoslovakia in August 1968. In the late 1980s, it also demonstrated to the federal government that there was probably still strong support for reunification among East Germans. However, it did not grasp the full extent of the GDR's economic crisis. West Germany's political leadership was deceived by the GDR's claim that it was one of the world's ten leading industrial economies and did not realize in the late 1980s that the East German economy was on the point of collapse.[57] Political intelligence collection on the GDR was also poor. So far as is known, in the last twenty-five years of the Cold War the BND failed to recruit any high-grade human sources in the GDR.[58]

The United States' intelligence collection on its friends was inevitably poor and led to grave misjudgments. One example is the IC's view of the shah of Iran, whom it regarded as secure from overthrow until a few months before his flight from Iran. As before Pearl Harbor in December 1941, poor intelligence collection enabled flawed presumptions—the "Pahlavi Premise" that the shah's position was strong, that his army and security police could keep him in power, and that religious fundamentalism would not win mass support—to prevail.[59]

Cognitive Errors

This volume provides much evidence of well-known cognitive errors. Mirror-imaging was common among American analysts during the Cold War. (They should not be censured too much for it: It shows that they were thinking for themselves at least, which the Soviet and East German foreign intelligence services were not.) The lack of high-grade political intelligence on the Soviet regime encouraged it. The misjudgments of the Soviet Union to which it led have been referred to above. Another cognitive bias is the tendency to assimilate new information into an existing understanding. This was encouraged by analysts' practice, to which Ben Fischer refers, of using precedents of Soviet conduct to predict trends in the USSR's internal politics and foreign policy. The reliance on precedent made Gorbachev a very hard target. Understandably, the intelligence community did not predict the end of the Cold War until it had already begun.[60]

In the Soviet Union, the lack of high-grade political intelligence gave free rein to the influence of Marxism-Leninism, the personality of the party leader, and bureaucratic interests pushing for hostility to the West and a continuing arms buildup. Of course, the conviction that the West was hostile to the Soviet Union was so entrenched in the Soviet mind that it might have overcome top-quality intelligence on American policy. It was entrenched within the Soviet government itself. The International Department of the Communist Party's Central Committee was a strong influence in favor of ideological orthodoxy. As a result, intelligence was usually ignored. The absence of evidence that the United States planned to make a nuclear first strike on the USSR was discounted, and the quest for such evidence continued.

The Marxist-Leninist assumption of Western hostility took disregard of intelligence—and disregard of the lack of it—to an extreme. However, this was an extreme form of a mental model of suspicion and mistrust that existed in the United States as well and distorted American perceptions of the Soviet Union. One example is Team B's worst-case estimate, in 1976, of Soviet strategic objectives. Team B regarded the USSR as trying to develop an offensive nuclear-missile capability, backed up by an effective civil defense system, which would enable it to make a successful first strike on the United States, absorb any American second strike, and thus win a nuclear war.[61] Actually, the USSR is believed then to have been pursuing only an effective retaliatory capability.[62] Another example is the conviction of President Lyndon Johnson and his successor, Richard Nixon, in the late 1960s and early 1970s, disregarding the lack of evidence to this effect, that the Soviet Union, China, and Cuba were orchestrating worldwide protest against the Vietnam War.[63] The latter is an example of the common mistake of attributing to an adversary more coordination than he has.

The Cold War provides resounding confirmation for a maxim that Ernest May distilled from the studies collected in *Knowing One's Enemies*: that presumptions that influence how intelligence is interpreted need to be carefully examined.[64] These presumptions are very often policies or part of the rationale for them; they reflect mirror-imaging. Intelligence will always be incomplete, and therefore attitudes and presumptions will always seep deeply into its interpretation. The failure of US intelligence analysts to understand Iraq's WMD programs in the years between the Gulf War and the Iraq War is a classic example of this. Very flawed presumptions were applied to weak intelligence, resulting in huge overestimation of the ambitions and capabilities of Saddam Hussein's regime.[65]

However, the collection shows that ideological thinking leads to graver, more persistent errors than mirror-imaging. Marxist-Leninist ideological axioms were written on tablets of stone and could not be challenged by the intelligence services. One was that capitalism had an inherent tendency to crisis and would collapse; communism would triumph and become the leading social system in the world. A related belief was that as capitalism's crisis deepened, the capitalists would try to escape from it by waging war on the Soviet Bloc. This belief prompted Yuri Andropov's decision in 1981 to order a worldwide intelligence operation to look for signs of an American first strike on the USSR. A further ideological bias was the belief of the Soviet leadership that the global "correlation of forces" was bound to turn in its favor. This caused it, in the mid-1970s, to overestimate the significance of the US defeat in Vietnam and the success of Marxist national liberation movements in the third world.[66]

The US intelligence community's failure to prevent the attacks by Al-Qaeda on the World Trade Center and the Pentagon resulted not from overestimation but from underestimation. As Mark Stout shows, the Cold War cast a long shadow over intelligence analysts. To their way of thinking, until September 2001 the gravest threats to the United States had to come from states and WMDs. Al-Qaeda, not being the one and not having the other, was not regarded as a threat of the first rank. The number of people it could kill without WMDs was also underestimated. Again, that demonstrates how important it is to challenge presumptions. Stout's conclusion, that understanding is a social process, is entirely in accord with the IC's current attitude toward analysis.

It is a well-known phenomenon that human beings overestimate the extent to which others are responding to their initiatives. Raymond Garthoff and Ben Fischer show that this mistake was made by both the United States and the Soviet Union during the détente period. The USSR's leaders regarded the United States as having been forced into détente by their country's strategic strength. Ben Fischer shows that, for their part, American policymakers and analysts overestimated the influence the United States had over the Soviet Union's international conduct.[67]

The academic literature stresses that error arises when the human mind follows its natural tendency of assimilating new information into knowledge it already has. This tendency makes it resist new interpretations. However, the lack of such knowledge is also a danger: The new information is simply not understood at all. Raymond Garthoff shows that Soviet leaders' assessment of the international situation was affected by the fact that they could not understand the US political system, having had no experience of it or of anything like it.

The Cold War provides much evidence in support of two more of May's maxims in *Knowing One's Enemies*: that prudence generally causes intelligence analysts and policymakers to overestimate their enemies' capabilities, understanding, and skill and that policymakers should rely on their intelligence services more for tactical warning and short-term predictions than long-term predictions (though the US analysts' poor performance, mentioned above, in predicting aggressive moves by the Soviet Union and other states should be borne in mind).

There are numerous examples of each side overestimating the other. Even as South Vietnam was being conquered by the North Vietnamese in 1975, for instance, KGB chairman Yuri Andropov thought that a new American invasion of the country was possible.[68] The same prudence, in the late Cold War, made the CIA's intelligence analysts slow to understand how much change Mikhail Gorbachev was willing to make to Soviet foreign policy to end the Cold War. President Reagan was persuaded to respond to Gorbachev's overtures, not by the intelligence community but by Gorbachev's own concessions. The State Department, under George Shultz, was quicker to see the opportunity presented by Gorbachev's new foreign policy than was the CIA's Directorate of Intelligence.[69]

This has continued into the post–Cold War era. Directly after the 9/11 attacks, as Mark Stout explains, the CIA was too willing to regard cooperation between Al-Qaeda and Saddam Hussein's regime as possible. It never concluded that the two were cooperating, but it saw this as possible because it did not want to be too complacent.

The Soviet regime presented the US intelligence community with the difficult task of monitoring the decay of Marxism-Leninism. Such a long-term trend is inevitably mysterious. The USSR began the Cold War as a highly ideological actor. Stalin was, at root, an ideologue who merely supplemented his ideological goals with pragmatic initiatives. He never ceased to believe in the international class struggle and the irreconcilability of communism and capitalism. For him, there were no universal human values uniting the communist and capitalist worlds. By the 1970s ideology and pragmatism were contending more as equals in the Soviet policymaking system. Each had its institutional champions. Pragmatism won out when Gorbachev became Soviet leader in 1985; he saw that the Cold War was not merely unwinnable but was also holding the Soviet Union in backwardness. His policy became to end it. The US intelligence community was slow to see this because, to quote Christopher Andrew, "scarred by forty years of Cold War" it was reluctant to let its guard down.[70]

The Obscurity of Intentions

Proclivities remain very obscure and hard to divine. Attempting to divine them commits an intelligence community not merely to obtaining secrets but also to comprehending mysteries. Ernest May pointed out in *Knowing One's Enemies* that the governments of the 1930s found one another harder to understand than those of the 1910s because they were more diverse and their workings more complicated and obscure. By contrast, the governments of the period before the First World War had resembled a gentlemen's club.[71] This trend continued in the Cold War era and continues today. The chapters in this volume demonstrate how, despite large intelligence communities and assessment staffs, the governments of West and East had a poor understanding of one another from 1945 to 1990 and, in the 1990s, were slow to grasp the rising threat of substate actors such as Al-Qaeda.

The Cold War provides much evidence that US intelligence analysts performed capably in alerting policymakers to problems. However, owing to the Cold War's astonishingly rapid end, they have been criticized for focusing too much on the Soviet Union's military and economic strength and not studying it sufficiently in the round. Examining it as a totality would have helped analysts realize the full significance of its weaknesses and particularly that of the ethnic tensions within it.[72]

This collection also stresses that, to estimate how security threats will develop, it is essential to study them comprehensively. Tamir Libel and Shlomo Shpiro demonstrate that Israeli analysts have examined Palestinian terrorism too narrowly; they have focused too much on giving warning of attack and have neglected the political development of Palestinian terrorism. Concerned, as they have been, with attacks by terrorist organizations, they have neglected "the street." The West German Federal Intelligence Service made the same mistake, as Matthias Uhl shows: Its practice, in the early 1960s, was to analyze political and military intelligence separately, which made the construction of the Berlin Wall harder to predict.

An urgent challenge for analysts and policymakers now is to understand youth. The youth of the Muslim world have been the motor behind Palestinian and jihadist terrorism and the uprisings since 2011 that have made up the so-called Arab Spring. Tamir Libel and Shlomo Shpiro point to the Israeli Military Intelligence Directorate's lack of collection capabilities on social and economic developments in the Palestinian community. Since such developments radicalize youth, they need to be monitored.

The need to see the situation and oneself as the target state sees them, and the difficulty of doing so, emphasize the importance of diplomats as sources of insight into the outside world. For security reasons, intelligence analysts spend little or no time in the countries they study. By contrast, diplomats are posted there and come to understand them well. In this collection, Eunan O'Halpin shows how much better than their political masters in London British ambassadors in Dublin understood the political situation in the Republic of Ireland and in the Irish Republican Army (IRA) in Dublin. Raymond Garthoff demonstrates how, throughout the Cold War, the Soviet Foreign Ministry played a large role in intelligence assessment and regarded itself as the regime's best source of information on international affairs. When Ronald Reagan was president of the United States, his wife's astrologer was also a rival. She provided the president with horoscopes of Gorbachev purporting to explain his character and his likely behavior. All four of Reagan's summit meetings with Gorbachev took place on days considered by the astrologer to be astrologically suitable.[73]

The collection also underlines the weakness of intelligence in comparison with personal experience.[74] Raymond Garthoff considers personal contacts to have been the most important influence on Soviet leaders' understanding of the United States. Intelligence is now growing in importance in decision making since political leaders have no contact with terrorists.

Most fundamentally, intelligence cannot influence policy if policymakers refuse to let policy give way to it. This point is made by Eunan O'Halpin in his chapter. He shows that Britain failed to take loyalist terrorism in Northern Ireland seriously enough early enough, even though it was the root of the problem. Britain focused too much on the Provisional IRA (PIRA). The main reason was policy, though PIRA's attacks on targets in mainland Britain were a further factor. Britain's commitment to the union of Britain and Northern Ireland doomed it to handling republican terrorism in Northern Ireland with a mixture of insensitivity and lack of self-understanding. Cultural affinity with republicanism was important; Britain's Conservative Party lacked it, though Celts in the Labour Party, such as James Callaghan, did not.

Reorganization and Self-Understanding

May put forward two further maxims: that reorganization offers little in the way of improved performance (certainly less than good working procedures) and that any analyst has to have a good understanding of his own country's strengths and weaknesses and of who its enemies are.[75] Both are very relevant to today. Mark Stout shows both that the US intelligence community was, prior to September 2001, slow to realize how dangerous an enemy of the United States Al-Qaeda was and that the US intelligence community's post-9/11 reorganization has had no effect on its understanding of the jihadists. The terrorist threat increases the need to understand one's own society since, as an asymmetrical threat, to do harm it relies on exploiting its enemy's weaknesses.[76] At the time of NATO's "Able Archer" exercise in 1983, the CIA's Office of Soviet Analysis did not know of the many "psyops" the Reagan administration was undertaking against the USSR and so did not know the full extent of the threat that Soviet leaders thought they saw.[77]

This collection also provides evidence of crude cognitive errors that have distorted understanding of foes. The US intelligence community's failure, analyzed by Mark Stout, to understand the importance of religion to jihadists prior to September 2001 was a profound cognitive error. It resulted from a lack of imagination and from political correctness. Analysts did not fully realize how fanatically religious their foes were (or how secular American society was, which created an imaginative gulf between them). The same lack of imagination made analysts slow to grasp during the Iranian Revolution of 1978–79 that the shah would be replaced by an Islamic fundamentalist regime. As Gary Sick, then the National Security Council staffer responsible for Iran, commented later, "the notion of a popular revolution leading to the establishment of a theocratic state seemed so unlikely as to be absurd."[78] Likewise, Julian Richards shows that the Pakistani army officers who have so often dominated their country's government have regarded their people as superior to Indians. This crude religious and ethnic prejudice has caused them to exaggerate their own strength and start wars with India that they have lost.

This collection underlines that the roads to error are many. The authors' hope is that it makes those roads harder to travel.

Notes

My thanks go to Raymond and Douglas Garthoff, Ben Fischer, and Mark Stout for their comments on this introduction, which have improved it. My further thanks go to Geoffrey Maddrell and Tatsuko Yamazaki. Responsibility for all errors made and opinions expressed remains my own.

1. Ernest R. May, ed., *Knowing One's Enemies: Intelligence Assessment before the Two World Wars* (Princeton, NJ: Princeton University Press, 1984), 8.

2. For an example of the dealings they do have, see Jonathan Powell, *Talking to Terrorists: How to End Armed Conflicts* (London: Bodley Head, 2014).

3. Roger Z. George, "Fixing the Problem of Analytical Mindsets: Alternative Analysis," in Roger Z. George and Robert D. Kline, eds., *Intelligence and the National Security Strategist: Enduring Issues and Challenges* (Lanham, MD: Rowman & Littlefield, 2006), 314–22.

4. National Commission on Terrorist Attacks upon the United States, *The 9/11 Commission Report* (Washington, DC: Government Printing Office, 2004), 339–60.

5. See Director of National Intelligence, *Vision 2015: A Globally Networked and Integrated Intelligence Enterprise* (Washington, DC: Director of National Intelligence, 2008).

6. Richards J. Heuer Jr. and Randolph H. Pherson, *Structured Analytic Techniques for Intelligence Analysis* (Washington, DC: CQ Press, 2011), xvi, 3–7, 22–24.

7. Lawrence D. Freedman, *US Intelligence and the Soviet Strategic Threat*, 2nd ed. (Basingstoke, UK: Macmillan, 1986), 184–85.

8. These are terms used to refer to the understandings of particular problems that intelligence analysts and policymakers have; they are ways of making a very complicated reality comprehensible to the human mind. Most analysts use the term "mindset." Heuer and Pherson prefer the term "mental model," arguing that such understandings are natural and inevitable and that the term for them should not have a negative connotation, as mindset has (see their *Structured Analytic Techniques for Intelligence Analysis*, 5).

9. May, *Knowing One's Enemies*, 537–42; Richards J. Heuer Jr., *Psychology of Intelligence Analysis* (Washington, DC: Center for the Study of Intelligence, 1999).

10. Robert Jervis, *Perception and Misperception in International Politics* (Princeton, NJ: Princeton University Press, 1976).

11. Richard K. Betts, "Analysis, War, and Decision: Why Intelligence Failures Are Inevitable," *World Politics* 31, no. 1 (October 1978): 61.

12. The communist party was known as the Socialist Unity Party (Sozialistische Einheitspartei Deutschlands, or SED).

13. On the sources now available on Soviet and US intelligence during the Cold War, see Raymond Garthoff, "Foreign Intelligence and the Historiography of the Cold War," *Journal of Cold War Studies* 6, no. 2 (Spring 2004): 22–29. The thousands of records declassified by the CIA and transferred to the National Archives and Records Administration are held in Record Group (RG) 263. An overview of the contents of RG 263 is available online at http://www.archives.gov/research_room/federal_records_guide/central_intelligence _agency_rg263.html. Garthoff refers (at p. 24n3) to the many volumes of declassified US intelligence records that have been published by the CIA History Staff.

On declassifications of intelligence records in the United Kingdom and their impact on the historiography of British intelligence, see Richard J. Aldrich, "Did Waldegrave Work? The Impact of Open Government on British History," *Twentieth Century British History* 9, no. 1 (1998), 111–26; Gill Bennett, "Declassification and Release Policies of the UK's Intelligence Agencies," in "British intelligence in the Twentieth Century: Missing Dimension?," special issue, *Intelligence and National Security* 17, no. 1 (2002): 21–32; and Christopher R. Moran and Christopher J. Murphy, eds., *Intelligence Studies in Britain and the US: Historiography since 1945* (Edinburgh, UK: Edinburgh University Press, 2013). On declassifications of pre-1990 intelligence records of the Federal Republic of Germany, see Bodo Hechelhammer, "Möglichkeiten und Grenzen des Zugangs zu Unterlagen der Nachrichtendienste: Geschichtsaufarbeitung des Bundesnachrichtendienstes im Spannungsfeld zwischen Geheimhaltung und Transparenz," in *Mitteilungen aus dem Bundesarchiv*, no. 1 (2013): 52–59. The archive of the Bundesnachrichtendienst at the Bundesarchiv (Federal Archive) is B 206.

On declassifications of intelligence records of the former GDR, see John Miller, "Settling Accounts with a Secret Police: The German Law on the Stasi Records," *Europe-Asia Studies* 50, no. 2 (1998): 305–33, and Paul Maddrell, "The Revolution Made Law: The Work since 2001 of the Federal Commissioner for the Records of the State Security Service of the Former German Democratic Republic," *Cold War History* 4, no. 3 (2004): 153–62. As later chapters in this book explain, there have been no declassifications of intelligence records in Israel and Pakistan.

14. James B. Bruce and Roger Z. George, "Intelligence Analysis: The Emergence of a Discipline," in *Analyzing Intelligence: Origins, Obstacles, and Innovations*, ed. Roger Z. George and James B. Bruce (Washington, DC: Georgetown University Press, 2008), 1–5.

15. See James G. Blight and David A. Welch, eds., *Intelligence and the Cuban Missile Crisis* (London: Frank Cass, 1998) (also published as *Intelligence and National Security* 13, no. 3 [special edition, autumn 1998]), and Richard K. Betts, *Surprise Attack: Lessons for Defense Planning* (Washington, DC: Brookings Institution Press, 1982). For a broader view of analytical error, see Michael Herman, *Intelligence Power in Peace and War* (Cambridge: Cambridge University Press, 1996), chap. 13. The US intelligence community has tried to correct this focus on analytical error by publishing collections of declassified intelligence analyses. They are listed in Garthoff, "Foreign Intelligence and the Historiography of the Cold War," 24n3. Analyses of the CIA's Directorate of Intelligence were the subject of a conference on "CIA's Analysis of the Soviet Union, 1947–1991," which was held at Princeton

University in March 2001. These documents were not only released to the National Archives and Records Administration, but were also made available online at http://www.foia.cia.gov/collection/princeton-collection.

16. Michael Herman, "Intelligence Effects on the Cold War: Some Reflections," in *Did Intelligence Matter in the Cold War?*, ed. Michael Herman, J. Kenneth McDonald, and Vojtech Mastny (Oslo, Norway: Institutt for Forsvarsstudier, no. 1 [2006]), 10; Garthoff, "Foreign Intelligence and the Historiography of the Cold War," 41.

17. Two recent studies of the influence of ideology on Soviet policy are Vladislav M. Zubok, *A Failed Empire: The Soviet Union in the Cold War from Stalin to Gorbachev* (Chapel Hill: University of North Carolina Press, 2007), and Jonathan Haslam, *Russia's Cold War: From the October Revolution to the Fall of the Wall* (New Haven: Yale University Press, 2011). Recent studies of its influence on American policy are Melvyn Leffler, *The Specter of Communism: The United States and the Origins of the Cold War, 1917–1953* (New York: Hill & Wang, 1994); Tony Smith, *America's Mission: The United States and the Worldwide Struggle for Democracy in the Twentieth Century* (Princeton, NJ: Princeton University Press, 1994); W. Scott Lucas, *Freedom's War* (New York: NYU Press, 1999); and Anders Stephanson, "Liberty or Death: The Cold War as US Ideology," in *Reviewing the Cold War*, ed. Odd Arne Westad (London: Frank Cass, 2000).

18. May, *Knowing One's Enemies*, 503–4.

19. Freedman, *US Intelligence and the Soviet Strategic Threat*, 185–87.

20. Richard K. Betts, *Enemies of Intelligence: Knowledge and Power in American National Security* (New York: Columbia University Press, 2007), 75–76; Gregory F. Treverton, "Intelligence Analysis: Between 'Politicization' and Irrelevance," in George and Bruce, *Analyzing Intelligence*, 99–102; Jack Davis, "Defining the Analytic Mission: Facts, Findings, Forecasts, and Fortunetelling," in George and Kline, *Intelligence and the National Security Strategist*, 296–97.

21. On the Team A / Team B dispute over Soviet strategic objectives, see US Congress, Senate, Report of the Senate Select Committee on Intelligence, Subcommittee on Collection, Production and Quality, *The National Intelligence Estimates A–B Team Episode Concerning Soviet Strategic Capability and Objectives* (Washington, DC: Government Printing Office, 1978); Freedman, *US Intelligence and the Soviet Strategic Threat*; and John Prados, *The Soviet Estimate: US Intelligence Analysis and Russian Military Strength* (New York: Dial, 1982). For claims that in 2001–3 the Bush administration put pressure on analysts to reach conclusions supportive of the administration's policy of war on Iraq, see James Bamford, *A Pretext for War: 9/11, Iraq, and the Abuse of America's Intelligence Agencies* (New York: Doubleday, 2004), and John Prados, *Hoodwinked: The Documents That Reveal How Bush Sold Us a War* (New York: New Press, 2004).

22. Richard J. Kerr, "The Track Record: CIA Analysis from 1950 to 2000," in George and Bruce, *Analyzing Intelligence*, 36.

23. Sherman Kent, *Strategic Intelligence for American World Policy* (Princeton, NJ: Princeton University Press, 1949), 7. That forecasting future developments is, in particular, the purpose of National Intelligence Estimates is emphasized in Harold P. Ford, *Estimative Intelligence: The Purposes and Problems of National Intelligence Estimating* (New York: University Press of America, 1993), 31–35.

24. Kerr, "Track Record," 41–42.

25. For a call for National Intelligence Estimates to contribute more directly to the policy process, see Treverton, "Intelligence Analysis," 102.

26. Kerr, "Track Record," 36–37.

27. Christopher M. Andrew and Vasili Mitrokhin, *The Mitrokhin Archive: The KGB in Europe and the West* (London: Allen Lane / Penguin Press, 1999), 720–23. "Main Adversary," a Soviet intelligence term of art, is capitalized in the present volume.

28. Zbigniew K. Brzezinski, *Ideology and Power in Soviet Politics*, rev. ed. (New York: Frederick A. Praeger, 1967), 134–35.

29. Klaus Eichner and Andreas Dobbert, *Headquarters Germany: Die USA-Geheimdienste in Deutschland* (Berlin: Edition Ost, 1997), 156, 176.

30. Herman, "Intelligence Effects on the Cold War," 17.

31. Brzezinski, *Ideology and Power in Soviet Politics*, 141–42.

32. Indeed, the Cold War ended with the claim that the West's ideology had been vindicated. See Francis Fukuyama, *The End of History and the Last Man* (New York: Free Press, 1992).

33. Kerr, "Track Record," 38.

34. Angus Maddison, "Measuring the Performance of a Communist Command Economy: An Assessment of the CIA Estimates for the USSR," *Review of Income and Wealth* 44, no. 3 (1998): 307–23.

35. George, "Fixing the Problem of Analytical Mindsets," 314–15.

36. May, *Knowing One's Enemies*, 538; Kerr, "Track Record," 39–42.

37. Betts, *Enemies of Intelligence*, 67.

38. J. Kenneth McDonald, "How Much Did Intelligence Matter in the Cold War?," in Herman, McDonald, and Mastny, *Did Intelligence Matter in the Cold War?*, 53–54.

39. The Commission on the Intelligence Capabilities of the United States Regarding Weapons of Mass Destruction (WMD Commission) and the Senate Select Committee on Intelligence state in their reports on the Iraqi WMD affair that American analysts did not adjust their findings in response to pressure from the George W. Bush administration to conclude that Iraq was developing WMDs. However, analysts would be loath to admit that they did succumb to pressure. They were strongly inclined, anyway, not to underestimate Saddam's WMD programs again, as they had done before the Gulf War. The pressure from the administration may have increased their inclination to be prudent but in a way so subtle that the analysts themselves were unaware of it.

40. Treverton, "Intelligence Analysis," 92–96. On the Iraqi WMD debacle, see Commission on the Intelligence Capabilities of the United States Regarding Weapons of Mass Destruction, *Report to the President of the United States*, March 31, 2004, http://govinfo.library.unt.edu/wmd/report/index.html (hereafter cited as WMD Commission Report), and US Senate, Select Committee on Intelligence, *The Report on the US Intelligence Community's Prewar Intelligence Assessments on Iraq*, June 2004, http://www.fas.org/irp/congress/2004_rpt/index.html.

41. See Anne Hessing Cahn, *Killing Détente: The Right Attacks the CIA* (University Park: Pennsylvania State University Press, 1998), 163–84; see also Prados, *Soviet Estimate*, 248–57.

42. Andrew and Mitrokhin, *Mitrokhin Archive*, 322–41, 721.

43. John Lewis Gaddis, *The United States and the End of the Cold War: Implications, Reconsiderations, Provocations* (Oxford: Oxford University Press, 1992), 100–102; Vojtech Mastny, "On the Soviet Side," in Herman, McDonald, and Mastny, *Did Intelligence Matter in the Cold War?*, 57–69.

44. The German courts that tried spies of the HVA who supplied intelligence on NATO referred in their judgments to the advantage their information would have given the Warsaw

Pact if there had been a war in Europe. See Georg Herbstritt, *Bundesbürger im Dienst der DDR-Spionage: Eine analytische Studie* (Göttingen: Vandenhoeck & Ruprecht, 2007), 303–6.

45. Andrew and Mitrokhin, *Mitrokhin Archive*, 723–25; Kristie Macrakis, "Does Effective Espionage Lead to Success in Science and Technology? Lessons from the East German Ministry for State Security," *Intelligence and National Security* 19, no. 1 (Spring 2004): 52–77.

46. Garthoff, "Foreign Intelligence and the Historiography of the Cold War," 35.

47. See Kent, *Strategic Intelligence for American World Policy*, 5.

48. Jens Gieseke, *Der Mielke-Konzern: Die Geschichte der Stasi 1945–1990* (Munich: Deutsche Verlags-Anstalt, 2006), 217–21, 244–46.

49. National Commission on Terrorist Attacks upon the United States, *9/11 Commission Report*, 353–60.

50. Ralph Jessen, "Staatssicherheit, SED und Öffentlichkeit," in *Staatssicherheit und Gesellschaft*, ed. Jens Gieseke (Göttingen: Vandenhoeck & Ruprecht, 2007), 161–62.

51. WMD Commission Report, http://govinfo.library.unt.edu/wmd/report/chapter7_fm.pdf.

52. On Venona, see John Earl Haynes and Harvey Klehr, *Venona: Decoding Soviet Espionage in America* (New Haven: Yale University Press, 1999). On the breakthroughs of the late 1970s, see Matthew M. Aid, *The Secret Sentry: The Untold History of the National Security Agency* (New York: Bloomsbury, 2009), 164–65, and Haslam, *Russia's Cold War*, 318–19.

53. Garthoff, "Foreign Intelligence and the Historiography of the Cold War," 37–38.

54. McDonald, "How Much Did Intelligence Matter in the Cold War?," 48–49.

55. See Oleg Bukharin, "US Atomic Energy Intelligence against the Soviet Target," *Intelligence and National Security* 19, no. 4 (2004): 655–79.

56. Cahn, *Killing Détente*, 144–47.

57. See Paul Maddrell, "The Economic Dimension of Cold War Intelligence-Gathering: The West's Spies in the GDR's Economy," *Journal of Cold War Studies* 15, no. 3 (Summer 2013): 85–88.

58. See Paul Maddrell, "Im Fadenkreuz der Stasi: Westliche Spionage in der DDR. Die Akten der Hauptabteilung IX," *Vierteljahrshefte für Zeitgeschichte* 61, no. 2 (2013): 141–71.

59. Christopher M. Andrew, *For the President's Eyes Only: Secret Intelligence and the American Presidency from Washington to Bush* (London: HarperCollins, 1995), 438–43.

60. See Benjamin B. Fischer, ed., *At Cold War's End: US Intelligence on the Soviet Union and Eastern Europe, 1989–1991* (Washington, DC: Central Intelligence Agency, 1999).

61. Freedman, *US Intelligence and the Soviet Strategic Threat*, 197–98.

62. Pavel Podvig, "The Window of Vulnerability That Wasn't: The Soviet Military Buildup in the 1970s; A Research Note," *International Security* 33, no. 1 (Summer 2008): 118–38.

63. Andrew, *For the President's Eyes Only*, 335–36, 354–55.

64. May, *Knowing One's Enemies*, 541–42.

65. WMD Commission Report, http://www.govinfo.library.unt.edu/wmd/report/overview_fm.pdf.

66. Mastny, "On the Soviet Side," 65–66.

67. For a further example of American intelligence analysts and military commanders wrongly estimating an adversary as responding to American initiatives, this time in war, see James J. Wirtz, *The Tet Offensive: Intelligence Failure in War* (Ithaca, NY: Cornell University Press, 1991), 111–39.

68. Christopher M. Andrew and Vasili Mitrokhin, *The Mitrokhin Archive II: The KGB and the World* (London: Allen Lane / Penguin, 2005), 12–13.

69. Andrew, *For the President's Eyes Only*, 495–500.

70. Ibid., 499.

71. May, *Knowing One's Enemies*, 528, 530–32.

72. See Gaddis, *The United States and the End of the Cold War*, 101. See also John Lewis Gaddis, *We Now Know: Rethinking Cold War History* (Oxford: Clarendon, 1997), 283–84.

73. Andrew, *For the President's Eyes Only*, 498.

74. On this, see Jervis, *Perception and Misperception in International Politics*, chap. 6. A recent study that makes the same point is Keren Yarhi-Milo, *Knowing the Adversary: Leaders, Intelligence, and Assessment of Intentions in International Relations* (Princeton, NJ: Princeton University Press, 2014).

75. May, *Knowing One's Enemies*, 532–34, 538–39, 541.

76. Treverton, "Intelligence Analysis," 97.

77. On these psyops, see Thomas C. Reed, *At the Abyss: An Insider's History of the Cold War* (New York: Presidio, 2004).

78. Gary Sick, *All Fall Down: America's Fateful Encounter with Iran* (London: Tauris, 1985), 164–65.

Soviet Leaders, Soviet Intelligence, and Changing Views of the United States, 1965–91

RAYMOND L. GARTHOFF

MARXISM-LENINISM POSITED an ineluctable conflict between the capitalist (imperialist) world and an emerging socialist (communist) world. That ideological framework did not preclude Soviet leaders from acting pragmatically, but it did lead them to believe there was an objective and historically determined underlying adversarial relationship. The conviction of successive Soviet leaders that they were on the right side of an inexorable revolutionary historical process engendered in Western leaders the counterconviction that they had no recourse but to accept the challenge of their self-declared adversary and engage in an imposed competition. There were unique features of the perceptions of each side, but most important was a feature common to both: a reciprocated image of the other side as an adversary and the attribution to it of hostile intent, fueling potential confrontation and a constant arms buildup.

This chapter examines the changing understanding of the American adversary that Soviet political leaders and intelligence services derived from their ideology, foreign intelligence, and interactions with the West during the final twenty-five years of the Cold War. It concludes that intelligence fared poorly in competition with other influences and sources of information and that, in the end, a bold decision by the last leader of the Union of Soviet Socialist Republics (USSR) to alter fundamentally the Soviet conception of international politics ended America's status as the Soviet Union's "Main Adversary," to use the formal Soviet term.

The Cold War Setting (1945–64)

Josef Stalin, the Soviet leader from the late 1920s until his death in 1953, was strongly interested in acquiring intelligence information but highly skeptical about reported information that did not accord with his preconceptions. When highly placed Soviet spies in the British government and intelligence services in the 1940s and 1950s correctly reported that there were no British agents in the USSR, he doubted the reports and suspected that such valuable sources as Kim Philby were double agents. The foreign intelligence "Center" often dared not pass to Soviet leaders intelligence it feared would be unacceptable to them. Stalin harbored suspicions about his own intelligence officers abroad as well as about their agents, later purging a number who had served in the West during World War II.

American chargé d'affaires in Moscow George Kennan commented in 1946 on "the unsolved mystery as to who, if anyone, in the Soviet Union actually receives accurate and unbiased information about the outside world. . . . I for one am reluctant to believe that Stalin himself receives anything like an objective picture of the outside world." Kennan noted that Stalin was subject to constant "misinformation and misinterpretations about us and our policies" from his advisers.[1] Stalin, of course, was responsible for this situation and indeed enforced it. Below the top political level, there were biases in collecting, selecting, and transmitting information to Stalin and his top advisers as well as competition among the several intelligence services and important elements of the government and the Communist Party.

Soviet intelligence, rather than moderating or correcting Stalin's misunderstanding of the West, reinforced it.[2] Lt. Gen. Vadim Kirpichenko, a former deputy chief of foreign intelligence, notes, with particular reference to Stalin's rejection of numerous intelligence reports warning of the impending Nazi attack in 1941, that "the leaders of the country had not required analytical information from the NKVD [People's Commissariat for Internal Affairs]. They required, so to speak, 'fresh facts,' without any working over or context. What we received from sources of information we reported without any commentary or analysis." He notes that at that time there was not any analytical service in the Soviet foreign intelligence organization, which undercut the value of its intelligence reporting to Stalin: "In general, on the eve of the war the Soviet leaders did not accord our Service high State significance."[3] Indeed, the principal Soviet intelligence analyst was Stalin himself, who in the 1930s reportedly had said, "Don't tell me what you think. Give me the facts and the source!"[4] Despite Stalin's bias, steps taken after the war built a still constrained but at least professional analytical capability in processing foreign intelligence, including in the departments of the Central Committee of the Communist Party concerned with foreign affairs as well as in the intelligence services.

From the early years of the Cold War, Soviet intelligence collection activities were targeted principally on the policies and plans of the main Western powers. Recruitments of Westerners declined sharply with the end of World War II, and wartime assets disappeared or lost their access to valuable information.[5] Nonetheless, after 1948 Soviet intelligence built extensive new espionage networks in the United Kingdom and the United States, and in Japan, France, West Germany, and elsewhere in Europe.[6] These efforts notwithstanding, there is little evidence of any significant contribution Soviet intelligence made to the basic understanding of the United States and its major allies held by Stalin and other Soviet leaders in the 1950s.

After Stalin's death in March 1953, Nikita Khrushchev gradually moved into a leading position in the collective leadership that took power. Stalin's successors shared his Marxist-Leninist worldview but showed a readiness to make departures in some areas of policy. Most basic was adoption in February 1956 of a policy of "peaceful coexistence," holding that while the conflict between the capitalist and socialist camps would continue, socialism could emerge victorious without war. The new formulation was an ideologically sanctioned recognition of realism in the nuclear age. Khrushchev and other Soviet leaders continued to believe that Western leaders were hostile to the USSR, and while not inevitable war could still occur, so a strong Soviet nuclear and overall military deterrent was required.

The first East-West summit meeting in ten years was held in Geneva in July 1955. Although no concrete agreements were reached, the Soviet leaders gained confidence. Khrushchev was bolstered by a belief he had taken the measure of his foreign adversaries. He later noted that the meeting had convinced him and his colleagues that "our enemies probably feared us as much as we feared them" and that it was "an important breakthrough for us on the diplomatic front. We had established ourselves as able to hold our own in the international arena."[7] Ambassador Charles Bohlen believed that the Geneva summit led Khrushchev to conclude the West was not planning to attack the Soviet Union.[8]

Khrushchev's aggressive diplomatic ventures owed nothing to intelligence. They resulted from his impetuous nature, faith in the political power of nuclear weapons, ideological view of world politics, and lack of understanding of the West. He gambled with nuclear brinkmanship in the Suez Crisis of 1956, warning Britain and France that if they did not cease their intervention, nuclear missiles could strike their countries. The Soviets had no deployed missiles capable of such a strike, and Britain and France called off their intervention owing to American insistence, not because of Khrushchev's threat.[9] But judging from indications in internal Soviet discussions and the testimony of his son Sergei, Khrushchev believed that his threat had led to the Anglo-French withdrawal.[10]

In 1957 Khrushchev's attraction to the use of nuclear bluff and blackmail was boosted by the USSR's first successful test of an intercontinental ballistic missile and orbiting of *Sputnik*, the first artificial satellite of Earth. The alarmed Western reaction to those developments magnified the strategic significance of Soviet entry into the missile age and encouraged Khrushchev to seek political advantages from the promise of not yet realized strategic nuclear strength.

Khrushchev's confidence became his nemesis in 1958 when he called for the Western powers to withdraw their military and political presence from West Berlin, convert it into a "free city," and recognize East Germany. The ensuing political crisis, which lasted four years, ended with no change in the city's status. Khrushchev's failed initiative, which he had undertaken without seeking any intelligence advice on possible Western reactions, stemmed entirely from his overconfidence in judging that the USSR's Main Adversary and its allies would acquiesce in a political defeat. If he thought he could play budding American concern about a possible "missile gap" to his advantage, the calculation failed. Although US concern about Soviet missile strength did grow during 1959–60 when Berlin was a focal point of American-Soviet confrontation and contributed to a sense of crisis, it became clear to all during 1961 that America actually had the lead in strategic missiles.

What altered Khrushchev's view of America during the Berlin Crisis was not intelligence but his own impressions. Above all, his twenty-day visit to the United States in September 1959—the first ever by a Soviet leader—provided him with a partial corrective and broadening of his understanding of the United States. Upon his return to the Soviet Union, he publicly stated that President Eisenhower "sincerely wishes to see the end of the Cold War." Khrushchev saw his reception in America (he received full honors as head of state even though he did not hold that title) as according himself and by extension the USSR equality with President Eisenhower and the United States, in his eyes reflecting a major advance.

Although the USSR's Committee for State Security (KGB) lacked high-grade sources of political intelligence on the United States that could correct his misperceptions, Khrushchev sometimes benefited from concrete and verifiable intelligence information as he conducted his erratic diplomacy. Soviet intelligence obtained good coverage of North Atlantic Treaty Organization (NATO) planning, including policy discussions and concrete military plans for various contingencies concerning Berlin. For example, KGB chairman Aleksandr Shelepin was able in July 1961 to report to Khrushchev that NATO was preparing, with serious contingency planning, to deal with the Berlin Crisis as a military problem and was also preparing various sanctions against the USSR and East Germany. Stiff personal letters on US resolve sent by President John F. Kennedy to the leaders of Britain, France, and West Germany as well as follow-up actions by Secretary of State Dean Rusk were all intercepted and rapidly reported to Moscow. Also, an American sergeant stationed at the Orly Armed Forces Crisis Center in Paris was copying for Moscow all the NATO top secret Live Oak military contingency planning documents for Berlin, and there were multiple other penetrations of NATO.[11] At the same time, Khrushchev was, according to his son, wary and dismissive of intelligence reports from vague undisclosed sources and possible hostile misinformation, perhaps because he himself had authorized intelligence disinformation and deception measures.[12]

In some respects Soviet intelligence on the West played a positive role. Extensive Soviet and other Warsaw Pact espionage penetrations of NATO headquarters and NATO member countries throughout the Cold War disclosed much to Moscow about secret NATO political and military deliberations and decisions relating to a whole range of East-West relations. These disclosures conveyed the firmness of the Western position in a way that open Western declarations could not. They also provided evidence that NATO had no offensive plans for war against the Warsaw Pact (although Soviet intelligence remained suspicious that the United States had ultrasecret offensive war plans not shared with its NATO partners).

After the Berlin Crisis wound down and as the American edge in strategic military power grew, Khrushchev in 1962 undertook his most dangerous foreign policy initiative, secretly deploying in Cuba nuclear-armed missiles that could at least temporarily shore up the weak Soviet strategic missile force in the strategic balance with the United States. Once again he miscalculated, overestimating the chances that US intelligence would not learn of the action until it was a fait accompli and underestimating his adversary's mettle. Once again he was compelled to retreat. Khrushchev embarked on this gambit, as he had with Berlin, without seeking any intelligence assessment as to whether the deployments could be successfully concealed and as to possible American responses. Soviet intelligence, in turn, did not discover that the United States had learned of the missile deployment for an entire week. During the crisis Soviet military intelligence did provide detailed data on the US military buildup and readiness for possible action, confirming American resolve. Khrushchev, however, had no intelligence information from espionage or other means concerning internal American deliberations, decisions, and intentions prior to or during the crisis, and thus on crucial questions of the other side's perceptions and willpower, he had to consider his actions to resolve the crisis virtually blindfolded.[13]

Khrushchev's behavior in his remaining two years in office showed an awareness of the need for both sides to "weigh its words more carefully and take into account" the other side's military strength, and "not incite conflict."[14] Both his assessment of the Main Adversary and his recognition of the need for prudence in policy were importantly affected by the chastening experience of the crisis. He and President Kennedy set a new tone for US-Soviet relations in 1963, reaching several agreements that lessened tensions, including a ban on atmospheric nuclear testing, and he seemed ready to move further. Then Kennedy's assassination changed the political landscape. Khrushchev and his colleagues considered how best to establish relations with Kennedy's successor, but before Lyndon Johnson's election as president in his own right, Khrushchev was ousted.

Brezhnev: Engagement and Détente (1965–79)

Leonid Brezhnev was first among equals in the collective leadership that replaced Khrushchev in October 1964. At Communist Party congresses in 1966 and 1971, the leaders adopted their general foreign policy line: War must be avoided, peaceful coexistence must prevail, and there should be détente between the capitalist and socialist countries. Nonetheless, they stepped up arms programs because they rejected Khrushchev's substitution of bluster for military spending as a path to the kind of equality that the United States would acknowledge and take into account. They accepted the case made by the military establishment and military-industrial complex—which had not fared well under Khrushchev—for expanded Soviet military programs. The increase in military spending and forces was not sudden or sharp, but it was sustained because it rested on persistent institutional advocacy as well as perceived requirements, which now included building up forces in the Far East to counter China as well as providing a deterrent vis-à-vis the Main Adversary. It was also fed by the dynamics of competition with the American buildup, abetted by a bias for exaggeration in Soviet intelligence on American military programs. Although his policies contributed to an arms race, Brezhnev eschewed Khrushchev's saber-rattling and attempts at coercive diplomacy.

Political leaders and other officials who were developing a greater appreciation of the realities of world politics hoped that increased Soviet military strength would engender greater acceptance of Soviet political influence in the world. For that goal, more interaction with the West was necessary, and Brezhnev led the way in developing détente first with Western Europe and then with the United States. America thus became a partner as well as an adversary, blurring the image of the enemy. Ideologically, there was no change in the traditional view of a rising socialist world pitted against a historically doomed but still powerful capitalist world, but in practice détente became the path to gaining respect and acknowledgment by the Main Adversary that the USSR had in fact "arrived" as an equal. Détente meant, of course, a relaxation of tensions but between two sides that remained counterposed in a systemic confrontation. Thus geopolitical competition continued, and a return to greater tensions and even war remained possibilities despite improved US-Soviet relations.

The wartime generation's adjustment of ideological assumptions to greater realism in the 1960s and adoption of cooperative measures to lower the risk of war in the 1970s affected the thinking of many officials in the postwar generation. To be sure, this development of a more realistic and enlightened understanding of the world was cautious and limited, and—unsurprisingly in light of the contradictions implicit in détente between ideological opposites—there remained countercurrents and setbacks. The change nonetheless came to shape the views of many officials, advisers, and academics serving in virtually all official institutions dealing with foreign affairs. Some of them would play important roles in the final phase of the Cold War.

To support this new policy, Soviet leaders took steps in the late 1960s to improve their understanding of, and to influence, the Main Adversary. In 1967 an Institute of the USA was established in the Academy of Sciences to cultivate influential Americans—a form of high-level academic propaganda—and, more important, to deepen Soviet knowledge about and ability to deal with the Main Adversary. Its head, Academician Georgy Arbatov, has disclosed that the institute's first major report, in April 1968, concluded that the United States had serious internal economic problems, that the next president might therefore seek better relations with the Soviet Union, and that the Soviet side could help bring this about. This assessment was bolder than any advanced by Soviet diplomats or intelligence analysts, but Arbatov believed that the institute should raise such viewpoints even if they were controversial or unwelcome to some leaders.[15]

Also in 1967, Brezhnev's appointment of Yuri Andropov as chairman of the KGB led to some improvement in intelligence analysis. Early on, Andropov requested a major KGB assessment of US policy and found it could not produce the kind of report he wanted both to inform the political leadership and to invigorate the foreign intelligence service.[16] That service, the KGB's First Chief Directorate (PGU), had by this time—two decades into the Cold War—developed its competence in espionage and covert action. Its headquarters in Moscow had evolved from a staff of only 120 in 1939, up to 248 when the USSR entered the war against Germany in 1941, down to 135 in 1942, 197 in 1943, up to 600 in 1946, about 3,000 by the mid-1960s, about 12,000 in the mid-1980s, and to its peak of about 20,000 in the second half of the 1980s.[17] Its analytical capability had not grown commensurately, however, leaving Soviet leaders to rely on the Foreign Ministry, Party Central Committee staff, and the Ministry of Defense, as well as academic experts, consultants, other advisers, and not least themselves, to evaluate important issues. Andropov's arrival helped to relieve the intelligence analysts from their reputation as a backwater for "burned" (exposed) and burned-out officers and give them a more respected status and role, albeit still subject to constraints imposed by ideological and political-bureaucratic considerations.

Andropov's appointments in 1973 of Vladimir Kryuchkov as head of the PGU (until 1988) and of Col. Nikolai Leonov (soon made major general) as head of the PGU's Information-Analytical Department (until 1983) led to further improvements in Soviet intelligence analysis, particularly on the Main

Adversary. They raised the standards, prestige, and career progression associated with analysis. Andropov stressed brevity in reports and initiated a daily intelligence digest, and Leonov raised both competence and morale among analysts, although he was unable to persuade Andropov and Kryuchkov to build it up as much as he believed was needed. Leonov bemoans that while the Central Intelligence Agency (CIA) had a roughly 1:1 ratio of analysts to operations officers, the KGB in the 1970s and 1980s had a comparable ratio of only about 1:10. Leonov does not state the number of personnel in the Information-Analytical Department, but former KGB colonel Oleg Gordievsky has estimated it to have expanded from fewer than seventy in the mid-1970s to more than five hundred by the mid-1980s.[18]

Kryuchkov recruited intelligence officers from graduates of Moscow State University, the Institute of International Relations, the Military-Political Institute, and the Institute of Foreign Languages (and sent junior KGB officers to such schools), and in the KGB's own Intelligence School he instituted a new department for training in analytical work. The KGB also increased contacts with the heads of the main civilian Academy of Sciences institutes—Arbatov at the USA and Canada Institute (Canada was added to its scope in 1974) and Nikolai Inozemtsev and later Yevgeny Primakov at the Institute on the World Economy and International Relations.

Leonov's headquarters analysts felt free to caveat or disregard KGB political reporting from the field, which was often poor. The New York residency, for example, made errors in the names and ranks of United Nations diplomats, showed lack of understanding of American and world political issues, and quoted sources in the Communist Party of the USA (CPUSA) as authoritative. Leonov is proud of what he describes as greater freedom to debate issues in his department, where he introduced brainstorming sessions, and some of his analysts developed a less ideologically deformed understanding of the Main Adversary as data about the West poured into the Center. They were, however, mindful of the biases of Leonov, Kryuchkov, and Andropov, and the views they expressed tended to be more hostile toward the United States than the attitudes of the political leaders they served.[19]

As détente with the United States advanced despite America's playing of the China card and continued engagement in a war against North Vietnam, KGB leaders worried that both the political leaders whom they served and the analysts who worked for them were not properly assessing the Main Adversary.[20] In his memoir, General Leonov states that his analysis department had to wage a constant battle against "illusions of détente with the United States."[21]

In the early 1970s Andropov developed "Theses of a Soviet Intelligence Doctrine for the 1970s," stating that the main task of intelligence was to learn enemy military strategic plans and warnings to prevent a surprise nuclear-missile attack on the Soviet Union.[22] By contrast, in 1968, in his first annual report to Brezhnev as KGB chairman, Andropov had stated that the first priority of KGB intelligence collection was political, not military, information, writing that "the intelligence services of the KGB attributed primary significance to the timely acquisition of secret information on subversive plots of the enemy." The report contained not a word about even the possibility of a surprise American attack.[23] Again, in late 1974 when détente was beginning to falter, Andropov exhibited his hostility toward America by railing in a speech against Western reactionaries for sabotaging Soviet peace overtures.[24]

Andropov was not above suppressing or distorting KGB information. For example, Gen. Oleg Kalugin has revealed that the Washington residency, at a time when he headed its political reporting, relying on good sources told the Center that the CIA had *not* acted to destabilize Czechoslovakia before the Soviet military intervention in 1968. Andropov chose not to pass this information to the Politburo since it contradicted his bias and the Soviet propaganda line. (The KGB was also then buttressing official propaganda by fabricating evidence of American plotting, including planting caches of US-produced small arms to be "discovered" and identified as a US contribution to a Czech uprising.)[25]

Our focus here is not on intelligence operations such as espionage or clandestine political measures, but several aspects of the East-West "intelligence war" bear mention for their impact on Soviet views. Lt. Gen. Vadim Kirpichenko, who ended his long service in the PGU as deputy chief from 1979 to 1991, tells us in his memoir: "The context of the term 'the main adversary' in our operational lexicon over the course of time has undergone changes, but at all times we meant by it above all the special [intelligence] services of the USA."[26] As détente with America was at its height, the KGB residency in Washington increased from about 120 officers in 1970 to about 220 in 1975.[27] In 1974 Kryuchkov established in the First Department (USA) of the PGU a special staff called "Group North" to coordinate espionage and other intelligence activities against American targets outside the United States. KGB residencies in most Western and some third world countries also set up "Main Adversary groups" to organize efforts against American targets and interests, although it appears this task was often treated as simply generating reports to meet a bureaucratic tasking requirement.[28]

Another consequence of the intelligence war was that the intense competition with the other side's intelligence services led Soviet intelligence officers to credit the American intelligence services with many US policies they deemed harmful to the USSR. Writing in his post–Cold War memoir, Lt. Gen. Leonid Shebarshin, head of the KGB's foreign intelligence service from 1989 through 1991, still saw the CIA as having been "the driving force" of the Cold War.[29]

The KGB's conduct of deception, disinformation, and propaganda operations around the world usually had the Main Adversary as a principal target.[30] This led to a tendency for KGB officers to seek out information that would assist missions such as genuine secret American documents that could be transformed with forged passages and used secretly in influencing third countries or publicly as "black" propaganda.

Perhaps the most important observation related to intelligence operations is that Soviet espionage was not able to produce high-level information on the adversary's thinking, intentions, and plans. Efforts to improve espionage against the United States had produced successful penetrations of the US military (especially individuals with access to top secret military documents and codes) and information on secret scientific-technical developments (especially concerning weapons and technology). But except for reports concerning high-level NATO alliance coordination, Soviet intelligence was unable to supply valid policy-relevant information as valuable as that obtained by the leaders and their policy advisers in increasing direct interactions with American and other Western leaders and officials. Although some three to four hundred pages of intelligence reporting and analysis were sent daily to the leadership (mostly via the Central Committee's General Department, headed by Konstantin Chernenko), Soviet leaders including Brezhnev received only the small fraction their personal staffs thought worth bringing to their attention, and its influence seems not to have been substantial.

In addition to being subject to the anti-American bias of Andropov and other senior KGB chiefs, Soviet leaders received biased information about the American scene provided by CPUSA leaders. These views came via the International Department of the Party's Central Committee but were sensibly ignored by all but the department's chief, Boris Ponomarev, and senior Politburo member Mikhail Suslov, the leader whose views were most affected by devotion to ideological orthodoxy. The International Department also evaluated political intelligence provided by the KGB and advised the General Department on what intelligence to bring to Brezhnev's attention. Information going to the leaders was subject to bias in selection as well as slanting by the intelligence services. Brezhnev was often given exaggerated or fabricated reports on how well his speeches were received by publics around the world, and General Kirpichenko states that pessimistic and unpleasant reports were often kept from Brezhnev in order not to "upset" him.[31] Also, the PGU was usually careful to avoid initiatives or even reporting that implied support for controversial changes in Soviet policy. Such caution further diminished the already limited influence of Soviet intelligence at the top political level. As General Kalugin has summarized the point, "the opinion of Intelligence was usually ignored or not even seen by political leaders deciding most important foreign policy questions."[32]

Foreign Minister Andrei Gromyko was prepared to deal with the United States as a partner *because* it was the Main Adversary. His personal role allowed his ministry to play an important part in Soviet policy decisions relating to the

United States in the 1970s and beyond. He created his own brain trust of advisers who, among other things, reviewed and briefed him on the intelligence provided to him by the KGB and the Main Intelligence Directorate (GRU) of the General Staff.[33] The Foreign Ministry did not produce intelligence evaluations per se, but its policy recommendations often were accompanied by relevant assessments of US affairs. Although not immune from a tendency to tell the leaders what they wanted to hear, Ambassador Anatoly Dobrynin in Washington offered more frank and informative appraisals of American policies and aims than his predecessors and exercised some influence on Soviet policy.[34]

The blurring of the image of the Western powers as Soviet policy embraced a serious effort to lessen tensions with them in the early 1970s was accompanied by leadership frictions. Brezhnev had consolidated his position as unchallenged leader by 1973 and brought into the Politburo—for the first time since 1953—the key guardians of Soviet national security (Foreign Minister Andrei Gromyko, Defense Minister Andrei Grechko, and KGB chief Yuri Andropov), all of whom supported his détente policy. Clearing the way for a sustained commitment to the policy, unreconstructed cold warriors such as Ukrainian party chief Pyotr Shelest, who had opposed the 1972 Moscow summit with Nixon, were removed from the Politburo in the early to mid-1970s. Even among those who supported détente there remained countercurrents of skepticism regarding the Main Adversary. Andropov remained ever the skeptic about US aims, and Mikhail Suslov was leery even of rhetoric that emphasized shared Soviet-American interests or downplayed Soviet support for world communist solidarity. Brezhnev's wartime crony Marshal Grechko weighed in to keep Soviet military strength a key element in the policy, supporting arms control only reluctantly and working until his death in 1976 to ensure that agreed constraints were not far-reaching.[35]

As noted, Brezhnev and his colleagues believed the correlation of forces had shifted in their favor, making the Soviet Union a second global superpower on a par with its Main Adversary. Thus, in their view, US presidents had improved relations with the USSR because they were compelled by their recognition of changed objective reality to turn to a more cooperative regulation of the continuing historical contest between the two world systems. A Politburo and government statement at the time of the 1972 Brezhnev-Nixon summit ascribed "great international significance" to the signed agreement on "Basic Principles of Relations between the United States and the USSR" precisely because it was seen in Moscow as registering this recognition.[36] A secret Central Committee letter to senior Communist Party officials went beyond the public commentary, stating that "the very fact that Nixon *had to sign* a document that speaks of both sides placing the principle of peaceful coexistence at the basis of their relations" reflected "an important change in the correlation of forces" and "bears witness to a strong moral-political victory for the Soviet Union, and a weakening of the position of American imperialism."[37]

Soviet leaders thus saw Brezhnev's summits with US presidents in the early 1970s as marking an important advance in Soviet power and prestige. Similarly, the fruits of détente in Europe, above all the successful conclusion of the Conference on Security and Cooperation in Europe (CSCE) in Helsinki in 1975, were seen at the time as a signal achievement of Soviet diplomacy in stabilizing the postwar restructuring of Europe, including implicit acceptance of its East-West division.[38] These perceived successes did not lead Soviet leaders to believe that the historically determined adversarial relationship between the USSR and the United States had ended, but they did create an expectation that America would moderate its international behavior while accepting prudent pursuit by the USSR of its own advantage. American perceptions mirrored this Soviet view, assuring future difficulties as leaders on both sides pursued courses of action with little regard for the other side's concerns and with undue expectations that their own actions would be acquiesced to by their adversary.

Political leaders on both sides of the Cold War were inclined to reach their own conclusions about their counterparts. Most members of the Soviet leadership right down into the 1980s continued to be influenced by such stereotypes as belief that monopoly capitalists really ran the US government behind the scenes, and they could not comprehend that presidents such as Richard Nixon could not make decisions that Congress would not support. As Ambassador Dobrynin has remarked, the understanding of the United States (and foreign affairs in general) of most Politburo members was essentially limited to what they read in *Pravda*.[39] Personal contact of the principal Soviet leaders with American presidents was always a key factor in Soviet policymaking, especially when the leader was in a strong political position (Stalin until his death in 1953, Khrushchev from 1958 to 1963, and Brezhnev from 1973 to 1980). Moreover, the position taken by the leader (except in time of shared leadership or transition) usually precluded serious deliberation of issues.

Brezhnev, Andropov: Tensions Revived (1979–84)

East-West détente peaked in 1975, following Brezhnev's summits with Presidents Nixon and Ford in the early 1970s and the Helsinki CSCE agreement that year.[40] The next ten years saw a decline in Soviet relations with the United States brought on by a series of events culminating in 1983 when tensions caused Soviet leaders to view the USSR's Main Adversary with alarm, wondering even whether America was preparing for military confrontation. Not even a final Brezhnev summit with an American president and signing of another strategic arms limitation agreement in 1979 could stop the downward trend, which accelerated after Soviet military forces invaded Afghanistan late in 1979 and Ronald Reagan became president in early 1981.

One factor in the downturn was the USSR's decision to involve itself more actively in support of national liberation movements and civil wars in the third world. Soviet leaders allowed ideologically stimulated hopes for a wave of progressive, loosely socialist, and anti-Western movements to guide this element of their policy, thinking that strategic nuclear parity with the Main Adversary gave them room to support those movements in prudent, limited ways short of direct intervention and might also restrain American countermoves. The KGB was generally skeptical of these involvements, but its views were neither sought nor, when cautiously advanced, given attention.

Soviet leaders were dismayed by Washington's playing of the China card in the late 1970s, when the United States abandoned a policy of balancing US relations with the Soviet Union and communist China and adopted a distinct "tilt" in favor of relations with China to the detriment of the USSR. Central Committee official Valentin Falin stated in 1980: "There is no doubt that China played an important part in the unfavorable turn of United States policy. China, as the White House expected, offered the United States a chance to change the correlation of forces." Similarly, a senior Soviet diplomat told me at the time that while China would not be a real military threat to the Soviet Union for many years, to Moscow the most seriously disturbing element was that the Sino-American rapprochement put the *United States* and its aims in a different light.[41]

The year 1979 and those that followed brought blows to détente that affected Soviet perceptions of the Main Adversary. At the fifth US-Soviet summit of the 1970s, a meeting in Vienna in June 1979 between Brezhnev and President Jimmy Carter, Brezhnev noted that the Soviet leaders had been careful not to categorize the United States as an "enemy" or "adversary" and asked for reciprocal treatment from American leaders. Carter, apparently caught off guard, did not comment or reply.[42]

In October 1979 the first volume of Henry Kissinger's memoirs (*White House Years*) was published, and in it Kissinger disclosed that Nixon and he had had a cynical attitude during the heyday of détente. Although practiced themselves in self-serving postures, the Soviet leaders had been sincere in détente as they conceived it and were disenchanted to learn of the American deceit by leaders with whom they had personally dealt multiple times and dismayed to find themselves open to potential charges of having been hoodwinked. Valentin Falin, in the 1970s first deputy chief of the International Information Department of the Central Committee, told me years later that Brezhnev had been "shocked" and that the "unmasking" of the American leadership by one of its central figures had in the 1980s given ammunition to opponents of détente, who held that Brezhnev and Gromyko had made a serious error in trusting US interest in détente. I was also told of this impact of the Kissinger memoir on other occasions by Georgy Arbatov and Georgy Kornienko.

Also soon following the Vienna summit, a political hornets' nest erupted in Washington about intelligence reportedly "finding" a Soviet army "combat brigade" in Cuba, raising suspicions in Moscow that some in the American leadership had contrived a crisis to undermine the strategic arms limitation treaty agreed to at Vienna.[43] Indeed, the United States did not ratify the treaty, and Soviet leaders wondered whether Carter himself was responsible.[44] Brezhnev declared that he believed the failure to obtain ratification was "not without connivance of Government circles in the United States"—that is, in the administration.[45]

Soviet leaders saw NATO's decision in December 1979 to deploy Pershing II ballistic and ground-launched cruise missiles in Western Europe as threatening the strategic balance by enhancing the US capability for launching a sudden nuclear attack on the Soviet Union. In particular, they believed the Pershing II missiles had the range, accuracy, and short flight time to strike key Soviet strategic and political command centers in the Moscow area.[46] The KGB and (especially) the GRU provided strong evidence that the missiles had such capabilities. Moscow's failure to prevent the missile deployments through propaganda in Western Europe maintained the concern that the aging Soviet leaders felt about Western motivations, which increasingly were even thought to include possible preparation for war.

In 1979 PGU chief Kryuchkov had opposed the idea of Soviet military intervention in Afghanistan, as did all key Soviet military leaders.[47] But KGB chief Andropov joined Brezhnev, Dmitri Ustinov, and Gromyko on December 12 in making the fateful decision. General Leonov has made clear that no one in the Information-Analytical Department of the PGU knew anything in advance about the move (and he would have opposed it). The GRU was also not informed or asked for an assessment, and no Foreign Ministry official except Gromyko was aware.[48] As had occurred before, no advance assessment of the impact on the Main Adversary was made, although Gromyko knew it would harm US-Soviet relations. General Kryuchkov has stated that the KGB and GRU had informed the Soviet leadership of US designs for using the Afghan-Soviet border area to replace US intelligence collection facilities recently lost in Iran and that the main reason for the intervention was defense of Soviet security interests on the southern border, including possible influx of extremist Islamic influence.[49] KGB analysts erroneously predicted that the strong negative American reaction would be brief. Brezhnev and other Soviet leaders—who had not anticipated the long-lasting negative American response—tried to ride out the unforeseen rough waters with the United States despite virtual American abandonment of détente, a stance soon reinforced by the election of Ronald Reagan as president.

Reagan's disdain for arms control and determination to intensify a US arms buildup fed enduring images of the Main Adversary that still persisted in the minds of Soviet leaders and caused some officials to see him as an anti-Soviet cold warrior or even an erratic gunslinger. Nonetheless, the foreign policy line enunciated at the Twenty-Sixth Communist Party Congress in February–March 1981 made a renewed plea for dialogue and détente while castigating the United States for pressing a course of "undermining détente, boosting the arms race, a policy of threats."[50]

Soviet leaders found their concerns heightened when the United States in 1981 initiated unprecedented and unpublicized provocative American naval and air exercises, some with mock attacks on Soviet borders. In January 1981, in one of his first actions, President Reagan approved a proposal to begin a program of psychological harassing actions against the USSR, including authorization in March of "military probes on the Soviet periphery." In August–September 1981 an armada of eighty-three US, British, and Norwegian naval ships passed through the Norwegian Sea, and part of the fleet went beyond into the Barents Sea, north of Russia. By avoiding normal communications, the ships succeeded in evading detection until they demonstratively made their presence known, to Soviet consternation and concern.[51]

Détente collapsed when leaders adopted policies they regarded as necessary or advantageous despite the other side's perceptions of those policies as hostile and directed against its security. Thus Soviet leaders regarded the US rallying of NATO on deployment of new missiles in Western Europe capable of striking key strategic targets in the Soviet Union without warning as a deliberate and dangerous tipping of the strategic balance that provided the foundation for détente. Similarly, American leaders regarded the Soviet military intervention in Afghanistan as a dangerous extension of the "Brezhnev Doctrine" beyond the boundaries of the recognized Soviet alliance system and as the first step in a new Soviet offensive into Southwestern Asia. These evaluations of the motivations of the other side were seriously off the mark. They indicated, however, how enduring images of the Main Adversary had remained in the minds of leaders on both sides even under détente. Thus, without a direct clash between the two superpowers, each saw actions by the other that it regarded as hostile and dangerous to its security interests. While these concerns were in most cases exaggerated or misplaced, each saw the other carrying out actions that bore adversely on its interests despite détente undertakings to avoid such practices. They also contained the seeds of possible direct confrontation.

Now facing an apparently determined American policy of pressure and confrontation, Soviet leaders decided they had to guard against the worst-case possibility—a decision by the Main Adversary to launch a surprise nuclear attack on the Soviet Union. Sometime between March and May 1981, the Politburo approved a proposal by Andropov and Ustinov to launch a new intelligence program by both the KGB and the GRU to monitor all possible indications of US preparations for a sudden nuclear-missile attack on the USSR. While not the most likely contingency, it was certainly the most dangerous one and represented a threat that required vigorous and constant but secret measures to discover if the adversary was embarking on such a course. It is not known whether other members of the Politburo shared Andropov's and Ustinov's concerns over such a dire if improbable contingency; most likely not, but no one would object to a secret and passive precautionary alert, especially in light of what was seen in Moscow as the provocative stance of the superpower adversary. As greater tension between the superpowers inflamed alarmists in the Soviet leadership, intelligence became a means not for allaying their fears but for heightening them.

In May, in an unprecedented appearance at a conference of KGB chiefs, Brezhnev led off by denouncing Reagan's policies, setting the stage for KGB chairman Andropov, who asserted that the new US administration was actively preparing for nuclear war and announced that the Politburo had decided that the KGB and the GRU would cooperate in a worldwide operation to monitor any indications of US and NATO measures for the initiation of a nuclear attack, in particular a surprise missile strike.[52] The PGU was placed in charge of the operation, called Surprise Nuclear-Missile Attack (VRYaN) or Nuclear-Missile Attack (RYaN). In early 1983 it was designated as a long-term project (in KGB parlance, a "permanent operational assignment"). KGB *rezidenty* (station chiefs) in all NATO capitals and some other countries were required to submit biweekly reports to the Center on any and all indications of possible Western preparations to launch nuclear war. In February 1983 new and more detailed instructions were sent to all *rezidenty* in NATO countries, emphasizing the increased danger owing to the forthcoming deployment of Pershing II ballistic missiles.[53]

The Center insistently pressed field operatives to look harder for, and report more fully on, a target that did not exist, disproportionately tying up collection assets. At its peak in 1983, more than fifty officers in the Center were dedicated to assessing vast amounts of VRYaN biweekly intelligence reporting, reviewing irrelevant indicators, and reaffirming there was nothing worth passing on to their leaders.[54] By 1985 the operation was in decline, and it was finally ended by the last head of the KGB, Vadim Bakatin, and the first head of the PGU's successor organization, the Foreign Intelligence Service (SVR), Yevgeny Primakov, on November 27, 1991, just a month before the Soviet Union ceased to exist.[55]

Yuri Andropov left his post as chairman of the KGB in May 1982 to become a party secretary, and when Brezhnev died in November, Andropov succeeded him. He soon found himself facing the most alarming year in US-Soviet relations since the Cuban Missile Crisis in 1962, as hostile American public polemics intensified in 1983 over the already charged level of 1981–82. President Reagan accused the USSR of being "the focus of evil in the world" and guilty of "the aggressive impulses of an evil empire," called for a "crusade for freedom" to "triumph over evil," and announced a Strategic Defense Initiative (known as SDI or "Star Wars") to devise a comprehensive antimissile defense system to make the United States invulnerable.

What brought matters to a head with respect to Soviet perceptions of the United States was the downing on August 31, 1983, by Soviet air defenses of Korean Air Lines (KAL) Flight 007, a South Korean civilian airliner that had strayed off course over Soviet territory, with the loss of 269 lives. The Soviet air defense chiefs believed the errant aircraft was on a military reconnaissance mission for the United States (which had recently been flying both reconnaissance and psychological warfare flights in the region). The speed and vigor with which the United States denounced the action alarmed Soviet leaders, who were further persuaded of American hostility and suspected that the United States might have deliberately provoked the whole incident, as did Reagan's use of the episode in lobbying successfully for enlarged defense programs.[56]

On September 28 Andropov issued an unusual formal statement, representing the first definitive and authoritative overall Soviet assessment of the Reagan administration. US policy, he said, constituted "a serious threat to peace" and sought "a dominating position in the world for the United States of America without regard for the interests of other states or peoples." Describing the KAL 007 incident as "a sophisticated provocation organized by the US special [i.e., intelligence] services" and "extreme adventurism in policy," Andropov made clear that any earlier allowances that the Reagan administration might come around to a recognition of realities could no longer be sustained: "If anyone had any illusions about the possibility of an evolution for the better in the policy of the present American administration, recent events have dispelled them once and for all."[57]

Precisely at this critical juncture, an important phenomenon occurred that plagued both Soviet and American military warning and alerting systems throughout the Cold War. On September 26, 1983, the Soviet military intelligence satellite surveillance and warning system seemed to indicate a US launch of intercontinental missiles toward the Soviet Union. A relatively junior Soviet duty officer at the Serpukhov monitoring station, Lt. Col. Stanislav Petrov, correctly evaluated the information as a false alarm rather than as evidence of an actual attack. Had he judged differently or simply reported it, some higher-level military commander would have had to decide within minutes to report it as an attack, and someone, possibly well below the top political leadership given the time pressure, could well have started the ultimate great war.[58]

Less than two months later, a NATO military exercise called Able Archer, testing the command and communication procedures for the release of nuclear weapons in case of war, led the Center and the GRU under VRYaN to send flash cables to key KGB and GRU posts calling urgently for all information relating to possible US preparations for an imminent nuclear strike on the Soviet

Union. After the exercise had ended, the specific report that had led to the flash messages was found to have been in error, and inasmuch as the Center did not receive indications of a possible attack, no action was taken by Soviet intelligence to alert top Soviet leaders. This was the closest that VRYaN ever came to reaching such a momentous conclusion.[59]

Mikhail Gorbachev has told me the matter never came to the attention of the Politburo. Georgy Kornienko told me it had not been brought up with the Foreign Ministry, and Marshal Sergei Akhromeyev, then first deputy chief of the General Staff, has said there had been no general military alert. Col. Gen. Ivan Yesin of the Strategic Missile Forces has, however, said that part of the Soviet intercontinental missile force was placed on alert.

During the tense moments of late 1983, Andropov was foremost in drawing attention to what he saw as threatening US policies and the danger of war. He told the Politburo in 1983 that the danger of war was then greater than at any other time since the Cuban Missile Crisis, and he was cited in a cable to KGB posts worldwide as stating that the danger was the greatest since World War II.[60] Other available KGB cabled reports from 1983 and early 1984 cite statements by PGU chief Kryuchkov that "the threat of an outbreak of a nuclear war has reached dangerous proportions" and "is reaching an extremely dangerous point."[61]

I found occasion years later to ask a number of senior Soviet officials whether they really meant what they had said. In a private conversation in 1999, I asked General Kryuchkov when he had considered the US-Soviet relationship to be most dangerous, and he promptly said 1983 was the most alarming time (citing SDI and KAL 007 but not Able Archer). When I asked about VRYaN, he downplayed it, saying it was really an intelligence watch, "just in case," rather than reflecting real expectation of an attack, even though it was couched in "sharp terms." I asked if he personally had *ever* believed that the United States would launch a nuclear strike on the Soviet Union, and after a moment's reflection he said that he had not. When I asked if other members of the leadership had ever really expected an attack, he said that he thought not. When I pressed, asking if there had been none, he replied, "Maybe Andropov. He was more fearful of an attack than others."

Maj. Gen. Oleg Kalugin, not himself concerned over a possible Western attack, has argued that Andropov was concerned not only because of all the indications in the early 1980s of American hostility to the Soviet Union but also because he was acutely aware of how far the USSR had fallen behind the West in science and technology. Above all, Andropov believed the United States and its Western allies were working day and night to destroy the Soviet Union, and he saw CIA plots and imperialist intrigues everywhere.[62] A number of former intelligence officers (with some exceptions in the GRU) had not considered VRYaN to be a serious program or a Western attack to be a serious threat.

Just as the growing tensions at the outset of the Cold War in 1946–50 gave rise to overstated rhetoric about the threat of war, when both Main Adversaries depicted the danger in terms "clearer than the truth" (as Dean Acheson elegantly phrased it), so too were the fears of a threatening war in 1981–83 fanned by VRYaN and other Soviet reactions to American expressions of alarm over an alleged "window of vulnerability" to Soviet attack portrayed by the conservatives on the Committee on the Present Danger and "Team B."

In apparent contrast to the intense hostility of the Soviet and American intelligence services, at the very peak of tension in 1983 the KGB took an initiative in approaching the CIA and reaching agreement to create an intelligence "hot line" for clarification of potentially dangerous misunderstandings. This contact, which the CIA called "the Gavrilov channel," allowed direct meetings on and off during the next several years.[63] This remarkable agreement testified to the depth of concern felt by intelligence professionals on both sides—especially the Soviet side—during this most tense political confrontation during the Cold War. It also demonstrated the ability of the Main Adversaries, in secrecy and without political posturing, on occasion to seek sensible and mutually useful clarifications aimed at dispelling potentially dangerous misperceptions.

Gorbachev: Back to Détente—and Beyond (1985–91)

Andropov died in February 1984 and was briefly succeeded by the colorless and ailing Konstantin Chernenko, who in turn died in March 1985 and was succeeded by Mikhail Gorbachev, a vigorous young leader who during a visit to London in November 1984 had been praised by Prime Minister Margaret Thatcher as "a man we can do business with."

Gorbachev and Reagan both wished to meet, and after some rocky diplomatic exchanges and hesitation in Moscow they agreed to a summit in Geneva.[64] It was clear that Gorbachev had seized the reins of Soviet policy. One day before the world learned of the planned meeting, it was announced that Eduard Shevardnadze, another young Soviet leader who was Gorbachev's friend and political ally, would be foreign minister, replacing Gromyko. When Gorbachev and Reagan met in Geneva in November 1985, no major agreements were reached (indeed, the major issue of arms control and SDI was confirmed to be in deadlock). But the two men initiated a dialogue and recognized each other as real persons, not as cardboard images of ideological adversaries in the thrall of Wall Street or an Evil Empire.

The most important effect of the Geneva summit, evident only in retrospect, was the launching of policy reevaluations, first in Moscow, then in Washington. This process of reappraisal continued at the two leaders' second meeting, in

TABLE 1   US-Soviet Summit Meetings, 1945–91

1945	Yalta*	Stalin-Roosevelt
1945	Potsdam*	Stalin-Truman
1955	Geneva*	Khrushchev-Eisenhower
1959	Washington	Khrushchev-Eisenhower
1961	Vienna	Khrushchev-Kennedy
1967	Glassboro	Kosygin-Johnson
1972	Moscow	Brezhnev-Nixon
1973	Washington	Brezhnev-Nixon
1974	Moscow	Brezhnev-Nixon
1974	Vladivostok	Brezhnev-Ford
1979	Vienna	Brezhnev-Carter
1985	Geneva	Gorbachev-Reagan
1986	Reykjavík	Gorbachev-Reagan
1987	Washington	Gorbachev-Reagan
1988	Moscow	Gorbachev-Reagan
1988	New York	Gorbachev-Reagan
1989	Malta	Gorbachev-Bush
1990	Washington	Gorbachev-Bush
1990	Helsinki	Gorbachev-Bush
1990	Paris*	Gorbachev-Bush
1991	Madrid*	Gorbachev-Bush
1991	Moscow	Gorbachev-Bush

*These meetings involved leaders of other nations as well.

Reykjavík in August 1986. Again, no agreements were reached, but unexpectedly radical possibilities for arms reductions were discussed. Both leaders began to see mutual interest in reconsidering not only far-reaching arms reductions but also the role of military power in the bilateral relationship. In fact, the change went even further: They were developing common aspirations for a radically changed US-Soviet political relationship.

Gorbachev's closest foreign affairs adviser, Anatoly Chernyayev, wrote in his diary that Reykjavík was the turning point in Gorbachev's evaluation both of Reagan and of the opportunity for overcoming the Cold War. He no longer thought the USSR faced an imperialist military threat, and he never again spoke or thought of Wall Street capitalists running American policy behind a façade of politicians.[65] As had occurred with his predecessors, personal contact and communication with a literally personified "adversary" brought about changed perceptions and new policies.

Gorbachev's first encounters with Reagan, along with other contacts and reevaluation of Soviet relations with the West, convinced Gorbachev that radical changes were needed in order to end the arms race, US-Soviet hostility, and the Cold War.

Early in 1986, before he had been in power a year, Gorbachev laid out a new conceptual basis for thinking about world affairs at the Twenty-Seventh Communist Party Congress, becoming the first Soviet leader to proclaim that with problems "on a global scale affecting the very foundation of the existence of civilization . . . cooperation on a global scale is required." He spoke of "the interdependent and in many ways integral world that is taking shape"—*one* world.[66] In fact, after the congress, he stopped referring even to two different and opposed political systems. He also alluded to a novel conception of Soviet security that eschewed confrontation and military power: "The task of ensuring security increasingly is a political task and can be resolved only by political means." This statement prefigured radical policy steps almost unimaginable in 1986. The Stalinist two-camp, two-world conception was now passé, and the foundation for seemingly endless arms programs had been removed.

"New thinking"—the literal translation of the term used by the Russians— had arrived with breathtaking speed. And it led Gorbachev to another startling conclusion: The new world he wanted to bring into being could come about only if the Soviet Union took the lead and assumed the main burden of establishing different relations, an approach that he made a fundamental task of his foreign policy. Gorbachev would meet three more times with Reagan and then six times with President George H. W. Bush, and surprising developments came one after another. Agreements, including a formal treaty destroying all intermediate-range nuclear ballistic missiles, and unilateral actions, such as greatly reducing the size of the Soviet army and withdrawing a large portion of Soviet forces from Eastern Europe, peppered political leaders in both Western and communist regimes with novel challenges, forcing them to deal with major changes made at Gorbachev's initiative.

Gorbachev's new thinking about Soviet foreign policy was grounded in decades of gradual change in Soviet evaluations of the world around the USSR and in Soviet policies to deal with that world, above all with the Main Adversary. Its roots were in Khrushchev's post-Stalin "thaw," including steps such as emphasizing peaceful coexistence. It also had been influenced by Western socialist and Eurocommunist ideas and by experiences gained from increased contacts with Western thinking and with life in the West, especially during the period of détente, which lasted into the 1980s in Europe.

Although some dissidents were involved in this conceptual transition, it was mainly accomplished by officials who came to view the world more pragmatically, including some of the best academics, journalists, and other professionals in the Academy of Social Sciences, the Central Committee's departments, and the Foreign Ministry.[67] There arose among them—especially among those who worked in institutions dealing directly with the outside world—a gradually growing recognition that they, and their country, were in a sense imprisoned by their ideology. They increasingly wanted the USSR to become part of the international community and not automatically see others as inherent adversaries. Moreover, many gradually realized that the Soviet Union had contributed to the Cold War and its tensions. Their abandonment of Stalinist-era views was gradual and slow to surface because official fealty to orthodoxy remained dominant into the 1980s, but the ideology had become increasingly brittle and pro forma. What brought change to the fore was the arrival in power of a Soviet leader willing to embrace the new thinking openly and use it as a basis for state policy. Gorbachev's deathblow to old thinking caused revolutionary change in international relations and tolled the final bell for the communist regimes in Europe—and the USSR.

New thinking included prominently a disavowal of the very concept of an adversarial relationship, seeing in a political confrontation bolstered by nuclear deterrence a real danger of war. The "image of the enemy" was now seen as itself contributing to enmity and therefore as something to be discarded—on both sides. This was a drastic change, but the old image was not compatible with the conception of one world and the need for cooperation in dealing with global problems—such as energy, ecology, the economy, and not least security. Security was now defined as eliminating threats of war and reliance on nuclear weapons and as "common security" for all. In practice, the Soviet Union and the United States had been uneasy partners as well as adversaries during much of the Cold War, but now partnership was to be integral to the relationship even though competition and sometimes opposing interests remained. A fundamentally adversarial relationship was simply not compatible with the new outlook.

As Gorbachev's foreign policy aide has noted, from the very outset the new thinking embraced a whole panoply of related guidelines for policy: "recognition of the impermissibility of nuclear confrontation and war, breaking the arms race and beginning disarmament, a new look at the very logic of Soviet foreign policy based on international class struggle, rejection of the 'image of the enemy,' and recognition of the absence of an imperialist threat to the USSR."[68] As another of the new thinkers put it to me in 1985, they now realized that the danger of war came not from imperialism but from the very existence of adversarial confrontation and deterrence based on alert nuclear weapons. The Main Adversaries of the Cold War needed to become main partners—which of course required realization and action by both sides.

In a meeting in Moscow in October 1987, Gorbachev, looking toward another summit meeting, challenged Secretary of State George Shultz: "Can't you [Americans] get along without continuing to portray the Soviet Union as an enemy? How can we continue to negotiate with you if you see us as an enemy?"[69] At a major leadership conference sponsored by the Foreign Ministry in July 1988, Shevardnadze and two of his chief deputies spoke about the need to eliminate "the image of the enemy."[70] First Deputy Minister Anatoly Kovalev emphasized that apart from encouraging and making it easier for the West to abandon such a perception of Soviet policy, "we ourselves have so far done little to demolish the analogous stereotype in the consciousness of the Soviet people. One without the other will hardly succeed."[71] In a mischievous twist, Georgy Arbatov on several occasions in the late 1980s, including one I personally recall, expressed this serious idea to Americans in a jocular way: "We are going to do something terrible to you—we are going to take away your Enemy!"

Intelligence played no role in promoting the new thinking that fundamentally recast Soviet policy. As Communist Party leader, Gorbachev of course received a steady flow of intelligence selected by the KGB, the GRU, and Central Committee departments. Kryuchkov, head of the KGB's foreign intelligence directorate when Gorbachev took power, records in his memoir that Gorbachev from the outset "showed great interest in [intelligence] information, was, one could say, greedy for it."[72] Partly for this reason but mainly because the political leadership had become so ossified, the intelligence chiefs welcomed Gorbachev's accession to power.[73] They later noted that Gorbachev often failed to apply intelligence in policymaking—at least not as the KGB chiefs believed it should be applied.[74]

Kryuchkov and KGB intelligence analysts did try to be responsive to the changes in policy under the new thinking. Soviet foreign intelligence had to adapt to new assignments in objectives, collection, reporting, and evaluations— above all with respect to the Main Adversary. Speaking at the Foreign Ministry conference in 1988 shortly before his promotion to chairmanship of the KGB, Kryuchkov tried to accommodate what he called the Communist Party's "new methodology for looking at the world" and even acknowledged the impact of new Soviet policies in the West: "The 'enemy image,' the image of the Soviet state as a 'totalitarian,' 'half-civilized' society, is being eroded and our ideological and political opponents are recognizing the profound nature of our reforms and their beneficial effect on foreign policy." But he balanced that observation with doubt about the depth of the US commitment to disarmament and with concern about the ongoing US-Soviet intelligence war, alleging there had been "in the first half of this year more than 900 provocation operations" (i.e., attempts to recruit agents) and "agent penetration into key Soviet installations such as the Ministry of Defense, the KGB, and the Ministry of Foreign Affairs." He even cited a familiar, but by 1988 rarely mentioned, danger—"the immediate danger of nuclear conflict being unleashed"—which he described as a *"former"* KGB tasking requirement but one that has "not been removed from the agenda."[75] This was a last-gasp reference to the VRYaN alert.[76]

Kryuchkov's speech shows that the KGB could not basically reform. It had existed for almost seventy years to engage enemies in mortal combat, and if the enemies were now declared not to exist, it lost its own raison d'être. Of course, it continued to ferret out Western political, military, and scientific-technical secrets and to provide support to the leadership in its foreign policy (albeit still in its accustomed way). And new tasks included seeking to identify Western opposition to renewed détente as well as to Soviet initiatives. Its dire warnings of external threats were no longer needed, however, and its "active measures" against the United States had to give way to some support for constructive relations.

The KGB annual report to Gorbachev for the year 1988 dropped all references to VRYaN and declared that it was "actively supporting the foreign policy of the Soviet state and has *adjusted its activity* with the aim of making a greater contribution to accomplishing the tasks of creating a universal system of international security and favorable conditions for deepening the processes of *perestroika* in the country."[77] From the available evidence, however, although KGB analysts sometimes addressed matters of interest to Gorbachev, they often cast doubt on Western readiness to cooperate and thus undercut the protestations of support for Soviet policies. Vadim Bakatin, the last head of the KGB (from August through December 1991), concluded after reviewing its reports that "the information that the KGB provided to the Soviet political leadership did not help to curb the arms race, or to enhance trust between states"—key objectives of Gorbachev's policy.[78]

Gorbachev's early interest in intelligence reports had quickly declined. On November 29, 1985, he had his Politburo colleagues discuss a memorandum "on the impermissibility of distortions of the actual state of affairs in communications and informational reports submitted to the Central Committee and other ruling bodies." The party organization itself was under fire. One result was to instruct the KGB to take measures to ensure that its information was accurate. The record of a follow-up meeting of the KGB leadership shows that all KGB components were tasked with taking "all necessary measures to preclude sending to [the leadership of] the KGB of the USSR unreliable information and non-objective evaluations of the state of affairs in concrete sectors and lines of operational service."[79] Gorbachev was not satisfied with the results.

In May 1987 Gorbachev convened KGB, GRU, and Foreign Ministry intelligence analytical chiefs and sharply criticized their performance. A former KGB officer reports the meeting had little impact; the head of the PGU's Information-Analytical Directorate simply told his people to improve their analysis.[80] Chernyayev cites from his diary a comment Gorbachev made in the spring of 1989 to a small circle of advisers (including General Kryuchkov) about the intelligence the leadership was receiving: "Reading a cabled report I immediately recognize the 'fingerprint'—whether it is the GRU, the KGB, the MID [Foreign Ministry] or the Party staff. Each has 'its own interests.' But we, the leadership, need to know the truth in order to make correct decisions. . . . I'm looking at you, Vladimir Aleksandrovich! [addressing Kryuchkov]."[81]

The value of intelligence reporting and analysis to the political leadership was diminished by the KGB practice, in the name of security, of providing only vague indications of information sources, often referring simply to a "reliable source" or "documentary evidence." The source might indeed be a trusted agent or an acquired document, but the information might have been a newspaper article, gossip, or a source's (or his case officer's) assumptions or beliefs. It might even have been invented out of whole cloth by the case officer, the *rezident*, the Center's information analysts, or Kryuchkov himself.

General Leonov, the head of the Information-Analytical Department of the PGU from 1973 to 1983, described its task as "filtering the flow of information in accordance with its significance and quality, systematically collecting the data and analyzing the collected documentation"—not intelligence assessment or estimates as understood in the United States.[82]

Although Gorbachev discounted much KGB reporting as distorted by self-interest or ideological correctness or as policy lobbying, he was sometimes susceptible to reporting about continued Western "old thinking" skeptical about his policies. In January 1989, dismayed that Bush had not yet responded to his dramatic UN speech the previous month, he told Italian Communist Party leader Achille Ochetto that Bush "has in mind a Western effort to undermine the Soviet Union's international initiatives." And in April he was cautiously receptive to a Kryuchkov report that the CIA and State Department had created a commission whose objectives reportedly included discrediting Gorbachev and even raised the matter with British prime minister Margaret Thatcher and Italian prime minister Giulio Andreotti, both of whom sought to reassure him.[83] Only at his meeting with Bush in Malta in December 1989 were Gorbachev's suspicions dispelled. Bush himself said at Malta that he had "turned 180 degrees from my previous position" and now fully supported Gorbachev. Gorbachev later remarked that "the United States and the USSR are 'doomed' [destined] to talk, cooperate and collaborate. There is no other way. But for that we have to rid ourselves of seeing each other as enemies."[84]

Just as intelligence had not been active in the development of new thinking, so it remained on the sidelines as new thinking manifested itself in new policies. Gorbachev selected Kryuchkov to head the KGB in 1988, promoted him to general of the army, and in 1989 brought him into the Politburo. He met with him fairly frequently but did not bring him into policy discussions. Nor did he rely upon intelligence beyond routine acceptance of reporting. General Leonov, one of the more astute intelligence chiefs who became keenly aware of their lack of relevance, has said he observed, beginning in 1986, a noticeable loss of interest by Gorbachev in intelligence, including even espionage successes: "Intelligence lost its consumers, and the consumers lost interest in intelligence."[85] Gorbachev increasingly ignored intelligence when it was different from what he wanted to believe. As General Shebarshin put it, "when the information confirmed Gorbachev's views, it was welcome. But when policy and reality started to diverge, with the situation in the country going from bad to worse, Gorbachev did not want to know."[86] By 1991, Leonov sadly noted, "foreign intelligence was no longer in the focus of the Government's [i.e., Gorbachev's] attention."[87]

Gorbachev rarely refers in his memoir and other publications to intelligence inputs to policymaking. In talking with George Shultz in 1987, he commented favorably on the overall role of intelligence in allowing each side to know the other better: "We are political leaders, not babes. We know why the CIA was created and what it does. You gather intelligence on us, and we gather intelligence on you. I'll say even more: the fact that you know a lot about us introduces an element of stability. It's better to know a lot about one another than only a little. . . . Intelligence, in its usual meaning [i.e., secret information], plays a constructive role by helping to avert precipitous political or military actions." He also indicated, however, that in playing this positive role, the Soviet and American ambassadors were "our intelligence chiefs, thank God!"[88] He clearly did not regard KGB reporting as a major source of key political information or assessment.

Gorbachev and some other Soviet leaders learned to discount or ignore intelligence reports, sometimes because they did not support their policy preferences, other times because they suspected they were of questionable validity or deliberately slanted or fabricated. In August 1990, when Iraq had occupied Kuwait and the United States was seeking international support to press Iraq to withdraw, the KGB, in an attempt to head off a joint US-Soviet stand, gave Gorbachev a false report that the United States was about to attack Iraq. Gorbachev and Shevardnadze ignored this report, which Gorbachev saw as a deliberate attempt to stymie Soviet policy—as indeed it was.[89] General Grushko, first deputy chief of the KGB, discusses another case of manipulation in his memoir in the course of complaining that Gorbachev ignored valid intelligence to which he should have paid attention. Gorbachev was seeking Western economic aid at a G-7 meeting in June 1991 amid public speculation about sizable Western credits to the USSR, and the KGB had concrete, accurate intelligence that the Western powers *had* decided *not* to provide such assistance. Gorbachev, burned before by bad information and believing the KGB was out to derail his policy with fabricated reporting, did not accept this intelligence as valid. In this case, the KGB had gilded the lily of good data by adding a false claim, telling Gorbachev it was part of a Western disinformation campaign to make him think he would get aid, which was not the case.[90]

Another problem KGB officers faced was that they often were not players in supporting important diplomatic negotiations. General Leonov, longtime head of the Information-Analytical Department of the KGB's foreign intelligence service, notes that the KGB was not tasked to help prepare for the 1986 Reykjavík summit. The KGB nonetheless volunteered materials, Leonov states, including a correct assessment that Reagan was not prepared to give in on SDI, leading Leonov to complain, "Obviously, our materials were not taken into account."[91] In this case, Gorbachev was already well aware that SDI was a likely US sticking point, but he wanted to open up the subject, and for that purpose the Defense Ministry and the Foreign Ministry materials were more relevant. Another example showing KGB irrelevance to issues important to Gorbachev was the role of the Defense Ministry in preparing Gorbachev's offer in January 1986 of a comprehensive program for eliminating all nuclear weapons by the year 2000. In this case, the proposal was based on a study by the General Staff. Some key military leaders were more prepared than other officials to engage in negotiations aimed at surrendering military assets in exchange for anticipated lowered threats from adversaries.[92]

The May 1987 meeting at which Gorbachev criticized the analytical work of all the intelligence agencies may well have prompted discussion of whether the very conception of a Main Adversary was still valid. Several senior KGB officials have said that at about that time the question arose. At the same July 1988 conference at which Shevardnadze talked about giving up the image of the enemy, while KGB chief Kryuchkov spoke of the need to erode the *Western* "image of the enemy" applied to the USSR, he made no reference to a need to dispense with the *Soviet* "image of the enemy" applied to the West and above all to the United States.[93] But change was coming. Looking back, senior KGB officers have acknowledged they gave in to the change, albeit reluctantly. Writing after the Cold War, General Kirpichenko noted: "Former friends and former adversaries have become partners. Ceasing to be someone's enemies, we rather calmly have rejected the concept of a 'main adversary.' The epoch of confrontation and hostility, it has turned out, could be ended."[94] General Shebarshin, however, noted in his memoir that it had been difficult to give up the concept and that dropping the designation of the Main Adversary for the United States came only after a long and serious debate, with considerable opposition in the KGB. He nonetheless stated that with the Paris CSCE summit meeting the Cold War was over and there was no longer doubt that the concept of a Main Adversary was also over.[95] At that meeting, on November 26, 1990, the United States and its NATO allies, together with the Soviet Union and its Warsaw Pact allies, formally signed a statement agreeing that they were "no longer adversaries." Gorbachev's statement to Bush in December 1989 at Malta that "we don't consider you an enemy any more" had finally elicited the Western reaction he had long sought.[96]

With the fading of the image of the enemy and of the concept of the Main Adversary, the external threat to the Soviet Union was seen as greatly diminished. This facilitated Gorbachev's policies of unilateral and negotiated reductions of military forces and redefinition of military requirements, including acceptance of momentous changes in Central and Eastern Europe. A month after the Paris summit, a Soviet journalist noted an important implication of the change: "We have lost our beloved enemy, whose existence guaranteed the economic and political interests of vast segments of Soviet society."[97] It was thus unsurprising that resistance to the new situation came not only from intelligence professionals but also from the military-industrial complex. On one occasion, Gorbachev reproached Oleg Baklanov, the head of the Defense Industry Department of the Central Committee (and later one of the abortive *putsch* leaders), telling him sternly, "You only see the United States through a gunsight." Baklanov unhesitatingly shot back, "Yes!"[98]

For the KGB, which was responsible for internal security in the face of growing unrest and other public expressions of dissatisfaction that eventually led to the USSR's collapse, it is hardly surprising that senior officers looked for and "found" foreign—including American—support for internal political dissidence, nationality conflicts, separatism, and other threatening activities. KGB chiefs repeatedly warned about the dangers of subversion and unrest, and many have also since alleged (and cited what they see as evidence of) Western intelligence support for this internal threat.[99] General Kryuchkov, for example, writes that in 1989 the KGB "received reliable information on the activities of the special [i.e., intelligence] services of Western countries against the Soviet Union and all of its union republics," which had "sharply heightened collection of information on the situation in our country." He further contends that as trouble in the country grew in 1990 and 1991, Western services stepped up incitement of nationality issues and engaged in "economic sabotage."[100] But nowhere does he define what kind of "reliable information" was obtained. Grushko also claimed that the KGB had "reliable data on the fact that the US and NATO greatly counted on weakening the Soviet Union" and that "in the Soviet Union the Americans supported any striving for separatism under cover of the slogan of democratization."[101] From reading many KGB reports, including some sent to Gorbachev, it seems clear to me that ambiguity about the validity of these charges characterized the original reporting as well as Kryuchkov's memoir. It is not surprising that Gorbachev ignored such reports.

The most vituperative KGB attack alleging American attempts to break up the Soviet Union was made in April 1991 by the KGB's analysis chief, Gen. Nikolai Leonov, in addressing (at Kryuchkov's suggestion) a caucus of ultraconservative parliamentarians (the Soyuz, or Union, faction). Leonov ranted about US attempts to destroy the USSR and virtually charged Gorbachev with ignoring intelligence warnings and imperiling the country as Stalin had in 1941: "The KGB has been informing the leadership of the country about this in a timely and detailed way. We would not want a repetition of the tragic situation before the Great Fatherland War against Germany [World War II], when Soviet intelligence warned about the imminent attack of Nazi Germany, but Stalin rejected this information as wrong and even provocative. You know what that mistake cost us. . . . *History will not forgive us for passivity and inaction*."[102]

This remarkable statement by Leonov, who had only recently been placed in charge of analysis and information for the entire KGB, was a sign of the hard-line faction's desperate desire to reverse Gorbachev's policies. Early in Gorbachev's tenure, many Soviet intelligence leaders had accepted his ambitious goals of managing the economy better, disengaging from costly foreign entanglements, and even enlarging personal liberties. But they became increasingly concerned by 1988 and 1989 that these goals had been pursued with insufficient attention to maintaining Soviet security. By 1990–91 most intelligence chiefs were alarmed over the deteriorating internal situation and what they saw as foreign policy failures (especially German reunification in NATO and the disintegration of the Soviet political-military position in Europe).

The paranoia of the KGB's chiefs contributed to the USSR's final crisis. In June 1991 there was an unsuccessful attempt in the USSR's parliament, the Supreme Soviet, by several of Gorbachev's closest colleagues at a "soft coup," which would have taken many of Gorbachev's powers away from him.[103] In the course of it, Kryuchkov cited a 1977 KGB report that contended the United States was embarking on a program to infiltrate and recruit Soviet citizens who could be trained and aided to become influential Soviet officials and eventually manipulate Soviet policies to serve American interests. By dragging this report out of the files, Kryuchkov hoped to suggest that CIA agents of influence were influencing Gorbachev's policies.[104]

Although Soviet intelligence leaders have maintained in memoirs published since the Cold War that there were real American and other Western efforts to weaken the Soviet Union, they have also almost unanimously asserted that the main causes of the USSR's collapse were internal failings of the system and the leadership.[105] In 1990–91, without addressing their concerns openly, they sought to persuade Gorbachev and other leaders of the external threat. After the end of the Cold War, even while clinging to an instinctive distrust of America, they recognized openly what they were unwilling to say at the time. General Kirpichenko, for example, has stated: "The bitter truth is that not the US Central Intelligence Agency, and not its 'agents of influence in the USSR,' but we ourselves destroyed our great state, and all our highest party and state figures continued to pursue chimeras, not wishing to distinguish myths from reality."[106]

The Main Adversary, it turned out, was not the main threat.

Conclusions

How did Soviet leaders move from seeing the world as two hostile camps with one destined to overcome the other to seeing it as a single entity sharing a common destiny? A key part of the explanation is the decline of the influence of ideology in the crucible of geopolitical realism and decades of interactions with the Main Adversary and other Western powers. Even the most ideologically influenced Soviet leaders of the Cold War, Stalin and Khrushchev, allowed pragmatism to guide policies despite the continuing influence of ideology in shaping their own appraisals and the assessments prepared for them by their intelligence services. Ideology led to the decision to designate a Main Adversary, but it did not provide a formula for how to deal with it.

The most important factor leading Soviet and American leaders toward pragmatic realism was the advent of nuclear weapons. Both sides built such weapons in great numbers so as not to become vulnerable to hostile political leverage or outright attack, but they also had to prevent their use in order to ensure survival. Because of the possibility of escalation to the nuclear level, all wars involving the two Main Adversaries had to be avoided, and containing the tensions associated with sometimes intense political conflicts became a supreme imperative for leaders on both sides.

Critical to the drastic final changes in Soviet policy was the maturation of a generation of officials who grew up questioning Soviet reality in ways that led them to see the old ideology as not just an increasingly unconvincing outdated façade but also as an obstacle to necessary change. Ideology continued to serve a legitimizing function for the political system, and paradoxically it justified the authority of Gorbachev, as general secretary of the Communist Party, to introduce radically new policies. In the end, however, its hold on Soviet views of foreign affairs faded as new thinking finally ground away some of its basic assumptions, including the need for a Main Adversary.

The end of the long US run as the USSR's Main Adversary in a cold war derived from the even more basic change of seeing the world as one, and one can see in retrospect that the path to that radical conception had been prepared by many years of Soviet diplomacy. Stalin had acknowledged the need for mixed rather than wholly adversarial relations with the main imperialist states, and the transition after his death marked a turning point of greater importance than either his successors or their Western adversaries appreciated at the time. Under Khrushchev, earlier orthodoxy was bent to take into account the impact of nuclear weapons and the inescapable reality that nuclear war could not serve any ideological or political purpose. Orthodox views of adversarial US-Soviet competition were cited in the 1970s but posed no obstacle to US-Soviet détente as Brezhnev and his colleagues sought international recognition of the USSR as a nuclear superpower capable of matching the influence of the United States. The shift of views as successive Soviet leaders moderated their images of American leaders was not uniform. Vyacheslav Molotov, Andropov, and Kryuchkov demonized US leaders, sometimes using intelligence to support their views while in fact basing their evaluations on ideological prescription (Molotov) or fears (Andropov and Kryuchkov).

To be sure, many factors sustained the near half century of cold war. Interests and objectives clashed, as did each side's perceptions and evaluations of its principal adversary. Persistent interactions and mutual misperceptions stimulated by ideological presumptions validated judgments about the adversary that perpetuated competition and confrontation. This chapter examines one side of the relationship, but the views it describes were part of a complex interrelationship of the actions, perceptions, and evaluations on *both* sides. Common to both sides was a perceived need for an adversary. As Georgy Arbatov put it, "the formation of an 'image of the enemy' was always important, even a key component of the policy of the 'Cold War.' It was possible to start it and then sustain it for decades as the centerpiece of the whole system of relations only under one condition—if the people believe in the existence of an aroused fear, and if possible also a detestable adversary."[107]

The ideological narrative influencing Soviet perceptions paradoxically also shaped US perceptions as American leaders recognized the importance of ideology in Soviet thinking and concluded it was necessary for the United States to counter the Soviet challenge. For both sides, intelligence was avidly sought and used to evaluate the adversary. At the same time, the prevailing image of an enemy profoundly affected the collection and interpretation of data by intelligence services and hence the assessments they offered political leaders. When year after year in the 1980s Soviet intelligence could find no real signs of Western preparation to attack, their chiefs, rather than congratulating their staffs for reassuring Moscow, urged them to redouble efforts to find evidence that was not there. The adversarial image trumped reality.

Even when an adversary's intentions are prejudged to be generally hostile and dangerous, they are nonetheless elusive—if not illusory. In such circumstances, intelligence does what it *can* do: derive an evaluation of intentions from capabilities. Nuclear deterrence, which served a defensive purpose, required a superoffensive capability since the requirement was to be able to retaliate in kind after absorbing an enemy attack. It is therefore unsurprising that intelligence services on both sides viewed and depicted such a capability by the *other* side as posing an offensive threat. On the Soviet side, when Western leaders spoke of pursuing a policy of deterrence, the term was consistently translated—for the Soviet leadership as well as publicly—as *ustrasheniye*, a word that connotes offensive intimidation or compellence. When Soviet leaders began to describe their own policy as deterrence, however, the word always used was *sderzhivaniye*, which connotes restraining a possible aggressor. The adversarial nature of the Cold War guaranteed that political leaders and intelligence officers on each side would tend to depict the other side in the worst possible light. Only after the advent of new thinking in the late 1980s did Soviet commentaries use the more defensive term to describe American deterrence policy.[108]

As security was redefined to rely less on military power, the idea of giving up familiar military assets (and later geopolitical ones) in exchange for better relations with former adversaries was disturbing to many. Nonetheless, the military leadership was more prepared than many political party chiefs to adopt new military doctrine—including mutual deterrence—and to engage in serious negotiations, even with heavy Soviet concessions.[109]

Until broken by Gorbachev, the assumption that the US-Soviet relationship *had* to be adversarial had pernicious influence not only in sustaining suspicion and massive investment in military power to deter an attack by the other side but also in distorting evaluations of the motives and policies of the putative enemy on a wide range of issues. It led to a tendency to see the adversary's motives and objectives as set and unchanging and thus to underestimate the impact of other parties or of one's own actions. It also tended, even when attempts were made to place oneself in the other side's shoes, to skew consideration of the other side's motives or options toward the more threatening or offensive end of the spectrum of possibilities.

One of the most explicit statements of recognition of the radically changed appreciation of the abandonment of the Cold War paradigm was made by Col. Gen. Nikolai Chervov of the General Staff in the authoritative journal *Military Thought* in mid-1990 in an article titled "On the Path to Trust and Security," with the superheading "New Thinking in Military Affairs." Chervov went so far as to acknowledge that the US and NATO Cold War doctrine of containment and deterrence "at one stage played a not unhelpful role in preserving peace. But new times require new policies." Chervov noted that containment and deterrence must be abandoned by both sides because that approach to seeking security "inherently embodies the conception of an evil enemy, the idea of confrontational mutual threat, mutual distrust, suspicion and hostility, a competition in mounting nuclear armaments."[110]

General Kirpichenko reported in 1993 that Russia's foreign intelligence service had "renounced the very concept of 'an adversary.' Today, Russian intelligence does not have a main or even secondary adversaries."[111] Similarly, the Russian military doctrine adopted in 1993 specifically stated that "the Russian Federation does not regard any state as its enemy."[112]

Intelligence did not play the primary role in shaping basic Soviet perceptions of the United States. In the final analysis, the Soviet experience in evaluating its Main Adversary in the Cold War depended on judgments made by Soviet political leaders that were informed increasingly over time by their own experience, especially in direct contacts with American and other Western political leaders. Although until Gorbachev they had quite limited exposure to the outside world, such contacts as they had, especially with Western leaders, were all the more important to their understanding, on balance outweighing inputs by intelligence officers, diplomats, or Communist Party apparatchiks. Few Politburo members other than the top leaders had significant interactions with the outside world. The Soviet leader with the most experience involving intelligence, Andropov, had no significant contact with the West and none with Western leaders. Not surprisingly, he was the most consistently suspicious and fearful leader. Although professional Soviet foreign intelligence officers became more knowledgeable and effective in the 1970s and 1980s, senior intelligence chiefs in Moscow rarely had experience in the West. (By contrast, leading Foreign Ministry figures almost all had considerable such experience.) Where intelligence did play a role was in providing a great deal of specific and valuable information about the Main Adversary's military technology, military operational planning, diplomatic measures, and various aspects of political information, albeit often accompanied by weak analysis, especially in assessments and estimates of basic US policies and intentions. Intelligence did not contribute to understanding the adversary.

The most extensive and significant experience of any Soviet leader with the West and his Western counterparts was that of Gorbachev, who developed rapport with Reagan at Reykjavík and Bush at Malta. His experience contributed to the development of his new thinking on international matters, and he understood that changes in American thinking were needed to radically transform the US-Soviet relationship. He was not as naive as some of his Russian critics have suggested, although he was overly optimistic in counting on American acceptance of common values as a basis for relations. He expected, for example, that after the dismantling of the Warsaw Pact, the United States, rather than expanding NATO, would help build a common European security structure encompassing Soviet as well as Western interests. Where he broke decisively from his predecessors was in seeing positive potentialities in a drastically different East-West relationship and in acting on that prospect. The depth of his conviction that the United States and the West were not necessarily adversaries surprised many, as did his determination not only to argue his point of view but also to prove it in the real world. His willingness to take bold actions based on new thinking about international affairs brought about not only the end of the Main Adversary as a conceptual polar star of Soviet policy but also the end of the Cold War.

Resentment in Moscow in recent years over lost superpower status, the continuing global role of the United States, and perceived American disregard for Russian interests in expanding NATO contribute to raising tensions. But these tensions do not represent a renewed Cold War. In the absence of an ideological commitment to a historically destined revolutionary change of the world order, there is no preordained struggle to the death between two political systems or two Main Adversaries. Russian leaders perceive the United States to be competitive and adversarial with respect to some Russian interests, but they do not see it as necessarily a permanent adversary, nor do they live in fear of a sudden American nuclear attack or, for that matter, of any war with the United States.

Instead, the United States has come to occupy a prominent place as the most powerful of a number of important countries with which Russia is variously partner, competitor, or adversary—depending on issues and events. And Russia pursues a traditional policy of seeking to protect and to advance its national interests, as it sees them.

Today, a quarter century after the end of the Cold War, conflicts of interest and reciprocated suspicions have arisen. Vladimir Putin has seen not only a challenge to his desire to restore a weakened Russia to the status of a great power but also an opportunity to gain personal authority at home by belligerent challenges abroad and specifically by provoking a degree of hostility toward the United States. He has spurned American attempts to "reset" and reestablish a more favorable mutual relationship. But it is not a declaration of cold war, nor is it a reconstitution of the danger of possible mutual extinction represented by the twentieth-century Cold War between two systems predestined to conflict and headed by two Main Adversaries.

Notes

This chapter is drawn from a larger study, Raymond L. Garthoff, *Soviet Leaders and Intelligence: Assessing the American Adversary during the Cold War* (Washington, DC: Georgetown University Press, 2015). The author, a lifelong scholar of Soviet affairs, has worked for the US government and research institutions, and the chapter is informed by numerous contacts and interviews with Soviet intelligence officers, military leaders, diplomats, and scholars, as well as research in Soviet and American published studies and archival sources. All statements of fact, opinion, or analysis expressed are those of the author and do not necessarily reflect the official positions or views of the Central Intelligence Agency or any other US government agency. Nothing in the contents should be construed as asserting or implying US government authentication of information or CIA endorsement of the author's views. This material has been reviewed by the CIA to prevent the disclosure of classified information.

1. See *Foreign Relations of the United States, 1946*, vol. 6, *Eastern Europe, The Soviet Union* (Washington, DC: Government Printing Office, 1969), telegram 408 (February 22, 1946), 707, and telegram 878 (March 20, 1946), 722.

2. See Christopher Andrew and Vasili Mitrokhin, *The Sword and the Shield: The Mitrokhin Archive and the Secret History of the KGB* (New York: Basic Books, 1999), 54.

3. See "Answers of the Chief of the Group of Consultants of the Foreign Intelligence Service of Russia, Lt. General V. V. Kirpichenko, to Questions from the Journal 'Modern and Contemporary History,'" *Novaya i noveishaya istoriya* [Modern and contemporary history], no. 4 (1997): 87–88. A modest analytical service was established only in 1943.

4. Stalin's comment is cited by Christopher Andrew and Julie Elkner, "Stalin and Foreign Intelligence," *Totalitarian Movements and Political Religions* 4, no. 1 (2010): 75.

5. A purge of Soviet intelligence officers cost their services information and expertise, and the defections of two key agents in 1945 caused the extended deactivation of most Soviet agents in North America. See Andrew and Mitrokhin, *Sword and the Shield*, 47–51, 144, 155–56.

6. Ibid., 150–54.

7. Strobe Talbott, ed., *Khrushchev Remembers* (Boston: Little, Brown, 1970), 400.

8. Charles E. Bohlen, *Witness to History, 1929–1969* (New York: Norton, 1973), 389.

9. See Aleksandr Fursenko and Timothy Naftali, *Khrushchev's Cold War: The Inside Story of an American Adversary* (New York: Norton, 2006), 99–137.

10. Ibid., 130. See also Sergei Khrushchev, *Nikita Khrushchev and the Creation of a Superpower* (University Park: Pennsylvania State University, 2000), 211; William Taubman et al., eds., *Khrushchev: The Man and His Era* (New York: Norton, 2003), 359–60; and Vladislav Zubok and Constantine Pleshakov, *Inside the Kremlin's Cold War: From Stalin to Khrushchev* (Cambridge, MA: Harvard University Press, 1996), 191.

11. See Fursenko and Naftali, *Khrushchev's Cold War*, 372–74, and Christopher Andrew and Oleg Gordievsky, *KGB: The Inside Story of Its Foreign Operations from Lenin to Gorbachev* (New York: HarperCollins, 1990), 460–62.

12. See Khrushchev, *Nikita Khrushchev and the Creation of a Superpower*, 535.

13. See James G. Blight and David A. Welch, eds., *Intelligence and the Cuban Missile Crisis* (London: Frank Cass, 1999), the chapters on Soviet intelligence by Aleksandr Fursenko and Timothy Naftali, 64–87, and on US intelligence by Raymond L. Garthoff, 18–63.

14. Khrushchev, *Nikita Khrushchev and the Creation of a Superpower*, 641.

15. Georgy Arbatov, *The System: An Insider's Life in Soviet Politics* (New York: Times Books, 1992), 172–74.

16. Andrew and Mitrokhin, *Sword and the Shield*, 203–4.

17. For the figures for 1939 and 1946, see Alexander Feklisov and Sergei Kostin, *The Man Behind the Rosenbergs* (New York: Enigma Books, 2001), 413, 164; for 1941–43, see Lt. Gen. Vadim Kirpichenko, *Razvedka: Litsa i lichnosti* [Intelligence: Its features and personalities] (Moscow: Geya, 1998), 235; for the mid-1960s and mid-1980s, see Christopher Andrew and Oleg Gordievsky, *Comrade Kryuchov's Instructions: Top Secret Files on KGB Foreign Operations, 1975–1985* (Stanford, CA: Stanford University Press, 1993), xiii; for an estimate of about twelve thousand in the mid-1970s, see Oleg Kalugin, *The First Directorate: My 32 Years in Intelligence and Espionage against the West* (New York: St. Martin's Press, 1994), 149; for the last half of the 1980s, see D. P. Prokhorov, *Razvedka ot Stalina do Putina* [Intelligence from Stalin to Putin] (Saint Petersburg: Dom Neva, 2004), 108.

18. [Lt. Gen.] Nikolai S. Leonov, *Likholet'ye: Sekretnye missii* [The troubled years: Secret missions] (Moscow: Mezhdunarodniye Otnosheniya, 1995), 129.

19. From multiple sources. General Leonov's memoir provides the most complete rundown; see ibid., especially 121–33. The comments on reporting from the New York residency are from Arkady N. Shevchenko, *Breaking with Moscow* (New York: Alfred A. Knopf, 1985), 206–7.

20. Kissinger's secret trip to Beijing in 1971 and Nixon's formal visit in 1972 came as an "intelligence surprise," shocking the Soviet leadership. Brezhnev dressed down Gromyko (who was himself greatly distressed) for not foreseeing it. See Shevchenko, *Breaking with Moscow*, 200–201. Soviet concern about China in the early 1970s, following armed border clashes, reached such a serious state that some intelligence officers even proposed that China rather than the United States should be considered the Main Adversary; it was decided that China should be regarded as a major, but not the main, adversary. See Andrew and Gordievsky, *Comrade Kryuchkov's Instructions*, 2.

21. Leonov, *Likholet'ye*, 162–63.

22. See Prokhorov, *Razvedka ot Stalina do Putina*, 397–402; Kalugin, *First Directorate*, 151–53; and Kalugin, *Proshchai Lubyanka!* [Farewell, Lubyanka!] (Moscow: Olymp, 1995), 167–71.

23. See Garthoff, "New Evidence on Soviet Intelligence: The KGB's 1967 Annual Report," *Cold War International History Project Bulletin* 10 (March 1998): 212.

24. See Kalugin, *Proshchai Lubyanka!*, 172–74.

25. Kalugin, *First Directorate*, 108.

26. Kirpichenko, *Razvedka*, 340.

27. Andrew and Gordievsky, *KGB*, 540.

28. Ibid., 540–41.

29. Lt. Gen. Leonid V. Shebarshin, *Iz zhizni nachalnika razvedki* [From the life of a chief of intelligence] (Moscow: Mezhdunarodniye Otnosheniya, 1994), 180.

30. See Shebarshin, *Iz zhizni*, 61–62. See also Christopher Andrew and Vasili Mitrokhin, *The World Was Going Our Way: The KGB and the Battle for the Third World* (New York: Basic Books, 2005), 17–19; Andrew and Gordievsky, *Comrade Kryuchkov's Instructions*, 91–106, 129–39; and Christopher Andrew and Oleg Gordievsky, *More Instructions from the Centre: Top Secret Files on KGB Global Operations, 1975–1985* (London: Frank Cass, 1992), 30–36.

31. Interview with Lt. Gen. Vadim Kirpichenko, *Vremya novosti* [The day's news] (Moscow), December 20, 2004.

32. Kalugin, *Proshchai Lubyanka!*, 131.

33. Shevchenko, *Breaking with Moscow*, 160, 244. This included intelligence addressed for Gromyko's eyes only.

34. See Anatoly Dobrynin, *In Confidence: Moscow's Ambassador to America's Six Cold War Presidents (1962–1986)* (New York: Random House, 1995); and see Shevchenko, *Breaking with Moscow*, 193–98, 256–62. The US Department of State has published a unique volume recording the exchanges between Henry Kissinger and Anatoly Dobrynin, as reported by each of them. See *Soviet-American Relations: The Détente Years, 1969–1972* (Washington, DC: Government Printing Office, 2007).

35. Grechko even went so far as to suggest that Deputy Foreign Minister Georgy Kornienko had to be an American agent because he pushed for a strategic arms agreement. Andropov had to reassure him. See Sergei F. Akhromeyev and Georgy M. Kornienko, *Glazami marshala i diplomata* [Through the eyes of a marshal and a diplomat] (Moscow: Mezhdunarodniye Otnosheniya, 1992), 41.

36. "On the Results of the Soviet-American Talks," *Pravda*, June 2, 1972.

37. Central Committee Archive TsKhSD, Fond 4, Opis 22, Delo 937, Letter of the CC CPSU ST 43, (archive) 115; (letter) 25 (emphasis added).

38. In post–Cold War evaluations, General Kryuchkov continued to cite the "positive role" of the Helsinki Accord in improving relations in Europe, while General Leonov saw it as a "disaster" for the Soviet Union because it raised the issue of human rights in an international agreement. See Gen. Vladimir Kryuchkov, *Lichnoye delo* [A personal account], vol. 1 (Moscow: Olymp, 1996), 100, and Leonov, *Likholet'ye*, 163–65.

39. See Dobrynin, *In Confidence*, 218–19.

40. General Leonov also judged 1975 to be the high point of the Soviet state, with a gradual decline sharpened in 1979–80 by events in Afghanistan and Poland. See Leonov, *Likholet'ye*, 134, 201.

41. Ibid., 1100–1101, citing both sources.

42. After the Soviet invasion of Afghanistan, Carter's highly critical remarks about the Soviet leaders were regarded by some senior Soviet officials as breaking a 1965 agreement that neither side would impugn personally the leaders of the other side. Carter was not aware of this informal understanding. See Garthoff, *Détente and Confrontation*, 809, 1105.

43. Ibid., 910–34.

44. Valentin M. Falin, *Bez skidok na obstoyatel'stvo: Politicheskiye vospominaniya* [Without allowance for circumstances: Political memoirs] (Moscow: Respublika, Sovremennik, 1999), 361–62.

45. "Answer by L. I. Brezhnev to Questions by a Correspondent of 'Pravda,'" *Pravda*, January 13, 1980.

46. The GRU estimate was ten to twelve minutes. The distance from Pershing II sites in Germany to targets near Moscow was greater than the range announced by the United States but within the range estimated by Soviet military technical experts, on the basis of their reading of US tests of the missile as well as assumptions as to US targeting priorities. See Garthoff, *Détente and Confrontation*, 935–74.

47. Ibid., 991–1046, especially 1014–17, and Kryuchkov, *Lichnoye delo*, 1:203–5.

48. Leonov, *Likholet'ye*, 201–2; Georgy M. Kornienko, *Kholodnaya voina: Svidetel'stvo ee uchastnika* [The Cold War: Testimony of a participant] (Moscow: Mezhdunarodniye Otnosheniya, 1994), 193–97; Garthoff, *Détente and Confrontation*, 1010.

49. Kryuchkov, *Lichnoye delo*, 1:199–201, 205.

50. Andrew and Gordievsky, *KGB*, 59.

51. See Ben B. Fischer, *A Cold War Conundrum: The 1983 Soviet War Scare* (Washington, DC: Central Intelligence Agency, Center for the Study of Intelligence, September 1997), 6–10, and Gregory L. Vistica, *Fall from Glory: The Men Who Sank the US Navy* (New York: Simon & Schuster, 1995), 8, 105–9, 116–32. The Soviets were shocked because the radio silence negated their advantage from having US Navy codes supplied by their agent John Walker. The commander, Adm. James "Ace" Lyons Jr., used the silent approach because he suspected Soviet intelligence was intercepting US naval communications.

52. The most authoritative account, based on information from former KGB colonel Oleg Gordievsky, is in Andrew and Gordievsky, *Comrade Kryuchkov's Instructions*, 67–69; also see Andrew and Gordievsky, *Sword and the Shield*, 433–34.

53. Andrew and Gordievsky, *Comrade Kryuchkov's Instructions*, 69–85.

54. Ibid., 85.

55. See Vadim V. Bakatin, *Izbavleniye ot KGB* [Getting rid of the KGB] (Moscow: Novosti, 1992), 89–90; A. Ivan'ko, "The End of VRYaN," *Izvestiya*, November 28, 1991, 1.

56. See Raymond L. Garthoff, *The Great Transition: American-Soviet Relations and the End of the Cold War* (Washington, DC: Brookings Institution Press, 1994), 118–31; also see Seymour Hersh, *"The Target Is Destroyed": What Really Happened to Flight 007 and What America Knew about It* (New York: Random House, 1986); Alexander Dallin, *Black Box: KAL 007 and the Superpowers* (Berkeley University of California Press, 1985); Fischer, *Cold War Conundrum*, 19–24; and David Hoffman, *The Dead Hand: The Untold Story of the Cold War Arms Race and Its Dangerous Legacy* (New York: Doubleday, 2009), 63–71.

57. *Pravda*, September 29, 1983.

58. This incident has been most fully researched by David Hoffman, on the basis of interviews with Petrov; see Hoffman, *The Dead Hand*, 6–11. The incident was first disclosed, although in error dated in July, in Col. Gen. Yuri V. Votintsev, "The Unknown Military Forces of a Vanishing Superpower," *Voenno-istoricheskii zhurnal* [Military-historical journal], no. 10 (1993): 38.

59. Andrew and Gordievsky, *Comrade Kryuchkov's Instructions*, 85, 87–88. See also Garthoff, *Great Transition*, 138–40; Fischer, *Cold War Conundrum*, 24–26; Fritz W. Ermarth, "Observations on the 'War Scare' of 1983 from an Intelligence Perch," unpublished paper,

Parallel History Project on NATO and the Warsaw Pact (November 11, 2003); and Len Scott, "Intelligence and the Risk of Nuclear War: Able Archer-83 Revisited," *Intelligence and National Security* 26, no. 6 (2011): 778–90.

60. On the Politburo statement, see Andrew and Mitrokhin, *World Was Going Our Way*, 414; on the KGB cable see Kalugin, *First Directorate*, 302.

61. Andrew and Gordievsky, *Comrade Kryuchkov's Instructions*, 4–6, 17, from a January 1984 meeting and a November 2, 1983, instruction. For other statements of alarm by political and military leaders, see Garthoff, *Great Transition*, 136–38.

62. See Kalugin, *First Directorate*, 256–60.

63. This arrangement was first disclosed by Milt Bearden and James Risen, *The Main Enemy: The Inside Story of the CIA's Final Showdown with the KGB* (New York: Random House, 2003), 189–90.

64. Garthoff, *Great Transition*, 197–234.

65. Anatoly Chernyayev, *Shest' let s Gorbachevym: Po dnevnikovym zapiskam* [Six years with Gorbachev: According to a diary record] (Moscow: Kultura, 1993), 114–15. See also Dobrynin, *In Confidence*, 610.

66. For a more full discussion and citations from Gorbachev's speech to the congress, see Garthoff, *Great Transition*, 254–64.

67. See ibid., 261–64, and on the 1970s, Garthoff, *Détente and Confrontation*, 40–57. For analysis of how "new thinking" developed, see Robert D. English, *Russia and the Idea of the West: Gorbachev, Intellectuals, and the End of the Cold War* (New York: Columbia University Press, 2000). On the role of transnational contacts, see Matthew Evangelista, *Unarmed Forces: The Transnational Movement to End the Cold War* (Ithaca, NY: Cornell University Press, 1999).

68. Chernyayev, *Shest' let s Gorbachevym*, 114, 144.

69. "From the Gorbachev Archives," *Mirovaya ekonomika i mezhdunarodnyye otnosheniya* [World economy and international relations], no. 11 (1993): 75.

70. E. Shevardnadze, in *Vestnik Ministerstva Inostrannykh Del SSSR* [Bulletin of the Ministry of Foreign Affairs of the USSR], no. 15 (1988): 32, 40; Anatoly Kovalev, ibid., 37; and Vladimir Petrovsky, ibid., 55.

71. Kovalev, ibid., 37.

72. Kryuchkov, *Lichnoye delo*, 1:333.

73. For example, see Lt. Gen. V. F. Grushko, *Sud'ba razvedchika: Kniga vospominanii* [The fate of an intelligence officer: A memoir] (Moscow: Mezhdunarodniye Otnosheniya, 1997), 190.

74. Ibid., 201. General Shebarshin also has noted that while relations between Gorbachev and Kryuchkov were initially good, they faded, and after 1989 Kryuchkov became more critical of Gorbachev. See Shebarshin, *Iz zhizni*, 22, 35–36.

75. For a translation of Kryuchkov's speech from *Mezhdunarodnaya zhizn'* [International affairs], no. 10 (1988), see Andrew and Gordievsky, *Comrade Kryuchkov's Instructions*, 213–17 (emphasis added). Kryuchkov also cited concern over SDI, which he told me in 1999 had in his view been a disinformation bluff from the outset.

76. The annual reports of the KGB to Gorbachev covering the years 1985, 1986, 1988, and 1989 are available; the one for 1986 (submitted in February 1987) was the last to refer briefly to "acquiring information in the interests of timely warning of a surprise nuclear-missile attack on the USSR." The issues reviewing 1988 and 1989 make no reference to the subject. See Raymond L. Garthoff, "The KGB Reports to Gorbachev," *Intelligence and National Security* 11, no. 2 (1996): 228.

77. See ibid., 230 (emphasis added).

78. Bakatin, *Izbavleniye ot KGB*, 176.

79. For reference to the document and KGB chairman Viktor Chebrikov's report of a meeting of KGB leaders on December 10 during which they pledged to correct their ways, see Garthoff, "KGB Reports to Gorbachev," 226–27, 242.

80. See Yuri B. Shvets, *Washington Station: My Life as a KGB Spy in America* (New York: Simon & Schuster, 1991), 236. The analytical office was raised from a "department" to a "directorate" in 1984.

81. Chernyayev, *Shest' let s Gorbachevym*, 285.

82. See Leonov, *Likholet'ye*, 121. For an evaluation of KGB (and CIA) threat assessments of the adversary in 1975–91, see Mikhail A. Alexeev, *Without Warning: Threat Assessment, Intelligence, and Global Struggle* (New York: St. Martin's, 1997), 181–225. For evaluations of Soviet intelligence assessment by two experienced British intelligence assessors, see Percy Cradock, *Know Your Enemy: How the Joint Intelligence Committee Saw the World* (London: John Murray, 2002), 281–89, and Gordon S. Barrass, *The Great Cold War: A Journey through the Hall of Mirrors* (Stanford, CA: Stanford University Press, 2009), 379–400.

83. Chernyayev, *Shest' let s Gorbachevym*, 281, 288, 301.

84. Ibid., 303, and see Dobrynin, *In Confidence*, 632–34.

85. Leonov, *Likholet'ye*, 317, 333.

86. Lt. Gen. L. Shebarshin, interview by John Kampfner, *Daily Telegraph* (London), December 1, 1992.

87. Leonov, *Likholet'ye*, 360.

88. Mikhail Gorbachev, *Zhizn' i reformy* [Life and reforms], vol. 2 (Moscow: Novosti, 1995), 36.

89. See Garthoff, *Great Transition*, 435.

90. Grushko has revealed that the KGB reporting to Gorbachev involved the Western disinformation claim. See Grushko, *Sud'ba razvedchika*, 201–2. In 1999 Kryuchkov recounted to me the same incident—but omitted mentioning that the KGB added the claim of Western disinformation.

91. Leonov, *Likholet'ye*, 320–22.

92. See Akhromeyev and Kornienko, *Glazami marshala i diplomata*, 86–90, and Dobrynin, *In Confidence*, 596–98.

93. E. Shevardnadze, in *Vestnik Ministerstva Inostrannykh Del SSSR* [Bulletin of the Ministry of Foreign Affairs of the USSR], no. 15 (1988): 32, 40; Anatoly Kovalev, ibid., 37. For a translation of Kryuchkov's speech from *Mezhdunarodnaya zhizn'*, no. 10 (1988), see Andrew and Gordievsky, *Comrade Kryuchkov's Instructions*, 213–14.

94. Kirpichenko, *Razvedka*, 340.

95. Shebarshin, *Iz zhizni*, 221–23, 257–59. General Grushko also stated that by 1990 the United States was no longer the Main Adversary but a partner: Grushko, *Sud'ba razvedchika*, 171.

96. For all the declarations, see Garthoff, *Great Transition*, 406, 432, 434.

97. Galina Sidorova, "A Non-Christmas Story," *New Times*, no. 52 (1990).

98. I had heard about this, and when I asked Baklanov about it in 1999, he proudly confirmed it.

99. In addition to former Soviet intelligence officers' later memoirs, there is much evidence of their warnings in 1989–91. See Andrew and Gordievsky, *KGB*, 606–8; 623–28.

100. Kryuchkov, *Lichnoye delo*, 1:353–60.

101. Grushko, *Sud'ba razvedchika*, 175, 195, 196, 201.

102. Leonov, *Likholet'ye*, 372, 375–76 (emphasis added).

103. Kryuchkov, a leading figure among the conservatives involved in the soft coup, also was a leader of the more drastic pseudo-coup in August, but he did not bring the KGB as an organization into his political activities. He did not involve other KGB leaders in the August attempt (which sought to coerce Gorbachev into abandoning the effort to negotiate a new union of constituent republics to replace the USSR) except for directing Lt. Gen. Yuri Plekhanov, the head of the security directorate, to isolate Gorbachev. He and his coconspirators had no "Plan B" when the plot failed.

104. Kryuchkov, *Lichnoye delo*, 1:414–20, citing his speech of June 17, 1991. (For an abridged text, see Kryuchkov, *Lichnoye delo*, 2:387–92.)

105. Ibid., 1:420. He also made this statement in December 1990 (cited in Andrew and Gordievsky, *Comrade Kryuchkov's Instructions*, 218). See also Shebarshin, *Iz zhizni*, 180; Gen. Army Filipp D. Bobkov, *KGB i vlast'* [The KGB and state authority] (Moscow: Veteran MP, 1995), 369; Grushko, *Sud'ba razvedchika*, 195; and Kirpichenko, *Razvedka*, 33.

106. Kirpichenko, *Razvedka*, 33.

107. Georgy Arbatov, *Zatyanuvsheyesya vyzdorovleniye (1953–1985 gg.): Svidetel'stvo sovremennika* [A long drawn-out convalescence, 1953–1985: The Testimony of a Contemporary] (Moscow: Mezhdunarodniye Otnosheniya, 1991), 267.

108. Even years later, the official *Essays on the History of Russian Foreign Intelligence* stated that *yadernoye ustrasheniye* (nuclear deterrence by intimidation) after 1945 became "the main political and military strategy of the United States." See *Ocherki istorii Rossiiskoi vneshnei razvedki* [Essays on the history of Russian foreign intelligence], vol. 5, *1945–1965* (Moscow: Mezhdunarodniye Otnosheniya, 2003), 36–37.

109. Akhromeyev and Kornienko, *Glazami marshala i diplomata*, 69–73, 86–90, 120–27; Hoffman, *Dead Hand*, 235–37, 270–72, 275; and see Raymond L. Garthoff, *Deterrence and the Revolution in Soviet Military Doctrine* (Washington, DC: Brookings Institution Press, 1990), 94–185.

110. Col. Gen. N. F. Chervov, "On the Path to Trust and Security," *Voennaya mysl'* [Military thought], no. 6 (1990): 14.

111. Lt. Gen. V. Kirpichenko, in "Foreign Intelligence: From the USSR to Russia," *Krasnaya zvezda* [Red star], October 30, 1993, 6.

112. See *Osnovnyye polozheniya voyennoi doktriny Rossiiskoi Federatsii* [Main provisions of the military doctrine of the Russian Federation], special issue, *Voyennaya mysl'* [Military thought] (1993), 4. Even earlier, evolving Soviet military doctrine from 1987 to 1991 did not specify that the United States or NATO was "the enemy."

2

The Stasi's Reporting on the Federal Republic of Germany

PAUL MADDRELL

THIS CHAPTER EXAMINES the reports to its political leadership of the German Democratic Republic's (GDR) foreign intelligence service on the main subversive threat to the GDR: the Federal Republic of Germany (FRG). The GDR's main foreign intelligence service was the Main Intelligence Directorate (Hauptverwaltung Aufklärung, or HVA) of the notorious Ministry for State Security (Ministerium für Staatssicherheit, or Stasi). The HVA's reports to the leadership of the ruling communist party, the Socialist Unity Party (Sozialistische Einheitspartei Deutschlands, or SED), were prepared by its Department VII (Abteilung VII). The SED's leaders received these reports (*Parteiinformationen*) daily. No copies survive in the party's archive, held in Berlin by the Stiftung Archiv der Parteien und Massenorganisationen der DDR (SAPMO-BA), because the recipients were instructed, in the interest of secrecy, to return each report. Their copies were then destroyed; the only copy that was meant to survive was that of the HVA itself. The HVA's archive was destroyed in 1990. However, some 60 percent of the *Parteiinformationen* have survived because the HVA was proud of its reporting and wanted to preserve it for posterity.[1] That the party archive holds so little on the leadership's relations with the security and intelligence services means that too little is known about how the SED's leaders reacted to the intelligence they received.

Department VII's principal subject was West Germany. This was so because the GDR's relationship with the Federal Republic was far and away its most important. Whatever their public pronouncements, the SED's leaders always realized that East Germans remained part of a larger German nation. Events in West Germany affected the stability and success of the GDR. Any success for

West Germany, in their eyes, menaced the GDR; any turn for the worse represented an opportunity. Ideology increased the subversive threat that the Federal Republic was considered to be. Since the SED insisted that the creation of a communist society had eliminated the basis for any opposition in the GDR, it followed that any opposition or instability had to result from the malice of the capitalist West and first and foremost the Federal Republic. The communist leaders were acutely sensitive to developments in West Germany. Any activities of the West German trade union movement that might appeal to East German industrial workers were alarming; the German Trade Union Confederation, (Deutscher Gewerkschaftsbund, or DGB) was accordingly closely monitored by the HVA.[2] The SED's concern extended to events in West Germany far removed from politics. The HVA monitored carefully the Federal Republic's preparations for the Olympic Games of 1972 (held in Munich), fearing that it might add to the country's prestige.[3] Young West Germans' growing hostility to serving in the federal armed forces, the Bundeswehr, and their increasingly poor discipline as soldiers were noted.[4]

This chapter is based on Department VII's reports from four periods in the life of the GDR. The first is the period 1959–61 when the GDR was caught up in the Second Berlin Crisis, which culminated in the closure of the Berlin sectoral border. During these years, the HVA kept Walter Ulbricht and other top leaders supplied with a constant stream of intelligence on the Berlin question and particularly on West German views of it. The second is 1972, when the GDR was reluctantly embracing détente. The third is 1983, when military developments made the international situation seem threatening; the SED was troubled by the deployment of medium- and intermediate-range nuclear missiles in West Germany and other member states of the North Atlantic Treaty Organization (NATO). The HVA was also then involved in the global operation of the Soviet Union's Committee for State Security (KGB) to obtain warning of a nuclear first strike by NATO (the operation was codenamed "RYaN"). The fourth is the GDR's final crisis of 1989. In all these periods the HVA was obtaining much intelligence on the Federal Republic and was reporting on it to the leaderships of the party, the armed forces, and the Stasi, as well as the leaderships of other Soviet Bloc states.

In 1989 Department VII consisted of six analytical staffs, of which one was concerned exclusively with the Federal Republic.[5] The department was very well supplied with intelligence on West Germany. Over thirty years, the HVA built up a formidable capability to obtain information from within the West German government, political parties, labor movement, armed forces, media, and industrial and scientific communities. Department VII prepared reports on political, economic, and military matters.[6] Its reports are on a full range of subjects: West German party politics, foreign and defense policy, the Federal Republic's relations with its major allies and other states, developments in NATO, NATO's weaponry and forces in West Germany, other military matters, the West German labor movement, industry,[7] Western European socialist parties and politics, international economic decision making in which West Germany was involved, West German views of developments in the GDR and elsewhere in the Soviet Bloc, and more.

A point that arises clearly from the reports is that the intelligence the HVA obtained from within the West German government, political parties, and companies was also its main source of information on the wider world. It reported on what West Germany's politicians, civil servants, and soldiers thought of events elsewhere. This became easier and easier as the Federal Republic increasingly became integrated into multilateral Western structures, chief among them NATO, the European Economic Community (EEC), the International Monetary Fund (IMF), and the World Bank (WB). This integration enabled the HVA to spy on the Federal Republic's Western allies.[8] As the Federal Republic, from the late 1960s, entered into relations with the Eastern European states, the HVA was able to provide the SED leaders with information on the thinking and dealings of their communist comrades.[9] Its intelligence reporting was that of a parasite.

One person appears more often in these reports than any other: Willy Brandt. Brandt's dismal lot was that his rise in West German and European politics moved in step with the HVA's penetration of West German political life. Only in the late 1950s did the HVA begin to enjoy substantial success in recruiting sources in West German political parties. Its success was greatest in the West Berlin Social Democratic Party (Sozialdemokratische Partei Deutschlands, or SPD), of which Brandt was chairman. So the HVA obtained much information on him. It had increasing success in the 1960s in penetrating the West German government; Brandt, of course, became foreign minister in 1966 and chancellor in 1969. At his side when he was chancellor was an HVA spy, Günter Guillaume, whom Brandt took with him on trips around the world (some of the reports of Department VII are said to come from a "traveling companion" [*Reisebegleiter*] of Brandt[10]). Karl Wienand, the SPD chief whip in the Bundestag, was another top-level HVA source who reported on Brandt. Brandt resigned as chancellor in 1974 when Guillaume was exposed but remained chairman of the SPD, in which the HVA still had valuable sources. He also played a prominent role in Western European socialist politics, in which the HVA took a close interest, and in international affairs, on which Department VII also reported fully. Brandt must have been one of the most spied-on Germans in history. The HVA followed him wherever he went. As far as West Berlin SPD politics in the late 1950s and early 1960s are concerned, the HVA quite literally followed him from meeting to meeting.

The Conventions That Governed the HVA's Reporting

Throughout the period under consideration, strict conventions governed the Stasi's intelligence reporting, including that of the HVA. These conventions were established in the 1950s and affected the Stasi's reporting on both domestic and foreign subjects. They were imposed by Erich Mielke, who was made minister of state security in 1957 by the SED's first secretary, Walter Ulbricht. Ulbricht was then concerned about the Stasi's reporting. In his view, it contained too much criticism. These conventions concerned both the content and the style of the reports. Reports on foreign subjects, though prepared by the HVA, went first to the ministry's principal intelligence assessment body, the ZAIG (Zentrale Auswertungs- und Informationsgruppe), which forwarded them on to the leadership. The ZAIG also prepared reports on domestic subjects, using information provided by the Stasi's domestic security departments.[11]

Intelligence reports could not criticize the regime or its policies or dispute the SED's legitimacy or whether it genuinely represented public opinion. If intelligence reports were too critical, they would undermine the party's legitimacy by implying that the party line was wrong or unpopular and that Marxism-Leninism was not as "scientific" as it claimed to be. Throughout the period 1959–89, most (72 percent) of the intelligence reporting to the party leadership concerned foreign rather than domestic subjects and came from the HVA. This was so even though more of the ministry's intelligence collection took place within the GDR than outside it. This reflects how sensitive reporting on the GDR was. It inevitably raised difficult questions of legitimacy, popular representation, and political stability.[12] An illusory justification was given for this practice. By the 1970s the party line on détente was that the Soviet Bloc's strength had forced the West into a policy of accommodation. The corollary of this was that the GDR had achieved an unprecedented degree of stability. This meant that there was little need to report on the political situation at home.

The department's staff took care not to criticize the party's outlook. Reports that might displease their readers were retained within the ministry. They can still be found in the archive, marked "*nicht rausgegangen*" (not gone out). Rather, they saw their job as to give the party opportunities for action by informing it of opportunities and threats. They are better described as reporters or newsmen than analysts. Reading their reports, one cannot help but be reminded of journalists, who summarize information and pass on the news quickly. This is different from the work of an analyst, who tries to pass on understanding rather than news. Journalists also know well what news their readers expect.

A further convention was that Department VII's staff did not report on whatever they wanted to. They reported only on subjects of interest to the party. In the early 1970s the HVA's political intelligence reporting chiefly concerned three subjects: the Federal Republic's policy toward the GDR, political develop-ments in West Germany, and the attitude of other states, mainly in the third world, to the diplomatic recognition of the GDR. The reports did not deal comprehensively with any particular topic; instead they were short and concen-trated on conveying information to the readers.[13]

The readership was not fixed. It was not the case that all Politburo members or all Central Committee secretaries received them. They were sent to a small and ever-changing group of party leaders (sometimes only a handful and never more than about twenty in number). Most were members of the Politburo. Most HVA reports also went to the KGB. The content of the report determined who received it. Political intelligence was sent to the top party leaders. Military intelligence reports (approximately 30 percent of the HVA's output) were sent to the defense minister and leading military commanders, not the top party figures. Economic and commercial information was sent to the leading eco-nomic officials. In the 1970s and 1980s, the principal recipient was Günter Mittag, the Central Committee secretary responsible for the GDR's economy.

Strict conventions also applied to the use of the intelligence. No recipient knew who else had received the same report (unless one went to the general secretary, in which case he was informed who the other recipients were). The information contained in the report could not be discussed, even in Politburo meetings. This must have greatly limited its value in decision making, as did the fact that some members had received the information while others had not. Its influence is certainly hard to discern since, naturally, the minutes of Politburo meetings do not record members referring to it.[14]

The ZAIG's reporting to the political leadership on domestic matters was also selective. It reported on particular topics, usually troublesome problems, individuals, or social groups (such as the churches or the young). Often the reason for the report was that the Western media had already taken the issue up; the Stasi provided the leaders with an official GDR view of the matter and prepared them to respond. Because it raised sensitive questions of popular representation and legitimacy, the ZAIG's reporting on public opinion in the GDR was relatively rare. It tended to concern particular groups in society rather than East German public opinion as a whole. The reports tended to present the situation positively. Reports making particularly sensitive findings were retained within the Stasi.[15]

Department VII's Reporting

How did these conventions affect the HVA's intelligence reporting? The party's claim to infallibility was a heavy burden on the entire ministry. In the 1950s, the Stasi's reporting of foreign intelligence was crude. The best example of how crude it could be comes not from the records of the HVA's Department VII but from those of the ministry's main assessment body in the late 1950s, the Information Department (Abteilung Information). In 1957 the party leadership was so alarmed by this department's reporting on public criticism of the regime that it required the Stasi strictly to restrict the dissemination of its reports, which it regarded as so subversive that they might undermine the loyalty even of Stasi officers. The party leadership introduced strict rules of its own regarding the dissemination of the HVA's intelligence reports.[16]

The Information Department did try to prepare actual assessments. That is to say, information from various sources was combined to form a view of a particular problem beyond the GDR's borders that was of interest to the leadership. A report that has survived is an assessment from March 1959 of the impact on the West Berlin population of the visit of the first secretary of the Soviet Communist Party, Nikita Khrushchev, to East Berlin. Although the Information Department's staff acted as assessors rather than newsmen, they were still not analysts in the Western sense. They did not try to reach conclusions of their own. Their approach to studying the matter was politically correct; so were their main findings, although they did not entirely disregard the information available to them. They were careful in how they examined the matter, what they wrote, and how they arranged it.

Since they were reporting to the party leadership, the view of the situation they presented was very much that which it wanted to see. They were also strongly influenced by the fact that Khrushchev was visiting the GDR to reinforce his ultimatum to the Western allies over Berlin. They were therefore commenting on a matter on which both the Soviet Communist Party and their own had clear, aggressive policies. They knew that their job was to uphold the party's rule and authority; they believed that the party was always right. Consequently, they did not intend to tell it what to think. Khrushchev, as the supreme representative of the mother party of communism, was a figure worthy of special respect.

The report crudely distorts the view of the West Berlin population about Khrushchev's visit. In so doing, it reflects the SED's policy on the Berlin question and the basic ideas of Marxism-Leninism. Political viewpoints are tied to social class (Uta Stolle has called this "social class theater").[17] Each social class is presented as holding the view Marxism-Leninism required that it should. Above all, the SED regime's standpoint is presented as attractive to the working class in West Berlin and utterly convincing for workers in East Germany. Opposition in East Germany is presented as small and confined to marginal social groups.

The visit is presented as a success with the West Berlin population (and chiefly with the workers and employees among them). These people had approved of what Khrushchev had said and how he had acted. Individuals are quoted expressing positive views; these views are said to represent those of a large part of the West Berlin workforce. This "positive reaction" came close to reflecting the SED's own policy on the German question; the report speaks of their condemnation of the distorted reporting of the West Berlin press on the issue and their view that there was a "need to normalize the status of West Berlin."

The reaction of the West Berlin population is examined by social category. Bank employees are said to want to do business with the GDR, not wage war on the Soviet Bloc. Employees in administrative offices (*Verwaltungsangestellten*) are said to be troubled by Khrushchev's visit because it showed his determination over West Berlin, which would force the Western allies to leave it. Consequently, these people, like business and professional people, are stated to be considering moving to West Germany. The West Berlin middle class is reported to believe that the best solution to the Berlin question was that it should become a free city (Khrushchev's policy). American army officers and soldiers are stated to be troubled by the visit, fearing that it was a sign of worse to come. All classes of the West Berlin population are presented as thinking well of Khrushchev's speeches.

"Negative arguments" (*negative Argumente*) are referred to in the report. However, they come in a short section at the end. They are also stated to be either merely the views of particular individuals or are simply listed as quotations that are not attributed to any person or social group. An indication of how widely these views were held is missing from the report. In sum, the report was "intelligence to please." It represented disinformation.[18]

The Stasi's reporting on the reaction of East Germans to Khrushchev's visit was even more politically correct. It was not only crudely distorted but tended toward hyperbole. East Germans, and above all the working class, were stated to be in "joyful agreement" with Khrushchev. The views of the working class were said to be entirely in accord with the official line of the SED and with the public statements of Khrushchev and Ulbricht on the German question. East Germans were also said to like Khrushchev and his conduct. Many expressions of opinion are listed in the report. Not all were supportive of the regime's propaganda, but the report treats these viewpoints as unacceptable deviations from a satisfactory norm. It refers to them as "*Unklarheiten*" ("uncertainties," which in communist language meant confused thinking). Hostile viewpoints are also reported, but they are said to be very few in number and heavily outnumbered by supportive ones.[19]

The reporting of Department VII of the HVA was never so crude. It did not so slavishly reproduce the regime's propaganda. However, throughout the years 1959–89 its reporting had severe weaknesses. The reporters tried not to antagonize their readers. Their principal concession to them was to write reports that were very factual in character. They passed on information rather than an analysis. The problem with an analysis was that it might give the party leaders the impression that the intelligence service wanted to take decisions for them. The reporters did not try to reach any conclusions that added substantially to the information they were reporting. Still less did they try to reach conclusions independent of the party's thinking. They saw their task as to summarize the information available to them.[20] In the 1950s they generally summarized reports obtained from a single source, and the source's code name appears at the end of the report. By the 1970s they were increasingly blending the information available to them from more than one source. The department's reports avoided prediction and concentrated on stating what was taking place or being planned at the time. In American terminology, they represented "current intelligence." Predictions were dangerous because they might contradict the wishful thinking of the leadership. It was safer to report on what was happening, being planned, or had happened. The reporters did not recommend any course of action. Consequently, the HVA had no view of the Federal Republic that was independent of that of the SED leadership. That view was generated by Marxism-Leninism.

Of course, it is not possible to summarize information without making judgments and Department VII did make them. However, they are better described as subjudgments: judgments necessary to make sense of, and organize, the information they had received and were passing on. Some of these subjudgments were important and stirred up controversy.

Another way of deferring to the leadership was to pass on to it the kind of information it wanted. Department VII's staff consistently passed on information that supported the leaders' delusion that all opposition in the GDR was inspired and directed by forces in the West. Only as the regime moved into its final crisis did this change.[21] The department's reports also reflect an avid interest on the part of the SED leadership in the activities of the political Left (in all its forms) in West Germany, Western Europe, and elsewhere. Even though the SPD was not in power in West Germany from 1949 to 1966, the HVA seems to have sent the party leadership more reports on it than on the conservative parties, the CDU/CSU (Christlich-Demokratische Union / Christlich-Soziale Union) and the FDP (Freie Demokratische Partei). In part, of course, this reflected the sources available to it. However, in part it also reflected the SED leadership's very high opinion of the political importance of the Left everywhere. The Left was the agent of history.

The department's reporting was also tailored to the interests of particular consumers. Walter Ulbricht seems to have been particularly interested in the doings of the West German trade union movement. Reports on it were sometimes sent to him posthaste, by special courier.[22] Ulbricht feared the influence on East German workers of West German trade unionists, led by the DGB. He never forgot the shock of the workers' uprising of June 1953. True believer in communism that he was, he feared that West German influence was luring the workers away from communism. He was also on the watch for signs that the

West German working class was turning toward communism; it never did. The SED's leaders were also very interested in intelligence on the thoughts, plans, and disputes of the West German SPD and on the activities of young socialists in the Federal Republic. In 1959 Ulbricht and other top leaders received reports on discussions within the SPD every few days. Sometimes they received more than one report a day.[23] Even at the very end of the Cold War, the SED was still using the HVA to monitor the SPD and its electoral performance.[24]

Department VII's concessions affected the phrasing of its reports as well. If the report was on a subject on which the party had a definite policy, the report might make clear that the reporters respected that policy.[25] The reports frequently concerned people who were fiercely critical of the SED and the GDR; this criticism was toned down. Politically incorrect terms, such as "the freedom of Berlin" and "consistent violation of human rights" (by the GDR), were often put in quotation marks.[26] A very good example is a report from 1972 on ethnic Germans living in states of the Soviet Bloc who wanted to migrate to the Federal Republic. This was a very sensitive matter since only a small proportion of the Germans wanted to migrate to the GDR. The report glosses over this with the words, "For various reasons their hopes for achieving resettlement have always chiefly focused on the Federal Republic and on a significantly smaller scale on the GDR."[27] The general secretary received a little flattery; the reporters wanted to make clear that they respected him.[28]

One category of report seems to be less factual than the others. They are reports on economic developments in the capitalist world, particularly on the West German economy. They were sent to top party leaders throughout the four periods with which this chapter is concerned.[29] The reports are distorted by a Marxist-Leninist understanding of economics. This flaw was not confined to intelligence reports, of course. It is equally visible in public pronouncements of the regime and in the GDR press. The distortion is present in all four periods examined, though it is slight by the 1970s. Slight, of course, does not mean uninfluential. The reports' readers were such diehard Marxists that they probably seized on this kind of information.

The distortion is evident in the late 1950s. A report from March 1959 about West German economics minister Ludwig Erhard's tour of East Asia maintains that the tour resulted from pressure from West German monopolies that were troubled by sales difficulties and wanted to open up new markets. This report was sent to top leaders, including Ulbricht.[30] Only three months later Ulbricht received a report on economic differences between the United States and Canada; the authors clearly started from the Marxist premise that the struggle for markets was an inherent flaw in capitalism.[31]

Reports from 1972 on the prognoses of West Germany's Federal Association of German Industry (Bundesverband der Deutschen Industrie) for the economy display the same flaw. The reports state that these prognoses were very pessimistic. There undoubtedly was bad economic news at the time, and pessimistic forecasts were made. However, nowhere in the reports do the strength of the West German economy and its weight in the international economy appear. A key feature of the department's reporting on economic matters is what it does not say. The same bias is evident in a report from 1972 on West German thinking about international currency reform following the collapse of the Bretton Woods system the previous year. It is implicit throughout the report that the dollar had been very successful as the international economy's linchpin currency; its success points to a highly successful international capitalist economy, but nowhere is this expressly stated.[32] The oil shock of the early 1970s must have greatly encouraged the Marxist-Leninists in the SED Politburo to believe that the capitalist economy was in severe and damaging crisis.[33] Some expressions in these reports smack of a Marxist understanding of economics rather than the thinking of West German industrialists. One report claims that "aggressive, vagabond dollars are lying in wait so as to bring down the German currency market."[34] By contrast, a report in 1972 to Erich Honecker, Horst Sindermann (then deputy chairman of the Council of Ministers), and other leaders on West German analyses of the performance of the GDR's economy is very superficial and tedious. It may be that the reporters were unwilling to make the leadership aware of the full contents of the West German analyses.[35]

Another aspect of the economic reporting of the HVA is worthy of note. It reported to top leaders on very unimportant matters. This was not actually specific to its economic reporting; top leaders received reports on all sorts of trivial matters. However, the triviality of the economic reports seems to be influenced by Marxist ideas of cutthroat capitalist competition. For instance, in February 1972 Hermann Axen and others received a report on the competition between West Germany and France over making the color television system each preferred (PAL in the Federal Republic's case, SECAM in France's case) the more popular in the Mediterranean area. It is hard to see why the HVA would be reporting to such senior figures in the regime on such unimportant and technical matters unless the information pandered to their Marxist delusion that market competition would undermine the close relations the two partner states had established.[36]

The tendency to let Marxist economics infuse reports on the Western economies quickly became weaker than Department VII's usual matter-of-fact approach. Certainly by the early 1970s, the reporting had become almost entirely factual. It may be that the HVA had become so used to reporting on the workings of the capitalist economy that the influence of Marxism on them had declined. Its officers were also abler and better-educated than they had been previously.[37] Its reporting avoids crude Marxist errors, such as a tendency to consider capitalist states similar because they are all capitalist. A report from 1983 about Western sanctions on trade with the Soviet Bloc differentiates accurately between Western European and American attitudes to them. It distinguishes between the moderate Western European policy on sanctions and the more extreme American policy. It maintains that in the United States, the Reagan administration's policy was to reduce trade with the Soviet Bloc so as to diminish the resources available to the Soviet military-industrial complex, while Western European governments wanted to increase trade so as to enhance opportunities for exercising influence. It also states that the foundation of the Western European view was that the free world's economies were clearly superior in many respects to those of the bloc—so superior that greater East-West trade could not undermine this superiority. Both the Western Europeans and the Americans believed that the Soviet economy suffered from severe weaknesses that could be exploited. The Reagan administration believed that these weaknesses were so great that the USSR could be forced into undertaking economic and social reforms. The report is clearly based on reports obtained in Western capitals and NATO; facts triumphed over Marxist economics.[38]

This was just as much the case at the very end of the GDR's life. A report from 1989 about discussions between member states of the International Monetary Fund and World Bank reads like a minute of their discussions—so much so that it is odd to find it in a communist archive.[39] Another, from September 1989, concerns the US government's thinking about the economic potential of the Asia-Pacific region. The information contained in the report seems to have been obtained chiefly from the National Security Council (NSC). The United States was very impressed by the region's economic potential and feared its competitive challenge. It planned to prepare itself for a "Pacific Century." The report is a well-informed survey of US foreign economic policy, very free of ideological language or assumptions. This is remarkable since it was addressed to the top leaders of the party, including Honecker (the party's general secretary), Willi Stoph (the chairman of the Council of Ministers), and Axen (a Politburo member and the Central Committee secretary responsible for international relations). Its description of US policy has turned out to be very accurate. The United States did indeed use the crisis of the Communist Bloc to reduce the military threat to Western Europe from the Warsaw Pact and turn NATO from a military alliance into primarily a political one. The United States did plan to use the resources released by this to prepare itself for the Asia-Pacific challenge.[40]

In 1989 the HVA summarized an analysis by a West German economic research institute on the policies on manufacturing and trading in high-technology goods of the states of the Council for Mutual Economic Assistance (Comecon). The HVA was at its most matter-of-fact when summarizing reports obtained in the West; its summary was an accurate one, uninfluenced by ideology. The report contained many statements that must have made its readers swallow hard: that the Comecon states were imitators but that trends in high technology indicated that the costs of imitation were rising faster than the costs of innovation; that the GDR had rested its entire economic policy on achieving the world standard in electronics, and yet in microprocessors and silicon chips it was at least a generation behind; and that the states of the Organization for Economic Cooperation and Development (OECD) were importing fewer high-tech goods from the Comecon states because developing countries had become more competitive.[41]

Nevertheless, a tendency (if only a slight one) to regard capitalist economies as crisis-wracked remains evident in the reports to the very end. A report from 1983 on the EEC's initiatives to overcome the economic recession of the early 1980s used terms—"in the light of the continuing capitalist world economic crisis," "the most difficult economic crisis since the 1930s"—that would have encouraged the SED's leaders to believe that the Western world was in profound crisis. The report maintained that "according to opinions of committed European politicians, voiced internally, the EC mechanism is showing itself in fact to be completely powerless faced with the problems of unemployment, combating the deficits and restoring the competitiveness of Western European industry." In short, it concealed the strength of the Western European economies.[42] A report from 1983 on high-level politics in Bonn, clearly drawn from information obtained from excellent sources, maintains that "the governing coalition's economic policy, directed at the strengthening of monopoly capital, is also leading to considerably greater social burdens on the working masses than the previous SPD-led government's policy."[43]

The department's reporting had strengths. It received very good intelligence from West Germany and recognized its value. Its reporting improved between the 1950s and 1980s and was always very matter-of-fact in character. The reports from the 1970s on were good reports: Though they contained some ideological language and concepts, they were overwhelmingly factual and true to the sources. The reporters claim that the HVA leadership expected them to put ideology to one side and report matter-of-factly; they largely achieved this.[44] They tried to draw on all the available information, not just one source. Very often the department merely summarized the contents of a West German report on a particular topic. Or it set out its sources' accounts of meetings they had attended. In both cases, it made much use of reported speech, and in these cases its reports are particularly factual in character. The German language uses the present subjunctive to indicate reported speech; the department's reports abound in its use. The reports' tendency to summarize information obtained in the West, rather than reach conclusions themselves, was so great that, as the GDR's foreign trade minister in the 1980s, Gerhard Beil, rightly pointed out, they must have resembled those of West Germany's Federal Intelligence Service (Bundesnachrichtendienst, or BND). Indeed, the better the HVA became, the more its reports resembled those of its adversary.[45]

The reporters were not afraid to pass on facts that the party leadership will not have liked. Indeed, they consistently did so.[46] The best examples are their reports on NATO's military planning, which consistently made clear that NATO expected to respond to an attack by the Warsaw Pact. This flatly contradicted the party line that the West was the threat to peace, yet the HVA did not distort its account of NATO's assumption and planning; it did not present NATO as more aggressive than it was.[47] The HVA was just as matter-of-fact in its reporting on political matters. The West German politicians and civil servants who were its main targets had a very low opinion of the GDR. So did foreigners around the world. While the reporters toned down criticism, it still shines through the reports. Willy Brandt was quoted in a 1959 report telling his party chairman, Erich Ollenhauer, that he did not trust the USSR and considered it extremely dangerous and aggressive, to the point of being capable of going to war.[48] A report on Brandt a little later implicitly concedes that his anticommunism increased his popularity in West Berlin.[49] A report from 1961 relates that Indian officials were not in the least supportive of the GDR's position on West Berlin.[50]

A report from 1972 makes clear that the West German government, then negotiating a recognition treaty with the GDR (the Grundlagenvertrag[51]), thought the trade between the two German states insignificant for the Federal Republic, though valuable for the GDR. The readers can have been left in no doubt as to the West German view of the small size of the GDR's economy as compared with theirs.[52] A report from the same month, June 1972, demonstrates that the French government thought little of Comecon and its chances of successfully integrating the economies of the bloc states.[53] Another report from 1972, on Egyptian president Anwar Sadat's visit to Moscow, was not afraid to present the visit in a way unfavorable to the Soviet Union and thus unwelcome to the GDR. Sadat's visit was declared to be a failure; he had not obtained the support he sought. Consequently, he had only one option: to improve Egypt's relations with the United States. This was a success for President Richard Nixon, who had seen that time was on his side in US relations with Egypt. The information was obtained from sources close to Sadat's vice president, Dr. Mahmoud Fawzi.[54]

During Erich Honecker's leadership (1971–89), the members of the SED Politburo regularly received much information that was equally critical of the GDR in the monthly reports on West German media broadcasts about East Germany of the latter's Institute for International Politics and Economics (Institut für Internationale Politik und Wirtschaft). These reports made clear how little the West German media thought of the legitimacy and stability of the SED regime.[55]

A surprising aspect of the HVA's archive is how much the SED relied on West German reports for information on communist Romania. A report from 1972 does not hesitate to show Nicolae Ceauşescu's regime as brutally repressive (just like the SED's own). In the report appears the striking phrase, "Party and government are of course endeavoring to monitor all signs of life on the part of the population and are accordingly resisting all efforts at liberalization with iron resolution."[56] Amnesty International might have been proud of this phrase. Of course, the authors of the report could write it only because there was no love lost between the communist regimes of East Germany and Romania.

Naturally, bad news abounds in the reports for 1989. As 1988 became 1989, the HVA was quick to obtain NATO secretary-general Manfred Wörner's end-of-year report. It reported accurately Wörner's view that the communist systems of the USSR and Eastern Europe were falling apart: Political pluralism was being introduced in the Soviet Union; communist rule was collapsing in China; and Poland and Hungary were carrying out genuine political reforms.[57] Prime Minister Stoph, Hermann Axen, and others will not have enjoyed reading, in September 1989, a report, expressed very matter-of-factly, that NATO countries thought that the GDR would not follow other bloc states in adopting reform but would try to preserve its "inflexible command economies [*sic*]."[58] Indeed, by that time not even that most small-minded of dogmatists, Erich Mielke, was insisting that the ideological pieties be observed. In October 1989 a report by the HVA to the party leadership about the agrarian economies of the communist states went out over his signature. It summarized, again matter-of-factly, the West German view that the agrarian sectors of the communist economies were in a worse state than any others.[59]

Inevitably, the department's reporting was not entirely of facts. Facts needed to be interpreted for a sensible report to be prepared. This required judgments about their significance. Since the department did not intend its reports to challenge the party's thinking, they are better called "subjudgments." A good example of such a judgment is provided by a report from January 1983 on political developments in Algeria. The report maintained that the Algerian leadership was increasingly dominated by "petit bourgeois–nationalistically oriented forces" led by the president, Chadli Bendjedid. "Nationalist-religious circles" were also on the rise. Both were gaining ground at the expense of the Marxist Left, or "the revolutionary-democratic forces," as the report called them. Consequently, forces in the leadership that wanted to encourage private business and open the economy to the West were growing. This would include expanding economic relations with the United States and using them to exercise political influence. In short, the report made use of Marxist concepts about social class but took an empirical approach to reporting on political conditions in Algeria and made statements that were unwelcome from the GDR's perspective.[60]

This report was sent to the chairman of the State Planning Commission, Gerhard Schürer, who had just returned from a visit to Algeria. There he had discussed political developments with the Soviet ambassador, Vasili N. Rykov, who was also a member of the Soviet Communist Party's Central Committee. Rykov's view had been different from that of the HVA. As he saw it, Algeria's leadership, though it had been forced to make some compromises in respect of private business, was still committed to a socialist course and opposed a procapitalist policy. In its foreign policy the regime still held to "fundamental anti-imperialistic positions." Economic dependence on the United States was actually in decline.[61]

Schürer did not know what to make of the differences between the two views and sent the note of his conversation with Rykov to Mielke.[62] Mielke asked Department VII to consider the note and comment. The department defended its report, arguing that Rykov's view was too simple and too much his own; it focused too much on how the Algerian leaders described themselves rather than on intelligence on what they were actually doing. Intelligence received established that "progressive" forces were actually being repressed; conservative and reactionary forces were playing significant roles in the leadership and government bureaucracy. There were policy discussions in the leadership about initiatives that were clearly not socialist. Reforms in the private sector of the economy were not mere concessions to internal and external pressure; they reflected a declining commitment to socialism. While Rykov maintained that Algeria's foreign policy remained anti-imperialist, the facts suggested that nationalism and pragmatism were playing a larger role in determining policy and that greater efforts were being made to expand economic relations with the West. Algeria was increasingly seeking to maintain a neutral position between the superpowers and was pressing for such a policy within the Non-Aligned Movement.[63]

Even at the end of the regime, though, reports suppressed truths of which the authors were aware. In October 1989, the HVA reported to Honecker, Stoph, Axen, Egon Krenz, and other party leaders about the Chinese Communist Party's view of the drastic turn of events in the Soviet Bloc. The report was signed by Mielke (as were other reports at this time), and he clearly played a role in its drafting. Much of what the Chinese were reported to have said—that Hungary seemed to be adopting a Western political system and that communism could be overthrown throughout Eastern Europe—is clearly an accurate report. So is the report of the Chinese view of the flood of emigrants from the GDR to the Federal Republic. Mielke quoted the Chinese as saying that in every country there were people who, for personal reasons, wanted to emigrate. The Federal Republic was certainly deliberately increasing this dissatisfaction, "but," the Chinese were reported to have said very delicately, "there had to be some other reasons for the desire of GDR citizens to leave." Mielke was glossing over the truth, knowing full well that the crisis went deeper. Indeed, the remark he made next points to this awareness. He wrote that "one could therefore say that identification with the currently existing form of Socialism in the GDR was lacking among many citizens."[64] He was deliberately deferring to Honecker's wishful thinking about the emigration crisis. Asked by a Swedish newspaper in 1984 why so many people wanted to leave the GDR, Honecker had replied that in every country there were people who thought that they would do better elsewhere. He added that every year some fifty-three to sixty thousand West Germans chose to leave the Federal Republic. In short, he used information he received to support his distorted view of reality, not to rethink it.[65]

Acceptance of Intelligence

Every indication is that the SED leadership had a severely distorted view of political developments. A dictatorship has the power to cut itself off from reality. So it was with the GDR's gerontocracy in the 1980s. The HVA's last chief, Werner Großmann, maintains that the leadership was very skeptical of his service's intelligence reports.[66] The reports on political and economic affairs evidently made little impression on their readers. Honecker's attitude toward the emigration crisis has been mentioned above. The most cherished delusion of all communist regimes was that dissent was stirred up from outside. Honecker took this so far that in the 1980s he insisted that the HVA find out the BND registration number of the prominent dissident Bärbel Bohley.[67]

The HVA's reports probably made little impact on Honecker. They will have been damned by the fact that they repeated too much information that was sent to him in surveys of the Western media. This information he rejected as false and malicious propaganda. He will have been no more inclined to believe intelligence reports on the outside world. Interviewed after the regime fell, he said that he had paid little attention to ZAIG reports on the GDR's domestic situation because they contained the same criticisms as the Western press. Foreign intelligence reports had the same flaw. All Honecker could tolerate was information he wanted to read. The analogy with the Western press applies very well to the HVA's reports: They were similar to newspapers and were based on sources in the West. Honecker was, in substance, reading a classified Western newspaper. Honecker expressed a higher opinion of information he received from the Socialist Unity Party and its Workers' and Peasants' Inspectorate (Arbeiter- und Bauern Inspektion). The latter provided factual information on the problems of everyday life in the GDR, such as the availability of consumer goods, their poor quality, and so on.[68] This was Honecker's great interest; he wanted to be seen as a man who had given East Germans a good standard of living.

Nevertheless, he was swayed by some foreign intelligence. Intelligence obtained from Günter Guillaume on Willy Brandt's eastern policy succeeded in overcoming Honecker's strong, ideologically influenced hostility to better relations with West Germany. Dogmatic Marxist-Leninist that he was, Honecker initially regarded Brandt's policy as hostile and reflective of a capitalist crisis in the Federal Republic, but he was persuaded by the HVA's intelligence that a measure of beneficial cooperation could be achieved.[69] Late in the Cold War, he was also encouraged to support Mikhail Gorbachev's first moves toward arms reduction in Europe by intelligence that the West German government did not think that high-tech conventional weapons would enable NATO to achieve any military superiority over the Warsaw Pact.[70]

The principal recipient of Department VII's reports on foreign political and economic matters in the 1970s and 1980s was not the SED general secretary but Hermann Axen. This was natural since, as the Central Committee secretary for international relations, he held the highest foreign policy job in the GDR and played a large role in shaping the GDR's foreign policy. He was just as much as true believer in Marxism-Leninism as Honecker. His comment to the Soviet leadership in 1984 "that we have a stronger influence on the FRG than it has on us" is proof of how deluded he was. (At the time, more and more East Germans were applying to emigrate to the Federal Republic, and the availability of the West German deutsche mark in the GDR was encouraging intense demand for Western consumer goods.)[71] At the very same time, the HVA accurately reported that the influence of the peace movement in Western Europe was declining. Axen said that the report was wrong and sent it back.[72] Just how doctrinaire the SED's leaders were is demonstrated by the fact that their intelligence reports presented them with much Western information on the weaknesses of the Soviet Union's economy, but they still obdurately opposed reform.[73] They probably pounced on information that accorded with their own views, such as that mass unemployment was a terrible problem in West Germany[74] or that the peace movement was on the rise there.[75]

Conclusion: Reporters, Not Analysts

Department VII's officers had a difficult job—that of reporting on what they knew to be good intelligence to people who were hostile to much of it. They took a middle course between challenging the leaders' thinking and distorting intelligence so that it reflected that thinking. The result was factual reporting, expressed in politically correct language and using politically correct concepts, that was meant to challenge the party's thinking as little as possible. This was neither independent thinking nor intelligence to please. It lay halfway in between: It was intelligence meant to displease as little as possible. However, the reports still did displease; the pill could not be entirely sugared. When they displeased, they were simply ignored or rejected.

The reports were too tame. Although they did not, for the most part, consciously provide information that reinforced the leaders' misconceptions, they did not try hard enough to challenge or eliminate them. The party leaders were men who deluded themselves; the Hauptverwaltung Aufklärung allowed them to do so. The HVA was a good foreign intelligence service. It consistently supplied the top leaders with intelligence relevant to their policy initiatives and concerns. It did not seek to persuade the party because the latter did not want it to. It therefore passed on the facts of information received from its sources, introducing its own interpretation as little as possible. Its factual reporting was thorough and good. Among the facts were plenty that should have caused Axen, Honecker, Ulbricht, and their colleagues to rethink their assumptions. They were never minded to do so.

The HVA itself had no view of the Federal Republic different from that of the SED leadership. That view was the official GDR view: The Federal Republic was a successor state to the Third Reich and was a capitalist state that, under the leadership of American capitalism, threatened the world again with war. As a capitalist economy, it was exploitative and so had a natural tendency toward crisis.

Department VII's staff were reporters, not analysts. Analysis in the American sense—independent thinking—was precisely what the HVA was not allowed to do. Least of all was it allowed to consider major problems such as are examined in US National Intelligence Estimates. On the available evidence, it was never told to pose itself the questions "Why is the West German economy such a success?" or "How will the strength of the Federal Republic's economy affect the interests of the GDR over the next ten years?" There are no such reports among those that survive. Instead, it was told to snoop around in the West German Economics and Finance Ministries and the Federal Association of German Industry and report on what the officials there were saying and planning. Their reports are remarkably free of any direct discussion of West Germany's economic strength. They are very much current intelligence; they do not look deeper than what was being said or planned at that time. They avoid the major issues—these had already been decided by the principles of Marxism-Leninism.

Indeed, the hardest subjects for Department VII's officers to report on were economic. Its understanding of economics is the most obviously flawed part of Marxism. Neither the reporters nor their political leaders understood or wanted to understand how the West German or international economies worked. Nor did they seek new answers to the big economic questions. Instead Department VII's officers described economic plans and discussions and provided lists of statistics. Their Marxist training still influenced their economic reporting, though, and for the worse. Fact and interpretation could not be entirely separated here. The reports for the 1970s and 1980s are better than the earlier ones because the department had learned to discuss economic and financial matters very factually. Its reports read like minutes of the meetings concerned.

The easiest subjects to report on were military and scientific. They raised no political issue. Military intelligence reports were long and useful to consumers.

Department VII also reported on people in a very particular way. The Communist Party had a very special status in every communist state. The HVA had to be careful in the way it presented communist leaders because they dominated and represented their parties. By contrast, Willy Brandt, Helmut Schmidt, Konrad Adenauer, and other West German politicians, ministers, civil servants, businessmen, and media figures appear as ordinary people in the reports because they are presented very matter-of-factly. Department VII's officers certainly had a far better understanding of them than they did of the distant and narrow-minded ideologues who abused and disregarded their reports. So much political intelligence did the HVA collect on the Federal Republic that the reader often has the sense that its staff felt more at home in the corridors of the Bundestag and Foreign Office than they would have been in those of the SED Central Committee or the GDR's parliament, the Volkskammer.

The HVA was, actually, freer in its reporting on West Germany than it or other departments of the Stasi were in their reporting on the GDR.[76] It could and did say that West German trade unionists had voted for conservative parties. It would have been impossible to say that East German industrial workers favored "bourgeois" policies and parties. It was made even easier in the West German case because it would be presented in a straightforwardly factual report; Department VII was not claiming that this was its own finding. By contrast, the HVA officers knew that they could not dispute that their regime had the support of its own working class.

The SED leaders' attitude toward foreign intelligence can be seen in these reports. Walter Ulbricht was interested in it. He received a lot of it in the late 1950s and early 1960s. However, he was a true believer in Marxism-Leninism and an utter dogmatist. Intelligence had to say the right thing. Honecker was much less interested in it. His main concern was to give East Germans a better standard of living and thus show them that they lived in a truly socialist society. Though sensitive to what the Western media were saying about the GDR, he was, in the view of some of his Politburo colleagues, even less able than Ulbricht to tolerate criticism of the state of affairs there.[77] Hermann Axen received much more foreign political intelligence than Honecker or any other Politburo member did. He was also a dogmatist who clearly regarded the sole function of intelligence as giving the party opportunities for action. He did not see its role as being to persuade the leadership to take a view different from that it wanted to. A constant of communism is the leaders' criticism of their intelligence services and rejection of their intelligence.

Notes

I am grateful to Jens Gieseke for reading and commenting on this chapter in draft and to Frank Joestel for his advice about the distribution of HVA reports. Responsibility for all opinions expressed, and errors made, remains my own.

1. Jens Gieseke, "East German Foreign Espionage in the Era of Détente," *Journal of Strategic Studies* 31, no. 3 (2008): 398, 408–10.

2. BStU, ZA, MfS-HVA 186, Einzelinformation zur Lage in Westberlin, Westdeutschland and im kapitalistischen Ausland—Betr.: Bestrebungen der Gewerkschaftsjugend zur Kontaktaufnahme mit der DDR und Maßnahmen zur ideologischen Diversion, June 18, 1959; BStU, ZA, MfS-HVA 192, Einzelinformation über Absichten einer sogenannten marxistischen Gruppe im DGB zur Forcierung der ideologischen Diversionsarbeit gegen die DDR, May 1961. "BStU, ZA" stands for the Central Archive (Zentralarchiv) of the Bundesbeauftragter für die Unterlagen des Staatssicherheitsdienstes der ehemaligen Deutschen Demokratischen Republik, Berlin (Federal Commissioner for the Records of the Security Service of the Former German Democratic Republic).

3. BStU, ZA, MfS-HVA 382, Information über die Hilfeleistungen der Bundeswehr für die Olympischen Spiele in München und Kiel, Nr. 330/72, April 6, 1972.

4. BStU, ZA, MfS-HVA 382, Information über Aufgaben, politisch-moralischen und militärischen Zustand des westdeutschen Territorialheeres, Nr. 335/72, April 11, 1972.

5. The other five staffs were concerned with NATO, the European Economic Community, and other developed countries; the third world east of Suez; the third world west of Suez; military affairs; and economic affairs. Most of the intelligence on which these staffs reported was obtained from sources in West Germany or from West German sources elsewhere.

6. The collection and assessment of scientific and technological intelligence were matters for a separate section of the HVA known as the Science and Technology Sector (Sektor Wissenschaft und Technik, or SWT). Three departments of the HVA formed the SWT's collection wing. A further department, Department V (Abteilung V), carried out some basic analysis in the course of its main job, which was the channeling of stolen technology and scientific secrets to East German industry.

7. BStU, ZA, MfS-HVA 192, Auskunft über die Lage der westdeutschen und westberliner Elektroindustrie, June 27, 1961 (sent to Ulbricht, Mielke, and others).

8. See BStU, ZA, MfS-HVA 382, Information über die Einschätzung aktueller Fragen der Militärpolitik und Streitkräfte Großbritanniens durch die Bundeswehrführung, Nr. 164/72, February 23, 1972; Information über die Militärpolitik und Streitkräfte der Türkei, Nr. 393/72, April 28, 1972; Information über eine Einschätzung der Innen- und Außenpolitik Großbritanniens durch westdeutsche Regierungskreise, May 3, 1972.

9. BStU, ZA, MfS-HVA 382, Information über die westdeutsch-rumänischen Konsultationen auf der Ebene der stellvertretenden Außenminister zu aktuell-politischen Fragen am 21 und 22 Februar 1972 in Bonn, April 6, 1972; Information über die Ergebnisse des westdeutsch-ungarischen Meinungsaustausches am 6./7. März 1972 in Budapest, Nr. 372/72, April 21, 1972.

10. BStU, ZA, MfS-HVA 382, Information über die westdeutsch-iranischen Beziehungen und über Angriffe des Schahs auf die Politik der DDR, Nr. 398/72, May 3, 1972.

11. The Stasi's first assessment department, the Information Department (Abteilung Information), came into being in the wake of the popular uprising of June 17, 1953; it had the job of reporting on public opinion (previously this job had been done by the post interception department). In 1959 the Information Department gave way to the Central Information Group (Zentrale Informationsgruppe, or ZIG), which in turn became the Central Evaluation and Information Group (Zentrale Auswertungs- und Informationsgruppe, or ZAIG) in 1965. The ZAIG continued in being until the Stasi's dissolution in 1989–90. For the history

of the Stasi's assessment departments, see Roger Engelmann and Frank Joestel, *Die Zentrale Auswertungs- und Informationsgruppe* (Berlin: BStU, 2009).

12. Reporting to the party leadership on the state of public opinion in the GDR was thin after the late 1950s (there were about fifteen reports every year). There was no reporting on this subject to the leadership throughout the whole of 1973 because Honecker was so hostile to it. It was thin and intermittent thereafter. See Jens Gieseke, "Bevölkerungsstimmungen in der geschlossenen Gesellschaft: MfS-Berichte an die DDR-Führung in den 60er und 70er Jahren," *Zeithistorische Forschungen* 5, no. 2 (2008): 243–47.

13. Jens Gieseke, "Annäherungen und Fragen an die 'Meldungen aus der Republik,'" in *Staatssicherheit und Gesellschaft: Studien zum Herrschaftsalltag in der DDR*, ed. Jens Gieseke (Göttingen: Vandenhoeck & Ruprecht, 2007), 81–87, 92–93.

14. Ralph Jessen, "Staatssicherheit, SED und Öffentlichkeit," in Gieseke, *Staatssicherheit und Gesellschaft*, 161–62.

15. Siegfried Suckut, ed., *Die DDR im Blick der Stasi 1976: Die geheimen Berichte an die SED-Führung* (Göttingen: Vandenhoeck & Ruprecht, 2009), 8–11, 16–18, 27–32. See also Daniela Münkel, ed., *Die DDR im Blick der Stasi 1961: Die geheimen Berichte an die SED-Führung* (Göttingen: Vandenhoeck & Ruprecht, 2011), and Frank Joestel, ed., *Die DDR im Blick der Stasi 1988: Die geheimen Berichte an die SED-Führung* (Göttingen: Vandenhoeck & Ruprecht, 2010).

16. Engelmann and Joestel, *Die Zentrale Auswertungs- und Informationsgruppe*, 22–25.

17. Uta Stolle, "Traumhafte Quellen. Vom Nutzen der Stasi-Akten für die Geschichtsschreibung," *Deutschland Archiv* 30, no. 2 (1997): 211.

18. BStU, ZA, MfS-HVA 184, Information Nr. 84/59, Reaktion der Westberliner Bevölkerung auf den Besuch und die Erklärungen des Gen. N. S. Chrustschow [*sic*], Abteilung Information, March 9, 1959.

19. BStU, ZA, MfS-HVA 184, Bericht über die Reaktion der Bevölkerung der DDR auf den Besuch und die Erklärungen des Genossen Chruschtschow, March 7, 1959.

20. This comes close to being one of the "sub-optimal" analysis strategies identified by Richards J. Heuer Jr. on page 58 of his book *Psychology of Intelligence Analysis* (New York: Novinka Books, 2006)—that of "avoid[ing] judgment by simply describing the current situation, identifying alternatives, and letting the intelligence consumer make the judgment about which alternative is most likely." The HVA's practice falls short even of this, since the reports do not identify alternative hypotheses. For Heuer, "the ideal is to generate a full set of hypotheses, systematically evaluate each hypothesis and then identify the hypothesis that provides the best fit to the data."

21. Werner Großmann, *Bonn im Blick: Die DDR-Aufklärung aus der Sicht ihres letzten Chefs* (Berlin: Das Neue Berlin, 2001), 174.

22. BStU, ZA, MfS-HVA 184, Unterredung des DGB-Vorsitzenden Richter mit dem Vorsitzenden des Vereins "Rettet die Freiheit," March 12, 1959; Sitzung des Geschäftsführenden DGB-Bundesvorstandes am 16. 2. 1959, March 12, 1959. See also BStU, ZA, MfS-HVA 186, Bestrebungen zur Ablösung des Generalsekretärs des IBFG, Oldenbroek, June 17, 1959, and Sitzung des DGB-Bundesvorstandes am 7.7.1959, July 17, 1959.

23. E.g., BStU, ZA, MfS-HVA 184, Verschärfungen der Spannungen zwischen Willy Brandt und dem SPD-Parteivorstand, March 4, 1959; BStU, ZA, MfS-HVA 186, Führende westberliner SPD-Funktionäre zu evtl. Übereinkünften der Genfer Außenministerkonferenz in der Westberlinfrage, June 9, 1959; Äußerungen führender westberliner SPD-Funktionäre zur Genfer Außenministerkonferenz und zur Situation nach dem Landesparteitag, June 13,

1959; Sitzungen des westberliner SPD-Landesvorstandes am 1 und 8. 6. 1959, June 13, 1959; Frankfurter Kongreß des SDS vom 23./24. 5. 1959, June 13, 1959; Auseinandersetzungen im Westberliner SDS, June 15, 1959; Parteivorstandssitzung der SPD am 13. 6. 1959, June 17, 1959; Sekretärkonferenz der Westberliner SPD am 11. 6. 1959, June 18, 1959.

24. BStU, ZA, MfS-HVA 813, Information über die Lage und die Politik der SPD nach der Europawahl sowie den Kommunalwahlen am 18. 6. 1989, Nr. 347/89 [date illegible].

25. An example is disarmament: See Information über den aktuellen Vorbereitungsstand der "2. Konferenz für europäische atomare Abrüstung" in Westberlin (9.-14. 5. 1983), Nr. 109/83, April 4, 1983.

26. In German: "*Freiheit Berlins*" and "*ständige Verletzung der Menschenrechte.*"

27. BStU, ZA, MfS-HVA 380, Information über eine westdeutsche Einschätzung der Umsiedlung und Familienzusammenführung deutscher Bürger aus den sozialistischen Ländern, Nr. 159/72, February 22, 1972. In German: "*Aus verschiedenen Gründen hätten sich die Hoffnungen auf Verwicklung des Übersiedlungswunsches in erster Linie stets auf die BRD, in erheblich geringerem Maße auf die DDR gerichtet.*"

28. E.g., BStU, ZA, MfS-HVA 24, Information über Äußerungen von BRD-Regierungskreisen zur weiteren Gestaltung der Beziehungen zur DDR, Nr. 94/83, April 4, 1983.

29. E.g., BStU, ZA, MfS-HVA 186, Die Stellung der AEG in der westdeutschen Elektro-Industrie [undated but evidently from June 1959].

30. BStU, ZA, MfS-HVA 184, Einschätzung der Ostasien-Reise Erhards durch den FDP-Bundestagsabgeordneten Lenz, March 16, 1959.

31. BStU, ZA, MfS-HVA 186, Wirtschaftliche Differenzen zwischen den USA und Kanada, June 3, 1959.

32. BStU, ZA, MfS-HVA 384 (Teil 1), Information über den Stand der Diskussionen um eine Reform des imperialistischen Währungssystems, Nr. 563/72, June 16, 1972.

33. BStU, ZA, MfS-HVA 380, Information über die Einschätzung der wirtschaftlichen Entwicklung der BRD 1972 durch die westdeutschen Unternehmerverbände, Nr. 190/72, March 2, 1972.

34. BStU, ZA, MfS-HVA 380, Information über die Haltung der westdeutschen Industrie zur Konjunkturpolitik der Bundesregierung, Nr. 176/72, February 24, 1972. In German: "*aggressive und vagabundierende Dollars auf der Lauer liegen, um sich auf den deutschen Devisenmarkt zu stürzen.*"

35. BStU, ZA, MfS-HVA 380, Information über Einschätzungen westdeutscher und westberliner Forschungsinstitutionen über die Entwicklung der Volkswirtschaft der DDR, Nr. 156/72, February 21, 1972.

36. BStU, ZA, MfS-HVA 380, Information über westdeutsche Bestrebungen zur Durchsetzung des PAL-Farbfernseh-Systems im Mittelmeerraum, Nr. 155/72, February 21, 1972.

37. Peter Siebenmorgen, "*Staatssicherheit*" der DDR (Bonn: Bouvier Verlag, 1993), 143.

38. BStU, ZA, MfS-HVA 24 (Teil 2), Information über aktuelle Aspekte der imperialistischen Sanktions- und Embargopolitik gegenüber den sozialistischen Ländern, Nr. 73/83, March 3, 1983.

39. BStU, ZA, MfS-HVA 813, Information über BRD-Aktivitäten zur Wahrnehmung des Außenvertretungsanspruchs für Berlin (West) auf dem Gebiet des Kulturaustauschs mit der DDR, Nr. 322/89.

40. BStU, ZA, MfS-HVA 813, Einschätzung zur Bewertung einiger Entwicklungen im asiatisch-pazifischen Raum aus amerikanischer Sicht, Nr. 405/89, September 14, 1989.

41. BStU, ZA, MfS-HVA 813, Information über BRD-Einschätzungen zu Produktion und Außenhandel der RGW-Staaten im Bereich der Hochtechnologie, Nr. 360/89 [date illegible].

42. BStU, MfS-HVA 24 (Teil 2), Einschätzung zu einigen aktuellen Aspekten der Lage und Entwicklung der Europäischen Gemeinschaften (EG), Nr. 50/83, February 11, 1983. In German: *"angesichts der anhaltenden kapitalistischen Weltwirtschaftskrise"*; *"[die] schwerste Wirtschaftskrise seit den 30er Jahren"*; *"nach internen Äußerungen engagierter 'Europapolitiker' zeige sich faktisch die völlige Machtlosigkeit des EG-Mechanismus gegenüber den Problemen der Arbeitslosigkeit, zur Bekämpfung der Defizite und der Wiederherstellung der Wettbewerbsfähigkeit der westeuropäischen Industrie."*

43. BStU, MfS-HVA 24 (Teil 2), Einschätzung zum innenpolitischen Kräfteverhältnis in der BRD vor der Bundestagswahl am 6. 3. 1983, Nr. 65/85, February 25, 1983. In German: *"die auf eine Stärkung des Monopolkapitals ausgerichtete Wirtschaftspolitik der Regierungskoalition hat darüber hinaus eine im Vergleich zur bisherigen SPD-geführten Regierung deutlich höhere soziale Belastung der werktätigen Masse zur Folge."*

44. Heinz Busch, "Die NATO in der Sicht der Auswertung der HVA," in Georg Herbstritt and Helmut Müller-Enbergs, eds., *Das Gesicht dem Westen zu: DDR-Spionage gegen die Bundesrepublik Deutschland* (Bremen: Edition Temmen, 2003), 240.

45. Günter Bohnsack and Herbert Brehmer, *Auftrag: Irreführung. Wie die Stasi Politik im Westen machte* (Hamburg: Carlsen, 1992), 251–52; Günter Bohnsack, *Hauptverwaltung Aufklärung: Die Legende Stirbt* (Berlin: Edition Ost, 1997), 80.

46. The ZAIG's reporting on domestic matters was similar. While the reporters made more use of ideological language and concepts (as they had to), from the 1970s they increasingly saw signs of crisis in East German society and gave much space to popular criticism. Of course, the reports still made criticism seem milder than it was. Knowing that there were informers among them, East Germans expressed their grievances cautiously to one another. The ideological character of the MfS's reporting further toned their criticism down. Moreover, the Stasi never presented the majority of the population as hostile to the regime. See Gieseke, "Bevölkerungsstimmungen in der geschlossenen Gesellschaft," 248.

47. Gieseke, "East German Espionage in the Era of Détente," 413–15.

48. BStU, ZA, MfS-HVA 184, Bericht Willy Brandts über seine Reise nach den USA und den Fernen Osten, March 10, 1959.

49. BStU, ZA, MfS-HVA 186, Äußerungen führender westberliner SPD-Funktionäre zur Genfer Außenministerkonferenz und zur Situation nach dem Landesparteitag, June 13, 1959.

50. BStU, ZA, MfS-HVA 192, Einzelinformation über Stellungnahmen ausländischer Politiker zur Deutschland- und Westberlinfrage, May 1961.

51. *Grundlagenvertrag* means "Treaty on the Bases of Relations." Recognition was de facto, not de jure.

52. BStU, ZA, MfS-HVA 384 (Teil 1), Information über Einschätzungen westdeutscher Regierungskreise zur weiteren Gestaltung der Handelsbeziehungen DDR-BRD, Nr. 552/72, June 12, 1972.

53. BStU, ZA, MfS-HVA 384 (Teil 2), Information über eine Darstellung der Entwicklung des RGW aus der Sicht französischer diplomatischer Kreise, Nr. 549/72, June 9, 1972.

54. BStU, ZA, MfS-HVA 380, Information über innen- und außenpolitische Probleme Ägyptens im Zusammenhang mit der Moskaureise von Präsident Sadat und seine sich daran

anschließenden Gespräche in Jugoslawien, Syrien und Libyen, Nr. 161/72, February 22, 1972.

55. Siegfried Suckut, "Seismographische Aufzeichnungen: Der Blick des MfS auf Staat und Gesellschaft in der DDR am Beispiel der Berichte an die SED-Führung 1976," in Gieseke, *Staatssicherheit und Gesellschaft*, 124–25.

56. See BStU, ZA, MfS-HVA 24 (Teil 2), Information über eine westdeutsche Einschätzung des Standes der Kulturbeziehungen zwischen der BRD und Rumänien, Nr. 452/72, May 10, 1972. In German: "*Partei und Regierung seien nämlich bemüht, alle Lebensäußerungen der Bevölkerung unter Kontrolle zu halten und stemmten sich daher mit eisernem Willen gegen alle Liberalisierungsbestrebungen.*"

57. BStU, ZA, MfS-HVA 813, Information über die politische Jahreseinschätzung 1988/89 des NATO-Generalsekretärs, Nr. 363/89 [undated].

58. BStU, ZA, MfS-HVA 813, Information über NATO-Wertungen zu den wirtschaftlichen Reformprozessen in den kleineren europäischen RGW-Staaten (Osteuropa), Nr. 419/89, September 1989. In German: "*starren Kommandowirtschaften.*"

59. BStU, ZA, MfS-HVA 813, Information über die Entwicklung der Landwirtschaft in der UdSSR und in den anderen europäischen RGW-Staaten, Nr. 423/89, October 4, 1989.

60. BStU, ZA, MfS-HVA 24 (Teil 2), Information über einige Aspekte der innen- und außenpolitischen Entwicklung Algeriens, Nr. 13/83, January 7, 1983. In German: "*kleinbürgerlich-nationalistisch orientierte Kräfte*"; "*nationalistisch-religiöse Kreise*"; "*die revolutionär-demokratischen Kräfte.*"

61. BStU, ZA, MfS-HVA 24 (Teil 2), Vermerk über ein Gespräch des Genossen Gerhard Schürer, Kandidat des Politbüros des ZK der SED, Stellvertreter des Vorsitzenden des Ministerrates der DDR, Vorsitzender der Staatlichen Plankommission, mit dem Mitglied des ZK der KPdSU und Botschafter der UdSSR in Algerien, Genossen Rykov, January 12, 1983, 327–32. In German: "*antiimperialistische Grundpositionen.*"

62. BStU, ZA, MfS-HVA 24 (Teil 2), letter from Schürer to Mielke, January 17, 1983, 323.

63. BStU, ZA, MfS-HVA 24 (Teil 2), Zur Einschätzung der Lage in Algerien durch den sowjetischen Botschafter, Gen. Rykov, gegenüber Gen. Schürer, 324–26.

64. BStU, ZA, MfS-HVA 813, Information über aktuelle Entwicklungen in einigen europäischen sozialistischen Staaten aus chinesischer Sicht, Nr. 425/89, October 4, 1989.

65. Ludwig A. Rehlinger, *Freikauf: Die Geschäfte der DDR mit politisch Verfolgten 1963–1989* (Berlin: Ullstein Verlag, 1991), 116.

66. Großmann, *Bonn im Blick*, 117–18.

67. Jens Gieseke, *Der Mielke-Konzern: Die Geschichte der Stasi 1945–1990* (Munich: Deutsche Verlags-Anstalt, 2006), 226.

68. Reinhold Andert and Wolfgang Herzberg, *Der Sturz: Honecker im Kreuzverhör* (Berlin: Aufbau-Verlag, 1991), 312–13.

69. Hermann Wentker, *Außenpolitik in engen Grenzen: Die DDR im internationalen System 1949–1989* (Munich: Oldenbourg Verlag, 2007), 322; Markus Wolf, *Spionagechef im geheimen Krieg: Erinnerungen* (Munich: List Verlag, 1997), 267–68.

70. Vojtech Mastny, "On the Soviet Side," in *Did Intelligence Matter in the Cold War?*, ed. Michael Herman, J. Kenneth McDonald, and Vojtech Mastny (Oslo: Institutt for Forsvarsstudier, no.1 [2006]), 68.

71. Quoted in Gieseke, *Der Mielke-Konzern*, 245. In German: "*daß wir heute auf die BRD stärker einwirken als sie auf uns.*"

72. Großmann, *Bonn im Blick*, 174.

73. For example, see BStU, MfS-HVA 24 (Teil 2), Information über die Wirtschaftsbeziehungen BRD-USSR, Nr. 32/83, January 14, 1983.

74. For an example of a report containing information to this effect, see BStU, MfS-HVA 24 (Teil 2), Einschätzung zum innenpolitischen Kräfteverhältnis in der BRD vor der Bundestagswahl am 6. 3. 1983, Nr. 65/85, February 25, 1983.

75. For an example of a report containing such information, see BStU, MfS-HVA 24 (Teil 2), Information über aktuelle Entwicklungstendenzen der Friedensbewegung in der BRD und in Westberlin, Nr. 106/83, March 29, 1983.

76. One of the department's tasks was to report on public opinion in the GDR. In doing this job, it knew that it had to conclude that the regime enjoyed strong popular support and always did so.

77. Siegfried Suckut, "Seismographische Aufzeichnungen," 118, 124–25.

3

"We May Not Always Be Right, but We're Never Wrong"

US Intelligence Assessments of the Soviet Union, 1972–91

BENJAMIN B. FISCHER

THE CORE MISSION of US intelligence during the Cold War was to monitor, analyze, and project trends in the internal politics and external behavior of the Union of Soviet Socialist Republics (USSR). The paramount task, however, was to assess challenges to the national security of the United States posed by Soviet foreign policy and military power. The most authoritative form of intelligence assessments was the National Intelligence Estimate (NIE) and its abbreviated or "fast-track" version, the Special National Intelligence Estimate (SNIE).

This chapter surveys NIEs and SNIEs on the Soviet Union during the last two decades of the Cold War. The historical trajectory of those years—the rise and fall of détente, the return to superpower confrontation, and finally the breakup of the USSR—encapsulated the Cold War as a whole and posed extraordinary challenges for US intelligence. Many observers have issued pronouncements, pro and con, on these estimates, which remain controversial because of allegations that they failed to predict the looming collapse of the Soviet Union. Critics and defenders alike, however, either have not bothered to read all the estimates or have resorted to cherry-picking examples that make them look either brilliant or foolish, depending on their predispositions.[1] Official secrecy, however, is no longer an impediment to determining exactly what US assessments said and when they said it; hundreds and virtually all of the most important NIEs have been declassified.[2] The first part of this chapter discusses the organization and procedures analysts used to prepare Soviet estimates. The second part examines the estimates themselves and how they dealt with major issues of the day.

The United States produced more and better intelligence on the Soviet Union than any other country, which is hardly surprising given its human and financial resources and threat perception of its superpower rival. It led the way with space-age technical collection programs and pioneered new intelligence disciplines, including estimative intelligence. There were remarkable successes in some areas and gaps in others. US intelligence was nothing short of brilliant in monitoring and assessing Soviet weapon systems. It was less successful in divining the motives and intentions of Soviet leaders and anticipating their behavior. In other words, estimative intelligence was better on capabilities than intentions.

The Estimative Process

Contrary to popular misconception, the Central Intelligence Agency (CIA) was not the sole producer of NIEs, although it played a leading role in the estimative process. NIEs were (and still are) interagency documents, which were reviewed and approved by the US National Foreign Intelligence Board (NFIB). The NFIB comprised "principals" or permanent representatives and "observers" from more than a dozen intelligence and law enforcement agencies ("elements") plus the CIA, which is an independent, nondepartmental national intelligence service without cabinet status.[3] The principals included ranking officials from the National Security Agency (NSA), the Defense Intelligence Agency, the National Photographic Interpretation Center, the State Department's Bureau of Intelligence and Research, the Federal Bureau of Investigation, and the Departments of Energy and Treasury, as well as the deputy director of the CIA and the deputy secretary of defense. Observers came from military intelligence services (of the US Army, the US Navy, the US Air Force, and the US Marine Corps) and from the National Reconnaissance Office (which managed satellite programs), if their interests were involved. These agencies and services were collectively referred to as the US intelligence community (IC).[4] During the Cold War the director of Central Intelligence (DCI) released NIEs as the chairman of the NFIB.[5]

From 1950 to 1973, the Office of National Estimates (ONE), located at CIA headquarters, prepared NIEs for the NFIB's review, approval, and release. The ONE's analytical staff did the actual drafting, and the Board of National Estimates (BNE), a panel of senior civilian and military members (so-called wise men) attached to the DCI's office, reviewed estimates before submitting them to the NFIB.

In 1973, DCI William F. Colby abolished the BNE and the ONE, claiming that they had become an "ivory tower" detached from policymakers' needs.[6] The real reason, however, was chronic complaints from the White House about the poor quality of estimative intelligence and especially Soviet estimates.[7] Colby acceded to a recommendation from the President's Foreign Intelligence Advisory Board (PFIAB), a blue-ribbon panel of outside advisers who reviewed US intelligence analysis and operations, to give other agencies a bigger role in drafting estimates and to promote competitive analysis. He appointed twelve national intelligence officers (NIOs), each responsible for a geographical region or subject of intelligence importance. The Soviet "account" was divided up among three NIOs, including one for regional issues (the Soviet Union and Eastern Europe) and two others for strategic and general-purpose military forces. Civilians were paired with military officers as NIOs and assistant NIOs in order to balance institutional interests.

Colby accomplished three things. He answered the PFIAB's complaint that the CIA dominated the estimative process, gained control over NIEs by handpicking NIOs who reported directly to him, and made drafting of estimates more competitive while keeping it intramural and free from outside interference. The word in the CIA's corridors was that Colby had replaced the College of Cardinals with the Twelve Apostles. The CIA, however, lost its status as the sachem of national intelligence estimates.[8] Six years later, DCI Stansfield Turner created the National Intelligence Council (NIC), which gave the NIOs a corporate identity but changed little. It still exists.

Sources and Methods

Michael Herman, a former practitioner turned scholar of intelligence, has made an important distinction between "message-like" and "observable" sources of information.[9] Message-like intelligence discloses plans, decisions, and intentions as revealed in documents, eyewitness or secondhand accounts, intercepted conversations, and other sources that in effect come from or near the horse's mouth. Observable intelligence reveals things that can be seen and usually counted or measured to one degree or another. Message-like sources are crucial for estimative intelligence but are rarely available or are at least unavailable in desirable quantity and quality. Observable intelligence is best suited for current analysis and especially military intelligence but less useful for forecasting or prognosticating.

During the Cold War, the United States used a variety of methods to acquire both types of intelligence on the Soviet Union. The most important methods were the triad of agent or human sources (HUMINT); signals intelligence

(SIGINT), which ranged from monitoring clear-text and encrypted communications to esoteric methods such as intercepting telemetry (radio transmissions) from Soviet missiles; and film and digital imagery (PHOTOINT and IMINT). None of the "INTs" was complete in and of itself, and to some extent they overlapped and complemented each other.

HUMINT refers to traditional clandestine agent operations but also includes overt reporting from foreign intelligence officers, diplomats, and attachés based on personal observations and professional contacts. Another source was intelligence sharing with allied foreign ("liaison") services. Additional sources included émigrés and defectors from the Soviet Union and Eastern Europe, as well as open sources such as newspapers, radio and television broadcasts, and official government statements.

One of the enduring myths of the Cold War is that cloak-and-dagger operations in the Soviet-American spy wars produced the bulk of critical intelligence on both sides. While this came close to reality on the Soviet side, the American situation was more prosaic.[10] With a few notable exceptions, US HUMINT collection was practically negligible. Extreme secrecy, superior counterintelligence, and world-class deception-and-denial operations made the Soviet Union a "hard target" in US intelligence jargon. It was well-nigh impossible to meet agents behind the Iron Curtain or abroad. Even when US intelligence managed to recruit Soviet agents, restrictions on time, space, and opportunity for agent meetings made such operations difficult and risky.

In theory, the CIA's operational doctrine was based on the so-called recruitment cycle in which intelligence officers compile a list of key intelligence requirements and then spot, develop, and recruit agents with corresponding access to secret information. In practice, however, this doctrine rarely applied to the Soviet case. As a former senior operations officer noted, the agency "wasted a lot of emotional energy trying to recruit Soviets during the Cold War." He could not recall a single Soviet agent who was "spotted, developed, and recruited from scratch by a CIA case officer."[11] Instead, CIA officers often had to settle for low-hanging fruit by targeting their counterparts in the Committee for State Security (KGB) and Main Intelligence Directorate (GRU, military intelligence), who, at best, could provide tactical counterespionage rather than strategic intelligence on political, economic, and military affairs.[12] Neither the CIA nor US military intelligence was able to recruit a single agent with access to the innermost secrets of the Kremlin or the Soviet high command; most agents with lower-level access were caught and shot.[13] A former senior CIA analyst noted that over the course of his twenty-four-year career, the agency failed to recruit a single Soviet agent with access to "trenchant information."[14] Two former directors of Central Intelligence, Stansfield Turner and Robert Gates, have stated that there were no significant Soviet recruitments during their tenures.[15]

America's reliance on technical collection began in the late 1950s and increased thereafter. By the 1970s, HUMINT accounted for only 13 percent of collection, and technical operations accounted for the remaining 87 percent.[16] That ratio probably obtained, or even increased in favor of technical collection, throughout the next decade.

Technical collection systems were wizardry marvels, and they undoubtedly helped to preserve the peace and to avoid a major conflict during the Cold War. "What saved us in my opinion was our adoption of technology. Not only overhead reconnaissance, but [also] SIGINT became valuable tools in the intelligence game," said James R. Schlesinger, who headed both the CIA and the Pentagon.[17] Science, technology, and engineering enabled the United States to monitor and assess Soviet strategic military capabilities and provided the means to verify compliance with strategic arms control agreements.[18] Assessments of Soviet strategic offensive and defensive weapons and force posture were the crown jewels of NIEs.

Reliance on technical collection created what one historian has called "technophilic hubris," the belief that technology can solve all or most intelligence collection problems, as well as a corresponding disdain for HUMINT.[19] Limitations were apparent but rarely considered. Imagery collection produced invaluable "observable" intelligence, and SIGINT produced equally valuable "audible" intelligence. Yet neither collection method was able to read the minds of Soviet leaders or gauge their intentions and peer into the future. That was left to estimative intelligence, which sometimes hit the mark and other times missed it altogether. Henry Kissinger's complaint of 1971 remained valid throughout the Cold War. "The greatest emphasis," in Soviet military estimates, Kissinger noted, "is still heavily on observed activity at test ranges, construction sites, and operational bases." They failed "to estimate Soviet objectives and strategies," which is "fundamental to understanding present Soviet programs and estimating future ones."[20]

Another issue concerned what SIGINT and imagery did not or could not detect, a problem compounded by the Soviet Union's extreme secrecy and effective deception-and-denial efforts. HUMINT, of course, was not immune to countermeasures, and all three collection methods were rendered less effective by Soviet efforts to reduce, and sometimes confuse and mislead, US intelligence. A key example was US targeting of Soviet nuclear research programs. As SIGINT and imagery collection capabilities improved in the 1970s, the Soviets met the challenge with offsetting deception-and-denial efforts and other security measures. While technical collection proved useful, the "lack of reliable on-the-ground intelligence made it difficult for the West to understand important developments inside the Soviet nuclear complex," which "resulted in significant gaps."[21]

Technical specialists believed that snatching electronic signals from the ether and snapping pictures from outer space were truly clandestine and invulnerable to penetration and compromise. It was, however, a hubristic view of technical collection. Soviet intelligence learned about both US collection and analytical methods from American spies.[22] In 1977 two Americans were convicted of selling to the KGB, before it was even launched, the secrets of a state-of-the-art satellite designed to collect Soviet missile telemetry.[23] The next year a CIA officer sold the GRU an operations manual for the first electro-optical imaging satellite that offered real-time coverage of the Soviet Union.[24]

Even the National Security Agency, the most secretive of all US intelligence services, was not immune. Soviet and East German intelligence penetrated the secrets of its worldwide collection mission and capabilities, as well as critically important SIGINT operations in frontline West Berlin.[25] One result was the crippling of "American electronic surveillance of Eastern Europe for six years."[26] At least one East German agent, known only by a cryptonym, has never been identified. An American who spied for the KGB was arrested thirty years after he had left the NSA. An NSA cryptanalyst revealed a US operation that employed submarines to place and recover sophisticated tapping devices on Soviet underwater communications cables on the ocean floor.[27] There may be others who got away.[28]

In December 1976, the PFIAB concluded that US intelligence had placed too much reliance on the technical INTs and too little on HUMINT. Soviet advances in science and technology were outpacing US intelligence technology. The board recommended that the IC devote more resources to HUMINT to correct the imbalance in technical collection. More agents, not more machines, the panel pleaded, were needed to determine Soviet intentions, as well as to uncover Soviet efforts to conceal strategic weapons programs.[29] The IC failed to heed the call, however.[30]

Estimative Methodology

Sherman Kent was the founding father of estimative intelligence. His legacy endures: The CIA's training center for analysts was named in his honor. Kent was a Yale professor of history before he joined the CIA, and his predecessor and the creator of the ONE, William L. Langer, was a Harvard historian. Not surprisingly, they adapted the historian's craft and methodology, deductive inference, to estimative intelligence.

Deductive inference searches for patterns in past events and behavior to determine trends, continuity, and change in the present or future. In the case of Soviet estimates, Kent defined it simply as looking for "indicators from precedents in Soviet foreign policy."[31] The method has strengths and weaknesses. On the one hand, it allows analysts to make tentative explanations for events and outcomes that reveal patterns, to generate testable hypotheses, and to hypothesize future developments—the essence of estimative intelligence. On the other hand, since it deals with probabilities rather than certainty, it allows different analysts to reach different conclusions from the same set of facts or circumstances. As Kent himself acknowledged, "estimating is what you do when you do not know."[32] In-house, cynics referred to NIEs as "guesstimates."

Estimative methodology has remained immune to change and criticism. One critic has complained that estimates "seem stuck in the 1950s through the 1960s deductive historical methods advanced by Sherman Kent, instead of adopting the latest social science knowledge."[33] Another has asserted the "traditional methodology of intelligence assessment and warning is obsolete."[34] Blue-ribbon panels, Congress, and some intelligence officials have pleaded for reform, arguing that traditional analysis is inadequate for warning of surprise and guiding policy, all to no avail.

Kent's "first rule" of estimating was "to try to cast yourself in his [the adversary's] image and see the world through his eyes," and it led to an egregious error that tarnished his reputation.[35] In September 1962 Kent oversaw an NIE that stated categorically that the Soviet Union would not deploy offensive nuclear weapons in Cuba. Such action, it argued, "would be incompatible with Soviet practice to date and with Soviet policy as we presently estimate it." One month later, a CIA U-2 spy plane returned from an overflight of the island nation with photographic evidence of construction sites being built for two types of Soviet missiles.

Not only would a high-risk Soviet action be unprecedented, Kent argued—it also would be "illogical." Here he fell into a notorious analytical trap known as mirror-imaging, or applying the logic of the analyst's own culture and experience without explicitly realizing it. It was a trap that would continue to ensnare Kent's successors throughout the Cold War.

The PFIAB conducted a postmortem that revealed other deficiencies. It concluded that Kent had ignored significant, albeit incomplete, information ranging from agent reports to sensitive SIGINT that did not square with his assumptions about Soviet behavior.[36] Sometimes called the mindset problem, it was evident in subsequent estimates as well. Abbott Smith, who served as Sherman Kent's deputy and later succeeded him, noted that "we had constructed for ourselves a picture of the USSR, and whatever happened had to be made to fit in that picture."[37]

The PFIAB also wagged a finger at Kent for ignoring evidence of the USSR's extensive deception-and-denial efforts to mask the missile deployments, which allowed Soviet leader Nikita Khrushchev to achieve "near total surprise." What saved the day in this case and many others was the American genius for developing technology, in this case the U-2, for intelligence collection.

Even after the PFIAB took Kent to the woodshed, he continued to defend the estimate, arguing that he had been right and Khrushchev had been wrong, because the Soviets were forced to withdraw the missiles. He ignored the fact that Khrushchev almost succeeded by bluffing, lying, and deceiving and brought the world to the brink of nuclear extinction. Kent's defense gave rise to the estimators' sardonic claim that "we may not always be right, but we're never wrong," which was repeated many times over the years.

Drafting and Coordination

Under the NIC system, the relevant NIO for a Soviet estimate drafted "terms of reference," a list of key issues to be addressed on a specific subject and then either prepared a draft or assigned the drafting to another analyst. With a draft in hand, the NIO would then convene a coordination meeting attended by interested agencies and analysts. The final product was then reviewed and submitted to the NFIB for approval before being released.

In theory, the coordination process was supposed to result in the best estimate available, involving as it did different views and multiple sources of information, as well as an opportunity for self-correction. However, the coordination "is too rarely used for this purpose."[38] Rather, there was often a bias toward seeking consensus and reconciling differing views in which "wordsmithing" took precedence over substance, resulting in the lowest common denominator to which all could agree: "Analysts and managers seek agreeable prose, words that may (or may not) help a policymaker but are crafted to get agreement among the parties in order to publish them."[39] One critic, and a former participant, went so far as to assert that such "time-consuming exercises in compromise . . . have largely outlived their usefulness" and "should be limited to a few special cases."[40]

The Détente Era (1972–79)

The Détente Parade

NIEs during the 1970s focused on the dawning of a new era in Soviet-American relations generally referred to as détente. For the United States, détente meant three things. The first priority was strategic arms negotiations aimed at limiting the number of nuclear warheads and missiles on both sides, as well as restricting antiballistic missile defense systems. Détente meant furthermore that the two superpowers would exercise mutual restraint where their interests clashed, "categorically" in Europe and "relatively" in the third world, where proxy wars were permitted so long as they remained local and limited and did not threaten to change the overall balance of power.[41] Finally, US policymakers envisioned using "soft power," ranging from trade and financial incentives to scientific and cultural exchanges, in order to entangle the Soviet Union in a web of accords that would create incentives to moderate its behavior while permitting access ("bridge building") to Eastern Europe in order to weaken Soviet hegemony.[42]

The Soviet view of détente was quite different. In the rearview mirror of history, the 1970s were a period of stagnation in which a "humdrum apparatchik" named Leonid Brezhnev marked time while the Soviet Union slouched toward collapse. Some signs of increasing problems were evident, but estimators focused on the military half of the Soviet paradox: a declining economic and industrial base combined with a robust accumulation of military power. Brezhnev presided over the largest and most rapid development of strategic nuclear and conventional military power in history, and no one knew where or whether it would end.[43] In Washington, nuclear missiles were considered instruments of deterrence and therefore guarantors of peace rather than weapons of war. On the Soviet side, however, "the Brezhnevite strategies of nuclear buildup and Third World advance were presented as two parts of an increasingly favorable 'correlation of forces' on a world scale."[44]

The Soviets were encouraged by what they perceived as a relative, and perhaps secular, decline in American power. They found confirmation in America's post-Vietnam "national malaise," compounded by political, economic, and social problems at home and the Arab oil embargo and price spikes of 1973–74. In President Richard Nixon's commitment to détente, the Soviets saw evidence of "a weakened America's need for peace, markets, and new sources of energy."[45]

In sum, for Americans détente signaled the attenuation, if not the end, of the Cold War. From the Kremlin's perspective, however, "with the capitalist world imploding, it seemed to Brezhnev that final victory in the Cold War required nothing more than avoiding risks at home while exploiting capitalism's weaknesses when and where they appeared."[46]

With few exceptions, NIEs during the 1970s offered positive assessments of Soviet behavior and Soviet-American relations, underscoring what they saw as the transformative effect of détente on Soviet policy. NIE 11-2-72, which appeared on the eve of the first summit meeting between Brezhnev and Nixon, asserted that achievement of "rough parity" in strategic military power had given the Soviets "a greater sense of security" that would moderate their international behavior.[47] Hedging slightly, estimators also expressed confidence that the United States could counteract Soviet actions that did not comport with détente. "Some leaders" might be tempted to go beyond parity, seeking some sort of "political-psychological leverage," but they would find themselves "in serious trouble if they press too hard."[48]

The first test of détente came in October 1973 during the Arab-Israeli Yom Kippur War. Both sides provided massive military support to their respective allies, and at one point Soviet leaders threatened to intervene unilaterally to prevent destruction of the Egyptian forces trapped on the Sinai Peninsula and facing destruction by the Israel Defense Forces. In response, the United States put its worldwide armed forces on enhanced alert for the first time since the Cuban Missile Crisis of 1962. Despite tense moments and the prospect of a superpower confrontation, the war ended with a United Nations–sanctioned cease-fire. The IC's postmortem concluded that détente had passed a severe test and proved that for the Soviet Union détente was "as much a need as a choice."[49]

The next estimate, NIE 11-5-75, examined the likely Soviet reading of deepening problems in US domestic and foreign affairs amid signs that détente was in trouble. The Watergate affair had ended with President Nixon's resignation, American military forces were withdrawn from Vietnam as Hanoi consolidated its victory in the south, Laos and Cambodia had joined "the socialist camp," and an imbroglio over Jewish emigration led the Soviets to cancel a trade agreement signed at the May 1972 summit.[50] The question posed was whether Moscow would attempt to take advantage of America's political turmoil and distraction, especially in the third world. The answer was an emphatic no. Soviet activities in the third world, the NIE concluded, "are of a lower priority . . . than [relations] with the highly industrialized countries, and Moscow will not wish to compromise relations with the latter by an overly aggressive pursuit of opportunities in the former."[51] Moreover, the estimate added, good relations with the United States were central to détente, and "arms control negotiations are central to those relations."[52]

The same estimate for the first time noted the Soviets' view that the "correlation of forces," a Marxist term for balance of international power, was shifting in their favor, only to dismiss it. Estimators acknowledged that Soviet leaders "remain convinced that their system will, by degrees, predominate," adding, however, they "do not accept, as a basis for policymaking, that the US is in permanent decline." America's "great strengths" in the economic, technological, military, and diplomatic areas plus the rapprochement with China ("a fairly useful lever in US hands") posed limits to Soviet ambitions. The Kremlin was "concerned to preserve the benefits of the détente relationship, and to avoid negative US reactions."[53]

A discordant note surfaced in SNIE 11-4-74, which was titled "Soviet Strategic Arms and Détente: What Are They Up To?"[54] It was commissioned by DCI James Schlesinger during his brief tenure at the CIA before he decamped to the Pentagon. Schlesinger was critical of the IC's and especially the CIA's analysis, believing it lacked realism and tended to view détente through rose-colored glasses.[55]

The same SNIE asserted that the Soviets were trying to have it both ways by pursuing "a far-reaching détente" and seeking "substantial improvements in . . . strategic capability."[56] It was the first estimate to suggest that the USSR was cheating on the 1972 Interim Agreement on Strategic Offensive Weapons Limitation (aka SALT I), the Holy Grail of détente. The SNIE cited evidence that the USSR was constructing large missile silos to accommodate "heavy missiles" prohibited since 1972 and was also using technical *maskirovka* (the Russian term for deception and denial measures) to deny US verification of Soviet compliance with the interim agreement.[57]

The authors concluded that the Soviets were bent on "testing US resolve on the rules of SALT." They remained confident, however, that if the Soviets were seeking strategic advantage, it would "require more optimism about declining US vitality and more faith in Soviet prowess than the leaders could confidently hold." Sooner or later, they would realize that they "could not continue building up their strategic capabilities and enjoying the benefits of détente." The estimate received a cool reception from intelligence officials as well as policymakers, since détente was still in vogue and troubling questions were not welcome. One of the drafters, Robert Gates, wryly noted that the SNIE put him and his coauthor "at the back of the détente parade."[58]

NIE 11-3/8 and the Team A / Team B Exercise

Until mid-decade, official estimates were sanguine that a continuing Soviet buildup of strategic missile forces was not an immediate cause for concern. NIE 11-8-72, for example, stated that the Soviets "are not likely to be able to negate the US deterrent under any circumstances we can foresee over the next ten years."[59] Two years later, the first of the new NIE 11-3/8 series stated that the USSR was seeking only "rough parity" with the United States.[60]

Critics inside and outside the government, however, challenged the estimates. They argued that the Soviet Union was engaged in a massive modernization program that called into question its commitment to SALT I and posed a threat to the US deterrent by creating a "hard target kill capability" that could destroy missiles in their hardened silos in a first strike with enough missiles left to deter a retaliatory blow.[61]

The primary threat, critics argued, was the USSR's first deployment of intercontinental ballistic missiles (ICBMs) with multiple independently targetable reentry vehicles (MIRVs); a MIRV is a ballistic missile payload that contains several warheads, each one of which is aimed at a separate target.[62] The modernization program included three new (fourth-generation) ICBMs, all of which were MIRVed, carried heavier payloads (throw weight), were equipped with enhanced guidance systems, and were more accurate than anything estimators had seen or anticipated. At the same time, the Soviets were engaged in hardening their own silos and enhancing their civil defense program, measures that could mean that the Kremlin was seeking to mitigate damage from an American retaliatory or "second" strike after destroying missile sites in the United States.

The IC was surprised on two counts. First, it had judged that the Soviet Union lagged well behind the United States in warhead technology and would not be able to deploy MIRVed missiles before the 1980s. Second, it now appeared that the Soviets had found a loophole in the SALT I accord, which imposed numerical limits on missiles but no limits on MIRVs. (The loophole was self-inflicted, however, since the American side, convinced of its own lead and the Soviet lag in technology, had excluded MIRVs from SALT negotiations.)

As outside criticism of the strategic estimates mounted, the PFIAB responded in two ways. First, it commissioned a study on the NIC's track record. The final report found that previous estimates had failed to convey an adequate sense of Soviet determination to continue building a sizable ICBM force and war-fighting capabilities. It also contradicted the most recent NIEs by claiming that the Soviets were more concerned with building up their strategic forces than achieving stability in the arms competition, that they viewed arms control measures primarily as a means for constraining US missile-force development, and that they were willing to jeopardize détente (or at least the US concept of détente) in the process.[63]

The PFIAB's other response was to press the NIC to open the estimative process to outsiders. DCI William Colby refused, but his successor, George H. W. Bush, complied shortly after succeeding Colby in 1976. Eight months later, the press announced that the NIC had agreed to let two groups, one from its staff and the other from outside later dubbed ("Team A" and "Team B") draft parallel versions of the next NIE 11-3/8. It was the first—and last—exercise in competitive analysis outside the IC.

Harvard professor Richard Pipes chaired Team B and one of its three panels labeled "Soviet strategic objectives." The other panels dealt with Soviet ICBM accuracy and air-defense issues and were relatively noncontroversial. Not so Pipes's panel, whose final report was as much a critique of previous estimates as a commentary on Soviet strategic forces and nuclear strategy. Pipes charged that the CIA team failed to understand that Soviet strategic culture was qualitatively different from America's and viewed Soviet developments through the distorted lens of mirror-imaging of US concepts and policy. He also argued that intelligence professionals failed to understand that the Kremlin believed that more missiles and more strategic power meant more clout in the international arena and that military might not only served to deter war (the US view) but also fight and win a war should deterrence fail. In sum, the Soviet Union was not committed to seeking parity with the United States in nuclear arms and therefore strategic stability—it was seeking superiority. Team B warned that within the next decade the Soviets would have a "window of opportunity" to strike with impunity, and the United States would be faced by a corresponding "window of vulnerability." Team A, led by a CIA officer and veteran chairman of estimates on Soviet strategic forces, demurred, claiming that such superiority was unattainable "except on the margins."

The NIC issued a separate report of Team B's conclusions ("An Alternative View"[64]) and included some of the report in the next NIE 11-3/8 in a section titled "Synthesis."[65] But there was no synthesis or reconciliation. The NIE simply recapitulated the opposing views without attempting to reconcile them or allow more debate.

Subsequent events and recent research revealed that Team B was more wrong than right, even if the questions it raised were more right than wrong. The Soviet modernization program was based on a decision made in the late 1960s to upgrade the USSR's second-strike rather than its first-strike capabilities, and "the evidence . . . strongly suggests that the Soviet Union had neither a plan nor the capability to fight and win a nuclear war."[66] The program was driven by inertia in the Soviet military and the military-industrial complex, whose inner workings remained concealed from US intelligence.[67]

Troubling Signs in the Third World

Next to Soviet strategic intentions, the most vexing issue for estimators was Soviet involvement in third world conflicts beginning in the mid-1970s. The American withdrawal from Southeast Asia and rising isolationist sentiment at home offered the Kremlin both motive and opportunity. As a Soviet diplomat put it, the "'Vietnam syndrome' . . . only served to whet appetites" in the Kremlin.[68] Opportunities abounded. Between 1974 and 1980, fourteen political upheavals and guerrilla insurgencies erupted in former colonial areas. By the end of the decade, the Soviet Union was allied, through "peace and friendship treaties," with Angola, Congo-Brazzaville, Ethiopia, Libya, Mozambique, the People's Democratic Republic of Yemen (South Yemen), and Syria and had established a presence in some thirty other countries. In 1975 alone, new pro-Soviet regimes seized power in Guinea-Bissau, Mozambique, Vietnam, Cambodia, Laos, and Angola.

The drive into the third world began in 1975 with Soviet and Cuban intervention in a civil war in Angola. Next, Moscow terminated its alliance with Somalia in favor of neighboring Ethiopia, where Soviet advisers directed the Ogaden War and aided their new ally in a civil war with a secessionist movement in the region of Eritrea. Finally, Soviet and Cuban advisers moved to the People's Democratic Republic of Yemen and aided its forces in battles against the Western-aligned Yemen Arab Republic (North Yemen).

The first estimate after the Angolan affair did not view Soviet-Cuban intervention as a challenge to US interests or as a portent of things to come.[69] It judged that "intense nationalism," resistance to outside interference, and the "vicissitudes of Third World politics" would constrain Soviet advances, a clear projection or mirror-imaging of the recent US experience in Vietnam. The estimate also claimed that Western political, economic, and cultural influence and the presence of US and other Western armed forces limited Soviet opportunities.

A second estimate, published in late October 1979, was more somber but still not alarmist.[70] It noted that the Kremlin's activities had reached "a new stage" since 1977 in the Horn of Africa, moving from military assistance to indigenous forces to direct engagement with Soviet military forces and advisers and Castro's foreign legions. The estimate acknowledged that Moscow was benefiting from a "perception" that the East-West balance of power had shifted to the detriment of the West, as well as US reluctance to use military force to counter the expansion of the Soviet and Cuban presence in the third world.[71] Still, it concluded that Soviet activities—"dramatic in scale and noteworthy for their use of Cuban forces"—did not "entail major risks for the Kremlin" and by implication made no major challenge to American interests.

Reassessment

The first estimate to take a comprehensive examination of Soviet foreign and military policy in the third world was NIE 11-4-78, "Soviet Goals and Expectations in the Global Power Arena."[72] It was the beginning of a reassessment of Soviet behavior and the previously upbeat view of détente. NIE 11-4-78 declared that Soviet policy was "essentially revolutionary" and based on a belief that the balance of power and influence had changed in the USSR's favor. It also judged that Soviet behavior in the next decade was likely "to include a purposeful, cautious exploration of the political implications of the USSR's increased military strength" and "will continue to be competitive and assertive in most areas of engagement with the West."[73]

The NIE was controversial. According to one of its authors, it ran headlong into "bureaucratic obscurantism" within the policy and intelligence communities, which held to the view that upheavals in the third world had mainly indigenous causes and that Soviet intervention was discreet, cautious, and reversible.[74] Nevertheless, it struck a responsive chord with President Jimmy Carter's national security adviser, Zbigniew Brzezinski. And it did so before the so-called geopolitical shocks of 1979—the Iranian Islamic revolution, the revolutionary guards' seizure of the American embassy in Teheran, and the Soviet invasion of Afghanistan—all of which, in many accounts, led to the Carter administration's growing disillusionment with détente.

Brzezinski used the estimates as the basis for two policy initiatives, one that dealt with strategy for nonmilitary competition in the third world and the other that aimed at enhancing the United States' global military presence and forces in critical areas. Former DCI Robert Gates, who helped draft the estimate, noted, "This is one of the few instances I can recall where a national intelligence estimate provoked such a strong reaction on the part of a president and senior policy-makers."[75]

Until mid-decade, Soviet estimates reflected a blinkered optimism regarding détente, which was the prevailing view in the White House and with public opinion in general.[76] Soviet behavior that, in the estimators' view, did not accord with "the rules of conduct" set forth at the first Nixon-Brezhnev summit was dismissed as temporary, aberrational, and subject to correction. NIE 11-5-75, for example, asserted that there was "constant conflict in the minds of Soviet leaders" between cooperating with and challenging the United States. But challenges so far, it claimed, were "on the margins of détente," adding that the Soviets were "somewhat more considerate of US attitudes and interests in certain [unspecified] areas than they would otherwise be."[77] The estimators almost certainly felt constrained to stop there during an administration that "took pains not to attack Soviet moves as contrary to the spirit or letter of détente while keeping US-Soviet tensions at a minimum."[78]

In the mid-1970s, estimates began to raise hard questions about Soviet conduct in the two areas of primary concern, strategic military power and intervention in the third world. NIE 11-5-75 was the first assessment to raise doubts about Soviet commitment to SALT I and the American view of strategic stability. Though controversial, it was exemplary because it took a comprehensive view of Soviet foreign and military policy and their interaction "in the global power arena" and took a better appreciation of the Kremlin's motives and goals. It also proved prescient by anticipating the coming period of Soviet-American relations after the collapse of détente.

From Détente to Confrontation (1980–84)

Détente Falters

The high tide of détente lasted from the first Nixon-Brezhnev summit in 1972 to the signing of the Helsinki Final Act on Security and Cooperation in Europe three years later. The final blow came during the last two years of Brezhnev's rule with the 1979 Soviet invasion of Afghanistan and a crisis in Poland in the years 1980–82. Faced by crises at home and abroad and rising American assertiveness, Kremlin leaders became convinced that the "correlation of forces" was turning against them and even questioned whether the United States might be planning a surprise nuclear attack against the USSR and the other Eastern Bloc countries of the Warsaw Pact.

Two months before the invasion of Afghanistan, NIE 11-10-79 stated that "we believe . . . that the Soviets are unlikely to invade a Third World country." It added, however, that Afghanistan was the one place "where the provision of limited Soviet ground forces in a hurry might well be undertaken."[79]

US intelligence had been watching for several months as the Soviet-backed regime in Kabul lost ground to the mujahideen, the indigenous Islamic resistance. The CIA issued an "alert memorandum" five days before the Soviets began airlifting troops into the capital city. It did not, however, issue an explicit warning of a full-scale invasion. The last alert appeared after Soviet forces had crossed the border, when, as one official mocked, the invasion was "already spectator sport."[80] Privately the White House complained that lack of clear warning constituted an intelligence failure.

The complaint was unfair. US intelligence reports prompted President Carter in June and July to warn Brezhnev against sending Soviet forces into Afghanistan. Thus Carter was fully aware that an invasion was possible, but his intelligence advisers judged that it was not likely. As a CIA participant noted, the problem was not US intelligence coverage, which was excellent—"it was that the operation being prepared was contrary to what intelligence analysts had expected Moscow was willing to do."[81] Analysts argued that the large-scale deployment of Soviet combat forces outside the Warsaw Pact area would be unprecedented and hence unlikely. They also judged that the Kremlin was not likely to risk what was left of détente and arms control, as well as opprobrium of world public opinion, just to shore up a dubious Marxist dictatorship.

Bureaucratic caution compounded mirror-imaging. Détente was in serious trouble, and the US Senate was withholding ratification of a second Strategic Arms Limitation Treaty (SALT II), which the White House later withdrew. An assessment that "Moscow was preparing another aggression in the Third World on the heels of Ethiopia was not something most US policymakers wanted to see casually aired."[82]

In August 1980, Polish workers on strike at the Lenin Shipyard in Gdańsk formed Solidarity, the first independent trade union in the Eastern Bloc. Warsaw granted legal status to the new trade union, which soon ballooned into a ten-million-strong national protest movement. What appeared to be an internal Polish affair became an international situation as the West worried that the Kremlin would dispatch Warsaw Pact forces to Poland. The Polish crisis transcended the transition in US administrations from Jimmy Carter to Ronald Reagan. A CIA task force rather than the NIC took the lead in monitoring the crisis and warning policymakers.[83]

In early December 1980, the CIA issued an alert memorandum saying that preparations for an invasion had been completed and would be implemented within days. The alert was on target. The information came from a CIA agent, a Polish army officer named Ryszard Kukliński, who had been engaged in martial-law planning since the previous August. What Kukliński did not— indeed could not—know was that in the meantime Warsaw Pact leaders decided at the last minute to stand down, at least for the moment.[84]

In March and April 1981, the CIA issued more warnings and another alert memorandum, convinced that Soviet-Warsaw Pact military exercises and logistical preparations signaled an imminent invasion. It was wrong again. The agency meanwhile ruled out the most likely alternative scenario, an internal crackdown, because it judged that Polish military and security forces would either refuse to act or, if they did, would prove to be incapable of suppressing Solidarity.

While technical collection played an important role in the CIA's coverage, this was one of the few instances in which "message-like" intelligence, from Kukliński, played a role. A Polish General Staff officer, the colonel had been cooperating with the CIA since the early 1970s.[85] He came under suspicion in November 1981, however, and the CIA exfiltrated him to the United States.

Despite Kukliński's information, US officials failed to anticipate martial law or attempt to ward off the crackdown by appealing to the Polish government or warning Solidarity. Senior policymakers later claimed that they had not been apprised of Kukliński's reporting or, more subtly, that the extreme secrecy of his reporting and the sensitivity of the source had rendered it useless. In fact, however, a CIA officer later claimed that some twenty senior officials were on the distribution list for reporting from Kukliński.[86]

CIA operations officers, moreover, mishandled Kukliński's defection by exercising such tight security that even the political analysts on the agency's Polish task force were not told of his departure from Warsaw and presence in a Washington-area safehouse. Rather, the colonel was closeted with military analysts for whom "martial law fell below such things as nuclear plans and posture," which "impeded the CIA's use of its own asset."[87]

On the night of December 12, 1981, as the crisis reached its dénouement, DCI William Casey, senior CIA officials, and analysts gathered in the agency's operations center to review news reports that all Polish telecommunications with Western Europe and the United States had been severed. Yet they could not decide what it meant. A debate over whether to alert the White House and the National Security Council ended with a decision to do nothing for fear of issuing another false alarm. The agency first learned of Warsaw's decision to impose martial law from international media reports.[88]

The Soviet War Scare

In May 1981, the Soviet Union ordered the KGB and the GRU to launch a joint "intelligence alert" codenamed RYaN, the Russian acronym for nuclear-missile attack. RYaN was an indications-and-warning-of-war exercise based on Kremlin suspicions that the United States might be planning a surprise attack on the Soviet Union and its Warsaw Pact allies. It remained in effect, with diminishing priority, until November 1991, but a critical episode occurred on the night of November 9–10, 1983, during an annual North Atlantic Treaty Organization (NATO) command-post nuclear-release exercise called Able Archer–83 in which "dummy missiles" were prepared for launch. Flash messages from KGB residencies (field stations) indicated that Able Archer might be a cover for the real thing.[89]

The following May, the NIC issued an SNIE, "Implications of Recent Soviet Military-Political Activities," that assessed that this episode, as well as other anomalous Soviet military moves, did not indicate an "abnormal Soviet fear of conflict with the United States."[90] Estimators concluded that the Soviets were edgy, but their limited reaction—putting fighter aircraft in the USSR, Poland, and East Germany on "strip alert"—indicated that they "did not in fact think there was a possibility of a NATO attack."[91] "We believe strongly that Soviet actions are not inspired by, and Soviet leaders do not perceive, a genuine danger of imminent conflict or confrontation with the United States."[92]

The SNIE was right about the Soviet reaction, but it was wrong in dismissing Soviet "war talk" as mere propaganda rather than an "authentic" view of the Soviet leadership. The NIC had put its faith in what it learned from SIGINT and IMINT, while rejecting intelligence from a senior Soviet intelligence officer in London named Oleg Gordievsky, who was secretly collaborating with British intelligence. Gordievsky was almost as close as it gets in the intelligence business to the horse's mouth. He handed over cable traffic on RYaN and the Able Archer episode. Yet the NIC rejected the messenger as well as the message. It dismissed RYaN as part of a KGB disinformation operation aimed at manipulating the Reagan administration to moderate its Soviet policy.[93] The national intelligence officer who drafted the SNIE suspected that Gordievsky was a disinformation agent and that British intelligence was either his victim or his collaborator, since London too was concerned that the Reagan administration's hard-line policy was raising Soviet-American tensions to the boiling point.[94] Six years later a PFIAB postmortem concluded that the SNIE had been dangerously wrong. The war scare was for real, and the IC had failed to take it seriously.[95]

The estimates on Afghanistan and Poland revealed that anticipating Soviet decisions and predicting their consequences—in other words, "thinking like the Soviets"—was not the IC's strong suit. In the first case, estimators believed that Soviet commitment to détente and arms control, though frayed, would deter an invasion outside the Warsaw Pact. It did not. After the invasion, they assumed that, with little left to risk, the Soviets would send troops to Poland to safeguard an ally in a critical security zone. In fact, as records of Politburo discussions later revealed, Soviet leaders concluded that sending troops to Poland would be fraught with political risks and economic sanctions that would finish off what, in their view, was left of détente. The Soviets were even prepared to accept Solidarity's advent to power rather than act against it.[96] This reasoning was not, of course, evident to US intelligence at time, but a better understanding of Solidarity's views might have led to a more accurate assessment. The union's leaders had been careful to assert that they were seeking political and economic reform, not the end of communist rule, and they had avoided challenging the

Soviet Union's hegemony or threatening to withdraw from the Warsaw Pact, the Kremlin's paramount concern that led it to move into Hungary in 1956 and into Czechoslovakia in 1968. With those precedents in mind, however, "the US government misjudged entirely what was happening. Mesmerized by the vision of Soviet troops marching into Poland, it had become blinded to the more probable alternative of martial law implemented locally."[97]

Inaccurate judgments on Poland and the war scare share a common thread. In both cases, estimators overlooked or discounted HUMINT from arguably the two best Western agents of the Cold War. A bureaucratic mistake and poor coordination between CIA operations officers and political analysts denied the latter access to Kukliński and the benefit of his information. The SNIE on the Soviet war scare revealed the estimators' absolute confidence in technical collection operations and rather curt dismissal of an agent, Gordievsky, who came prepared with documentary evidence of Soviet fears. The drafters almost certainly would have given Soviet "war talk" more weight had they known about a series of very aggressive and highly compartmented US and NATO air and naval maneuvers called "psyops," or psychological operations, reminiscent of the early Cold War and conducted close to Soviet airspace, territorial waters, and borders. They were not cleared for this "close-hold" information, however, and therefore had a limited understanding of the action-reaction dynamic of Soviet-American relations.[98]

The war scare made more of an impression on Reagan than on intelligence professionals. The Soviet reaction to Able Archer, he claimed in his memoirs, was an epiphany that led him to cancel the intimidating psyops and open a dialogue with Soviet leaders that culminated in three summit meetings with the new leader, Mikhail Gorbachev, during his second term.[99]

In retrospect, Soviet restraint in Poland and trepidation reflected in the RYaN alert offered clues that the Kremlin was beginning to reassess the "correlation of forces." The systemic problems that would bring down the Soviet empire and end the Cold War were "well advanced when the Polish crisis brought them to the fore."[100] An ailing and often incapacitated Leonid Brezhnev was clinging to his "superficial belief in the Soviet Union's irresistible global ascendancy," while his "more somber colleagues and successors knew better" and "acted accordingly."[101] Such clues were esoteric, however, and certainly not obvious to outside observers, least of all to US intelligence, which was still focused on Soviet assertiveness.

A Harder Inflection

The first comprehensive review of Soviet-American relations issued after Ronald Reagan entered the White House in 1981 was an update of the final estimate prepared for the previous administration, NIE 11-4-78 M/H, or Memorandum for Holders.[102] The NIC apparently decided that an estimate that had been deemed too hard-line by Democrats would find a better reception by Republicans who had campaigned against détente (or what candidate Reagan had denounced as "a one-way street") and vowed to rebuild American military power before negotiating with the Kremlin. The revised version was the first estimate to state categorically that the previous decade had witnessed a power shift in which the Soviet Union had achieved "unprecedently [sic] favorable advances across the military spectrum" at US expense. The Soviets were "now more prepared to accept the risks of confrontation in a serious crisis, particularly in an area where they have military or geopolitical advantages."[103] The M/H singled out the Persian Gulf as a potential flashpoint where Moscow was believed to be seeking control over Western oil supplies. It also asserted that the Kremlin now saw Central America as the "Achilles' heel of the West," where the Soviets and Cubans were aiding the Sandinista government in Nicaragua and backing guerrilla movements in El Salvador and Guatemala.

The next assessment, NIE 11-4-82, which projected likely Soviet behavior for the next three to five years (1985–87), took an even starker view.[104] Its key judgments: Soviet-American relations were "fundamentally adversary [sic]," détente was a dead letter, and the USSR was challenging the United States in every sphere. With a nod to Soviet troubles (economic problems, the defense burden, a rising dissident movement, and an approaching leadership succession), the estimate said that the Kremlin would remain "assertive" and chances of a confrontation, "most likely in the Third World, had increased."[105]

NIE 11-4-82 put a harder inflection on the Soviet military threat, no doubt because several members of the former Team B now held top positions in the new administration. It asserted that while the Soviets believed nuclear war would be catastrophic, they also believed that it was possible, adding that they rejected the American doctrine of mutually assured destruction and were striving to build superior capabilities to fight and win a nuclear war.[106]

SNIE 11-9-84 appeared just before the end of the first Reagan term.[107] It judged that the Soviets maintained a "deep hostility" to US interests but asserted that this stemmed less from ideology than from what they saw as American efforts to alter the balance of strategic power, strengthen alliances in the third world, and conduct regional security initiatives to counter and then reverse Soviet gains. The Soviets were on the defensive and realized that their efforts to exploit détente at US expense had been stalemated. The implication was not hard to miss. Reagan's hard-line policy was succeeding. Nevertheless, the estimators added, under pressure the Soviets were more, not less, dangerous; hostile actions in areas such as Central America and Pakistan were "a distinct near-term possibility."[108]

Two estimates, 11-10/2-84 and 11-6-84, declared that Soviet-American competition in the third world was now "an essential element" in bilateral relations.[109] The first estimate cited a laundry list of Soviet gains. The USSR now had air and naval facilities in eight countries, military assistance programs in thirty-four more, and alliances (peace and friendship treaties) with ten countries. There were new pro-Soviet governments in southern Africa, Central America, and South and Southeast Asia. Meanwhile, the Soviets had augmented their air- and sealift capabilities, allowing them to challenge the United States in distant areas.

Taken together, 11-10/2-84 and 11-6-84 provided the analytical underpinning for the Reagan administration's increasing engagement in regional conflicts. The first estimate asserted, for example, that "it is by no means certain that all pro-Soviet regimes can maintain power in their own countries."[110] Ad hoc at first, the policy of backing resistance movements opposing pro-Soviet regimes became known unofficially as the Reagan Doctrine.[111]

NIE 11-6-84 assessed Soviet capabilities for distant military operations and intervention over the next five to ten years. It drew a distinction between "global reach" and "power-projection" capabilities. The Soviets, according to the estimate, had extended their reach by providing arms and military advisers, by acquiring air and sea access, and by deploying their own forces and Cuban and East German proxies. But their power-projection capabilities—defined as prepositioned equipment, rapid deployment and amphibious forces, overseas staging and logistical bases, aircraft carriers, and aerial refueling—lagged behind those of the United States. The estimate concluded that the USSR would have difficulty mounting and sustaining distant operations even in the face of limited opposition. Its forces were spread too thinly, were vulnerable to counterforce, and lacked offensive punch. The Soviets could challenge the United States but only up to a point and not for long.

"Cooking the Books"?

Later, with the benefit of hindsight, critics seized on the gap between US perceptions and Soviet realities to charge that DCI William Casey had "politicized" intelligence by slanting, shading, or tendentiously shaping assessments "to support the confrontational style and politics of the Reagan administration."[112] By exaggerating Soviet military and economic strength and underestimating the economic burden of defense spending, the same critics asserted, the IC missed the coming collapse of the Soviet Union.

Accusations that Casey "cooked the books" stemmed in part from his unique role in the Reagan administration. He was a powerful DCI, the man credited with helping Reagan win the White House in 1980, a cabinet member with a central role in policymaking, and a hard-liner with strong anti-Soviet views. Robert Gates, who oversaw all Soviet analysis as deputy director for intelligence and chairman of the NIC under Casey, conceded that his boss "had his own foreign policy agenda" and used Soviet estimates as a "powerful instrument in forcing the pace in the policy arena."[113] That said, however, critics ignore the fact that Casey's influence was in decline during the second Reagan administration and well before his incapacitation in late 1986 and death several months later. From the mid-1980s onward, moreover, the IC was preoccupied with prospects for a new détente in Soviet-American relations and then with unmistakable evidence that the Soviet system was in crisis.

Soviet Collapse and the End of the Cold War (1988–91)

The Soviet Death Spiral

The second Reagan administration (1985–89) was a time of transition in Washington as well as in Moscow. During his reelection campaign, the president signaled his readiness to negotiate with the Soviets. The policymaking community split into two camps, the "squeezers" and the "dealers."[114] The former advocated continuation of the first term's hard-line policy, seeking to force the Soviets to negotiate from a position of weakness. The latter believed that a new opportunity to reach agreements had appeared and should be explored.

The transition in Moscow—and the new perceived opportunity—was the advent of Mikhail Gorbachev, a different kind of leader who professed "new political thinking" in domestic and foreign affairs. The squeezers were skeptical of Gorbachev's rhetoric and intentions, arguing that his policies signified yet another temporary retreat until the Kremlin could resume the Cold War from a stronger position. The dealers argued that Gorbachev was serious and that he needed better relations with the United States and stability abroad in order to advance reform at home. They believed that there was little risk, and potentially much gain, in opening a dialogue.

Reagan stood somewhere between the two camps and indeed played them off against one another. Both factions felt vindicated. The dealers claimed credit for the improvement in relations with Moscow during three Reagan-Gorbachev summit meetings and for the 1987 treaty that eliminated Soviet and American intermediate- and short-range missiles in Europe. The squeezers could point to the 1986 escalation of CIA support for the mujahideen in Afghanistan that led two years later to the Soviet Union's humiliating retreat and to covert support for Solidarity that allowed it to survive and force the communist regime to enter negotiations on political and economic reform.[115]

Both factions "tried to imprint the official Soviet estimate [sic] with their own interpretation of the developments in Moscow," and accusations of politicization surfaced again.[116] Secretary of State George Shultz, the leading dealer, accused DCI Casey of providing policymakers with "bum dope" intended to justify his anti-Gorbachev views. The debate over Gorbachev's intentions and sincerity continued into the next administration, of President George H. W.

Bush. William Webster, who succeeded Casey after his death in 1987 and served under Reagan and Bush, acknowledged the IC's ambiguity. When he asked for an assessment of Gorbachev, he said, "I had my glass half-full guys and my glass half-empty guys," he said later. "On the one hand this, on the other hand that."[117] Bush's national security adviser, Brent Scowcroft, dismissed Gorbachev as "Brezhnev with a humanitarian paint job" before subsequently embracing the Soviet leader as the best hope for ending the Cold War.[118]

Behind the scenes in Moscow, a struggle was brewing between Gorbachev and diehards in the military, the military-industrial complex, and the security agencies. Yet it, like other indications of serious problems affecting the warp and woof of the Soviet system, was elusive before 1989–90, making it difficult for Soviet watchers to evaluate Gorbachev's political debut and to agree on where the Soviet Union was headed.

Meanwhile, disaster struck the CIA. In mid-1985, Aldrich Ames, a counter-intelligence officer in the operations directorate, sold to the KGB the names of the agency's entire cadre of Soviet agents. To make matters worse, the Soviets replaced the agents Ames betrayed with double agents under their control; they fed the agency disinformation that made the USSR look stronger and more resilient than it actually was.[119] John Deutch, a later DCI (1995–96), commented that the tainted information "made it much more difficult to understand what was going on in the Soviet Union at a crucial time in its history."[120] Another intelligence official added that Soviet deception raised "the disturbing possibility" that US intelligence had been duped into overestimating the USSR's military and economic strength and political stability even as it was tottering on the brink of collapse.[121]

Gorbachev: Real Reformer or Sorcerer's Apprentice?

The pivotal year for the Soviet Union was 1989. Gorbachev introduced major changes in Soviet domestic and foreign policy and joined President Bush in a new "strategic partnership." It also was the year in which the Soviet Union entered the death spiral that led to its disappearance two years later.

In December 1988 Gorbachev delivered the most important foreign policy speech of his career. Addressing the United Nations General Assembly, he renounced Marxism-Leninism and class warfare as the basis of Soviet foreign policy, embraced "pan-humanist values" and "global interdependence," and pledged to convert an "economy of armaments into an economy of disarmament." He invited the United States to cooperate in ending the Cold War by halting the arms race and seeking settlements of regional conflicts. Then he made dramatic unilateral concessions, pledging to reduce Soviet ground forces by five hundred thousand and to withdraw fifty thousand troops from Eastern

Europe, as well as ten thousand tanks, eighty-five hundred artillery systems, and eight hundred combat aircraft, over a two-year period.

Gorbachev's speech caught US intelligence by surprise. The chief of Soviet analysis at the CIA told Congress straightforwardly that despite Gorbachev's initiatives in domestic and foreign policy, the agency had "never really looked at the Soviet Union as a political entity in which there were factors building which could lead to at least the initiation of the political transformation that we seem to see [at the present time]. . . . Had we said a week ago that Gorbachev might . . . offer a unilateral cut of 500,000 in the military, we would have been told we were crazy."[122]

NIE 11-4-89, the first estimate prepared for the Bush administration, appeared as the White House was completing a review of its Soviet policy, and it reflected still divided opinions about how seriously to take Gorbachev.[123] It also was unusual; rather than seek a consensus, the NIE spelled out contending views in the body of the estimate in a section labeled "Disagreements."

The drafters agreed that prospects for reaching favorable agreements with the USSR were good. One group, citing previous failed reforms and the "transient nature of past détentes," argued that "there is a serious risk of Moscow returning to traditionally combative behavior when the hoped-for gains in economic performance are achieved." The opposing view held that "Gorbachev's policies reflect a fundamental rethinking of national interests and ideology as well as more tactical considerations." It cited the withdrawal from Afghanistan and the Kremlin's tolerance of power-sharing arrangements in Eastern Europe as evidence of "historic shifts in the Soviet definition of national interest" that "are likely to have sufficient momentum to produce lasting shifts in Soviet behavior."[124]

The second view prevailed and was reflected in President Bush's announced policy of moving "beyond containment" and seeking agreements with the Soviet Union. It also paved the way for a Bush-Gorbachev summit meeting held in Malta in December.

Just as the NIE appeared, however, the CIA injected a new tone of skepticism about Gorbachev's prospects, not by asking if he was a genuine reformer but by questioning whether his reform efforts could succeed and, by implication, whether he could hold on to power. In a memorandum titled "Gorbachev's Domestic Gambles and Instability in the USSR," the CIA's Office of Soviet Analysis (SOVA) argued that *perestroika* (restructuring) was based on "questionable premises and wishful thinking" and that "the social and political unrest that has punctuated Gorbachev's rule is not a transient phenomenon. Conditions are likely to lead in the foreseeable future to continuing crises and instability on a larger scale."[125] The memorandum also noted that labor unrest and food riots were on the rise, but the severest challenge would come from ethnic violence or secessionist movements. A coming Kremlin crackdown "is most likely in the

Baltic region, but could also come in the Caucasus, Moldavia, or—down the road—even in the Ukraine."[126]

"Domestic Gambles" was the first assessment to look beyond Gorbachev and examine developments in the Soviet system as a whole. It also was the first to address the rise of nationalist and ethnic tensions, which it presciently saw as the key factor in a building crisis that could tear the multinational Soviet Union apart. Singling out the Baltic region proved to be prophetic when the Kremlin dispatched regular army forces and paramilitary units to the capitals of Lithuania and Latvia, which ended in the deaths of peaceful demonstrators.

SOVA's pessimistic assessment was not only insightful but also courageous. It was not well received by the White House, which had based its policy on the assumption that Gorbachev would remain in power for the foreseeable future. And whether right or not, the administration believed that it was an implicit endorsement of Boris Yeltsin, the recently elected president of the Russian Republic, who was Gorbachev's challenger and soon became his successor.

Reaction to "Domestic Gambles" was apparent in the next comprehensive estimate, NIE 11-18-89, "The Soviet System in Crisis: Prospects for the Next Two Years," which appeared in November 1989. It asserted that "[Intelligence] Community analysts hold the view that a *continuation and intensification of the current course is most likely* and believe that, despite the obvious difficulties, the turmoil will be manageable without the need for repressive measures so pervasive that the reform process is derailed" (emphasis in original).[127]

In an unusual departure, the CIA refused to concur and registered a detailed dissent in the body of the estimate. Sensing perhaps that it was swimming against the tide of consensus, the CIA designated Deputy Director for Intelligence John Helgerson, the agency's senior analysis official, to present the rebuttal. "We believe," he declared, that "there is a significant chance that Gorbachev, during the period of this Estimate, will progressively lose control of events. The personal political strength he has accumulated is likely to erode, and his political position will be severely tested." The dissent went on to say that "neither the political system Gorbachev is trying to reform nor the one that is likely to emerge will be able to cope with the surge of popular demands and a deepening economic crisis."[128]

The next estimate, 11-18-90, revealed just how far the rest of the IC had moved toward SOVA's position as the situation in the USSR deteriorated. Reviewing events of the previous year, it stated flatly that the "old communist order is in its death throes" and that the crisis of *perestroika* was now threatening "to tear the country apart."[129] It was remarkably candid about the difficulty of anticipating the future in a rapidly changing situation: "In such a volatile atmosphere, events could go in any number of directions. Because of this, the Intelligence Community's uncertainties about the future of the Soviet system are greater today than at any time in the forty years we have been producing Estimates on the USSR. Accordingly, our projections for the next year will be highly tentative."[130]

The estimators cited four possible scenarios: deterioration short of anarchy, anarchy, military intervention, and "light at the end of the tunnel," or muddling through.[131] They rated the first and the fourth scenarios as the most likely.

In April 1991, SOVA issued another pessimistic assessment in the form of a "typescript," an informal memorandum that was not coordinated with the rest of the IC. "The Soviet Cauldron" stated flatly that "Gorbachev's credibility has sunk to near zero" and that "anti-Communist forces are breaking down the Soviet empire and system of governance."[132] Four months before an assembly of government, military, and intelligence officials calling themselves the State Committee for the State of Emergency tried to overthrow Gorbachev, SOVA anticipated the coup owing to public statements and indications that the military and security organs were making logistical preparations to move large numbers of troops into Moscow at short notice.[133] SOVA predicted that a coup, if it occurred, would probably fail, which of course it did. It anticipated that Gorbachev's main opponent on the left, Yeltsin, was about to become the first popularly elected leader in Russian history and would challenge the old order.[134]

"The Soviet Cauldron" was an exemplary assessment, not so much because of its prediction as because of its analysis of the fissiparous forces that were driving the Soviet Union toward collapse. It also showed once again that the CIA was ahead of the rest of the IC.

NIE 11-18-91, the final comprehensive estimate before the Soviet breakup, appeared three months later.[135] It judged that the "USSR is in the midst of a revolution" and that events "will sweep the Communist Party from power and reshape the country." This would happen, the drafters said, "within the five-year time frame of this Estimate."[136] Gorbachev was gone within a few weeks, however; Yeltsin emerged triumphant and outlawed the Communist Party. On Christmas Day 1991, at 7:35 p.m., the Soviet hammer-and-sickle flying over the Kremlin was lowered and replaced by the new Russian tricolor. The USSR officially ceased to exist on December 31. The Cold War was over.

The NIEs were more conservative than the CIA's assessments during 1989–90. The bias toward consensus led estimators to focus on Gorbachev's string of successes and his staying power. Indeed, the rest of the world was in the throes of Gorbymania at a time when *Time* declared the Soviet leader "Man of the Year" and the Norwegian Nobel Institute awarded him the Peace Prize. Estimates were right about some things and wrong about others, and they missed completely one major development, Gorbachev's rash decision to surrender East Germany and allow a reunified German nation to join NATO. Analysts were trying to make sense of events in what SOVA called a "revolutionary whirlpool," which made their accurate predictions all the more remarkable while mitigating their misjudgments and failure to capture a turbulent situation in all its complexities. The CIA in particular documented the problems and, more important, the underlying causes of Gorbachev's problems and the general direction in which the Soviet Union was headed. What it could not predict was exactly where, when, and how the endgame would play out. But then neither could Gorbachev.

Final Thoughts

US intelligence estimates during the final two decades of the Cold War stand up well in light of what is now known about the rise and fall of détente, the Gorbachev conundrum, and the Soviet breakup. The NIEs of the early to mid-1970s exhibited the pitfalls of mirror-imaging. Estimators viewed Soviet-American relations and Soviet behavior primarily through the prism of US assumptions about détente. They believed, wrongly as it turned out, that the USSR would settle for parity and stability in strategic weapons according to the precepts of American strategic thought and that it would subordinate its interest in détente to its ambitions in the third world. Behavior that did not comport with their view was dismissed as aberrational or the result of the lingering but diminishing nonrational ideological factors. Some NIEs took for granted that the United States had the power and the resolve to counteract Soviet behavior that it found unacceptable, which was questionable during the 1970s but seemed like a self-fulfilling prophecy during the first Reagan term.

From mid-decade on, however, the estimates began to reflect a more accurate understanding of Kremlin motives and goals. The prime example was 11-4-78, which captured the essence of the nexus between Soviet strategic power and the drive into the third world that was motivated by both ideology and by opportunity to exploit this "unprotected flank of the Western domain."[137] That estimate and its follow-on version, 11-4-78 M/H, marked a reassessment of the balance of military and political power between the United States and the USSR based on a perceived erosion of the American deterrent vis-à-vis continuing augmentation and enhancement of Soviet ICBMs and projection of power into the third world. The view that relations were now fundamentally adversarial and might lead to a confrontation was overwrought, but it anticipated the rise in tensions during the early 1980s.

The most damning—and damaging—criticism of the Cold War estimates holds that the IC failed to alert the White House to new opportunities offered by Gorbachev's ascendancy and then compounded its error by ignoring the Soviet leader's diminishing hold on power as the Soviet Union lurched toward collapse.[138] An objective reading of US intelligence assessments shows, however, that this was not the case.

In 1989 estimators disagreed over Gorbachev's ultimate intentions—whether he had abandoned Marxism-Leninism as the basis of Soviet foreign and domestic policy or whether he just wanted to call a temporary truce before returning to the fray from a stronger position. Nevertheless, both sides agreed that in the meantime the United States should seek agreements when and where they were possible. It was the right call. By the time of the August 1991 coup attempt against Gorbachev, the Soviet Union had withdrawn from Afghanistan, Solidarity was in power in Poland, all the other Eastern Bloc communist regimes had fallen, and the Warsaw Pact was history. The United States and the USSR signed new treaties on conventional and strategic weapons. Washington, in close cooperation with Bonn, negotiated German reunification within NATO. Gorbachev joined the Bush administration in opposing Iraq's occupation of Kuwait. Finally, the Soviet Union's unexpectedly rapid and on the whole peaceful retreat from empire led to its demise and the end of the Cold War. All these results, which were unimaginable in mid-decade, occurred between 1988 and 1991.

When the first signs of Gorbachev's problems appeared, the consensus held that, despite challenges to his power, he would prevail. That view proved wrong but was not unreasonable at the time. The world stood in awe of Gorbachev's success to date and hoped for more. The CIA's skeptical, and more sophisticated, analysis was prescient. It offered a premonitory warning that reform, too little and too late, might lead to the end of, rather than to a new beginning for, the Soviet Union, and within a year the rest of the IC embraced the CIA's analysis. Even though the CIA's view was not initially well received by the White House, it led the Bush administration to accelerate negotiations with Gorbachev on the premise that even when he left the scene, his successor, whoever he might be, would honor any agreements he had signed. It also led the administration to begin thinking of ways to prepare a "soft landing" for the Soviet empire.[139] After the Cold War, it was revealed that, given CIA analysis, the White House created a secret committee to explore the consequences and foreign policy implications of a Soviet collapse.[140]

The Soviet estimates of 1989–91 eschewed bland compromises and searched for consensus while allowing real debate between conflicting interpretations of rapidly changing events. Rather than blur differences of opinion or consign dissents to footnotes, they incorporated disagreements in the body of estimates. Prodded by the CIA's maverick assessments, the IC was able to give policymakers grounds to hope for the best while preparing for the worst.

Notes

1. See, for example, John M. Diamond, *The CIA and the Culture of Failure: US Intelligence from the End of the Cold War to the Invasion of Iraq* (Stanford, CA: Stanford University Press, 2008), 89. A different example of selective use of NIEs is Keren Yarhi-Milo, in her

article, "In the Eye of the Beholder: How Leaders and Intelligence Communities Assess the Intentions of Adversaries," *International Security* 38, no. 1 (2013): 7–51. The author asserts that "the bulk of integrated intelligence estimates . . . on the Soviet Union throughout the Cold War focused on aspects of the Soviet military arsenal," which allegedly led their authors "to infer Soviet political intentions primarily from military capabilities" and therefore "to overstate Soviet hostility." The military estimates did not address political intentions or levels of hostility. The far more numerous nonmilitary NIEs cited in this chapter show that US intelligence agencies continually reassessed Soviet foreign policy on the basis of multiple indicators, including military and nonmilitary factors.

2. The US intelligence community has declassified 558 National Intelligence Estimates, totaling 13,710 pages, on the former Soviet Union and Eastern Europe: Gerald K. Haines and Robert E. Leggett, eds., *CIA's Analysis of the Soviet Union 1947–1991* (Washington, DC: Center for the Study of Intelligence, 2001), 13.

3. The sole exception was William J. Casey, who, as director of Central Intelligence from 1981 to 1987, was a member of President Ronald Reagan's cabinet.

4. For most of the Cold War, the term "intelligence community" was a widely used but informal expression. In 1981, President Ronald Reagan signed an executive order formally recognizing the "United States Intelligence Community."

5. The United States Intelligence Board (USIB) was the releasing authority for NIEs from 1958 until 1976, when the NFIB replaced it. From 1947 to 2005 the director of the Central Intelligence Agency also had the title of director of Central Intelligence, in which capacity he oversaw and coordinated the work of the entire IC.

6. John H. Hedley, "The Evolution of Intelligence Analysis," in *Analyzing Intelligence: Origins, Obstacles, and Innovations*, ed. Roger Z. George and James B. Bruce (Washington, DC: Georgetown University Press, 2008), 28.

7. Records released in 2007 reveal that President Richard Nixon and his national security adviser Henry Kissinger were frequently critical of national estimates. In a memorandum to Nixon, for example, Kissinger complained that the 1969 NIE on Soviet strategic offensive weapons suffered from "serious defects" in its analysis and evidence. He noted some improvement in the next estimate but still found it "ponderous . . . almost fatuous." FoxNews.com, "CIA Shortcomings Infuriated Nixon, Newly Released Documents Reveal," December 2, 2007, accessed September 20, 2009, http://www.foxnews.com/story/2007/12/02/cia-short comings-infuriated-nixon-newly-released-documents-reveal/.

8. NIOs were recruited from throughout the IC and could assign drafting responsibilities to any agency or individuals. In practice, most NIOs and most drafters still came from the CIA. See Hedley, "Evolution of Intelligence Analysis," 28.

9. Michael Herman, *Intelligence Power in Peace and War* (London: Royal Institute of International Affairs / Cambridge University Press, 1996), 83–88.

10. Raymond L. Garthoff, a former senior intelligence official and diplomat, noted that the Soviets and their Warsaw Pact allies were more successful than their American counterparts when it came to traditional agent operations. Nevertheless, he added, HUMINT did not play a key role in any of the critical US-Soviet crises. Neither side managed to penetrate the decision-making levels of the other, and no major US or Soviet political and military decisions were discovered and thwarted by human agents. Raymond L. Garthoff, "Foreign Intelligence and the Historiography of the Cold War," *Journal of Cold War Studies* 6, no. 2 (2004): 29.

11. Melvin A. Goodman, *Failure of Intelligence: The Decline and Fall of the CIA* (Lanham, MD: Rowman & Littlefield, 2008), 111.

12. Garthoff, "Foreign Intelligence and the Historiography of the Cold War," 33–34.

13. Tim Weiner, *Legacy of Ashes: The History of the CIA* (New York: Doubleday, 2007), xv.

14. Goodman, *Failure of Intelligence*, 111.

15. Ibid.

16. Herman, *Intelligence Power in Peace and War*, 30.

17. "Address by Former DCI, Conference on *CIA's Analysis of the Soviet Union, 1947–1991*, Princeton University, March 2001," in *Watching the Bear: Essays on CIA's Analysis of the Soviet Union*, ed. Gerald K. Haines and Robert E. Leggett (Washington, DC: Center for the Study of Intelligence, 2003), 255.

18. Garthoff, "Foreign Intelligence and the Historiography of the Cold War," 43–44. The same author noted, however, that technical collection was of little use in monitoring Soviet conventional forces.

19. Kristie Macrakis, "Technophilic Hubris and Espionage Styles during the Cold War," *Isis* 101, no. 2 (2010): 378–85.

20. "CIA Shortcomings Infuriated Nixon."

21. Oleg A. Bukharin, "The Cold War Atomic Intelligence Game, 1945–70," *Studies in Intelligence* 48, no. 2 (2004): 2.

22. Abram N. Shulsky and Gary James Schmitt, *Silent Warfare: Understanding the World of Intelligence* (Washington, DC: Brassey's, 2002), 49.

23. Jeffrey T. Richelson, *A Century of Spies: Intelligence in the Twentieth Century* (New York: Oxford University Press, 1995), 338, 344–46. The electronic interception of telemetry, or radio signals from onboard monitoring systems, allowed US intelligence to gauge the capabilities and performance of Soviet missiles while in test-flight status.

24. Ibid., 346–47.

25. Benjamin B. Fischer, "Deaf, Dumb, and Blind: The CIA and East Germany," in *East German Foreign Intelligence: Myth, Reality and Controversy*, ed. Thomas Wegener Friis et al. (London: Routledge, 2010), 60–62.

26. Markus Wolf with Anne McElvoy, *Man without a Face: The Autobiography of Communism's Greatest Spymaster* (New York: Times Books / Random House, 1997), 295–96.

27. Operation Ivy Bells tapped a Soviet military communications cable on the floor of the Sea of Okhotsk that ran between the Soviet Far East and the Kamchatka Peninsula. David Wise, *Nightmover: How Aldrich Ames Sold the CIA to the KGB for $4.6 Million* (New York: HarperCollins, 1995), 123, 123n.

28. Fischer, "Deaf, Dumb, and Blind," 60.

29. John Prados, *The Soviet Estimate: US Intelligence Analysis and Russian Military Strength* (New York: Dial, 1982), 276.

30. Ibid., 277.

31. Sherman Kent, "A Crucial Estimate Relived," *Studies in Intelligence* 36, no. 5 (1964): 115.

32. Weiner, *Legacy of Ashes*, 50.

33. Michael Collier, "A Pragmatic Approach to Developing Intelligence Analysis," *Defense Intelligence Journal* 14 (2005): 31.

34. Timothy J. Smith, "Predictive Warning: Teams, Networks, and Scientific Method," in George and Bruce, *Analyzing Intelligence*, 266.

35. Kent, "Crucial Estimate Relived," 117.

36. The scathing critique of Kent's estimate is "President's Foreign Intelligence Advisory Board: James R. Killian Jr., Chairman, Memorandum for the President and Report; 4 February 1963," in *CIA Documents on the Cuban Missile Crisis 1962*, ed. Mary S. McAuliffe (Washington, DC: Central Intelligence Agency, 1992), 361–71.

37. Weiner, *Legacy of Ashes*, 154.

38. James B. Bruce, "Making Analysis More Reliable: Why Epistemology Matters to Intelligence," in George and Bruce, *Analyzing Intelligence*, 185.

39. Ibid. Herman, *Intelligence Power in Peace and War*, 264–65, argued that the American estimative process, which is centralized under the NIC, allows for more diversity and dissent and therefore results in more trenchant conclusions than its British counterpart, which, in contrast, is decentralized and biased toward seeking consensus among government departments and agencies. Bruce's understanding of the process, which is based on years of practice and observation, is more convincing.

40. John H. Hedley, *Checklist for Intelligence* (Washington, DC: Georgetown Institute for the Study of Diplomacy, 1995), 17.

41. Martin Malia, *Russia under Western Eyes: From the Bronze Horseman to the Lenin Mausoleum* (Cambridge, MA: Belknap Press of Harvard University Press, 1999), 386.

42. President Richard Nixon told Congress that "economic cooperation with the Soviet Union would create interdependence between our economies which provides a continued incentive to maintain a constructive relationship." See Richard B. Day, *Cold War Capitalism: The View from Moscow 1945–1975* (Armonk, NY: M. E. Sharpe, 1995), 264.

43. Brezhnev's early years in power "saw the most intensive arms race of the Cold War." See Steven J. Zaloga, *The Kremlin's Nuclear Sword: The Rise and Fall of Russia's Strategic Nuclear Forces, 1945–2000* (Washington, DC: Smithsonian Institution Press, 2002), 101. According to US estimates, from 1965 to 1970, the number of Soviet strategic missiles capable of attacking the United States increased from 234 to 1,229.

44. Fred Halliday, *From Kabul to Managua: Soviet-American Relations in the 1980s* (New York: Pantheon, 1989), 15.

45. Day, *Cold War Capitalism*, 274. This important but obscure book notes that Kremlin advisers based their assessment of the "correlation of forces" on the orthodox Marxist-Leninist theory of the general crisis of capitalism, which they believed had entered a new, higher, and perhaps final phase of crisis.

46. Ibid., 275.

47. National Intelligence Estimate 11-72, "Soviet Foreign Policies and the Outlook for Soviet-American Relations," April 20, 1972, 1, accessed October 6, 2014, http://www.foia.cia.gov/sites/default/files/document_conversions/89801/DOC_0000273224.pdf.

48. Ibid.

49. Intelligence Analytical Memorandum, NIAM 11-9-74, "Soviet Détente Policy," May 12, 1974, 2, accessed October 6, 2014, http://www.foia.cia.gov/sites/default/files/document_conversions/89801/DOC_0000283803.pdf.

50. National Intelligence Estimate 11-5-75, "The Soviet Assessment of the US," October 9, 1975, accessed October 6, 2014, http://www.foia.cia.gov/sites/default/files/document_conversions/89801/DOC_0000273312.pdf.

51. Ibid., 11.

52. Ibid.

53. Ibid., 1.

54. Special National Intelligence Estimate 11-4-74, "Soviet Strategic Arms Programs and Détente: What Are They Up To?," September 10, 1974, accessed October 6, 2014, http://www.foia.cia.gov/sites/default/files/document_conversions/89801/DOC_0000268106. pdf.

55. See "Address by Former DCI," 258.

56. "Soviet Strategic Arms Programs and Détente," 1.

57. The Soviets were encrypting telemetry from certain missiles during test flights, making it impossible to measure their capabilities and performance.

58. Robert M. Gates, *From the Shadows: The Ultimate Insider's Story of Five Presidents and How They Won the Cold War* (New York: Simon & Schuster, 2006), 43.

59. National Intelligence Estimate 11-8-72, "Soviet Forces for Intercontinental Attack," October 26, 1972, 1, accessed October 6, 2014, http://www.foia.cia.gov/sites/default/files/ document_conversions/89801/DOC_0000268105.pdf.

60. National Intelligence Estimate 11-3/8-74, "Soviet Forces for Intercontinental Conflict through 1985," vol. 1, November 14, 1974, 1, accessed October 6, 2014, http://www .foia.cia.gov/sites/default/files/document_conversions/89801/DOC_0000268105.pdf. Prior to 1974, the NIC issued separate estimates for Soviet strategic defensive systems, designated 11-3, and for strategic offensive systems, designated 11-8. Thereafter, the two estimates were combined and designated 11-3/8.

61. A good short discussion of this complex issue is Pavel Podvig, "The Window of Vulnerability That Wasn't: Soviet Military Buildup in the 1970s; A Research Note," *International Security* 33, no. 1 (2008): 118–38.

62. Since MIRVed missiles carry multiple warheads that can be aimed at separate targets, they are force multipliers. The new Soviet ICBMs—the SS-17, SS-18, and SS-19—carried four, six, and eight MIRVs, respectively. Under the terms of the 1972 SALT interim agreement, the USSR was permitted a relatively higher number of missiles to offset the US lead in MIRVed missiles. The sooner-than-expected Soviet deployment of MIRVs on those missiles raised the prospect of what some observers called a Soviet "breakout" in the arms race.

63. Robert L. Hewitt et al., "The Track Record in Strategic Estimating: An Evaluation of the Strategic National Intelligence Estimates, 1966–1975," February 6, 1976, in Haines and Leggett, *CIA's Analysis of the Soviet Union 1947–1991*, 278–87.

64. "Soviet Strategic Objectives: An Alternative View, Report of Team 'B'" (December 1976), in *Estimates on Soviet Military Power 1954–1984*, comp. Donald P. Steury (Washington, DC: Central Intelligence Agency, 1994), 329–35.

65. National Intelligence Estimate 11-4-77, "Soviet Strategic Objectives," January 12, 1977, 15–16, accessed October 6, 2014, http://www.foia.cia.gov/sites/default/files/docu ment_conversions/89801/DOC_0000268137.pdf.

66. Podvig, "Window of Vulnerability That Wasn't," 122–23.

67. Ibid., 138.

68. Andrey Kosolov, "Reexamining Policy in the 'Third World,'" *International Affairs*, April 1990, 39. Kosolov was the pseudonym of an aide to First Deputy Foreign Minister Vladimir Petrovsky.

69. National Intelligence Estimate 11-10–76, "Soviet Military Policy in the Third World," October 21, 1976, accessed October 6, 2014, http://www.foia.cia.gov/sites/default/ files/document_conversions/89801/DOC_0000273313.pdf.

70. National Intelligence Estimate 11-10–79, "Soviet Military Capabilities to Project Power and Influence in Distant Areas," October 1, 1979, accessed October 6, 2014, http:// www.foia.cia.gov/sites/default/files/document_conversions/89801/DOC_0000278536.pdf.

71. Ibid., 2.

72. National Intelligence Estimate 11-4-78, "Soviet Goals and Expectations in the Global Power Arena," May 9, 1978, in *Intentions and Capabilities: Estimates on Soviet Strategic Forces, 1950–1983*, ed. Donald P. Steury (Washington, DC: Central Intelligence Agency, 1996), 400.

73. Ibid.

74. Gates, *From the Shadows*, 74–76.

75. Ibid., 76. The estimate also inspired Brzezinski to coin the term "Arc of Crisis," which referred to the vast area of political instability ranging from the Horn of Africa through the Arabian Peninsula to the Persian Gulf and beyond to the Asian subcontinent (Afghanistan, Pakistan, and India), linking what had appeared to be disparate events to a new Soviet effort to undermine American interests.

76. A 1973 Gallup poll showed that 78 percent of respondents believed that the United States should go further in negotiating with the Soviet Union. About half (48 percent) thought that the two countries were about equal in terms of military power, and nearly the same number (44 percent) believed that they would be equally strong in five years. See Anne Hessing Chan, *Killing Détente: The Right Attacks the CIA* (University Park: Pennsylvania State University Press, 1998), 7.

77. "Soviet Assessment of the US," 2.

78. William Bundy, *A Tangled Web: The Making of Foreign Policy in the Nixon Presidency* (New York: Hill & Wang, 1998), 442.

79. National Intelligence Council Interagency Intelligence Memorandum NI IIM 79-10022J, "Soviet Options in Afghanistan," September 28, 1979, 5, 6, accessed October 6, 2014, http://www.foia.cia.gov/sites/default/files/document_conversions/89801/DOC_000 0278533.pdf.

80. Douglas J. MacEachin, *Predicting the Soviet Invasion of Afghanistan: The Intelligence Community's Record* (Washington, DC: Central Intelligence Agency, 2002), 39.

81. Ibid., 37.

82. Ibid., 39.

83. The NIC issued only one SNIE before the Polish government declared martial law on December 13, 1981: Special National Intelligence Estimate 12-6-81, "Poland's Prospects over the Next Six Months," January 30, 1981, was ambiguous, saying that the crisis would be "protracted" with no resolution in sight. Accessed October 6, 2014, http://www.foia.cia.gov/sites/default/files/document_conversions/89801/DOC_0000273319.pdf.

84. Vojtech Mastny, "The Soviet Non-Invasion of Poland in 1980/81 and the End of the Cold War," Working Paper No. 23 (Washington, DC: Cold War International History Project, 1998), 14–15.

85. See Benjamin B. Fischer, "Entangled in History: The Vilification and Vindication of Colonel Kuklinski," *Studies in Intelligence* 9 (2000): 19–34.

86. Douglas J. MacEachin, *US Intelligence and the Polish Crisis 1980–1981* (Washington, DC: Center for the Study of Intelligence, 2000), 225–26.

87. Ibid., 227–28.

88. Ibid., 32, 103, 107–8, 152, 173, and 177–78.

89. Benjamin B. Fischer, *A Cold War Conundrum: The 1983 Soviet-American War Scare* (Washington, DC: Center for the Study of Intelligence, 1997) and "The Soviet-American War Scare of the 1980s," *International Journal of Intelligence and Counterintelligence* 19, no. 3 (2006): 480–518.

90. Special National Intelligence Estimate, "Implications of Recent Soviet Military-Political Activities," SNIE 11-10-84JX, May 18, 1984, accessed October 6, 2014, http://www.foia.cia.gov/sites/default/files/document_conversions/89801/DOC_0000278546.pdf.

91. Ibid., 4. "Strip alert" meant that pilots started their aircraft but remained parked on runways.

92. Ibid.

93. See Oleg Gordievsky, *Next Stop Execution: The Autobiography of Oleg Gordievsky* (New York: Macmillan, 1995), 377.

94. See Benjamin B. Fischer, "Anglo-American Intelligence and the Soviet War Scare: The Untold Story," *Intelligence and National Security* 27, no. 1 (2012): 72–93.

95. Gates, *From the Shadows*, 273.

96. Mastny, "Soviet Non-Invasion of Poland," 34.

97. Ibid., 34.

98. Fischer, *Cold War Conundrum*, 6–12.

99. A week after the Able Archer episode, Reagan noted in his diary that "I feel the Soviets are so defense minded, so paranoid about being attacked that without being soft on them we ought to tell them no one here has any intention of doing anything like that." Ronald Reagan, *An American Life* (New York: Pocket Books, 1990), 588–98.

100. Mastny, "Soviet Non-Invasion of Poland," 34.

101. Ibid.

102. National Intelligence Estimate, Memorandum for Holders, NIE 11-4-78 M/H, "Soviet Goals and Expectations in the Global Power Arena," July 7, 1981, accessed October 6, 2014, http://www.foia.cia.gov/sites/default/files/document_conversions/89801/DOC_00 00268220.pdf. A "memorandum for holders" is issued when new information has become available that supplements, but does not substantially change, a previous assessment.

103. Ibid., 1.

104. National Intelligence Estimate 11-4-82, "The Soviet Challenge to US Security Interests," August 8, 1982, accessed October 6, 2014, http://www.foia.cia.gov/sites/default/files/document_conversions/89801/DOC_0000268223.pdf.

105. Ibid., 7.

106. This view was probably inspired by Team B chairman and member of Reagan's National Security Council staff Richard Pipes. See his article "Why the Soviet Union Believes It Can Fight and Win a Nuclear War," *Commentary* 32, no. 1 (1977): 21–34.

107. Special National Intelligence Estimate 11-9-84, "Soviet Policy toward the United States in 1984," August 14, 1984, accessed October 7, 2014, http://www.foia.cia.gov/sites/default/files/document_conversions/89801/DOC_0000681976.pdf.

108. Ibid., 3.

109. National Intelligence Estimate 11-10/2-84, "The USSR and the Third World," September 19, 1984, accessed October 7, 2014, http://www.foia.cia.gov/sites/default/files/document_conversions/89801/DOC_0000518056.pdf, and National Intelligence Estimate 11-6-84, "Soviet Global Military Reach," November 1984, accessed October 7, 2014, http://www.foia.cia.gov/sites/default/files/document_conversions/89801/DOC_0000278544.pdf.

110. "USSR and the Third World," 8.

111. The term was coined by journalists and pundits. The White House never used it in official statements.

112. Goodman, *Failure of Intelligence*, 151.

113. Gates, *From the Shadows*, 286.

114. Ofira Seliktar coined these terms in *Politics, Paradigms, and Intelligence Failures: Why So Few Predicted the Collapse of the Soviet Union* (New York: M. E. Sharpe, 2004), 107.

115. On the CIA's covert support for Solidarity, see Benjamin B. Fischer, "Solidarity, the CIA, and Western Technology," *International Journal of Intelligence and Counterintelligence* 25, no. 3 (2012): 427–69.

116. Seliktar, *Politics, Paradigms, and Intelligence Failures*, 136.

117. Weiner, *Legacy of Ashes*, 417.

118. George Bush and Brent Scowcroft, *A World Transformed* (New York: Knopf, 1998), 155.

119. KGB efforts to protect Ames by planting false leads and disinformation on the CIA resulted in near paralysis of the agency's Soviet operations for the rest of the Cold War. See Benjamin B. Fischer, "Spy Dust and Ghost Surveillance: How the KGB Spooked the CIA and Hid Aldrich Ames in Plain Sight," *International Journal of Intelligence and Counterintelligence* 24, no. 2 (Summer 2011): 268–306.

120. "Director of Central Intelligence John Deutch Statement to the Public on the Ames Damage Assessment, CIA Press Statement, October 31, 1994," accessed September 20, 2009, https://www.cia.gov/news-information/press-releases-statements/press-release-ar chive-1995/ps103195.html.

121. "Washington Whispers," *US News & World Report*, May 5, 1994, 26.

122. Cited in Kirsten Lundberg, *CIA and the Fall of the Soviet Empire: The Politics of "Getting It Right,"* Case Study C16–94–1251.0 (Cambridge, MA: Harvard University Press, 1994), 30–31.

123. National Intelligence Estimate 11-4-89, "Soviet Policy toward the West: The Gorbachev Challenge," April 1989, accessed October 7, 2014, http://www.foia.cia.gov/sites/de fault/files/document_conversions/89801/DOC_0000265622.pdf.

124. Ibid., v.

125. Central Intelligence Agency, Office of Soviet Analysis "Gorbachev's Domestic Gambles and Instability in the USSR," SOV 89–10077, September 1989, iv, accessed October 10, 2009, https://www.cia.gov/library/center-for-the-study-of-intelligence/csi-publications/ books-and-monographs/at-cold-wars-end-us-intelligence-on-the-soviet-union-and-eastern-europe-1989–1991/16526pdffiles/SOV89–10077.pdf.

126. Ibid., vii.

127. National Intelligence Estimate 11-18-89, "The Soviet System in Crisis: Prospects for the Next Two Years," November 1989, vi, accessed October 7, 2014, http://www.foia.cia .gov/sites/default/files/document_conversions/89801/DOC_0000397625.pdf.

128. Ibid., vii.

129. National Intelligence Estimate 11-18-90, "The Deepening Crisis in the USSR: Prospects for the Next Year," November 1990, 1, accessed October 7, 2014, http://www.foia.cia .gov/sites/default/files/document_conversions/89801/DOC_0000397624.pdf.

130. Ibid., 3.

131. Ibid., 14–18.

132. Central Intelligence Agency, Office of Soviet Analysis, "The Soviet Cauldron," April 1991, 2, 5, accessed September 21, 2010, https://www.cia.gov/library/center-for-the-study-of-intelligence/csi-publications/books-and-monographs/at-cold-wars-end-us-intelligence-on-the-soviet-union-and-eastern-europe-1989–1991/16526pdffiles/SOV91–20177.pdf.

133. Ibid., 5.

134. Ibid., 1.

135. National Intelligence Estimate 11-18-91, "Implications of Alternative Soviet Futures," July 1991, accessed October 7, 2014, http://www.foia.cia.gov/sites/default/files/document_conversions/89801/DOC_0000265647.pdf.

136. Ibid., iii.

137. Jonathan Haslam, *Russia's Cold War: From the October Revolution to the Fall of the Wall* (New Haven: Yale University Press, 2011), 397.

138. See, for example, William Safire, "Bashing the Spooks," *New York Times*, April 6, 1995, 31.

139. James A. Baker III, *The Politics of Diplomacy: Revolution, War, and Peace, 1989–1992* (New York: G. P. Putnam's Sons, 1995), 478.

140. Benjamin B. Fischer, *At Cold War's End: US Intelligence on the Soviet Union and Eastern Europe, 1989–1991* (Washington, DC: Central Intelligence Agency, 1999), 18.

East Germany in the Sights of the West German Federal Intelligence Service

Four Examples from As Many Decades

MATTHIAS UHL

THIS CHAPTER EXAMINES the manner in which the Federal Intelligence Service (BND), West Germany's foreign intelligence agency, conducted its operations against the communist East German state during the forty years of the German Democratic Republic's (GDR) existence. Of particular interest are the assessments of political, military, and societal events at which the BND arrived at key moments in East German history, as well as the resulting information it provided to the West German federal government.

While the history of East German espionage against West Germany has been relatively well researched, the investigation of the intelligence activities conducted by the larger of the two German states against the smaller one is only just beginning.[1] This is largely due to the hitherto unsatisfactory accessibility of the sources, a situation that has only in recent years improved somewhat, now that the BND has released numerous files to the Federal Archive in Koblenz.

These records show that the intelligence activity directed against East Germany, like that which the Ministry for State Security (MfS; popularly known as the Stasi) conducted against West Germany, was initially strongly marked by ideological demonization. A large share of the BND's staff had previously served in the Wehrmacht, the SS, and the Security Service (SD) of the Third Reich and could not easily shed the attitudes acquired there.

All in all, the BND did not do at all poorly, compared with its counterpart. For while it was unable to place any top agents in the upper ranks of the party and state of the GDR, it could, at least until 1961, depend on a large number of sources who, taken together, were able to provide a situation assessment that was no less accurate. Yet even after the Berlin Wall went up, the BND was able to describe the situation in East Germany concretely and to provide political decision makers in Bonn with a largely comprehensive and detailed assessment of the situation.[2]

West Germany's intelligence service was able to deliver accurate information to the federal government during the four key events in East German history: the workers' uprising of June 17, 1953, the construction of the Wall on August 13, 1961, the invasion of Czechoslovakia in 1968, and the fall of the Wall in 1989. As a result, the West German government had important supporting information for its decision-making processes at its disposal. That indicates that the quality of work of a secret service depends not only on the number of its sources and their access to information but also to a considerable degree on its assessment of the information obtained. The BND's assessment process was no worse than that of the Stasi. However, the West German political elite, in accordance with German tradition, took virtually no account of intelligence information in its decision-making process.

The BND Sources in the Federal Archive

Not until 1983 did the BND organizationally establish an archive system. A year earlier, it and the Federal Archive had for the first time arrived at an administrative agreement regarding the transfer of declassified papers to the Federal Archive. Previously the service's security-relevant documents had for decades been destroyed after the conclusion of an operation in order to protect its sources and methods—a total loss of information, from the point of view of historical research.[3] Among the papers transferred to the Federal Archive were several studies from the stock of the Historical Division of the US Army and related institutions[4] and a collection of approximately twenty-six thousand file cards from the Wehrmacht's Army General Staff, Foreign Armies / East Directorate, with information on the Red Army and the Polish People's Liberation Army.[5] This card file system was not terminated in 1945 but rather served the Gehlen Organization, and later the BND, as a military evaluation tool.[6] A further serial source, finally, was the location card file on the GDR, some ten thousand densely written file cards.[7] It is witness to the efforts of the BND to systematically monitor, starting during the 1950s, some 120 military locations of the Soviet forces in East Germany.[8]

The documents that provide information about the construction of the Wall, the invasion of Czechoslovakia, and other matters are, first of all, the "Military Situation Reports East," with a total of 298 volumes in three component series (Weekly Reports, Monthly Reports, and Annual Reports). As "finished intelligence," however, they provide no insight into the acquisition and internal processing of information. Their purpose was "the transfer of information to a more or less broad external dissemination circle, with the naming of sources and the revealing of intelligence gathering methods consciously omitted."[9] To whom exactly these situation reports were addressed cannot be determined from the existing BND documentation; moreover, the BND sees itself as not in a position to provide information about this matter.[10] At least the question of the distribution schedule can be clearly specified on the basis of the second, partially evaluated stock of sources, the reports on the political situation by the BND. The current daily intelligence reports were usually transmitted by teletype to the Federal Chancellery, the Foreign Office, the Ministry of Defense, and the Ministry for All-German Affairs. In urgent cases, the appropriate authorities could also be informed by telephone. However, in certain cases, other government offices could also obtain access to the information reports of the political analysis staff. Evidently, at least in some cases, the dissemination was quite broad; for example, reports were also sent to Egon Bahr, a section chief in the West Berlin state chancellery. The addressees, moreover, included BND residencies in Germany and abroad, embassies, the Ministry of Economics, and generally the BND's Western partner agencies, which were collectively subsumed under the cover designation "Fleurop."

While the BND's Weekly, Monthly, and Annual Reports do not permit any statements to be made regarding sources and internal information assessment, the daily reports do provide some insight into the everyday life of intelligence gathering and processing at the BND. At least until the 1960s, the bulk of all of the information passed on to Bonn came from top organs of the East German Communist Party (SED) and from certain East German ministries. The fact that the classification of the reliability of sources was, in all available documents, either B ("reliable") or C ("fairly reliable") suggests that there was no direct intelligence access to top functionaries themselves but that such access did exist to people in their immediate surroundings—such as assistants, interpreters, and secretaries—and that these were exploited in a targeted manner. Generally the intelligence value of these reports was assessed as positive by the BND Analysis Center.[11]

These accounts have been supplemented by summary BND analyses from the 1970s and 1980s, in which the service attempted to analyze its own procedure during focal intelligence situations. These files very clearly show the strengths and weaknesses of the organization. Thus the situation reports, together with the report summaries, constitute a valuable stock of sources since they make clear what the actual situation of the BND's information policy toward the federal government was and also how information gathering functioned. There is no reason to assume that the reports did not express internal BND analysis. Finally, the documents show that the BND informed the federal government comprehensively, not only about the immediate processes involved but also about the overall political situation behind the Iron Curtain and particularly in East Germany.

The Gehlen Organization and the Uprising of June 17, 1953

The Gehlen Organization, which emerged from the Foreign Armies / East Section of the Wehrmacht, received its name from its former chief, Reinhard Gehlen, and starting in 1946 took over intelligence assignments for the United States.[12] In 1948 its headquarters were moved from the Taunus Mountains outside Frankfurt to the Munich suburb of Pullach; hence, the "Org." (its official abbreviation) was predestined for military espionage. As regards its character, it was a thoroughly military organization since, first of all, Germany had hardly any tradition of a civilian secret service that might have served as an example for the construction of a postwar intelligence service and, second, it recruited its personnel from among former intelligence and General Staff officers of the Wehrmacht. It may indeed have been Gehlen's intention to actively ensure the postwar survival of the spirit and working methods of the army General Staff.[13] Former personnel of the Gestapo, the SD, and the Reich Security Main Office (RSHA) generally, who also found jobs in Pullach, were likewise familiar with military structures. The American side, moreover, which financed the operation, first through the US Army and then through the Central Intelligence Agency (CIA), was primarily interested in military information about East Germany and Eastern Europe. Gehlen's men, while they had no eye for political nuances or ideological motives and often had a distorted view of the innermost mentality of the Eastern superpower due to a view of the enemy that verged on demonology, nonetheless had a masterly command of the ABCs of military intelligence about enemy operations.[14] The almost one thousand employees of the Org. and the approximately four thousand agents they handled therefore concentrated primarily on the observation of Soviet and East German forces on the other side of the Elbe but also on the political and economic situation in the GDR.[15]

After Pullach's human intelligence (HUMINT) had already proved its effectiveness in the Berlin Crisis of 1948–49,[16] a second test of the effectiveness of the Gehlen Organization came in the early summer of 1953. Indeed, reports from its operatives were the only source for its comprehensive reports about the military operations of the Group of Soviet Occupation Troops in Germany (GSOTG) against the popular uprising of June 17, 1953.[17]

In mid-June 1953 large sections of the East German population spontane-ously rose up against the SED dictatorship, which was able to retain power only because Moscow ruthlessly committed its occupation forces to suppress the uprising.[18] This was done primarily through massive intimidation. At the orders of their commander in chief, Marshal Andrei A. Grechko, all twenty-two divi-sions of the GSOTG were committed to combating the revolt according to a prepared emergency plan, starting in the early hours of June 17, 1953. Soviet military commanders proclaimed a state of emergency in 167 of the country's 217 cities and rural districts. In Berlin alone, some six hundred armored vehicles of the Second Mechanized Guard Army, consisting of the First and Fourteenth Mechanized Divisions and the Twelfth Armored Division, were sent into action.[19]

For the Org. and its operatives in East Germany, June 17 became the supreme test, for, like all crises, it mercilessly tested the service's strengths and weaknesses. First of all, it is clear that Gehlen's service had knowledge of the looming crisis in East Germany at an early date. In 1952 the top-level source V-3000, one of fifteen people who had drafted the National Economic Plan for 1953, had informed Pullach "that this plan will lead to very great difficulties, and is not implementable."[20] That showed clearly that the Gehlen Organization had greatly expanded its areas of competence since the time of the First Berlin Crisis (the Berlin Blockade of 1948–49). The service had not only succeeded in effectively monitoring the Soviet and East German forces in Germany but had also increasingly gained knowledge about the difficult economic situation in the country.

In April 1953 news arrived of the first strikes in the Mansfeld district, a copper-mining area in central Germany, and in Hennigsdorf, a factory town north of Berlin. The information came from a site observer, who evidently also had a sense of political understanding (a site observer is a source who reports on a particular target like an army base). On June 10, 1953, Gehlen came close to achieving a news scoop. Two days earlier, BND subsource V-8126/11 had informed his agent handler: "Politburo SED decides to reduce expansion of metal and heavy machinery industries. Instead, more production of necessities and consumer goods. Goal is rapid increase of living standards in Soviet Zone of Germany. Plans 1953 thru 1955 to be revised by June 10 for submission [to] Politburo."[21] That agent was being handled by the General Representation in Darmstadt (known as GV-H), and a GV-H staff member responsible for eco-nomics, who happened to be in West Berlin at the time, strongly urged that this important message be immediately radioed to headquarters instead of being sent by courier; however, the item remained caught in red tape. While the Economic Analysis Desk considered the report important, it did not pass it on, since it had not yet evaluated the source nor confirmed the information. As a result, the government in Bonn only learned of the East German "New Course" from the press. That showed that while the Org. was indeed capable of gathering politically important information in East Germany by intelligence means, its cumbersome structure massively hampered the rapid passing on and analysis of that information.

Indeed, Gehlen was working organizationally with a complicated system of subsidiary units scattered at locations all over West Germany. Subordinate to the headquarters in Pullach ("General Directorate") were the so-called General Representations, which were responsible for foreign intelligence and counterintelligence. The GV-H in Darmstadt, for example, was responsible for the intelligence area East Germany, Poland, and the Soviet Union. These GVs in turn had district representations (BVs) in virtually all major West German cities, such as the BV-E in West Berlin. Finally, the subrepresentations, also known as the examination offices, were the "actual frontline staffs of active espionage," responsible for recruiting, training, and handling spies.[22] Below that, along the border between the two German states and in West Berlin, there were also outposts, which served as easily accessible contact points for informants. All offices were disguised as commercial enterprises (as insurance, tax-advisory, translation, or advertising agencies) or as sections of government agencies—a complex network of branches designed for internal compartmentalization based on the need-to-know principle, for the purpose of protecting sources.[23] This convoluted system was repeatedly criticized by insiders, as it made management difficult and an overview virtually impossible, even by its own employees. Moreover, it was expensive, owing to the large number of offices it required, which, when their cover was blown, had to move to new locations. The exchange of mail was complicated by the fact that couriers were not permitted to know where these offices were. So, the conspiratorial system could not be maintained.[24]

Further information arriving in Pullach soon indicated that as of the early summer of 1953, completely new possibilities for intelligence operations in Germany were arising. The increasing hopelessness of the SED leadership created "ideal possibilities for our own intelligence approach,"[25] so that in the future it would be easier for Pullach to recruit intelligence sources in East Germany. Nonetheless, the Gehlen Organization for the time being continued to operate routinely, as a result of which the service was then taken by surprise by the ensuing events in Berlin and East Germany.

On June 16, around 8 p.m., the first reports of demonstrations in East Berlin arrived at headquarters in Pullach—fifteen minutes after the Bavarian Broadcasting System had broadcast that same information. Since most of the staff had already quit for the day, necessary decisions were delayed, so that the local agent handlers largely had to operate on their own. Not until the afternoon of June 17 did the Org. start getting its operation into gear. But in spite of all efforts, news from East Germany came only in a trickle, largely because of the Soviet security cordon around West Berlin. As a result, on June 18 the Americans complained, "Where are the reports? We've invested so much money!"[26] As a result, Gehlen decided at noon on June 19 to put into operation the agent radio network, conceived for an emergency, which at that time included twenty-three so-called radio agents (AFUs).

It took almost a week after the outbreak of the uprising for the first written source reports to arrive at the service, another indication of how complicated the communication paths within the Gehlen Organization were. Now, at long last, an "Uprising Staff" was finally created within the Analysis Directorate. It was largely to its credit that it was possible by July 5, 1953, when the staff was dissolved, to put together a mosaic from the separate source reports and thus, ex post facto, to permit "conclusions and assessments of possible intentions" to be drawn.[27]

While this depiction of intelligence operations may appear sobering at first glance, a thorough evaluation provides a more mixed picture. June 17 was a "spontaneous" event that surprised not only the Western intelligence services but also the SED leadership, as well as Moscow. The Org.'s chances of finding out anything about the demonstrations in advance had been close to zero. Nonetheless, Directorate 50D, which was responsible for intelligence gathering in East Germany, was able, between June 17 and July 5, 1953, to activate at least 548 of its approximately 600 East German sources to submit reports; ultimately, a total of 1,288 reports came in. The considerable activity of these agents is shown by the fact that during the period of the uprising in East Germany, each of them delivered an average of three reports. During that period, Gehlen's service radioed for approximately one hundred hours, sending important information that required rapid transmission between West Berlin and West Germany. Seventeen radio agents in East Germany broadcast a total of forty-one messages to their handling centers and received twenty-three messages with further instructions. In the military realm, 320 agent reports on the army alone were submitted to the Analysis Directorate.[28] In comprehensive reports, the analysts of the Gehlen Organization then attempted to put together an ex post facto political situation analysis of the uprising.[29]

Overall, the great extent of the agent operation used for the observation of Soviet troop movements for the suppression of the June 17 uprising is surprising. The Org. hoped to make up for the existing lack of real top sources, or the interrupted ties to those sources, through the use of a large number of site observers. According to an internal assessment, an operative in the political sphere could "to a certain degree be replaced by the central compilation of all the pieces of a mosaic provided by all sectors of intelligence work."[30] This succeeded with some delay, caused largely by the circuitous communication paths. The conclusion to be drawn for the future was therefore that, particularly in view of the sealing off of West Berlin—the center around which all intelligence activity directed against East Germany and the Soviet troops stationed there revolved (up to 95 percent of the Org.'s intelligence information traffic from the Soviet zone ran through the former Reich capital)[31]—the buildup of a reliable radio network was an absolute necessity. Every important source in the ministries and railway directorates was therefore in the future to be tied to the radio agent system.[32]

With that, the important lessons for the future had been learned. As a result, the Gehlen Organization, and its later successor the BND, after 1953 worked in a targeted manner in expectation of the ever-threatening interruption of the most important connection between the agents and their handlers: the meeting point West Berlin.

The service also realized that it was perhaps overly concentrated on acquiring military information and might therefore have neglected the collection of political information: "In such a situation, only the *essential political source* is useful, since the 'average consumer'—and that means most of our top sources, outside their areas of specialty—are much too harmless and clueless to be able to look behind the scenes in the case of events such as the current ones. . . . By the time you have pieced together the mosaic into a coherent picture, it no longer has any immediate relevance."[33]

However, the Gehlen Organization had great difficulty reorienting itself. Even after 1953, the acquisition of military secrets had top priority for the West German intelligence service. Even in 1960, only two of the fifteen major intelligence goals defined for the agents in Pullach were not oriented explicitly toward military or armaments-industry fields of observation.[34] Gehlen still primarily saw himself as the head of a military intelligence service.

His organization was, however, able to depend on highly motivated agents in East Germany, as the following example shows: "In spite of her handicapped leg—*she can walk only with crutches*—source traveled to Berlin twice in a vain attempt to make contact with her agent handler. Only at the third attempt did she succeed in crossing Glienicke Bridge to West Berlin, and was able to transfer her message with A 1 writing to the cover address."[35] In the secret service contest between East and West, the BND was, more than any other Western intelligence service, able to recruit its former compatriots in East Germany for active espionage activities and thus to achieve an advantage that should not be underestimated.

The Org.'s reporting on the events of June 17, 1953, which was considered a success, also helped Gehlen to realize his most important project up to that time: the transformation of the Gehlen Organization into the BND, as the only West German foreign intelligence service. For this purpose, the chief of the Org. had already forged connections with the Chancellery during the Korean War. He repeatedly attempted to establish close and permanent contacts with Chancellor Konrad Adenauer. A key role here was played by Gehlen's main contact, Hans Globke, who, in spite of his Nazi past, had since 1953 been serving as a state secretary in the Chancellery. The two men apparently agreed to a kind of quid pro quo: While Gehlen provided Globke not only with intelligence information but also with "dirty" material about political opponents and friends of Adenauer, the latter, as an administrative specialist, used his influence to ensure that the institutional decision on the creation of a West German intelligence service would favor the Org.[36]

On July 11, 1955, Gehlen achieved his goal. The federal cabinet decided to incorporate the Org. into the federal service "as an agency attached to the Federal Chancellery." The fact that, unlike the other federal agencies, the Org. was not established on a firm legal foundation would prove to be a birth defect that was almost impossible to overcome.[37] Ultimately there was no appropriate control or supervision, and Gehlen was able to run the BND as a sort of private enterprise, with all the negative consequences that that entailed.

When the BND was officially founded on April 1, 1956, and attached to the Federal Chancellery, it immediately established a kind of official liaison office to the Pullach headquarters in a small room under the roof of Schaumburg Palace, the chancellor's official residence. Through that office, Globke was supplied with the latest intelligence information daily. Adenauer and the head of his chancellery initially had great trust in Gehlen and his service, since he repeatedly proved to be a well-informed intelligence authority.[38]

All the same, the BND had by this time already passed the peak of its success.[39] As the only West German foreign intelligence agency, it was still too strongly fixated on military intelligence on the Eastern Bloc. Nonetheless, in the summer of 1961, it would once again be able to provide a precise prognosis of events surrounding West Berlin, since they had been planned by the Soviet Union and East Germany as a large-scale army, police, and state-security operation.[40]

The BND and August 13, 1961

During the first half of 1961, the Western secret services assumed that the Soviet Union would now finally attempt to drive the Western powers out of Berlin in order to strengthen the regime of Walter Ulbricht and not leave East Germany to disintegrate, as it threatened to do owing to the continuing exodus of its population.[41] In the frontline city Berlin, however, everybody seemed to be surprised by the events of August 13. In view of the lack of any effective ad hoc countermeasures, the outraged mayor of West Berlin, Willy Brandt, called on the Western city commandants to launch vigorous protests. Only later would Brandt realize, "Had I been somewhat less hot-blooded on August 13, I would have noticed that the honorable commandants were confused, helpless and lacking in instructions."[42] As the newly accessible BND files show, this confusion was possibly only playacting, for—as the service reported with respect to a meeting of the federal cabinet on August 17—the commandants had been informed about the measures for sealing off the city on August 12 at the latest.[43]

Gehlen had always insisted that his agency had previously reported "the upcoming hermetic sealing off of the zonal boundary, particularly in Berlin," except for the exact date.[44] According to the latest information, the BND had on January 13, 1961, for the first time informed the Federal Chancellery about the rerouting of streets near the inner-city sectoral boundary in Berlin, stating that the East German leadership planned "to turn the sectoral boundary in Berlin into a state boundary."[45]

On the other hand, it is only in retrospect that the closing of the West Berlin loophole by forceful separation appears as a measure with virtually no alternative. "Based on reports from our own Allied services,"[46] the West German political leadership believed that there were three possible ways in which the Second Berlin Crisis could reach a climax: first, a total blockade, as in 1948–49; second, the demand by Moscow for control of West Berlin's airports by Soviet or East German forces; or third, the closing of the sectoral boundary. A fourth alternative, the military occupation of West Berlin, was, on the other hand, dismissed.[47]

Steps toward the physical isolation of West Berlin had for years been expected by the Western powers as a possible reaction by East Germany and the USSR to the special status of the politically divided city. During the last third of January 1953, for example, the Gehlen Organization had announced that the complete shutoff of Berlin would occur that month. In 1957 the CIA, too, considered the possibility of a closure of the sectoral boundary.[48] At the end of 1958, the BND once again noted "that new measures by the GDR to isolate West Berlin must be expected in the foreseeable future."[49] As a precaution, the number of radio agents was increased. In spite of the success of East German counterintelligence, hundreds of operatives of the West German intelligence service remained active east of the Elbe, and the BND even succeeded in replacing its losses so that the "stock of sources necessary to fulfill the mission has remained virtually unchanged, qualitatively and quantitatively."[50] Nonetheless, at the end of 1958, all BND staff members were withdrawn from West Berlin. And finally, at the end of April 1959, Gehlen began sending situation reports on the Berlin Crisis every two weeks to the Federal Chancellery, the Foreign Office, the Ministry of Defense, the Ministry of the Interior, and the American, French, British, and Danish partner services. However, on August 12, 1959, when Khrushchev allowed his ultimatum to lapse without having achieved any results, this regular reporting was terminated again, owing to "decreased interest." Nonetheless, for the end of the year, Gehlen had a report on the situation of West Berlin sent out that stated, "The technical and organizational preparations for the cut-off of passenger and freight traffic . . . have been virtually completed."[51]

It is thus possible to posit that over time a certain habit and routine developed among Western politicians with regard to intelligence reports. It can even be assumed that the repeated warnings gradually lulled political decision makers to sleep with regard to such reports. Although the dramatic worsening of the Berlin Crisis in the summer of 1961 was clearly registered in Bonn and West Berlin, the construction of the Wall represented, for the Western side, "the realization of a development which had been considered only marginally likely."[52] The fact that BND reports, according to the current state of knowledge, favored precisely this development seems not to have received much attention from some political leaders, since the analysis of the information collected in Pullach highlighted the ultimately narrow scope of options, especially for West German policy, with respect to Ulbricht's and Khrushchev's actions in Berlin.[53]

The BND's Military Situation Report of July 1961, at any rate, indicates that the service was well-informed. By way of introduction, it summarized Soviet goals in case of a separate peace treaty with East Berlin very precisely: the political and economic isolation of West Berlin, a cutoff of the flow of refugees there, and the termination of air travel by refugees to West Germany, and "hence a consolidation of the Soviet zonal regime" and the "de facto recognition of the Pankow regime."[54] In the view of the BND, the SED leadership was preparing to put into action the preconditions "which have long since been prepared, for the closing off and/or control of the access routes from East BERLIN and the SBZ to West BERLIN,"[55] either by concluding a separate peace treaty between the USSR and the GDR or even prior to such a measure: "In case of a further increase in the flow of refugees to West Berlin, the possibility that the Soviet regime would, even prior to such a date, decide to impose closure measures cannot be dismissed."[56] The BND received an increasing number of reports from its military spies about numerous troop movements and transports of matériel from the Soviet Union to East Germany and the western areas of Poland.[57]

Finally, a report drafted in late June, in which the urgent problem of "flight from the Republic" was once again stressed, was available by August 1, 1961. The BND analyst confirmed that the SED leadership was making intensive efforts to obtain Moscow's approval, the consequences of which would have "included the closing of the Berlin sectoral boundary and the interruption of urban railway and subway traffic." The report, first considered "urgent" but then downgraded to a normal telex, was sent to the key decision-making bodies of the Federal Republic, the Federal Chancellery, the Foreign Office, and the Defense Ministry. The Ministry for All-German Affairs and the Western partner services, too, were informed of the upcoming "truly thorough closure actions."[58]

A report of the conference of Warsaw Pact countries held in Moscow from August 3 to 5 arrived in Pullach on August 9.[59] Although Khrushchev's decision had by this time already been made and Pullach had sources in the Soviet capital,[60] it was necessarily not aware of this decision, since only very few top Soviet and East German leaders had knowledge of the date of the border closure. The BND apparently also heard nothing about a meeting between the chief of staff of the Group of Soviet Forces in Germany (GSFG), Lt. Gen. Grigori Ariko, and the chief of the main staff of the East German National People's Army (NVA), Maj. Gen. Sigfrid Riedel, at which the details of the closure of the sectoral boundary were agreed to; this meeting had already taken place on July 25, 1961.[61] However, sources assigned to military espionage did continue to report on extensive troop movements by the Soviet forces in Germany and the NVA in the greater Berlin area.[62] Moreover, the troop movements from the Soviet Union to East Germany and the western border of Poland, which had been ascertained in July, continued. According to BND information, which has also been confirmed by Bundeswehr files, the Soviet Union strengthened its troop presence in East Germany by more than 37,500 men between May and August 1961 to a total of 380,000 men. An additional 70,000 soldiers were also stationed on the western border of Poland, having been transferred there from military districts in the Soviet Union. Thus Soviet troop strength in Central Europe in the time leading up to the construction of the Wall had been increased by some 25 percent, to more than 545,000 men. The Soviet Union had mobilized almost one-third of its entire land forces to militarily secure the border closure in Berlin.[63] Another demonstrative action by the Soviet side was the nomination of Marshal Ivan S. Konev as commander in chief of the GSFG. This highly decorated World War II general had been brought out of retirement specifically for this task. Recalling Konev, Khrushchev was sure, would have especially great symbolic effect in both foreign and security policy. It was also perceived accordingly by the BND.[64]

The service almost succeeded in ascertaining the date of the border closure. On August 11, a report stated "that measures are being prepared to close off the sectoral boundary between August 12 and 18, 1961, in order to cut off the no longer controllable flood of refugees."[65] Moreover, the BND's signals intelligence had since August 8, 1961, ascertained suspicious changes in the radio traffic of the GSFG. For example, the divisions of the Third Shock Army, which covered the important area between Magdeburg and Berlin, were now under the direct command of GSFG headquarters in Wünsdorf, which was very unusual and, according to the assessment of the analysts, "was connected with the Berlin crisis." Even more unusual was the fact that the Soviet General Staff in Moscow now communicated directly with the corps and divisions of the Twenty-Fourth Soviet Airborne Army, stationed in East Germany.[66] In spite of these warning signals, the Western partner services at a meeting with BND representatives on August 11 nonetheless arrived at the conclusion that "we are currently internally not assuming that the border will be closed." The most important issue was rather that of a revolt in East Germany.[67]

That shows that the service evaluated the information received from its sources not without a touch of self-censorship. Moreover, the acquisition of political and military intelligence information and their respective assessments were separate, so that important indicators for a sudden change in the situation were simply lacking. The fact that the BND was not able to provide information about the exact date of the border closure was therefore due not to any faulty acquisition of information but rather to insufficient—indeed, totally lacking—comparative analysis of incoming information.

It can thus be stated that in the run-up to August 13, the BND at least correctly transmitted the "shape of events" (Willy Brandt) to the political decision-making bodies in Bonn. There was intensive activity on the part of the service's sources, which evidently still reached into the highest levels of the SED. This activity and the continued acquisition of information on the part of the BND after August 13 show that the connection to sources did not suddenly break off owing to the physical division of Berlin. Overall the BND, even according to its internal assessment, was, as the Wall went up, "able to contribute considerably to the federal government's ability to counteract widespread panic and unrest, which was being fed by ever new rumors."[68]

However, the contribution of the BND to the overall situation assessment of the Western alliance was evidently very small. In the concert of Western intelligence agencies, Pullach was certainly not playing the lead violin. Franz Josef Strauß indeed had good reason for writing in his memoirs that "the reports that General Reinhard Gehlen and his service prepared . . . were certainly not the determining factor in the alliance's overall assessment. . . . Here, the reports of the American intelligence service the CIA essentially set the tone."[69]

This was also evident in the run-up to the Cuban Missile Crisis. Since June 1962 the service had continually reported on the stationing of Soviet medium-range missiles, basing its reports on information from agents on the spot. Finally, on August 20, 1962, Gehlen, in a personal discussion in Bonn, pointed out the enormous political consequences of this move: "Under these circumstances, a dangerous worsening of the worldwide situation is possible in the coming days and weeks, which could lead us to the brink of an armed confrontation over Berlin and Cuba."[70] But even in this case, it was clear that the US agency either did not appropriately appreciate the capabilities of its junior partner, the BND, or that it paid no attention to reports from Pullach and simply filed them away.

Neither the accurate BND information on the construction of the Wall nor that on the Cuba crisis could counteract the fact that Gehlen's influence in Bonn and among political decision makers in West Germany was already in decline.

In November 1961, Heinz Felfe, head of the Soviet counterintelligence section, was exposed as a Soviet spy. His was precisely the kind of case of which the American military intelligence services had repeatedly warned—that of former Nazi secret police and SS agents who had entered the service via the "old-boy network" and whose past made them susceptible to blackmail by Eastern secret services.[71] Nonetheless, Gehlen had repeatedly supported Felfe and protected him against internal doubters.

Felfe's treason not only caused the BND to lose its contacts in the Soviet Union and almost a hundred of its agents. Worse than that, the manner of operation of the service had been exposed, owing to the transfer of hundreds of top secret documents to Moscow, which for years did severe harm to the BND's spying operations against the Soviet Union.[72] As late as 1970, the BND was "more like an open informational institute" than a secret service, in the words of Richard Meier, who assumed control of the BND's Intelligence Collection Directorate in that year.[73]

Although the BND was the secret service best prepared for the closure of the border, having even prior to that event experimented with new communication methods for its agents in East Germany,[74] it nonetheless suffered heavy losses after the Wall was built. Between August 1961 and December 1965, the MfS succeeded in arresting 156 of the West German intelligence service's agents. By conservative estimates, Gehlen thus lost more than one-quarter of the sources who had previously been active in East Germany. The CIA suffered the arrest of fifty-four of its agents during that same period, which meant, however, that the MfS was able to eliminate more than half of the US intelligence service's operatives. All in all, it was apparent that the new communication paths to the agents made necessary by the Wall were increasingly vulnerable to the intensified monitoring by East German counterintelligence and that an end to conventional HUMINT activities against East Germany was in the offing. Over the long term, losses of such dimensions would prove to be impossible to sustain, so that Pullach would have to largely shut down its espionage activities in East Germany.[75]

During the Felfe crisis, Adenauer and the head of his chancellery, Globke, had still backed Gehlen up. In the fall of 1962, however, came the final break between the chancellor and his secret service chief. In the context of the so-called *Spiegel* affair, Adenauer even wanted to have "Mr. Gehlen" arrested for treason. Nonetheless, even after the affair, he did not dare to fire the BND president, who had, during his years in office, gathered compromising material about numerous Bonn politicians.[76]

Adenauer's successor, Ludwig Erhard, had no sympathy for the BND and justifiably feared that additional official internal documents might trickle to Pullach through the BND liaison office in the Chancellery. He therefore had the intelligence officials removed from Schaumburg Palace, his official residence, thus breaking the direct contact between the BND leadership and the chancellor. Not until the days of Helmut Kohl, almost twenty years later, would any BND president present the intelligence situation directly to the head of government. Only by way of the weekly situation conferences chaired by the chief of the Chancellery could the West German intelligence service now impact upon the policy of the federal government. Here the service's influence on the Chancellor's decisions should not be overestimated. Only on very rare occasions did the BND present the political leadership with "exclusive" secret information, for it was in competition with a large number of other "suppliers" of information intending to support policy decisions, who had better access to key figures in Bonn than did the intelligence service.[77] At the end of April 1968, Gehlen, who was by then badly damaged politically, finally stepped down. His successor, Gerhard Wessel, took office with the mission of at long last reforming the service and building it into a functional foreign intelligence service once again. First, however, he had to master his first test as the new BND chief, which came in the form of the Soviet invasion of Czechoslovakia.

BND Intelligence Operations and the Suppression of the Prague Spring

On August 20, 1968, in Operation Danube, thirty-three Warsaw Pact divisions marched into Czechoslovakia to suppress the Prague Spring and end the experiment of "socialism with a human face."[78] Secret service experts have claimed that no Western agent noticed the marching orders; hence, the Soviet-led invasion to this day ranks among the great failures of Western espionage.[79]

What, however, do the newly accessible BND files reveal about the success or failure of the service during the suppression of the Prague Spring? Although key portions of the BND's secret files for this period are presumably not yet available to researchers, it is possible to state on the basis of those files that are available that the image of the bumbling spooks from Pullach is no longer tenable.

As early as May 1968, the service reported in its Monthly Military Report that the Polish and Soviet troop movements along the Czechoslovak border were conceived as a means of putting pressure on the reform-communist regime of Alexander Dubček. Moreover, the BND reported that the Soviet Union was attempting to station certain units in Czechoslovakia. The purpose, according to the analyst, was that "in case of developments in Czechoslovakia which crossed the line of what was acceptable to the USSR, the Soviets would be able to circumvent the question of intervention, and the stationing of troops would be disguised as 'fraternal aid.'" The troop movements, the BND added, were intended to push developments in Czechoslovakia in the Soviet direction, constitute an open demonstration of power as pressure on the reformist forces, and ensure that the Warsaw Pact would be prepared for "any event."[80]

As this situation developed, the BND in the summer of 1968 dispatched numerous operatives and "opportunity informants" to Czechoslovakia. Moreover, the order went out to all residencies to report "any indications of military movements by rail or road," under the code word "Nepomuk."[81] Starting in July 1968, the German Defense Ministry and the Supreme Headquarters Allied Powers Europe (SHAPE) were kept informed about the military situation in Czechoslovakia.[82]

Soviet information now available also confirms that the BND was able to gain information about the Soviet deployment plans against Czechoslovakia at a relatively early date. On April 8, 1968, for example, the command of the airborne troops received a directive signed by Defense Minister Andrei Grechko and Chief of the General Staff Matvei V. Zakharov.[83] The commander and staff of the airborne troops thereupon drafted a plan, under the direct and immediate supervision of the General Staff, for the commitment of paratroopers in the context of Operation Danube.

But it was not only the paratroopers, considered the crack units of the Soviet Army, who were to be used against the reformers in Prague; large parts of the Soviet ground forces were also deployed against Czechoslovakia. The Twenty-Fourth Motorized Rifle Division of the Carpathian Military District in Rovno (now Rivne, Ukraine), which, according to Soviet documents, had received orders to move into Poland on May 7, 1968, was soon thereafter identified in the Katowice area by the BND. The 128th Motorized Rifle Division, which was moved from the Soviet Union to Hungary just one day later, was shortly thereafter observed by the West German intelligence service. The Soviet Union was thus also systematically beefing up its own forces for military operations.[84]

In its further reports, the West German intelligence service pointed to the continual further reinforcement of the troops along the Czechoslovak border, designed to put pressure on that country; these forces by that time had a total strength of ten or eleven divisions. There were increased indications that Soviet troops in East Germany that were not part of the GSFG were being deployed. The BND categorized this information as "significant."[85] Finally, at the end of July 1968, the West German intelligence service concluded in a further Weekly Report that an invasion could no longer be ruled out and that the Soviet Union was prepared "to use all necessary forceful means" to put an end to the dispute with the Czechoslovak reformers, "even if that meant serious negative consequences for the policy of coexistence and possibly upheavals in the communist realm."[86] The BND military situation report for the month of July 1968 stated in the same vein that, "with the currently unchanged massing of Soviet troops at the borders of Czechoslovakia, a military intervention is possible at any time."[87]

At this point, the Soviet General Staff had continued its planning for the occupation of Czechoslovakia. The West German intelligence service in its situation reports also registered the continued buildup of invasion forces, with signals intelligence playing a key role.[88] The BND was especially alarmed in late July and early August by a large-scale exercise of the rear echelons of the Soviet army, covering the entire western portion of the Soviet Union, Poland, and East Germany, which "is equivalent to the practical implementation of certain mobilization measures." Moreover, the service clearly saw that these war games "were presumably connected with the Soviet measures to exert pressure on Czechoslovakia that have been ongoing since the beginning of this year."[89]

Only shortly thereafter, the service reported that the troops exerting pressure on the Czechoslovak border had again been reinforced in late July and now included from twenty to twenty-two divisions. With these forces, according to a West German intelligence analyst, a military invasion of Czechoslovakia would be possible at any time. The secret service also pointed out that at the border between East Germany and Czechoslovakia temporary bridges were being built in order to enable crossings on a major scale.[90] With this knowledge the BND was one up on the CIA: According to BND information, "leading CIA personnel" believed that "'consideration' for world opinion would force the Soviet Union to dispense with a military invasion."[91] The other partner services, too, and even the federal government entertained considerable doubts about the BND's analysis regarding a violent solution to the Czechoslovak crisis.[92]

Pullach registered warning signals for an ever more probable military action on the part of the Warsaw Pact. By the first week in August, the number of deployed divisions had grown once again. According to BND information, the still continuing logistical operation served to "cover special troop reinforcement measures for Central Europe in the form of a mobilization of troops and matériel for the Western Military District, Poland, and the Soviet land and air forces in the Soviet Zone [i.e., East Germany], in order to create increased operational readiness for those forces. The forces deployed in connection with the CSL [Czechoslovak] situation must be considered to be at full operational readiness."[93] Moreover, the service continued, the Bratislava Declaration, in which Dubček had acceded to certain Soviet demands, "did not rule out military intervention by the orthodox states as a future possibility; rather, it legalized such action in case of transgression of the risk limit once again specified in the Bratislava Declaration."[94]

However, in spite of the numerous extant secret service reports, the BND did not succeed in predicting the exact date of the invasion of Czechoslovakia. The currently accessible files do however show that the reason for that was not any lack of information but rather inadequate analysis. On August 18 and 19, at any rate, BND signals intelligence was able, in spite of the strict radio discipline maintained by the Soviet Twenty-Fourth Air Army stationed in East Germany, to ascertain the redeployment of ten air regiments to air bases in the southern part of East Germany. These intelligence personnel were even more surprised by the fact that six of these air bases hosted two air regiments each, although other areas were available to them. Moreover, it was notable that in the western part of East Germany, a strip of land seventy kilometers wide along the border had been cleared completely of Soviet troops. In spite of this alarming sign, the analysts merely concluded that "considering the intended pressure and the securing of possible military consequences, this massing of tactical air units in a very small area contradicts the Soviet Union's own principles of loose dissemination of forces and is hence incomprehensible."[95] The fact that the occupation of Czechoslovakia was immediately in the offing escaped the analysts.

It is possible at least to conclude that the BND was not surprised by the Soviet invasion. The German defense minister, the command staffs of the Bundeswehr, and hence also the Chancellery were sufficiently informed of the situation in and around Czechoslovakia by the BND's military situation reports. Overall, as Strauß, who in 1968 had been minister of finance, stated at an event marking the thirtieth anniversary of the founding of the BND, the service had, during the suppression of the Prague Spring, "familiarized the federal government regarding the preparation of the other side down to the last detail."[96]

With this palpable success, Gerhard Wessel, the new BND chief, should actually have experienced a good start for his reform program. However, it was quickly clear that the political leadership in Bonn was still dissatisfied with the results of the BND's work. Especially the collection of political intelligence on East Germany and the Warsaw Pact left much to be desired, in the view of the Federal Chancellery. Owing, above all, to their new *Ostpolitik*, what the new chancellor Willy Brandt and the head of his chancellery, Horst Ehmke, needed was not so much reports about the military armament of the Eastern Bloc as solid information on its political, economic, and societal constitution. As Ehmke put it in his typically drastic manner, "I need GDR, GDR, GDR!" However, that was information that the service was at that time able to provide only to a limited extent.[97]

The new BND chief was aware of these shortcomings and tried to remedy them, for instance by merging the previously separated intelligence collection directorates.[98] However, his reform of the service proved to be exceedingly difficult and tedious, particularly since its results often ended up being caught between the millstones of political infighting in Bonn and conflicts between the old Org. staff and the young secret service personnel. While Gehlen had still been able to depend on political backing in Bonn, Wessel, as a conservative, now saw himself increasingly isolated, for the political landscape had also changed fundamentally since the 1950s. For the first time, the Social Democrats headed the government, and neither Chancellor Willy Brandt nor his successor, Helmut Schmidt, put much stock in the reports of their intelligence service, so their relationship to the BND remained very cool. They were interested less in factual matters than in increasing the political control of their party, the SPD, over the BND.[99] The service was unable to win any friends among the new decision makers in Bonn with its intelligence service products, such as special intelligence briefings for the top political leadership in Bonn, for these concepts were far too general to be usable for political purposes.[100]

However, it should not be forgotten that the political leadership in Germany has traditionally set little store in the advice of intelligence services. Chancellor Helmut Schmidt, for instance, once announced that he received better information from reading the *Neue Züricher Zeitung* than he did from his own intelligence service. The reasons for this mistrust lay both in the German historical tradition and in the country's Nazi past. In addition, as former BND president August Hanning said, there is a heritage of German idealism, of the German romantic period, that seeks to lend the impression that Germany's foreign and security policies are guided solely by high ideals, which in turn require no underpinning from the intelligence services. Moreover, foreign policy was of less importance in the West German political landscape. For these reasons, the intelligence services had low status in the political system of the Federal Republic, and the most important decisions were made without their expert advice, since these services were unable to compete with other advisory bodies. And the shift to a Social Democratic government certainly did not make this situation any better.[101]

By 1978, when Wessel retired, he had indeed steered the service through some stormy political waters with a steady hand and had also begun to dump some of Gehlen's baggage overboard. However, the reforms he had initiated were largely stalled halfway, so that the service once again sank into a hibernation phase.[102] For example, the BND was unable to predict the Soviet invasion of Afghanistan.[103] However, Wessel was, according to internal assessments of the Foreign Office, able to acquire competence in the areas of East German foreign, domestic, and economic policy.[104] Still, diplomats complained that "the BND's experts in Pullach lead a fairly isolated life"; rarely did they avail themselves of expertise from that quarter.[105] If reports did actually reach Bonn, both the BND and the Foreign Office regularly ascertained that their analyses "were not evaluated by the federal government."[106]

The BND and the End of the GDR

In 1985, after a brief interlude during the early 1980s when the service was headed by Klaus Kinkel, Hans-Georg Wieck took office as BND president.[107] That meant the end of the Org. generation at the service, which was now radically transformed and further expanded, with a special focus on intelligence regarding East Germany. Wieck, a former NATO defense expert who had moreover served as ambassador to Moscow during the early 1980s and thus had firsthand experience of the stagnation of "real-existing socialism," wanted to open the service up to the outside, so that for the first time not only diplomats but also politicians, business representatives, and journalists were allowed to attend selected BND briefings. Moreover, the new president used his administrative experience and the ever greater efficiency of West Germany's foreign intelligence service to finally increase its importance among political decision makers in Bonn. For the first time since Gehlen's day, he regained the privilege, in his capacity as BND president, of briefing the chancellor personally on the international situation. According to available information, these intelligence briefings for the chancellor took place regularly once a week.[108]

Although it was generally assumed that Chancellor Helmut Kohl was not particularly interested in the BND, a look behind the scenes reveals a different picture.[109] For example, Gabriele Gast, a staff member at the Soviet Analysis Desk and also an MfS spy, reports that Kohl showed himself to be extremely well informed during BND briefings. During these meetings with the BND president and his top staff, the chancellor also raised aspects of interest for political decision making and often requested additional information in order to get a more thorough picture of certain issues.[110]

The BND gained much of its knowledge of the East German situation by systematically questioning GDR citizens who were visiting West Germany or who had abandoned their country for good.[111] Using a carefully developed questionnaire, the BND examined the extent to which citizens of the GDR still identified with their state. Hence, up to six hundred persons were interrogated every six months, and their statements analyzed by the GDR Analysis Section of the BND, with its approximately thirty staff members. The result was surprising, both for Wieck and for the West German political leadership, for in spite of the apparent stability of the East German state, "between 72 and 78 percent of all those questioned desired reunification."[112] Nonetheless, these figures sparked vigorous resistance, especially in the Chancellery and in the Ministry of Intra-German Relations (formerly the Ministry of All-German Affairs), since the question of reunification had become increasingly "unpopular" in West Germany during the 1980s. Thus the BND reports were swimming against the political mainstream and were therefore not taken seriously in large parts of the government for a long time.[113]

The service was, moreover, able to gain information on numerous details about the actual situation in East Germany and especially on the mood of the population there, thanks to its ever more extensive monitoring of the mail between the two German states.[114] During the mid-1980s, more than 250 staff members of the BND's Subdirectorate ID, Desk 2, examined countless letters from East Germany for any information that might be useful for intelligence purposes. By the end of 1989, a total of more than 250 staff members were engaged in postal and telephone monitoring. In the Hamburg control office alone, ten thousand postal items per day were examined. The total number of letters from East Germany read every year by BND staff members came to 1.6 million.[115]

Another major source of information for the BND was signals intelligence, with which it succeeded in tapping into the telephone connections of the SED apparatus, which operated on the basis of a radio-relay link system. Together with other radio-technology intelligence tools, the service was able, by the end of the 1980s, to filter out of the ether 450 usable information items per day.[116] As a result, the BND was especially well informed about the SED cadres at the administrative level of cities and rural districts and their view of the problems of the East German state, since they usually sent their reports as telexes via the SED's own radio-relay system. However, the service thus at times became a victim of East German politics. For in order to pressure the SED leadership to institute reforms, Communist Party district leaders would, for instance, report enormous increases in the numbers of applications for emigration to West Germany, which caused the BND to assume that there were some half-million would-be emigrants, while their actual number was only around 125,000.[117]

Owing to the ever-increasing amount of travel between the two German states, the service increasingly depended on the questioning and exploitation of East German scientists, economics experts, and industrial representatives. The Stasi quickly realized that citizens of the GDR traveling abroad were being approached by the BND. Indeed, many "travel cadres" were in fact MfS informers (known officially as "unofficial employees with enemy contact") and tasked to collect information about the personnel and mode of operation of the BND.[118] However, this double game was intentionally planned by the BND, for if East Berlin wished to play it, it would of course be forced to equip its agents with the necessary "chips"—that is, real information—as a result of which Pullach could gain real knowledge.[119] For this reason, the BND was ready to accept the fact that nine out of ten of its East German sources were "carrying loads on both shoulders"—that is, were double agents for the MfS. Finally, the knowledge "thus gained with no risk" through this double game could be tapped by the BND and used as information for the political decision makers in Bonn.[120]

The BND stepped up its own HUMINT operations against East Germany. These operations were relatively safe from discovery because the BND sources limited themselves to engaging East Germans in conversation and making their own visual observations. Consequently, they made no contact with handlers on East German territory and were able to do without such technological tools of the intelligence trade as cameras, radios, or invisible ink. That was an increasingly serious problem for East German counterintelligence.[121]

What former BND president Hans-Georg Wieck saw as the most important strategic innovation was the questioning of directors of state enterprises and professors of economics regarding the situation in East Germany, since this once again made it possible to provide Bonn with a high-quality situation assessment.[122] What he saw as the decisive factor, however, was the linkage of critical analysis on the East German economy with following the political reform process in the Soviet Union. Thanks to this, the BND abandoned the hitherto dominant view that the GDR was a stable state and for the first time considered it possible that the East German state might collapse. This prognosis, according to Wieck, placed the BND closer to East German reality than the GDR Department in the Federal Chancellery or the West German Permanent Representation (Embassy) in East Berlin, both of which vigorously criticized the results provided by the service. The Kohl government in Bonn therefore was initially not responsive to these BND reports. Policymakers during the late 1980s, unimaginatively stuck in the established thinking of the late 1960s, which accepted the division of Germany into two states, were unwilling to believe the BND reports about the dilapidated East German industrial plant and therefore sought to distance themselves as much as possible from the BND.[123] Only in 1989, when the situation in East Germany reached the crisis stage, did at least the chancellor and the foreign minister, Hans-Dietrich Genscher, dare to place any faith in the analyses of their intelligence service.[124]

When the GDR collapsed in the fall of 1989, Kohl had three important pieces of information available to him, thanks to the BND's extensive knowledge of the East German state. On June 5, 1989, the BND had informed the Chancellery that CPSU general secretary Mikhail Gorbachev had stated in a conversation with SED general secretary Erich Honecker "that every country had the sole and exclusive responsibility for its own internal security. Under his leadership, the USSR would not intervene to protect the party and/or government from the dissatisfied masses."[125] It was thus clear that an East German revolution would not, as in 1953, be suppressed by a Soviet military operation.

When the Wall fell on November 9, 1989, surprising all politicians and intelligence services, Kohl had two more trumps in his hand. First of all, he knew that the majority of the East German population wanted not a reformed second German state but rather reunification. Second, the BND reports showed clearly that the East German dissidents were not going to be able to implement their idea of a "third path" of liberalization and humanization of the East German state.[126] On the basis of this information, the chancellor was able, shortly thereafter, to present his Ten-Point Plan for the reunification of Germany and push forward the process of reunification with the power of a bulldozer.[127] As later foreign minister Klaus Kinkel put it, "it was as if Kohl were sitting in the cab of a Caterpillar with huge wheels that ran over everything, and nothing could stop him. There was no hindrance that could not be pushed out of the way. It was he who was blessed with an uncannily certain view of his goal, who saw what needed to be done and what could be done."[128]

The chancellor's "certain view of his goal" he owed to the in-depth reporting of the BND.

Conclusion

A view of the historical progress over time of the BND reveals that during the 1950s and early 1960s the service conducted successful military intelligence operations against East Germany. However, the West German intelligence service, even before the building of the Wall, also had knowledge of other processes in East Germany. Until 1961 a large number of sources provided reports about virtually every event occurring on the territory of East Germany. The information thus gained permitted the piecing together of a current and accurate situation assessment, which was passed on to the political decision-making bodies.

The construction of the Wall changed the situation decisively. The closure of the border gave the Stasi the opportunity to take control of the remaining connection routes—postal contacts and broadcasts and increasingly also the transit routes by land and water—very thoroughly.[129] This thoroughness had evidently been underestimated by the BND. It can hardly be doubted that the Western intelligence services, including the BND, "did not always operate with the necessary professionalism and conspiratorial caution."[130] Certainly the MfS profited from the physical segregation of the espionage center West Berlin and was able in the following decade to achieve considerable counterintelligence successes.[131]

But even during this period, Pullach scored renewed successes by changing its strategies, as 1968 was to show. This included the recruitment of transit and travel spies from West Germany in West Berlin and the increased use of SIGINT. Starting during the 1980s, the BND increasingly switched to obtaining information by questioning visitors and refugees and to recruitment of GDR officials in third countries. It also made targeted covert approaches to prospective sources. The service again concentrated on recruiting sources in the GDR. The BND's intelligence operations thus created considerable problems for the Stasi during the last decade of its existence, in spite of the numerous East German counterintelligence successes. Nonetheless, this success was purchased dearly, for Pullach lost a large number of its sources, but it also learned from its own mistakes. In 1984, for example, Department II of the MfS (counterespionage) stressed the "clever, skillful conspiratorial operations of the enemy."[132]

Starting in the mid-1980s, BND chief Wieck consistently applied the strategy for the acquisition and analysis of information based on the comprehensive in-depth collection of intelligence about East Germany that covered all important areas. Wessel, the second BND president, had already seen this as the most important weapon in the intelligence arsenal and had definitively set the BND on a new course, transforming it from a military intelligence service to a foreign intelligence service:

> The continual observation of the potential of foreign powers must also include the observation of their internal political situations. The permanence of state and societal structures, the identification of the population, especially the social strata that support the state, with an ideology or doctrine, effective internal and external influences on these basic factors, and their current or expected effects will always be important for those who have been called upon to take action in the area of foreign policy. To be instructed in a qualified manner about this is often more important to the foreign policy leadership than access to some document that, while it may provide revealing information about the intentions of a foreign power, may also soon be obsolete.[133]

The true quality of a secret service is accordingly measured especially by the continuity and the longtime quality of its reporting performance and the capacity of its analysts. Fundamentally, however, every intelligence product that is fed into the political process after having successfully been acquired and evaluated faces the problem of whether and how it will be received and taken into account by decision makers.[134]

But it was precisely here that the BND showed its greatest weakness during the mid-1960s, since it was unable to overcome the "nonrelationship" between Bonn and Pullach that had begun to emerge under Adenauer and was to continue for decades. The main reasons for Bonn policymakers' disregard of the BND's analyses related to the service itself: (1) It had emerged from the Org. and was considered to be dominated by the Americans; (2) it had remained in Pullach, so that no personal or professional relationship of trust could develop between policymakers and ministry bureaucrats in Bonn on the one hand and the BND leadership on the other; (3) especially after the Felfe incident, it was considered to be infested with Eastern Bloc agents; (4) it was usually able to transmit its reports to Bonn only by means of time-consuming courier routes, so that the information generally arrived too late to be of any significance for the opinion-building and decision-making processes of the government; and (5) Gehlen had, with his internal spying on the political parties in Bonn, permanently destroyed the relationship of trust between his service and the political world.[135]

Moreover, the only office in Bonn that was really interested in the intelligence information provided was basically the Ministry of Defense, so that the service was largely intentionally excluded from the opinion-building process within the government. As a result, the long-lasting view in Bonn was that "the Service isn't any good anyway."[136] Only when the looming collapse of the GDR required new thinking and a policy that departed from the beaten track did the results of the BND's work become items in demand among decision makers.

Decisive for an evaluation of the successful activity of the service is thus not only its evident ability to acquire important intelligence information and present it in comprehensive analyses but also whether the BND's analyses were adequately incorporated into the political decision-making process and whether decision makers took sufficient account of them. The answer to these two questions is definitely no. As has been shown, the BND had in the 1960s lost the confidence of the political leadership and could therefore, in spite of its largely accurate assessment of the situation, exert little influence on the decisions being made in Bonn.[137]

Notes

1. Hubertus Knabe, *West-Arbeit des MfS. Das Zusammenspiel von "Aufklärung" und "Abwehr"* (Berlin: Ch. Links Verlag, 1999); Hubertus Knabe, *Die unterwanderte Republik: Stasi im Westen* (Berlin: Propyläen, 1999); *Das Gesicht dem Westen zu: DDR-Spionage gegen die Bundesrepublik*, ed. Helmut Müller-Enbergs and Georg Herbstritt (Bremen: Edition Temmen, 2003); and Georg Herbstritt, *Bundesbürger im Dienst der DDR-Spionage: Eine analytische Studie* (Bremen: Edition Temmen, 2007).

2. Gabriele Gast, "Im BND hieß es: Wir sind keine Keksfabrik," in *Angriff und Abwehr: Die deutschen Geheimdienste nach 1945*, ed. Klaus Eichner and Gotthold Schramm (Berlin: Edition Ost, 2007), 500.

3. Elke-Ursel Hammer, "'Archivwesen' im Bundesnachrichtendienst und Bestand B 206 im Bundesarchiv: Von Quellen/Methodenschutz und dem historischen Interesse," *Mitteilungen aus dem Bundesarchiv* 12, no. 1 (2004): 42.

4. On the Historical Division, see Bernd Wegner, "Erschriebene Siege: Franz Halder, die 'Historical Division' und die Rekonstruktion des Zweiten Weltkrieges im Geiste des deutschen Generalstabes," in *Politischer Wandel, organisierte Gewalt und nationale Sicherheit*, ed. Ernst Willi Hansen, Gerhard Schreiber, and Bernd Wegner (Munich: Oldenbourg, 1995), 287–302.

5. On the Foreign Armies / East Section: Helmut Roewer, Stefan Schäfer, and Matthias Uhl, *Lexikon der Geheimdienste im 20. Jahrhundert* (Munich: Herbig, 2003), 14; Dieter Krüger, "Reinhard Gehlen (1902–1979): Der BND-Chef als Schattenmann der Ära Adenauer," in *Konspiration als Beruf: Deutsche Geheimdienstchefs im Kalten Krieg*, ed. Dieter Krüger and Armin Wagner (Berlin: Ch. Links Verlag, 2003), 208–14.

6. See Federal Archive Koblenz, B 206/1–24.

7. On the value of these sources, see Armin Wagner and Matthias Uhl, *BND contra Sowjetarmee: Westdeutsche Militärspionage in der DDR* (Berlin: Ch. Links Verlag, 2007), 43.

8. From 1945 to 1954, the Group of Soviet Occupation Troops in Germany, then the Group of Soviet Forces in Germany, and from 1989 to 1994, the Western Group of Forces; see Kurt Arlt, "Sowjetische (russische) Truppen in Deutschland (1945–1994)," in *Im Dienste der Partei: Handbuch der bewaffneten Organe der DDR*, ed. Torsten Diedrich, Hans Ehlert, and Rüdiger Wenzke (Berlin: Ch. Links Verlag, 1998), 593–632.

9. Hammer, "'Archivwesen' im Bundesnachrichtendienst," 43.

10. Response to a query by the author to the Archive Desk of the BND, January 24, 2006.

11. For an official evaluation of the BND agent reports, see Federal Archive Koblenz, B-136/4869, "Schema für die Bewertung nachrichtendienstlicher Meldungen in Bezug auf Quelle und Inhalt," September 13, 1956.

12. For Foreign Armies and Gehlen, see Magnus Pahl, *Fremde Heere Ost: Hitlers militärische Feindaufklärung* (Berlin: Ch. Links Verlag, 2012).

13. Alaric Searle, *Wehrmacht Generals, West German Society, and the Debate on Rearmament, 1949–1959* (Westport, CT: Praeger, 2003), 105.

14. Hermann Zolling and Heinz Höhne, *Pullach intern: General Gehlen und die Geschichte des Bundesnachrichtendienstes* (Hamburg: Hoffmann und Campe, 2010), 135. For the economic intelligence of the Org., the BND, and other Western agencies against the GDR, see Paul Maddrell, "The Economic Dimension of Cold War Intelligence-Gathering: The West's Spies in the GDR's Economy," *Journal of Cold War Studies* 15, no. 3 (Summer 2013): 76–107.

15. *Annual History Report*, July 1, 1954–June 30, 1955, Historical Division, Headquarters, US Army Europe (1956), 165.

16. Hans-Henning Crome, "The 'Organisation Gehlen' as Pre-History of the Bundesnachrichtendienst," *Journal of Intelligence History* 7, no. 1 (2007): 34; Jens Wegener, *Die Organisation Gehlen und die USA: Deutsch-amerikanische Geheimdienstbeziehungen 1945–1949* (Berlin: Lit Verlag, 2008), 83–84; Wolfgang Krieger, *Geschichte der Geheimdienste: Von den Pharaonen bis zur CIA* (Munich: Beck, 2009), 268–70.

17. Federal Archive Koblenz, B 206/933, "Bericht der Organisation Gehlen: Juni Aufruhr 1953 in Ost-Berlin," July 1953, 34–43; see also Matthias Uhl, "Die militärischen Informationen der 'Organisation Gehlen,'" www.17juni53.de, July 16, 2003, and October 14, 2014, http://www.17juni53.de/chronik/5306/UHL-BND.pdf.

18. Letter from Ivan A. Fadeykin, plenipotentiary for Germany of the Soviet Ministry for State Security, to Lavrenty Beria, June 17, 1953, 2 p.m., in Valeriy Stepanovich Khristoforov, "Dokumenty Zentral'nogo arkhiva FSB o sobytiach 17 ijunja 1953 g. v GDR," *Novaya i noveishaya istoriya*, no. 1 (2004): 90.

19. Reports by Grechko and Tarasov to Bulganin of June 17, 1953, 11 a.m., in Christian F. Osterman, "'This Is Not a Politburo, but a Madhouse': The Post-Stalin Succession Struggle, Soviet Deutschlandpolitik and the SED; New Evidence from Russian, German and Hungarian Archives," *Cold War International History Project Bulletin* 10 (1998): 89.

20. Federal Archive Koblenz, B 206/934, "Bericht der Auswertungsabteilung der Organisation Gehlen: Die Unruhen in der Ostzone," late July 1953, 14.

21. Ibid., 81.

22. Zolling and Höhne, *Pullach intern*, 168; Heinz Höhne, *Der Krieg im Dunkeln: Die deutsche und russische Spionage* (Augsburg: Weltbild Verlag, 1998), 504; Julius Mader, *Die graue Hand: Eine Abrechnung mit dem Bonner Geheimdienst* (Berlin: Kongress Verlag, 1961), 125.

23. Ibid., 166–71; Heinz Felfe, *Im Dienst des Gegners: Autobiographie* (Berlin: Verlag der Nation, 1988), 171, 240–41.

24. Waldemar Markwardt, *Erlebter BND: Kritisches Plädoyer eines Insiders* (Berlin: Anita Tykve Verlag, 1998), 65–70.

25. Federal Archive Koblenz, B 206/934, "Bericht der Auswertungsabteilung der Organisation Gehlen," July 1953, 16. For instance, on June 14, 1953, at 5:36 a.m., Afu "Paicos" reported, "Course in zone changed 180 degrees stop comrades still unsure stop regards Paicos."

26. Ibid., 23.

27. Ibid., 67.

28. Ibid., 42–44; Federal Archive Koblenz, B 206/1990, 38–43, telex of March 17, 1953.

29. Federal Archive Koblenz, B 206/933, "Bericht über den Aufstand 1953," 1953; B 206/934, "Bericht der Auswertungsabteilung der Organisation Gehlen," July 1953.

30. Federal Archive Koblenz, B 206/934, "Bericht der Auswertungsabteilung der Organisation Gehlen," July 1953, 51. For agent operations during the 1950s, see also Paul Maddrell, "Blütezeit der Spionage: Westliche Nachrichtendienste im geteilten Deutschland 1945–1961," in *Duell im Dunkeln: Spionage im geteilten Deutschland*, ed. Stiftung Haus der Geschichte der Bundesrepublik Deutschland (Cologne: Böhlau, 2002), 25–32; Paul Maddrell, "Im Fadenkreuz der Stasi: Westliche Spionage in der DDR; Die Akten der Hauptabteilung IX," *Vierteljahreshefte für Zeitgeschichte* 61, no. 2 (2013): 141–71.

31. Federal Archive Koblenz, B 206/1990, 38–43, telex of March 17, 1953.

32. Federal Archive Koblenz, B 206/934, "Bericht der Auswertungsabteilung der Organisation Gehlen," late July 1953, 54–55.

33. Ibid., 154 (emphasis in original).

34. Mader, *Die graue Hand*, 175–76.

35. Federal Archive Koblenz, B 206/934, "Bericht der Auswertungsabteilung der Organisation Gehlen," late July 1953, 80.

36. Wolfgang Krieger, "'Dr. Schneider' und der BND," in *Geheimdienste in der Weltgeschichte: Spionage und verdeckte Aktionen von der Antike bis zur Gegenwart*, ed. Wolfgang Krieger (Munich: Beck, 2003), 239–41; Krüger, "Reinhard Gehlen," 223–26; Helmut Roewer, *Im Visier der Geheimdienste: Russland und Deutschland im Kalten Krieg* (Bergisch-Gladbach: Lübbe, 2008), 121; Franz-Josef Strauß, *Die Erinnerungen* (Berlin: Siedler, 1989), 153.

37. Harald Nielsen, "The German Analysis and Assessment System," *Intelligence and National Security* 10, no. 4 (1995): 60.

38. Hans-Peter Schwarz, *Adenauer. Der Staatsmann: 1952–1967* (Einbeck: DVA, 1991), 386–87.

39. Höhne, *Krieg im Dunkeln*, 542.

40. Matthias Uhl, *Krieg um Berlin? Die sowjetische Militär- und Sicherheitspolitik in der zweiten Berlinkrise 1958 bis 1962* (Munich: Oldenbourg, 2008), 114–40; Manfred Wilke, *Der Weg zur Mauer: Stationen der Teilungsgeschichte* (Berlin: Ch. Links Verlag, 2011), 312–41.

41. Bernd Stöver, "Mauerbau und Nachrichtendienste: Die CIA und der Wandel der US-Politik in Ostmitteleuropa," in *Mauerbau und Mauerfall: Ursachen-Verlauf-Auswirkungen*, ed. Hans-Hermann Hertle, Konrad Jarausch, and Christoph Kleßmann (Berlin: Ch. Links Verlag, 2002), 139–40.

42. Willy Brandt, *Erinnerungen* (Frankfurt/Main: Ullstein, 1989), 10; see also his account in Willy Brandt, *Begegnungen und Einsichten: Die Jahre 1960–1975* (Hamburg: Hoffmann & Campe, 1976), 11.

43. Federal Archive Koblenz, B 206/1996, "Report of August 28, 1961," 656–57.

44. Reinhard Gehlen, *Der Dienst: Erinnerungen 1942–1971* (Munich: Hase & Koehler, 1973), 285–86.

45. Confidential BND report of January 13, 1961, published in *Der Spiegel*, no. 32 (2011), 14.

46. Strauß, *Die Erinnerungen*, 382.

47. Paul Maddrell, *Spying on Science: Western Intelligence in Divided Germany, 1945–1961* (Oxford: Oxford University Press, 2006), 239.

48. Otto Lenz, *Im Zentrum der Macht: Das Tagebuch des Staatssekretärs Lenz 1951–1953*, ed. Klaus Otto (Düsseldorf: Droste, 1988), 539, and *13.8.1961: Mauerbau; Fluchtbewegung und Machtsicherung*, ed. Bernd Eisenfeld and Roger Engelmann (Bremen: Edition Temmen, 2001), 41.

49. Federal Archive Koblenz, B 206/1988, 11, excerpt from Overview 30/58.

50. Ibid., 113.

51. Federal Archive Koblenz, B 206/1991, "Situation Report Berlin, April 30, 1959," 14; ibid., "Situation Report Berlin, August 12, 1959," 69; ibid., "Stichworte zur Situation um Berlin," undated (late 1959), 85–94.

52. Strauß, *Die Erinnerungen*, 389.

53. Klaus Wiegrefe, "Sehr ernste Risiken," *Der Spiegel*, no. 33 (2011): 38–39.

54. Federal Archive Koblenz, B 206/181, "Military Situation Report, July 1961," 22. This terminology is typical West German Cold War language: Neither "East Germany" nor "GDR" were used, nor was its capital called "East Berlin," as all that would have implied recognition. Instead, the eastern German state was called the "Soviet (or 'East') Zone" (abbreviated SBZ), and its capital was ostensibly the Berlin borough of Pankow, site of a palace where the GDR's powerless president resided. (Most government offices were, of course, in central Berlin.)

55. Ibid., 25.

56. Ibid.

57. Ibid., B 206/107, "Überwachung Garnison Altengrabow," 3; B 206/109, "Überwachung Standort Dresden," 8.

58. Ibid., B 206/842, Telex PA 90012-k, of August 1, 1961: "Republikflucht aus der Sicht der SED"; Klaus Wiegrefe, "Die Schandmauer," *Der Spiegel*, no. 32 (2001): 72.

59. Federal Archive Koblenz, B 206/822, Telex PA 90172-k of August 9, 1961: "Zur Moskauer Konferenz der KP-Führer der Warschauer-Pakt-Staaten vom 03.-05.08.1961"; Wiegrefe, "Die Schandmauer," 72–73.

60. At least until 1960, the BND certainly did have top agents in Moscow who had access to internal documents from the inner circle of the Central Committee. For example, the BND source there learned on May 8, 1960, that Khrushchev was planning to let the Paris summit conference collapse. However, this information did not reach Pullach until May 16, 1960—that is, the day of the meeting. Federal Archive Koblenz, B 206/1995, 243–45, BND Report from Moscow, May 16, 1960.

61. Matthias Uhl and Armin Wagner, eds., *Ulbricht, Chruschtschow und die Mauer: Eine Dokumentation* (Munich: Oldenbourg, 2003), 33–34, 89–93.

62. Federal Archive Koblenz, B 206/107, "Situation Berlin, 64/61: Transporte und Kolonnen nach Berlin, Information CCFFA," August 4–5, 1961.

63. Ibid., B 206/118, "BND Military Situation Report, December," which was also the concluding Annual Report for 1961, dated December 15, 1961, 2–4; ibid., B 206/181, "Monthly Military Report for August of September 4, 1961," 9–15; Federal Archive–Military Archive Freiburg, BW-2/2226, "Berlin-Krise 1961/62" (personal file of Gen. Gerhard Wessel and supplement to the Army Situation Report of September 10, 1961), no page number.

64. Russian State Archive for Contemporary History Moscow, 3/14/494, 90–91, "Resolution P 340/93 of the Presidium of the CC of the CPSU 'on the Commander-in-Chief of the GSFG,'" August 9, 1961; Nikita Sergeevich Khrushchev, *Khrushchev Remembers* (Boston: Little, Brown, 1970), 459; Federal Archive Koblenz, B 206/822, Telex no. 11931 on the appointment of Konev as commander in chief of the GSFG, August 3, 1961, no page number.

65. Federal Archive Koblenz, B 206/1996, Report no. 90712, August 11, 1961, 2.

66. Federal Archive Koblenz, B 206/1989, "Der Einsatz der BND Funkaufklärung im August 1961," 1974, 16–28.

67. Federal Archive Koblenz, B 206/1996, "Fernschreiben über die Ergebnisse einer Besprechung mit westlichen Nachrichtendiensten zur Berlin-Lage," August 11, 1961, 305–10.

68. Federal Archive Koblenz, B 206/1971, "Ausarbeitung: Die Absperrung Ost-Berlins," 1986, 57.

69. Strauß, *Die Erinnerungen*, 358. A significant indication is provided by the fact that in Tim Weiner's history of the CIA, the BND is mentioned only in connection with the Felfe affair. Tim Weiner, *Legacy of Ashes: The History of the CIA* (New York: Anchor, 2007), 212.

70. Federal Archive Koblenz B 206/1975, "Die Kuba-Krise im Meinungsbild des BND," 1987, 20.

71. Although no official cases of blackmail are known today, it can be assumed that the KGB and the Stasi intensively examined the Nazi pasts of West German intelligence officers to be able to blackmail them, if necessary. In addition, § 37 of the Stasi records law does not allow access to former MfS files if active or former BND employees are affected. See Andreas Förster, "Brauner Sumpf," *Berliner Zeitung*, July 12, 2010, and Russian State Military Archive, 460-P, file 1873831, 21, letter of the First Chief Directorate of the KGB to the head of the Prison Department of the Soviet Ministry of Internal Affairs, asking for information on Hans Bernhardt Crome, October 27, 1957. Crome, an officer of the Wehrmacht and Abwehr who was captured at Stalingrad, became, after his return from Soviet prison in 1955, a BND officer.

72. Krüger, "Reinhard Gehlen," 231.

73. Richard Meier, *Geheimdienste ohne Maske: Der ehemalige Präsident des Bundesverfassungsschutzes über Agenten, Spione und einen gewissen Herrn Wolf* (Bergisch Gladbach: Lübbe, 1992), 45.

74. Paul Maddrell, "The Western Secret Services, the East Germany Ministry of State Security and the Building of the Berlin Wall," *Intelligence and National Security* 21, no. 5 (2006): 838–41.

75. Maddrell, *Spying on Science*, 253–62; George Bailey, David Murphy, and Sergei A. Kondrashev, *Battleground Berlin: CIA vs. KGB in the Cold War* (New Haven: Yale University Press, 1999), 443–46; Strauß, *Die Erinnerungen*, 358. For the BND's connection paths to its agents during the 1960s, see Albrecht Charisius and Julius Mader, *Nicht länger geheim: Entwicklung, System und Arbeitsweise des imperialistischen deutschen Geheimdienstes* (Berlin: Militärverlag der Deutschen Demokratischen Republik, 1969), 406–47.

76. The *Spiegel* affair was sparked by the cover article "Bedingt abwehrbereit," *Der Spiegel*, no. 41 (1962): 35–51, which exposed weaknesses in the Bundeswehr. Adenauer's heavy-handed response to this "treason" ultimately led to his own resignation. Schwarz, *Adenauer*, 788–90; Krieger, "'Dr. Schneider,'" 272.

77. Michael Herman, *Intelligence Power in Peace and War* (Cambridge: Cambridge University Press, 1996), 266; Hans J. Vorbeck, "Nachrichtendienste als Faktoren in politischen Entscheidungsprozessen," in *The Influence of Intelligence Services on Political Decision-Making*, ed. Volker Foertsch and Klaus Lange (Munich: Hanns-Seidel-Stiftung e.V., 2010), 19–21. For the possibilities of influence of the BND on policy, see also Hansjörg Geiger, "Erfahrungen eines BND-Präsidenten," ibid., 15–18.

78. Valery Vartanov, "Die militärische Niederschlagung des 'Prager Frühlings,'" in *Prager Frühling: Das internationale Krisenjahr 1968*, Bd. 1: *Beiträge*, ed. Stefan Karner et al. (Cologne: Böhlau, 2008), 665.

79. Klaus Wiegrefe, "Pleiten, Pannen und Legenden," *Spiegel Online*, April 2008 and October 14, 2014, http://www.spiegel.de/einestages/geheimdienste-und-prager-fruehling-a -947780.html.

80. Federal Archive Koblenz, B 206/192, "Military Situation Report–Monthly Report," (for May 1968), June 4, 1968, 43–44.

81. Wiegrefe, "Pleiten."

82. Federal Archive BA Koblenz, B 206/1972, "Der BND und die ČSSR-Krise," 1986, 19.

83. *Vozdushno-desantnye voyska Rossii* (Moscow: Fond Sodeystviya vozdushno-desantnym vojskam, 2005), 62; Aleksandr V. Margelov and Vasily V. Margelov, *Desatnik no. 1 general armii Margelov* (Moscow: Olma-Press, 2003), 410.

84. Excerpt from the historical information letter on the 849th Artillery Regiment of the Twenty-Fourth Motorized Rifle Division in *Voni zakhishchali mir u Evropi*, ed. Volodimir A. Ulyanchenko, Vladislav P. Suncev, Oleskiy O. Yurchenko, Volodimir L. Tkachenko, Nina Ya. Vorobjova, and Oleksandr P. Remezov (Zhitomir, Russia: Vidavnictvo, 2003), 142; excerpt from the historical information letter on the 398th Armored Regiment of the 128th Motorized Rifle Division in ibid., 144–45; Federal Archive Koblenz, B 206/192, "Military Situation Report–Monthly Report" (for May 1968), June 4, 1968, 50–52.

85. Federal Archive Koblenz, B 206/413, "Military Situation Report–Weekly Report," no. 30/68 (July 17–23, 1968), part A, General Matters (Summary), 3–4.

86. Federal Archive Koblenz, B 206/413, "Military Situation Report–Weekly Report," no. 31/68 (July 24–30, 1968), part A, General Matters (Summary), 3–4.

87. Federal Archive Koblenz, B 206/192, "Military Situation Report–Monthly Report" (for July 1968), August 7, 1968, 7.

88. For the signals intelligence collection of the BND and the Bundeswehr, see Erich Schmidt-Eenboom, "Empfänglich für Geheimes: Die (west)deutschen Nachrichtendienste im Äther," www.desert-info.ch, 1999 and October 14, 2014, http://www.desert-info.ch/download/pdf/PDF-Forum/Kreipe.pdf, and Günther K. Weiße, *Geheime Funkaufklärung in Deutschland 1945–1989* (Stuttgart: Motorbuch-Verlag, 2005).

89. Federal Archive Koblenz, B 206/413, "Military Situation Report–Weekly Report," no. 31/68 (July 24–30), 1968, part B, Overall Forces (Summary), 6–7.

90. Federal Archive Koblenz, B 206/192, "Military Situation Report–Monthly Report" (for July 1968) August 7, 1968, 6–8, 37.

91. Wiegrefe, "Pleiten."

92. Federal Archive Koblenz, B 206/1972, 19, "Der BND und die ČSSR-Krise," 1986.

93. Federal Archive Koblenz, B 206/413, "Military Situation Report–Weekly Report," no. 32/68 (July 31–August 6, 1968), part A, General Matters (Summary), 1–2.

94. Ibid., 4.

95. Federal Archive Koblenz, B 206/298, "Military Situation Reports East–Weekly Report," no. 34/68; ibid., Report USR 04–05–12, "Verlegung von Fliegerkräften 24. FrontLA, 5a–5b."

96. Federal Archive Koblenz, B 206/1972, "Der BND und die ČSSR-Krise," 1986, 5–6.

97. Meier, *Geheimdienst*, 41–44.

98. Erich Schmidt-Eenboom, "The Bundesnachrichtendienst, the Bundeswehr and Sigint in the Cold War and After," *Intelligence and National Security* 16, no. 1 (2001): 135–38.

99. Notes by Chancellor Kurt Georg Kiesinger regarding a conversation with the then foreign minister Brandt on December 2, 1968, in *Akten zur Auswärtigen Politik der Bundesrepublik Deutschland* (hereafter cited as *AAPD*), 1968, Bd. 2: *1. Juli bis 31. Dezember 1968*

(Munich: Oldenbourg, 1999), 1548. The conversation concerned the position of vice president of the BND, for which Brandt proposed an SPD candidate. He rejected Kiesinger's proposal of Günther Nollau as "too nervous"—probably also because Nollau was a CDU man.

100. Federal Archive Koblenz, B 206/929, "Nachrichtendienstliche Führungsorientierung zur Wirtschaftslage in der DDR," September 19, 1973, 108–25. Notably, Helmut Schmidt does not mention the BND in his memoirs, *Freiheit verantworten* (Düsseldorf: Econ, 1983) and *Ausser Dienst: Eine Bilanz* (Munich: Siedler, 2008).

101. Ambassador Wieck, Moscow, to State Secretary van Well, February 4, 1980, in *AAPD*, 1980, Bd. 1 (Munich: Oldenbourg, 2011), 223.

102. Dieter Krüger, "Gerhard Wessel (1913–2002): Der Ziehsohn Gehlens an der Spitze des BND," in *Konspiration als Beruf: Deutsche Geheimdienstchefs im Kalten Krieg*, ed. Dieter Krüger and Armin Wagner (Berlin: Ch. Links Verlag, 2003), 275–82.

103. August Hanning, "Die Bedeutung nachrichtendienstlicher Informationen für die Sicherheit der Bundesrepublik Deutschland," in *The Influence of Intelligence Services on Political Decision-Making*, ed. Volker Foertsch and Klaus Lange (Munich: Hanns-Seidel-Stiftung e.V., 2010), 31–38.

104. Notes of senior legation counselor Elbe on a service visit to the BND, March 19, 1979, in *AAPD*, 1979, Bd. 1 (Munich: Oldenburg, 2010), 373–76, and notes of ministry director Müller regarding a letter from BND president Kinkel on the foreign aid provided by East Germany to the third world, June 24, 1980, ibid., 980–82.

105. Notes of ministry director Haas on consultations regarding Africa with the BND, September 11, 1980, *AAPD*, 1980, Bd. 2 (Munich: Oldenbourg, 2011), 1656. The diplomats were particularly surprised during these consultations by the very detailed situation assessment of East German efforts in Africa. This indicates that the BND had again acquired increased competence in political analysis.

106. Wieck to van Well, February 4, 1980, *AADP*, 1980, Bd. 1 (Munich: Oldenbourg, 2011), 223.

107. On the Kinkel era at the BND, see Erich Schmidt-Eenboom, "Von Militärs und Maulwürfen: Die 'Ostarbeit' des BND," in *Duell im Dunkeln: Spionage im geteilten Deutschland*, ed. Stiftung Haus der Geschichte der Bundesrepublik Deutschland (Cologne: Böhlau, 2002), 59–60.

108. Hermann Wentker, "Die DDR in den Augen des BND (1985–1990): Ein Interview mit Dr. Hans-Georg Wieck," *Vierteljahrshefte für Zeitgeschichte* 56, no. 2 (2008): 350–52.

109. This legend has also been cultivated by Kohl himself. For instance, in his three-volume memoir there is only one reference to the BND, in which he merely states regarding state secretary Waldemar Schreckenberger, responsible for supervising the BND, "that the infighting between the secret services and the Federal Chancellery . . . repeatedly caused unedifying disputes." Helmut Kohl, *Erinnerungen 1982–1990* (Munich: Droemer, 2005), 335.

110. Gabriele Gast, *Kundschafterin des Friedens* (Frankfurt/Main: Eichborn, 1999), 278–82; Klaus Wiegrefe, "Volten im Wendejahr," *Der Spiegel*, no. 49 (2009): 47.

111. Jens Gieseke, *Der Mielke-Konzern: Die Geschichte der Stasi 1945–1990* (Stuttgart: DVA, 2001), 231–32.

112. Wentker, "Die DDR in den Augen des BND," 339.

113. Ibid., 350–52.

114. Monitoring of letters from East Germany had been going on since at least 1951. Between 1956 and 1971, for example, the customs service confiscated some 151 million postal

items from East Germany. See "Gesetzlose Praxis," *Der Spiegel*, no. 53 (2009): 14–15, and Josef Foschepoth, "Postzensur und Telefonüberwachung in der Bundesrepublik (1949–1968)," *Zeitschrift für Geschichtswissenschaft* 57, no. 5 (2009): 413–26. Unfortunately, however, very little is known about postal supervision by the BND during this later period.

115. Reinhard Grimm et al., eds., *Die Sicherheit: Zur Abwehrarbeit des MfS*, Bd. 1 (Berlin: Edition Ost, 2002), 457–56. Especially with regard to the daily working conditions in postal evaluation, see Norbert Juretzko, *Bedingt dienstbereit: Im Herzen des BND; Die Abrechnung eines Aussteigers* (Berlin: Ullstein, 2004), 60–76.

116. Schmidt-Eenboom, *Empfänglich für Geheimes*, 5; Weiße, *Geheime Funkaufklärung in Deutschland*, 95–99.

117. Wentker, "Die DDR in den Augen des BND," 340–41.

118. Werner Großmann, *Bonn im Blick: Die DDR-Aufklärung aus der Sicht ihres letzten Chefs* (Berlin: Das Neue Berlin, 2001), 143–45; Klaus Eichner and Andreas Dobbert, *Headquarters Germany: Die US-Geheimdienste in Deutschland* (Berlin: Edition Ost, 2008), 260.

119. Ullrich Wössner, "Angriffe des MfS auf den Bundesnachrichtendienst," in *Das Gesicht dem Westen zu: DDR-Spionage gegen die Bundesrepublik*, ed. Helmut Müller-Enbergs and Georg Herbstritt (Bremen: Edition Temmen, 2003), 401–2. This is also confirmed in the memoir of the West German counterintelligence chief Günther Nollau, *Das Amt: 50 Jahre Zeuge der Geschichte* (Munich: C. Bertelsmann, 1978), 251.

120. Wössner, "Angriffe des MfS," 401.

121. The Federal Commissioner for the Records of the State Security Service of the former GDR (BStU), MfS-HA II 24300, "Erkenntnisse über die Spionagetätigkeit des Bundesnachrichtendienstes der BRD auf der Grundlage der im Jahre 1977 erzielten Ergebnisse des MfS der DDR," December 1977, 1–13, 11.

122. Interview with Hans-Georg Wieck, May 10, 2012.

123. As Wieck noted elsewhere regarding the reception of BND information in Bonn, "many things, however, did not fit into the political landscape, and were therefore blocked out." See Karl-Rudolf Korte, *Deutschlandpolitik in Helmut Kohls Kanzlerschaft: Regierungsstil und Entscheidungen 1982–1989* (Stuttgart: DVA, 1998), 415–16, and Hans-Georg Wieck, "The GDR: As Seen by the Federal German Foreign Intelligence Agency (BND) 1985–1990," *Journal of Intelligence History* 6, no. 1 (2006): 98.

124. Wentker, "Die DDR in den Augen des BND," 346.

125. Quoted in Wiegrefe, "Volten," 45.

126. Wentker, "Die DDR in den Augen des BND," 339–41.

127. For good reason, Kohl quoted in his memoir the BND figures regarding East German citizens who favored reunification. Kohl, *Erinnerungen*, 317–18.

128. Quoted in Rolf Steininger, "Deutschland und der Fall der Mauer," in *Stationen im 20. Jahrhundert*, ed. Ingrid Böhler, Eva Pflanzelter, and Rolf Steininger (Innsbruck: Studienverlag, 2011), 222.

129. Paul Maddrell, "British Intelligence through the Eyes of the Stasi: What the Stasi's Records Show about the Operations of British Intelligence in Cold War Germany," *Intelligence and National Security* 27, no. 1 (2012): 69–73.

130. Karl-Wilhelm Fricke, "Spionage als antikommunistischer Widerstand," *Deutschlandarchiv* 35, vol. 4 (2002): 571–72; Maddrell, *Spying on Science*, 253–62.

131. Hanns Labrenz-Weiß, *Hauptabteilung II: Spionageabwehr* (Berlin: BStU, 2001), 42–48; Karl-Wilhelm Fricke and Roger Engelmann, *"Konzentrierte Schläge": Staatssicherheitsaktionen und politische Prozesse in der DDR 1953–1956* (Berlin: Ch. Links Verlag, 1998), 42–60.

132. BStU, MfS-HA II 30818, "Zur inhaltlichen Gestaltung und weiteren Qualifizierung des politisch-operativen Zusammenwirkens mit der Verwaltung der Sonderabteilungen des KGB der UdSSR bei der GSSD," 1984, 158.

133. Gerhard Wessel, "BND: Der geheime Auslandsnachrichtendienst der Bundesrepublik Deutschland," *Beiträge zur Konfliktforschung* 15, no. 2 (1985): 12.

134. Gehlen, *Der Dienst*, 310; Markwardt, *Erlebter BND*, 45, 424–25. Gabriele Gast, during her service as senior staff member in the Federal Chancellery under Helmut Schmidt, did ascertain that he considered BND reporting economic and military issues, in spite of his public statements to the contrary; see Gabriele Gast, "Aufgaben und Bedeutung der Lagebeurteilung Ost," in *Spionage für den Frieden: Eine Konferenz in Berlin am 7. Mai 2004*, ed. Klaus Eichner and Gotthold Schramm (Berlin: Edition Ost, 2004), 98–99, and Gast, "Keksfabrik," 501–2.

135. Wentker, "Die DDR in den Augen des BND," 344.

136. Ibid., 346; Wolfgang Krieger, "German Intelligence History: A Field in Search of Scholars," in *Understanding Intelligence in the Twenty-First Century: Journeys in Shadows*, ed. Len V. Scott and Peter D. Jackson (London: Routledge, 2004), 43–44.

137. Andreas Hilger and Armin Müller, *"Das ist kein Gerücht, sondern echt": Der BND und der "Prager Frühling" 1968* (Marburg: Unabhängige Historikerkommission zur Erforschung der Geschichte des Bundesnachrichtendienstes 1945–68, 2014), 103–14.

British Intelligence, PIRA, and the Early Years of the Northern Ireland Crisis

Remembering, Forgetting, and Mythologizing

EUNAN O'HALPIN

IN 1996 A FORMER HEAD of the British domestic security service (often known as MI5), when asked about his service's worst failing in the preceding thirty-five years, replied, "Not taking the IRA seriously enough early enough." In 2011, in a Reith Lecture broadcast just a few days before the tenth anniversary of 9/11, Dame Eliza Manningham-Buller, another former MI5 chief, said that Britain was especially well equipped to combat Islamic fundamentalism because of its lengthy experience of counterterrorism relating to Northern Ireland. She pointed to the eventual success of the Northern Ireland peace process, which culminated in Sinn Féin and the Democratic Unionist Party, groups representing opposite ends of the political spectrum in Northern Ireland, coming together to form a power-sharing administration along with more centrist parties. The only terrorist group that she mentioned by name in the course of her lecture other than Al-Qaeda, and she mentioned it on a number of occasions, was the Provisional Irish Republican Army (PIRA).[1]

But PIRA, born at the end of 1969 after a split within the all-island Irish republican movement, was the product, not the cause, of the Northern Ireland crisis. It did not even exist when serious intercommunal violence erupted in Belfast in the fall of 1969, and the Dublin-dominated IRA from which it emerged had played little part in either fomenting or reacting to events in

Northern Ireland before the Belfast outbreak. That violence was, as the British government acknowledged at the time, organized and initiated mainly by loyalist groups, who targeted Catholics living in mixed areas of the city and attacked adjoining Catholic districts without effective hindrance from the local security forces.[2]

PIRA was by far the most deadly single actor during the Troubles, responsible for 48 percent, and with other Irish republican groups for 58.6 percent, of all fatalities. Loyalist terrorists were responsible for 29.2 percent of deaths, including over forty cross-border killings in the Republic of Ireland between 1969 and 1998. Yet they seldom receive even a mention in public discourse outside Ireland, being considered a purely local phenomenon despite their own external links and support networks in Canada, Scotland, South Africa, and elsewhere.[3]

Why, then, has PIRA registered in the collective memory of the British intelligence community not only as a synonym for all terrorist organizations involved in the Northern Ireland conflict but also as an organization comparable in menace, purpose, and capacity to Al-Qaeda? The answer is primarily because for over twenty years PIRA posed a real though intermittent threat to Britain itself, as distinct from Northern Ireland. As one retired British official put it in 2008, attempting to explain the distinction between republican and loyalist terrorism, PIRA was "threatening to invade the mainland."[4] PIRA came very close to assassinating Prime Minister Margaret Thatcher in Brighton in 1984 and was not that far away from killing Prime Minister John Major when it mortared 10 Downing Street in 1991. The organization mounted a number of significant bombing operations in Britain, including both indiscriminate terrorist attacks and more targeted exercises intended to cause economic disruption (the Baltic Exchange in 1992, Bishopsgate in 1993, and Canary Wharf and Manchester in 1996). Yet Irish republican terrorist activities in Britain, mainly PIRA's, resulted in 126 fatalities, just 0.34 percent of the 3,661 fatalities worldwide associated with the Northern Ireland conflict and perhaps 0.4 percent of all PIRA killings.

An additional reason why PIRA so dominates British recollections is, of course, that the Provisionals' political arm, Sinn Féin, eventually became key participants in the Northern Ireland peace process, which saw the emergence of cross-community governance in Northern Ireland and decommissioning of terrorist arsenals as well as other important legal, institutional, and constitutional innovations in the Republic of Ireland and in the United Kingdom. The Provisional movement turned out to be people with whom Britain emphatically could do business, although only in conjunction with other interested parties, particularly the Irish government and the Unionist and loyalist communities in Northern Ireland. The best contemporary analogue for the Provisional movement, consequently, is not Al-Qaeda but the Taliban.

One key element in the emergence of a broadly accepted settlement in Northern Ireland was a trusted communication channel (known as "the Link"), established in the early 1970s, between PIRA and Britain's foreign intelligence service, MI6. It was through the Link that the PIRA leadership conveyed their willingness to eschew force in 1993, albeit in disputed terms.[5]

Experience of countering Northern Ireland–related terrorism, while simultaneously developing ways of "talking to terrorists," certainly renders British security and intelligence agencies very well placed to analyze and confront other contemporary terrorist threats. Nevertheless, the available records indicate that in the prelude to and the first years of the Northern Ireland conflict, London's intelligence machinery performed rather poorly in both tactical terms and in wider analysis of the underlying causes of the turmoil and the aims of the various nonstate protagonists. It also failed in its inability to appreciate the likely negative political impact for the beleaguered Irish government of significant British intelligence activities that came to light, specifically the Joint Intelligence Committee (JIC)–approved interrogation regime employed against a number of detainees when internment was introduced in Northern Ireland in August 1971, the bungled penetration of the Garda Síochána (Irish police) security section C3 in 1972, and the embarrassing claims of the criminal Littlejohn brothers in 1973–74 that British officials had connived in their plans to rob banks in Ireland.[6] The controversy surrounding the one-sided introduction of internment—in the words of MI6's Frank Steele, making the case for its abolition in 1972, the measure had been "directed mainly if not wholly against Catholics"—and the interrogation abuses that followed had the collateral effect of removing from the Dublin government's armory what had previously been its own trusted weapon of last resort against the republican movement, internment without trial, which had been deployed at various times to great effect and without great controversy in 1923–24, the 1930s, 1939–45, and 1957–58.[7] It is perhaps as much in problems of prevailing mindsets in Whitehall in the early years of the Troubles as in the undoubted eventual success of sophisticated intelligence and security operations against both republican and loyalist paramilitary organizations that there are general lessons to be learned.

This is not to argue that, had intelligence analysis on Northern Ireland as the crisis grew been more astute, particularly as regards underlying political conditions, the dismal course of events would have been very different. Most of the key decisions and mistakes made by the British, Northern Ireland, and Irish governments in the first years of the crisis were not based on intelligence assessments, good, bad, or indifferent, but on political judgments that proved to be disastrous. Until the prorogation of the Northern Ireland government in March 1972, furthermore, London could exercise only limited authority and control over security policy and operations in the province. The pivotal events of October 5, 1968, when a civil rights march in Londonderry (hereafter "Derry") led to serious clashes with the Royal Ulster Constabulary (RUC) (much of the police violence being captured by television cameras), were the direct responsibility of the Stormont administration. Harold Wilson's Labour government in London could only look on uneasily. The Cameron Commission hastily established to inquire into these early disturbances was unequivocal in its conclusions. While it noted the increasing involvement of Trotskyite and other leftist groups in civil rights agitation, a trend seen around the world, the commission concluded that the civil rights movement was agitating against manifest injustices, that the Stormont administration's approach to public order enforcement was one-sided and arbitrary, and that Catholic grievances about policing and the sectarian character of the part-time Ulster Special Constabulary were well founded.[8]

This chapter also looks at what two other countries, the United States and Ireland, contributed—or failed to contribute—to British efforts to understand, to anticipate, and to thwart terrorism in the early years of the Troubles. In places this strand of the discussion runs beyond those early years. This is done in order to explore the crucial point that Britain's relentless pressure for more effective interstate cooperation against PIRA, in combination with other factors, unavoidably contributed to a slow growth in autonomous American government interest in the substantive issues underlying the Troubles. By 1985 Washington was willing publicly to help both the British and Irish governments on Northern Ireland. The Republican president Ronald Reagan and his ideological nemesis Tip O'Neill, the Democratic speaker of the House of Representatives, held a photo-call to mark bipartisan American political and financial support for the Anglo-Irish Agreement, and in the 1990s the "peace process" was greatly facilitated by direct American government sponsorship of all-party negotiations and by cross-party support in Congress for American involvement as an honest broker.[9]

In the Republic of Ireland, similarly, as time passed, overt cooperation in security and law enforcement, if not explicitly something to be bargained, was certainly associated with Dublin's requirement that London would continue efforts to find an acceptable cross-communal political settlement of some kind.

Assessing the British Assessment Machine's Response: The Available Evidence

Thorough evaluation of the role of intelligence assessment in the prelude to and in the first years of the Troubles would require access to all the assessments themselves, together with the intelligence and other reporting on which these were based. We do not have such material. Tony Craig's *Crisis of Confidence* makes admirable use of records in the National Archives in London.[10] These often include the end product of intelligence analysis as well as diplomatic reporting and other material. Prime Minister's Office and Foreign Office files cast a good deal of light on how intelligence helped to frame policy decisions, while Ministry of Defence records are useful on questions such as police/army intelligence cooperation on the ground in Northern Ireland, on interrogation controversies, and on security forces' estimates of various paramilitary groups' strengths, capabilities, and intentions from 1969 onward. Cabinet Office records are also useful up to 1982, especially the minutes of the weekly JIC meetings.

Unfortunately, JIC records are heavily redacted before release, particularly in respect to Irish affairs. Associated memoranda and annexes are almost never to be found, other than when spare copies or drafts turn up in the files of other Whitehall departments. Files showing the work of the assessment staff, the key level for our purposes, are still closed. This makes material on security issues available in the private papers of British politicians involved with Northern Ireland more significant. The single most useful such ministerial collection for the early years of the Troubles are the Merlyn Rees papers, which include a frank if self-pitying journal that he dictated periodically while secretary of state for Northern Ireland from 1974 to 1976. His predecessors dealing with Northern Ireland were more reticent.[11]

The available records show there were a number of significant strands of information and analysis relating to the Northern Ireland crisis available to London's intelligence assessment machine in London from the mid-1960s onward. The most important were the following:

(a) material from the government of Northern Ireland (up to its demise in March 1972) and its police force, the RUC

(b) material secured by the British army, by mainland police forces, and by MI5, MI6, and other agencies including Customs and Excise

(c) material provided in reports by the British embassy in Dublin

(d) material provided by the Garda Síochána, or Garda, through liaison channels to the Metropolitan Police Special Branch and by Irish army intelligence to MI5

(e) material provided through liaison channels and otherwise by agencies of the US government and occasionally by Canada, Australia, and other friendly states

Intelligence on the IRA and Other Irish Terrorist Groups up to 1969

British intelligence was well aware of the IRA's leftward drift following the dismal failure of its sporadic "Border Campaign" of 1956 to 1962. The reasons for the conversion of some of the IRA's leadership to a broadly Marxist world-view have been much debated by historians in recent years, as has the related question of whether Moscow encouraged this development for Cold War purposes. Through its surveillance of the Communist Party of Great Britain (CPGB) and associated organizations and groups, including the "Connolly Association" established in London to mobilize the Irish in Britain, MI5 had some evidence that the CPGB had long aspired to exert substantial influence on the Irish republican movement. The initiation of the IRA's Border Campaign was greeted respectfully in January 1957 by the *Daily Worker*, which commented, "You may disagree with their methods, but the IRA have just aims."[12] In the wake of the ignominious tailing-off of that campaign in 1962, the IRA's new chief of staff, Cathal Goulding, became a convinced Marxist. What is not clear is the extent to which Goulding's conversion reflected a concerted strategy of communist penetration of the republican leadership. A recent academic study that lends weight to that argument has met with a flurry of outraged criticism by some veterans of the republican Left who maintain that the IRA's leftward swing after 1962 owed absolutely nothing to manipulation by Moscow or its British proxies.[13] In any case, no one in London seems to have taken the idea of the IRA as a Soviet pawn very seriously in the 1960s, while from 1970 PIRA was believed to follow the entirely pragmatic approach of previous Irish republicans in pursuing help from any quarter hostile to Britain, irrespective of ideology or geopolitics.[14] British analysts would have drawn comfort from the acidulous observations of a senior Soviet official on representatives of the Irish communist movement, which after the IRA split and the formation of PIRA still sought to stimulate Soviet interest in the Northern Ireland crisis. Anatoly Chernyayev, who later became Mikhail Gorbachev's principal foreign policy adviser, recorded his despair at the caliber of foreign representatives at celebrations for the fiftieth anniversary of the Soviet Union in 1972: One of the Irish delegates was "primitive and doltish," and "in general, the squalor of 'our' communist movement struck me particularly forcibly. . . . O'Riordan [the veteran leader of the Communist Party of Ireland] . . . spoke at the celebrations, they practically worshipped the ground he walked on. . . . But in Ireland nobody knows him—not the left, nor the right, nor the people who are throwing bombs, not the English. Nobody takes him seriously."[15]

The elephant in the corner of the Whitehall committee room was neither red nor green but orange. Loyalist terrorism seems barely to exist in Whitehall's collective memory of the Troubles and not at all in public and academic recitations of the wider lessons for intelligence analysis. Yet loyalist terrorism was a central, violent, and persistent element. Various loyalist terrorist groups killed over a thousand people; they mounted attacks in the Republic of Ireland, including those that on May 17, 1974, produced the largest total of fatalities on a single day in the entire conflict; and in combination with the wider loyalist community they provided the muscle and the menace during the Ulster Workers' Council strike that brought down Brian Faulkner's power-sharing Executive, the centerpiece of the 1973 Sunningdale Agreement so painstakingly negotiated by the British and Irish governments, just weeks after Harold Wilson's Labour Party took office in March 1974. In the wake of that disaster, which many blamed on the unwillingness of the Wilson government to use force or the threat of force to keep the roads open and to maintain vital services, the supine Merlyn Rees, newly appointed as secretary of state for Northern Ireland, noted defensively that "it's one thing to fight . . . the IRA, it's another to fight the Community as a whole which is what was happening with the Protestants."[16]

So why have loyalist terrorists been forgotten, and why did they never feature in discourse on international terrorism, as republican groups did, despite their own external connections? Part of the explanation lies in the fact that the cross-border dimension aside, loyalist terrorism was so downright provincial in its aspirations and operations. Because the loyalists did not threaten the mainland, they seem seldom to have registered in Whitehall's collective consciousness as a fundamental problem. The JIC certainly discussed loyalist terrorism from time to time, although records of their conclusions and the papers on which these were based have been so heavily redacted as to make it impossible to determine how loyalist terrorism was analyzed as compared with the threat from PIRA and other republican groups. What is clear is that loyalist terrorism was always seen as a second-order problem, something provoked by fears of republicanism and of betrayal and abandonment by Britain.

Intelligence Available from Northern Ireland and Dublin up to 1969

JIC and other papers show that during the 1960s London was reasonably well briefed on the Dublin IRA's development, in particular the growth of Marxist influence, as well as the organization's aspiration to profit from the growing civil rights movement in Northern Ireland. Andrew Gilchrist, the ambassador in Dublin from 1966 to 1970, took a particular interest in the question of a possible intersection between left-wing political activism and republicanism in Ireland, and he provided London with a number of well-informed reports that touched on efforts by the Dublin IRA and its associates to initiate and manipulate industrial, agrarian, and human rights protests. In 1967 Gilchrist discussed "the remnants of the old-guard IRA." He observed that "there are still surviving militants with good supplies of arms," but these "are very much in the background. . . . Young people are beginning to find all the blood and murders of their recent past tedious and uninteresting, perhaps a little incomprehensible." They were concerned with economic modernization and societal liberalization, not with the old grievance of partition.[17]

Gilchrist was an atypical diplomat. He had served in the Special Operations Executive in Thailand from 1944 to 1945 with resistance groups, giving him direct experience of subversion and irregular warfare, while his posting immediately prior to Dublin had been as ambassador in Indonesia during the "konfrontasi" (the Indonesian-Malaysian confrontation of 1963–66), in the course of which his embassy was attacked by a Djakarta mob while he and the military attaché stood armed inside the chancery ready to defend it if necessary. His experiences and sangfroid stood him in good stead when in June 1968 the Garda warned him of a significant kidnapping threat from a splinter republican group. Gilchrist, who found his protectors "extremely conscientious and efficient," built up a good rapport with the head of the Garda Special Branch, Superintendent John Fleming. This insight into Garda thinking helped him in framing a well-informed and perceptive report on the IRA and on the Irish government's "cat and mouse" approach to various republican activities within the state. Gilchrist also noted the very positive public attitude toward the civil rights campaign in Northern Ireland and also public appreciation of the efforts of the Northern Ireland government to address some of the grievances highlighted—in January 1969 the Northern Ireland prime minister, Terence O'Neill, was voted "man of the year" by readers of a leading Dublin newspaper for his modestly reformist approach. Such a development appeared to reflect a surprisingly realistic Irish public attitude toward the Northern Ireland state, one far removed from traditionalist nationalist irredentism; yet a year later the same readership chose Bernadette Devlin, the fiery left-winger who had come to international prominence during the Derry disturbances of August 1969. In terms specifically of the republican movement in 1968–69, Gilchrist's analysis broadly reflected the Garda view (i.e., that the IRA, while not sufficiently strong or equipped to mount a serious campaign against the Irish state and with its Dublin leadership largely focused on social and economic agitation, still had the potential to fan the flames in Northern Ireland and aspired to do so by penetrating and manipulating the civil rights movement).[18] The JIC was inclined to downplay Gilchrist's estimate of the drift of affairs in Ireland when it finally met him in September 1969, while his unusual direct link to the Garda Special Branch was lost when he retired in April 1970. His successor, John Peck, though markedly less forthright and irreverent, also gradually fell out of favor. Commenting on the ambassador's valedictory dispatch from Dublin in 1973, JIC chairman Sir Stewart Crawford wrote that Peck "tended to believe that HMG [Her Majesty's Government] did not give [Taoiseach (Prime Minister)] Mr Lynch sufficient credit for what he had done to support us," while "his ignorance of events in Northern Ireland" colored his outlook. In other words, he had gone native.[19]

The British government had no comparable sources in Belfast in the three years leading up to 1969 to report dispassionately on political and security developments. Consequently, while JIC proceedings show considerable interest in the wider potential for disorder generated by the civil rights agitation in 1968 and 1969, they also indicate that London had only a hazy view of political and security conditions in Northern Ireland itself.

There had been a brief flurry of Cabinet Office and JIC interest in the province in 1966, on foot of a warning from Terence O'Neill that the IRA was preparing to mount a series of attacks, most likely to include assassinations, to mark the fiftieth anniversary of the 1916 Rising. Arrangements to contain that threat were supervised by cabinet secretary Sir Burke Trend.[20] The Dublin government was consulted, but both Belfast and London were inclined to discount what they were told by the Garda and the Department of Justice—that is, that the IRA leadership had no plans for violent commemorative action north or south of the border and that the limited increase in training camps and other activities that had so alarmed O'Neill were not harbingers of a new campaign but essentially a diversion generated by the IRA leadership to maintain discipline and morale. Although London may not have been aware of this, the Garda had very good sources within the IRA leadership in these years. This was perhaps connected to the bitter factional disputes about the leftward direction of the movement that were to culminate in the split in December 1969, antagonisms that may have seen both leftists and traditionalists selectively leaking information designed to discredit their opponents.[21] The Garda estimate of IRA intentions in 1966 proved far more accurate than either Belfast's or London's, a point not reflected in the JIC's self-congratulatory conclusion that the absence of republican terrorist outrages in Northern Ireland in that potentially incendiary year of anniversaries was due to well-timed precautionary security measures.[22] The RUC inspector general did warn the Stormont government in June 1966 that "while there is always the IRA and its splinter groups in the background ready to seize any opportunity to disturb the peace . . . the fact is that an equal or even greater threat at present is posed by extremist Protestant groups," an observation borne out by three sectarian killings by loyalists, mainly ex-servicemen.[23] That group, headed by the former military policeman Augustus "Gusty" Spence, later an icon of loyalist remorse for political violence, was apparently not considered worthy of separate analysis in London. Its actions were considered a purely local phenomenon of no wider significance. The tendency to overlook or to discount loyalist terrorism was seen again in the spring of 1969. A number of bomb attacks targeted against strategic infrastructure—Belfast's electricity and water supplies—were assumed to be the work of the IRA. In fact they were loyalist actions, something that it took the RUC an embarrassingly long time to determine.[24]

Whitehall, 1969: Sir Humphrey Girds His Loins

One reason for London's difficulty in gauging the lay of the land in Northern Ireland in the late 1960s was unsatisfactory arrangements for liaison with Belfast. The prime minister of Northern Ireland corresponded with the Home Office, while the RUC dealt directly with the Metropolitan Police Special Branch and to a limited and highly secret extent informally with the Garda in Dublin and along the border. This meant that London had only very limited and somewhat partial official sources of information on affairs in Northern Ireland. By 1969 it was becoming clear that the hegemonic Unionist government in Belfast was part of the higher political problem that was already destabilizing the province and therefore not always a reliable rapporteur on events and issues. The chief of the General Staff reported, after a visit to Belfast, that the RUC was understrength and poorly led. The Special Branch in particular was "badly organized and run, with the result that speculation and guesswork largely replace intelligence." Furthermore, "the RUC is jealous of its independence; the Inspector General objects to what he calls 'interference from Ministers,' with the result that there is no mutual confidence or trust." Two months later, the director-general of MI5 cautioned the JIC about "the danger of friction" if the RUC and the Stormont administration felt that they were being pushed around. His warning that the police must be coaxed, not coerced, into sharing intelligence was to become a security policy mantra for at least the following decade.[25]

London therefore had some warning not only that trouble might escalate but also that the Belfast authorities were ill-equipped to contain it. But it was not until after sustained intercommunal violence erupted that London secured dispassionate political intelligence through the dispatch to Belfast in September of Sir Oliver Wright, soon to be joined by a deputy, Frank Steele of MI6. Wright, recently returned from a posting as ambassador in Denmark, recounted in a 1996 interview how he received a telephone call from the Foreign Office: "He said: 'What are you doing?' And I said: 'I'm up a ladder with a bucket of Flash'"—he was cleaning up after tenants had vacated his London home. Wright was summoned to a meeting with home secretary James Callaghan: "Mr Callaghan was surrounded by a group of officials from Permanent Under Secretary downwards and we sat in total silence for what seemed a very long time. Point number one was that the officials had no idea at all what to do."[26]

As "UK [United Kingdom] Representative" in Northern Ireland, Wright filled the political intelligence vacuum very effectively, quickly coming to grips with the intricacies of the situation and providing London with a clear view of the substantive issues in the province. "In my time it was still a civil rights movement," he recalled, and his main task was to draw up a list of legitimate minority grievances that should successively be addressed through legislation. Wright blamed the subsequent spiral of violence on two factors. The first was the emergence of PIRA and its initiation of a sustained bombing campaign in the course of 1970. The second, which happened almost simultaneously, was that "the Conservative Party came to power [in Britain]. Whereas [home secretary] Mr Callaghan came from a slightly Celtic background and had a sort of empathy for the Northern Ireland problem . . . I'm afraid [home secretary] Mr Maudling did not. He was a strictly 'south of Watford' man and couldn't begin to understand what these people were up to. . . . The combination of the [P]IRA and the change of government here led to a rapid deterioration in the whole situation which became an armed struggle."[27]

When civic unrest in Northern Ireland became significant in the fall of 1968, the central machinery of intelligence assessment was very slow to respond. Mired in a Cold War mindset and struggling to adapt to reforms to the assessment system introduced following the Soviet invasion of Czechoslovakia, the JIC barely noticed the emerging problem on its doorstep. In the view of Brian Stewart, secretary to the JIC from the fall of 1968 until January 1972, the response of the intelligence and security agencies was characterized by "extraordinary ignorance" and inertia, coupled with vague hopes that the problem might go away of its own accord. Some steps were taken shortly after Stewart's appointment as political conditions in Northern Ireland deteriorated. An Ulster Working Group was created early in 1969 under Stewart's chairmanship and met about a dozen times before the JIC decided, in October, that it be succeeded by a Current Intelligence Group on Northern Ireland. Despite objections from the Home Office and MI5, it was agreed that the RUC should have direct representation. The head of RUC Special Branch became a regular attender. This gave the JIC assessment staff direct, unfiltered access to police thinking on the crisis. Stewart, who had gained considerable experience of the travails of civil/military counterterrorism cooperation during the Malayan Emergency, took a proactive interest in intelligence arrangements in Northern Ireland. He believed that the key was effective liaison between the police and army at the local level. This proved impossible to achieve.[28]

In the spring of 1969, some steps were taken to improve matters on the security side. An MI5 officer and a military intelligence liaison officer were sent to Belfast, though they had to tread warily for fear of upsetting RUC susceptibilities. A director of intelligence was also appointed, based at army headquarters in Lisburn. This innovation did not result in the anticipated immediate improvement in reportage and analysis of events, but by the end of September two regular series of reports on Northern Ireland were reaching Whitehall. These were the director's summary, essentially a list of incidents, and the Home Office's Northern Ireland Papers. At some point what Sir Burke Trend termed an "Intelligence Committee" was established in Belfast to provide immediate information and analysis to the RUC and the army. MI6's Frank Steele did the groundwork that established a long-standing covert channel of communication with PIRA—the Link.[29]

In January 1972 Stewart visited Northern Ireland just before he stood down as JIC secretary and submitted a valedictory report. Security force morale was now high, and coordination had improved, it said, but "all action has to be achieved by persuasion rather than by direct intervention" so "the rate of progress in some fields remains regrettably slow." Trend, who always encouraged Stewart's activist approach to his role as JIC secretary, commended the report to Prime Minister Edward Heath as coming from someone who "has been one of the sharpest critics of intelligence arrangements in Northern Ireland in the past." According to Trend, Heath found the report "very interesting and asked that the points raised be followed up."[30] Stewart's direct involvement with Northern Ireland ended when he left the Cabinet Office. In 1979 his friend and former MI6 chief Maurice Oldfield was appointed to the new post of security coordinator in Northern Ireland. He asked Stewart to give him a paper setting out how police/military cooperation had worked in Malaya. Stewart did this, although he felt that circumstances in Northern Ireland were so different as to make direct comparisons impossible. Oldfield spent a week studying the issues hampering interagency cooperation in Belfast and wrote in a memorandum: "I always knew that Northern Ireland had many religions but I never realized that it could give rise to so much theology—and a good deal of it pretty dogmatic. I shall try to produce a framework of practical measures." After ten years of attempting to get the police and military to work together in counterterrorist operations in Northern Ireland, not all that much had changed.[31]

Talking to Terrorists: The Link and Its Uses, 1974–93

In July 1972 the government of Edward Heath took an astonishing initiative in response to a PIRA cease-fire, bringing over a group of PIRA leaders for face-to-face discussions in London with Secretary of State for Northern Ireland William Whitelaw and a number of officials, including MI6's Frank Steele. The Irish government was not consulted or informed. We know nothing of the intelligence background to this exercise, which produced nothing, affirmed PIRA's estimate of itself as the only party to the Northern Ireland conflict other than Britain that really mattered, and strengthened it in its belief that escalation of its armed campaign would soon force the British government to come to terms.[32]

The Labour government of Harold Wilson that came to power in March 1974 had no appetite for the Northern Ireland issue. While in opposition in March 1972, Wilson had visited Dublin for secret talks with PIRA leaders, accompanied by Merlyn Rees. When he returned to power, he appointed Rees as secretary of state for Northern Ireland. Rees by then privately favored British withdrawal. The attractiveness of what Wilson's special adviser Bernard Donoghue called "the unmentionable" policy option within Wilson's inner circle of advisers grew as the Ulster Workers' Council strike in May 1974 succeeded in destroying the power-sharing "Sunningdale" Northern Ireland Executive. Just a month previously, a Colonel Mears had assured the prime minister that although "the mood amongst Protestant extremists was bitter . . . there was general acceptance of power-sharing amongst the Protestant population," one of the more unfortunate instances of poor intelligence analysis that Northern Ireland produced.[33] For about a year thereafter, unilateral withdrawal appears to have been the prime minister's personal preference. On 30 May he wrote to his principal private secretary, Robert Armstrong: "I am addressing this minute to you only, and it is for you to advise on who else should see it." Wilson went on to discuss British withdrawal: "What I would envisage" was that once withdrawal was decided on, "we should proceed to prepare a plan for Dominion status for Northern Ireland." Reflecting on the prime minister's ideas in 2012, Armstrong observed that "it was not always easy to fathom what he thought strategically as opposed to tactically. . . . For what it is worth, I advised Harold Wilson strongly against the idea."[34]

Shortly after PIRA announced a cease-fire in February 1975, British ambassador Sir Arthur Galsworthy had a difficult meeting in Dublin with Foreign Minister Garret FitzGerald and Irish officials. The Irish were "suspicious" of the British explanation that there had been no direct negotiations with PIRA but merely contact through intermediaries to "provide . . . detailed explanations of HMG's position" and to put in place arrangements to manage the cease-fire effectively. Galsworthy also gave Taoiseach Liam Cosgrave assurances on the same lines.[35] These were lies. The Link was used for a sustained covert dialogue between the British government and the Provisionals not simply about the modalities of a cease-fire but also about the circumstances in which Britain would withdraw from Northern Ireland. This was relayed by republican sources to the media at the time. In February 1975 the German news magazine *Der Spiegel* actually named the two British officials then involved in the Link; one, MI6's Michael Oatley, has spoken publicly of his role in recent years.[36] PIRA Army Council notes of the discussions that led to and maintained the 1975 cease-fire are now available in the papers of Brendan Duddy, the Derry businessman involved in the Link. If they are an honest record, they show that PIRA was absolutely persuaded that the British government wished to withdraw from Northern Ireland but needed republican help to do so. One note reads: "A firm (public) understanding is totally and absolutely out of the question. This would lead to a Congo-type situation which both Brits and RM [Republican Movement] wish to avoid. . . . If on the other hand RM helps HMG to create circumstances out of which the structures of disengagement can naturally grow, the pace quickens immensely once the ground is laid. The only way to develop is to get the ground work right. HMG cannot say that they are leaving Ireland because the reaction will prevent that happening. They cannot make a stark, definitive statement."[37]

On other occasions, the British side asked: "How do you think industry should be re-sited? Do you see a role for foreign investment?" It also probed PIRA's attitude to the European Economic Community and promised a paper that would "show how the tie-up between Britain and NI is being unraveled." The Irish government was mentioned only in passing almost as an irritant that could be ignored. While parallel conversations were held with loyalist paramilitaries, these appear to have been of rather less substance.[38]

Some authors have argued that PIRA may have been misled about British intentions, deliberately or otherwise, by its MI6 contacts. But it seems likely that Harold Wilson was personally set on a policy of withdrawal, even if some colleagues and most officials thought this would be a disastrous approach. (Bernard Donoghue's published diaries are particularly useful on this.) The available British records do not disclose what instructions were given to the MI6 officers involved or what they reported back to London. After the breakdown of the 1975 cease-fire, some republicans became very critical of what they portrayed as the gullibility of their political leader, Ruairí Ó Brádaigh, in believing MI6 assurances that the British government had really contemplated withdrawal. Yet the two men who eventually wrested control of the Provisional movement away from him, Gerry Adams and Martin McGuinness, evidently had no qualms about using the Link for their own crucial exchanges with the British government in the early 1990s.[39]

British use of the Link to deal directly with the Provisionals again became an issue in 1993, during the Anglo-Irish negotiations that culminated in the "Downing Street Declaration." As the British official Jonathan Powell recalled, the British government had lied to the Irish about its covert dealings with the Provisionals. When this became clear, Taoiseach Albert Reynolds subjected Prime Minister John Major to a furious tirade at a bilateral meeting in Dublin. Major famously snapped his pencil but held his temper, and eventually an accommodation was reached.[40]

Dermot Nally, at the center of Anglo-Irish dealings on Northern Ireland for twenty years, explained Irish antagonism toward the British predilection for periodic secret dealings with PIRA. He maintained that the British never grasped the consistent Irish position that PIRA posed a far greater existential threat to the Irish state than to the United Kingdom and that for as long as PIRA denied the legitimacy of the Irish state and conspired against it, direct negotiations between PIRA and London behind Dublin's back would be disastrous.[41] Much the same issues arise in contemporary Afghanistan, where the government in Kabul is understandably apprehensive that the Western powers may be willing to sacrifice its vital interests in order to buy off the Taliban.

Documenting the Dublin Dimension

The Irish security forces played a crucial role in the two states' struggles against various terrorist organizations from the start. As well as the republican menace, there was a substantial cross-border threat from loyalist terrorism. These factors provided an incentive for quiet cooperation even at times when the British and Irish governments disagreed profoundly on higher political issues. Thus the ambassador-designate to Washington, Sir Nicholas Henderson, was much surprised, when undertaking a familiarization tour in Northern Ireland prior to leaving for the United States in 1979, to find that the RUC commander in Derry was in regular touch with his Garda opposite number across the border in Donegal. His Whitehall briefing had apparently led him to expect otherwise.[42]

Liaison with British security forces and agencies, a particularly delicate aspect of management of the conflict, was often obscured—to Dublin's great relief—by the more public and contentious issue of Anglo-Irish cooperation on law enforcement and in particular the lengthy saga of British efforts to secure the extradition of terrorist suspects to the United Kingdom. Contemporary scholars have given little consideration to the modalities, practicalities, and limitations of Anglo-Irish security force cooperation, other than some analysis of the frequent and visible diplomatic tensions that arose between the two states on matters such as extradition and cross-border terrorism, particularly during Mrs. Thatcher's premiership. Dermot Nally, described by his British Cabinet Office analogues Sir Robert Armstrong and Sir Robert Wade-Gery as a man of "remarkable" capacity, believed that from 1979 Mrs. Thatcher was always "90%" preoccupied with security, whereas successive Irish governments maintained that satisfactory security would ultimately be a result, not the cause, of some kind of intercommunal settlement in Northern Ireland.[43]

Researching security aspects of the early years of the Northern Ireland crisis in Irish archives is challenging. The records of the Department of the Taoiseach—the Irish equivalent of the Cabinet Office—from 1969 on contain almost no high-level security material such as police or military threat assessments, nor papers disclosing the substance of North-South or Anglo-Irish security cooperation. The relevant army and Garda records are almost all closed to research. Such records as have been released very often consist only of a file cover and newspaper cuttings.[44] A certain amount of material about the modalities of police-to-police dealings in border areas has emerged since 2011 through the work of the Smithwick Tribunal, established to investigate allegations of Garda collusion in the murder of two senior RUC officers in 1989.[45] The evidence given tends strongly to support the view that before and throughout the conflict, the RUC and Garda managed cooperation as much as possible on a local and highly informal basis, without reference to higher authority. As one Irish official put it in the 1950s, "the more informal it was and the less that was known about it the better."[46] This is also the impression I gained from a brief perusal of still-closed Irish records on Anglo-Irish security liaison in the first decade of the conflict. It is clear that, whatever their bilateral tensions, neither police force wanted their respective bureaucratic and ministerial masters to inquire or intrude into such matters other than at the most general level. Such attitudes had prevailed in both police forces for decades before 1969.[47]

Documentary traces of such Anglo-Irish and North-South security and police links are, consequently, rare. Patrick MacEntee's 2007 commission of inquiry on the state's original investigation of the Dublin and Monaghan bombings of May 1974 offers a striking picture of the grossly overstretched Garda security section, C3.[48] Among its difficulties was an inability to manage its own records effectively: In 1970, 55 new files were opened; in 1971, 89; in 1972, 1,595; and in 1973, 1,575. Many of these records had not survived or proved to consist only of file covers. By contrast, MacEntee found army intelligence records management to be good.[49] But in both organizations it seems highly likely that much of the most sensitive material was never committed to paper: MacEntee was informed by the Department of Justice in 2006 that in the 1970s it was probable that Garda "briefings on security matters . . . would have been done orally. . . . It may well have been the case that details of these briefings would not be recorded in the Department." This was also "the present practice, oral briefings are sometimes preferred where the purpose is to provide the Minister with information of a highly sensitive nature and where it is considered inappropriate . . . to present a written brief or to maintain an account of the information supplied."[50] A similar picture emerges from this writer's interviews with a range of former political figures. Four attorneys general who served at various times from the early 1980s described receiving only oral briefings by senior Garda officers. Garret FitzGerald, foreign minister from 1973 to 1977 and taoiseach from 1981 to 1982 and from November 1982 to 1987, recalled mainly oral briefings on security issues. Professor Jim Dooge, minister for foreign affairs from 1981 to 1982, described impressive oral briefings from Garda officers on terrorist operations and intentions that made him reflect on the risks that must have been taken by people to secure such material. John Bruton, taoiseach from 1994 to 1997, was unavailable for an arranged interview but wrote that he had "the highest regard" for the army intelligence briefings he received periodically on security issues. One Irish army director of intelligence said that he deliberately never brought so much as a scrap of paper when briefing the minister for defense in the late 1980s and early 1990s, for fear that he might be asked to hand it over.[51]

Dermot Nally was firmly of the view that security and liaison matters were the business of the functional Irish police and army agencies and that the less political involvement there was, the better. He deliberately left it to one of his deputies and to the Departments of Justice and Defence to handle policy issues in that area: The extensive political intelligence on which he and other Irish policymakers relied was gathered through officials of the Department of Foreign Affairs, the "travelers," who developed extensive contacts with all shades of opinion, including loyalist paramilitarism, from 1970 onward. Nally never so much as had a meeting with the Garda commissioner even when security cooperation was at the top of Mrs. Thatcher's Anglo-Irish agenda in the early 1980s. He described how, after one or two quite detailed intelligence briefings for the taoiseach came across his desk, he asked to be removed from the circulation list. Nally was also critical of what he regarded as the British bureaucratic disease of committing highly sensitive matters to paper in the first place, stamping a document "top secret" or "UK eyes only" and then copying it across a myriad of Whitehall departments each crammed with photocopiers and junior staff without adequate security clearance.[52] (For their part, a British assessment of security in Irish government departments and the security forces in 1976 rated "the state of security in the Republic as 'moderate to poor' by British standards, except in the case of the Special Detective Unit and the Departments of Foreign Affairs and Justice, where it is reasonably good.")[53]

In the 1970s and 1980s Britain was inclined to complain of Irish security deficiencies, both through anonymous media briefings and occasionally at the intergovernmental level. Even when action was agreed at the political level, the American embassy in London reported in March 1974 that the "practical" results were few, and a month later the army commander in Northern Ireland told Prime Minister Wilson that while "there were regular meetings with the Irish army . . . he had to face facts, and the Irish armed forces were not able to do much."[54] On the other hand, after some loyalist bombings of hotels in the Republic in 1976, apparently intended to discourage foreign tourism and thereby to damage the Irish economy, the American ambassador in Dublin reported the somewhat more fatalistic, and perhaps realistic, view of the Irish security forces. No matter what steps the British authorities might take in Northern Ireland to disrupt loyalist bomb plots against the Republic of Ireland, the reality was that the "border is like a sieve and complete control is impossible."[55]

MI5 and Irish army intelligence had worked closely on counterespionage issues during the Second World War, and relations remained good in subsequent decades irrespective of changes of government in Dublin.[56] In MI5 the connection was maintained by Guy Liddell until his retirement in 1953 (in 1951 he recorded warnings about IRA plans for attacks on Royal Air Force (RAF) bases in Northern Ireland from "Liam" [Archer, the Irish army chief of staff] and Dan [Bryan, the Irish army director of intelligence]. The Irish clearly had a good source which they were anxious to safeguard." Dick White took over Irish liaison in 1953 and was succeeded in 1956 by Brig. Bill Magan, himself an Irishman from County Westmeath, who managed Irish liaison until his retirement in 1968: It amounted to little more than "a good lunch" once or twice a year. The liaison functioned satisfactorily in respect of Cold War security and espionage issues but seldom as regards the republican movement, although there must have been some crossover in the 1960s as Marxist influence grew within the IRA.[57] Despite the involvement of a maverick junior Irish army officer in the "arms crisis" of 1970—a scandal that has often been construed, incorrectly, as demonstrating a "twin-track" Irish approach to the growing Northern Ireland crisis as distinct from showing how poorly organized and weakly led the army was at the time—the Irish army intelligence directorate deepened its links with MI5 in the early years of the crisis.[58] In 1975 Secretary of State for Northern Ireland Merlyn Rees noted that the two armies "do in a very cloak and dagger way talk together" in London but "not Northern Ireland army to army" and recorded the optimistic view of the Irish army's director of intelligence that "PIRA are in their death throes." By 1976 Irish army intelligence had "secure telex links with London." Some Irish officers also took courses at the Intelligence Corps training establishment at Ashford.[59]

In the specialized matter of bomb disposal, the Irish army had long-established training and technical links with their British military counterparts in the Royal Observer Corps and Royal Electrical and Mechanical Engineers. A former Irish army director of ordnance recently described how such links were quietly developed and maintained irrespective of the political temperature through personal visits and technical dialogue, unsupervised by higher military or political authorities, dealing with both republican and loyalist bomb-making and deployment techniques and practices. There was a great deal of operational cooperation in border areas, where bombs were sometimes laid in Northern Ireland to be detonated by command wires or signals from the Republic. Such collaborations were largely undocumented, though the 1985 Anglo-Irish Agreement specifically permitted British and Irish personnel to cross the border where necessary for bomb disposal operations.[60]

Recalled from retirement to investigate allegations by a disgraced Garda about supposed Irish intelligence failures around the time of the Omagh bombing in 1998, Dermot Nally was struck by the remarkable leeway accorded to individual Garda officers working against terrorist organizations, a custom that on balance he thought justified because it protected informants, although it could also lead to abuses. His investigation threw some light on the workings of RUC/Garda cooperation, which by the late 1990s was held by both forces to be extremely close and effective: The senior Garda handling liaison testified that on occasion he would be in direct communication with his RUC opposite number "up to ten or twelve times a day," quite apart from a myriad of local bilateral exchanges. An RUC officer confirmed this general picture.[61]

Historians may have to content themselves with such crumbs of information and recollection. It appears highly unlikely that substantive Irish police or military records on the management of intelligence sharing with the RUC, MI5, and the British army will ever emerge. In any case, we have already seen that as a matter of policy a great deal of business was done by word of mouth and through personal contacts. An Irish official centrally involved in the Northern Ireland peace process recently characterized the Department of Justice as the "greenest" arm of Irish government because it committed so little to paper. Consequently Irish security records from the 1960s and 1970s are unlikely to be much help. Thus, even if relevant British records do emerge, it is unlikely that it will be possible to identify material or analysis originating from the Irish security forces.[62] From all of this it should be clear that the history of North-South and of Dublin-London security liaison before and during the Troubles will have to be written largely from British records, problems of balance notwithstanding, perpetuating a trend in scholarly writing where what might be termed the "Dublin dimension" of counterterrorism operations is simply ignored.[63]

The Intelligence and Security "Special Relationship" and the Onset of the Northern Ireland Conflict

Irish America had been the principal external source of support for Irish republicanism throughout the twentieth century, before and after the Anglo-Irish Treaty of December 1921, which saw the granting of independence to the southern part of Ireland. Because Northern Ireland remained part of the United Kingdom, many Irish Americans were sympathetic to the Irish grievance about partition.

Irish republicanism in the United States had a venerable troublemaking pedigree. The IRA's American supporters came under considerable scrutiny during the Second World War because of the IRA's entanglement with Germany, a relationship that, as in 1914, had been initiated by the Irish American secret society Clan na Gael with the German embassy in Washington. Federal Bureau of Investigation (FBI) records show that long-standing links with the British police and MI5, managed through the FBI's "legal attaché" offices in the US embassy in London, included fairly frequent low-level exchanges on matters relating to Irish republicanism. Material traced from the 1950s and 1960s consists mainly of reports on the identities and movements of suspect individuals with Irish links. For example, in 1964 the London office told headquarters that "London [i.e., the British authorities] would like to commend those responsible for these investigations [into IRA suspects in the United States] and to express appreciation for the work done." The FBI's London office also liaised with the Garda on IRA matters, while its legal attaché in Ottawa occasionally handled exchanges with Canadian authorities on Irish individuals and republican organizations active in Canada.[64]

During the IRA's desultory Border Campaign of 1956–62, the issue of the illegal export of arms from America by IRA supporters was investigated and discussed by federal agencies, although no prosecutions followed. In the mid-1960s, American agencies observed the leftward ideological shift of the republican movement in Ireland, at least as espoused by the Dublin leadership in speeches and publications. In 1963 the FBI took note of a visit by the IRA's chief of staff, Cathal Goulding, by then on the way to becoming a convinced Marxist. When in America, he downplayed this element of his thinking. It was just as well, because the IRA's American support base was rabidly anticommunist. A Clan na Gael ballad of 1964 complaining of federal surveillance reflected this:

> They are following the Fenians,
> While Commies wander free.
> They're harassing conscientious men,
> While England plies the sea.
> And ships her goods to Castro,
> Who sits right at our door.
> We asked Lord Hume [sic] to end the trade,
> He smirks, and sends them more.[65]

Central Intelligence Agency (CIA) records indicate that that agency did not analyze the IRA through a Cold War prism. In an interview in 1998, Dr. Cleveland Cram, a former head of the CIA's London station who also handled liaison with Irish army intelligence for almost a decade in the 1950s and 1960s, offered the view that the CIA always regarded the IRA as the FBI's business. This was a disappointment for their Irish army contacts, who could get no worthwhile information on the IRA's external links from their ultrasecretive rivals in the Garda security section and hoped that the CIA could help.[66] Marxist some of the IRA leaders may have been by 1969, but no one in the American intelligence community saw this as having any significant bearing on the Northern Ireland issue.

The papers of Richard Helms, the career intelligence officer who became director of the CIA in 1967, testify to the very close links between British intelligence and the CIA in the era when the Troubles broke out. Helms's papers include many warm personal letters from senior British intelligence figures such as Dick White, Maurice Oldfield, and John Bruce Lockhart. In 1965 Roger Hollis, the recently retired head of MI5, wrote of "the close relationship between our two Services," while in 1968 JIC chairman Sir Edward Peck looked forward "to a continuation of the close ties between the Agency and ourselves." In 1971 Sir Burke Trend wrote to "Dear Dick" to applaud a public lecture he had given defending the work of intelligence services: "I suppose it would be tempting providence to say that little by little the intelligence community seems to be being accepted as both 'respectable' and worthwhile. . . . In so far [*sic*] as this isn't an illusion, much of the credit must go to you and to people like yourself who are prepared to defend it with such vigour and conviction." In the same year Helms congratulated "Dear Jack"—Sir John Rennie, the head of MI6—on the number of MI6 officers included in the New Year's Honours List: "It was particularly gratifying to see Brian Stewart honored. We enjoyed having him with us for a few days in December, and I hope you will pass along my congratulations to him and to other officers similarly recognized." Stewart was especially valued in Washington for his knowledge of China and the Far East— during the 1960s he had served in Beijing and Shanghai, and from 1967 to 1968 he was Britain's sole representative in Hanoi, making do without staff or secure communications. During short trips out and upon his withdrawal, Stewart spent a good deal of time giving the Americans his views on Vietnamese morale and political strategy. But in his dealings with the Americans, Northern Ireland was never on the agenda. It was a strictly domestic question into which the United States intelligence community had no wish to pry.[67]

Although it is outside the time frame of this discussion, we should note the centrality of intelligence liaison in Anglo-American relations. Thus in the late 1970s, the British ambassador Peter Jay, despite his unusual background as a journalist and commentator, cultivated close links with American intelligence officers. At 7 a.m. most mornings he played tennis with Adm. Stansfield Turner, President Jimmy Carter's selection as a reforming director of the CIA, and he sometimes played with Bill Webster, then the FBI director: "The CIA was a most important relationship."[68] By 1981 the Irish embassy had gotten in on the act. CIA director William Casey, an Irish American, was a dinner guest of the exceptionally energetic ambassador, Sean Donlon, and of leading Irish business-man Tony O'Reilly.[69]

Available CIA records reflect the fact that the Northern Ireland crisis was seen primarily as a bitter conflict of religious and political identities and loyalties, not as a phenomenon attributable to wider geopolitical tensions or an issue into which the United States should seek to interpose itself. PIRA's appearance and rise to dominance on the republican side was seen as evidence of the weakness and internationalist ideological fixations of the Marxist-dominated Dublin IRA leadership. As the decade progressed, PIRA's burgeoning Middle Eastern and Eastern European links and its contact with terrorist organizations across the world were interpreted as evidence of opportunism and pragmatism, not of Cold War geopolitics. The marginalization of the old-guard Marxist leadership of the pre-split IRA, who as the "Official IRA" continued to throw revolutionary shapes and intermittently to beseech Moscow for money, weapons, and support, was probably significant in framing the CIA's assessment of PIRA as a primarily nationalist movement that had many foreign friends, from Libya to Cuba, but no foreign controllers.

There are, nevertheless, traces of growing linkages from the mid-1970s in official American minds between the IRA and the problem of terrorism internationally. For example, in 1976 the American consulate in Belfast forwarded a telegram "indicating the link" between Provisional Sinn Féin and the Palestine Liberation Organization. Yet there is little evidence to suggest that, in seeking help in combating the international machinations of republican terrorism, Britain sought to tar PIRA with a Cold War brush. On the contrary, the available British assessments of PIRA's fairly extensive international links in the 1970s with Middle Eastern and European terrorist groups was that these were overwhelmingly functional and pragmatic (in contrast to the small breakaway Irish National Liberation Army [INLA], a self-consciously leftist revolutionary group). A 1982 CIA report on terrorism noted the INLA's links with the Rote Armee Fraktion (Red Army Faction, or RAF) and other German terrorist groups, pointing to evidence of cooperation in training and in operations against British targets in Germany. They also quoted "the Dublin police" as reporting that in March 1982 "six Germans—all of them women—tried to establish contact with Irish terrorist organizations." The INLA's reported aim, "according to its own pronouncements," was to continue the struggle "until an authoritarian Irish state modeled after socialist Cuba has been set up—Ireland, a new Cuba in the Irish Sea." But PIRA continued to be assessed in Washington as primarily an organization defined by its hostility to British rule in Northern Ireland.[70]

The other side of the coin of polite American official disinterest in the substance of the Troubles in their first years was a certain institutional inertia on issues where the British government did want firm action by federal authorities: Irish republican arms purchasing and fund-raising. From 1969 onward, Britain sought to interest American security and law enforcement agencies in these matters. Here considerable difficulties arose.[71] It seems probable that, just as at the diplomatic level, the challenge was to stimulate vigorous action by a range of American agencies, federal and local, without encouraging any wider engagement with the substance of the Northern Ireland issue.

In reality, in 1969 there was no danger that the Americans would offer to lend a political hand, let alone to play the role of honest broker that became so important in the vastly different circumstances of the 1990s. When Taoiseach Jack Lynch threw out a hopeful hint that he would welcome an invitation to the White House in the fall of 1969, the National Security Council observed that "it would be best to delay it at least until the problems in Belfast were a bit closer to resolution than they now appear." National Security Adviser Henry Kissinger concurred: "The unfortunate situation in Northern Ireland is a complicating factor." The Richard Nixon administration had no intention of being drawn into that mess, although one National Security Council staffer did prepare an options paper stating that "if the situation in Ulster so worsens that we believe we should act, then the best course might be to go for outright mediation."[72]

FBI records do show, however, that in May 1969 regional offices were directed to develop sources that would help to determine if efforts were being made to involve American citizens in the Northern Ireland issue. That fall visits by a number of prominent Northern Irish civil rights activists including Bernadette Devlin were monitored, while the Justice Department requested an investigation of one freelance republican who mounted a series of eccentric protests as the steam locomotive *Flying Scotsman* toured American cities to promote British exports. In the next few years more serious inquiries were mounted following the discovery in Britain and Ireland of weapons smuggled from the United States, but such efforts often appeared somewhat halfhearted and became mired in jurisdictional disputes. For example, in November 1973 the FBI's New York office, which by default had acquired a lead role in monitoring Irish republican activities in America, said that it would "endeavor to develop quality informants" on PIRA fund-raising and "the methods used to funnel this money into Northern Ireland" but warned that "there is no statutory jurisdiction," as these were "matters under the primary control of the Internal Revenue Service and the Bureau of Alcohol, Firearms and Tobacco [BAFT]." The document acknowledged the need for "closer cooperation and coordination" between agencies, but a year later another FBI office stated that beyond passing on information received by the legal attaché in London from "the Irish federal police" to US Customs, the FBI had no competence to investigate Irish republican activities. After further internal debate, in 1974 FBI headquarters instructed its Chicago office to drop all investigations into possible Irish arms smuggling until Customs had completed its own.[73]

As a result of pressure from both the British and the Irish governments in 1973, the State Department organized an interagency meeting in New York on the problem of Irish republican fund-raising and arms smuggling. Customs, the BAFT, the Treasury, the CIA, and the FBI were among those involved. The official organizing the meeting pointed to an underlying problem: Despite the Nixon administration's general assurances to the British and Irish governments that the US government was doing all that it could to cut off the supply of weapons and money, the reality was that there was a serious practical subtext that inhibited vigorous action: "Before taking specific action, we believe that we should seek White House guidance because of the widespread impression within the Federal agencies concerned that individual Members of Congress would come down hard on civil servants who attempt to curb even illegal IRA fundraising."[74]

There is evidence that as the decade progressed, federal law enforcement agencies grew more willing to investigate illegal PIRA activities in the United States—in April 1976, Customs officials paid a "successful and useful" visit to Dublin to establish "a liaison . . . on illegal activities and persons suspected of illegal activities" such as "arms/money smuggling"—but prosecutions proved problematic well into the 1980s.[75]

From 1970 onward, British diplomats privately bemoaned, and British politicians publicly deplored, the apparent unwillingness of the United States to take firm and consistent action against Irish republican support networks and activities in America. Presidents Nixon and Gerald Ford were briefed periodically on the question, in preparation for meetings with Prime Ministers Wilson and Heath. Yet, as noted above, this was in a sense the natural concomitant of the American government's disinclination to interfere in any way in the internal affairs of its closest Cold War ally. The Anglo-American understanding that Northern Ireland was an exclusively British matter entirely divorced from Cold War geopolitics carried with it a license for successive American administrations to steer clear of the issue altogether. That was to produce much frustration for British diplomats in Washington for the succeeding two decades, as they attempted to encourage the American government to be more active against PIRA's support networks while dissuading it from taking any wider political interest in Northern Ireland. The contradictions in this approach became manifest in the 1980s when the Reagan White House paradoxically became a guarantor of a new departure in conflict management in Northern Ireland. After the Brighton bombing in October 1984 that so nearly killed Mrs. Thatcher, President Reagan sent her a message explicit not only in condolences but in practicalities: "Acts such as the one last night are a growing threat to all democracies. We must work together to thwart this scourge. . . . In the context of our special relationship, I have directed that my experts be available to work with yours to assist in bringing the perpetrators to justice."[76]

The positive in this, from a British perspective, was that America now fully acknowledged the evil of Irish terrorism. Yet with increased support against terrorism came increased interest in the underlying political issues. Just two months later, Reagan's briefing notes for a meeting with Mrs. Thatcher at Camp David stated that while he should assure her that "US policy has not changed" and that he had "no intention of commenting on this complex, historical question," nevertheless there had been widespread unease at Mrs. Thatcher's ill-chosen "Out, out, out" remarks at a press conference where she dismissed various Irish proposals for political development put to her by Taoiseach Garret FitzGerald. Reagan was briefed to say "Know this can be a difficult problem, but hope Anglo-Irish dialogue can be intensified: need at least appearance of progress at next spring's Anglo-Irish summit." Robert Armstrong and Dermot Nally, two officials then at the center of Anglo-Irish dialogue, regarded Reagan's intervention as decisive in persuading Mrs. Thatcher to continue with the radical departure in policy that resulted in the Anglo-Irish Agreement of 1985.[77]

Conclusion

This chapter set out to evaluate the performance of the intelligence assessment system regarding the development of the Northern Ireland Troubles, with particular reference to the emergence and rise to terrorist preeminence of PIRA.

The intelligence assessment machinery can hardly be blamed for the rise of PIRA or for the general course of events. These were the product of deep-rooted historical forces inside and beyond Northern Ireland. It is, however, clear that some key problems identified by London, such as weaknesses in civil-military cooperation in Northern Ireland, were not effectively addressed despite many years of earnest analysis and committee meetings. In their interrogations of internees in 1971, furthermore, the army and police in Northern Ireland were following guidelines established and revised by the JIC, so responsibility for the humiliating international controversy that arose must be laid partly at the JIC's door. Again, although it is difficult to be certain about this in the absence of records, whoever made the decision to mount intelligence operations against the Irish state should have considered the likely political implications for both the British and the Irish governments if such activities were exposed. On the other hand, the Link established by MI6 in Derry ultimately played an important if disputed role in ending the PIRA campaign, although London's propensity to negotiate through back channels with PIRA and to lie about such exchanges also generated a good deal of friction with the Irish government. Finally, in the realm of interstate cooperation against terrorism, London seems not to have realized that the likely cumulative result of constantly pressing Washington to do more against PIRA activities in the United States was to invite increased American interest in the substance of the Northern Ireland issue, thereby aiding in the internationalization of a conflict that British policy had always defined as an internal domestic matter. Knowing one's enemies is not enough: It is also necessary to know what your friends may think and do once you involve them, however obliquely, in your affairs.

Assessments made and analysis prepared in haste in Whitehall during the course of the complex and rapidly changing circumstances of the first years of the Troubles were bound to appear limited, naive, and overoptimistic when inspected by historians forty years later. What is more alarming is that contemporary memory of the Troubles within the British intelligence community, at least as adduced in this chapter, seems scarcely more nuanced or better informed than was London's view of them in September 1969. PIRA was certainly the greatest terrorist threat to confront the British state in the three decades from 1970 to 1998. To that extent, intelligence and security officials may legitimately invoke the struggle against PIRA as a central feature of those years. But to reduce the grand narrative of counterterrorism during the Troubles to Britain's doughty battle against PIRA, entirely forgetting both loyalist terrorism and the

Dublin dimension, is to ignore history and the lessons that could be drawn from it for today's vastly broader, more amorphous, and more perilous struggles against borderless terrorism across the world.

Notes

1. Dame Eliza Manningham-Buller, Reith Lecture on "Terrorism," BBC Radio 4, September 6, 2011.

2. *Violence and Civil Disturbances in Northern Ireland in 1969: Report of Tribunal of Inquiry* [The Scarman Report] (Belfast: Her Majesty's Stationery Office, 1972).

3. "The Loyalists get their money from Canada," journal entry, undated, covering May and early June 1974, Merlyn Rees Papers 1/4, London School of Economics (hereafter cited as LSE).

4. Comment by Humphrey Crum Ewing, a former intelligence officer, Oxford Intelligence Group, February 25, 2008, responding to my paper later published as "'A Poor Thing but Our Own': The Joint Intelligence Committee and Northern Ireland, 1965–72," *Intelligence and National Security* 23, no. 5 (2008): 658–80.

5. Ferghal Cochrane, *Northern Ireland: The Reluctant Peace* (New Haven: Yale University Press, 2013): 126–27.

6. Eunan O'Halpin, *Defending Ireland: The Irish State and Its Enemies since 1922* (Oxford: Oxford University Press, 1999): 265; Anthony Craig, *Crisis of Confidence: Anglo-Irish Relations in the Early Troubles* (Dublin: Irish Academic Press, 2010), 146–48.

7. Steele to Woodfield (Northern Ireland Office), August 9, 1972, National Archives, UK (hereafter cited as TNA), CJ 4/209; journal entry, June 16, 1974, Merlyn Rees Papers 1/4, LSE. See discussion of the 1971 interrogation issue and its longer-term Anglo-Irish and international ramifications in Samantha Newbery, "Intelligence and Controversial British Interrogation Techniques: The Northern Ireland Case, 1971–72," *Irish Studies in International Affairs* 20 (2009): 103–19, and Samantha Newbery, Bob Brecher, Philippe Sands, and Brian Stewart, "Interrogation, Intelligence and the Issue of Human Rights," *Intelligence and National Security* 24, no. 5 (2009): 631–43.

8. *Disturbances in Northern Ireland: Report of the Commission Appointed by the Governor of Northern Ireland* [The Cameron Report] (Belfast: Her Majesty's Stationery Office, 1969).

9. White House Diary, November 15, 1985, Reagan Presidential Library, http://www.reaganfoundation.org/whdpdf/111585.pdf.

10. Craig, *Crisis of Confidence*; O'Halpin, "'A Poor Thing but Our Own.'"

11. These are in the Merlyn Rees Papers at the LSE.

12. Metropolitan Police Special Branch report, November 7, 1954, TNA, KV 2/3358.

13. Matt Treacy, *The IRA 1956–1969: Rethinking the Republic* (Manchester: Manchester University Press, 2011). I supervised the PhD thesis upon which this book is based.

14. Eunan O'Halpin, "The Geopolitics of Republican Diplomacy in the Twentieth Century," in *From Political Violence to Negotiated Settlement: The Winding Path to Peace in Northern Ireland*, ed. Maurice Bric and John Coakley (Dublin: University College Dublin Press, 2004), 127–45.

15. Diary of Anatoly S. Chernyaev, December 16 and 30, 1972, National Security Archive, George Washington University, accessed via http://www2.gwu.edu/~nsarchiv/

NSAEBB/NSAEBB379/1972%20as%20of%20May%2024,%202012%20FINAL.pdf, August 18, 2013. Chernyayev was then deputy head of the International Department of the Central Committee of the Communist Party of the Soviet Union.

16. Journal entry, June 2, 1974, Merlyn Rees Papers 1/4, LSE.

17. "A Slow Look at Ireland," August 1, 1967, Gilchrist Papers, GILC 962/14A, Churchill College Cambridge Archives Centre, UK (hereafter cited as CCCA).

18. Note of discussion between Gilchrist and Sir Denis Greenhill, July 19, 1968, and dispatch on "The IRA and the Republic," July 5, 1968, TNA, FCO 23/192.

19. Minute by Sir Stewart Crawford, March 19, 1973, TNA, FCO 87/209.

20. Material on this episode is in TNA, PREM 13/49.

21. Craig, *Crisis of Confidence*, 146.

22. O'Halpin, "'A Poor Thing but Our Own,'" 678.

23. Simon Prince and Geoffrey Warner, *Belfast and Derry in Revolt: A New History of the Start of the Troubles* (Dublin: Irish Academic Press, 2011), 75.

24. Scarman Report, para. 1.13; *Belfast Telegraph*, September 25, 2011.

25. General Baker to Secretary of State for Defence, May 19, 1969, and minute by "NC" for Sir Philip Allen (Home Office), July 31, 1969, TNA, CJ 3/55.

26. Interview with Sir Oliver Wright, September 18, 1996, British Diplomatic Oral History Project, CCCA.

27. Ibid.

28. Interview with Brian Stewart CMG, Dublin, October 6, 2011. See his *Smashing Terrorism in Malaya: The Vital Contribution of the Police* (Subang Jaya, Malaysia: Pelanduk, 2004).

29. JIC(A)(69), forty-second, forty-fourth, and forty-fifth meetings, October 16, October 30, and November 6, 1969, TNA, CAB 185/9, Trend to Prime Minister, July 9, 1970, TNA, PREM 15/100; Jonathan Powell, *Great Hatred, Little Room: Achieving Peace in Northern Ireland* (London: Vintage, 2008), 68–73; John Bew, Martyn Frampton, and Inigo Gurruchaga, *Talking to Terrorists: Making Peace in Northern Ireland and the Basque Country* (New York: Columbia University Press, 2008), 59.

30. Interview with Brian Stewart CMG, Dublin, October 6, 2011; Trend to Peter Gregson, January 21, covering report by [redacted: Stewart], January 12, and minute to Gregson conveying prime minister's appreciation, January 25, 1972, TNA, PREM 15/998.

31. Memorandum by Oldfield headed "BUT ME NO BUTS," October 16, 1979, TNA, PREM 19/83.

32. Richard English, *Armed Struggle: The History of the IRA* (Oxford: Oxford University Press, 2003), 157–58.

33. Minutes of prime minister's meeting at Army Headquarters, Lisburn, April 18, 1974, TNA, PREM 16/145.

34. Bernard Donoughue, *Downing Street Diary: With Harold Wilson in No. 10* (London: Jonathan Cape, 2005), 127 and 129 (May 22 and 27, 1974); Wilson minute to Armstrong, May 30, 1974, TNA, PREM 16/148; Lord Armstrong to the author, September 15, 2012.

35. British ambassador, Dublin, to London, February 15, 1975, TNA, CJ 4/865.

36. British embassy, Bonn, to Foreign Office, February 17, 1975, TNA, CJ 4/865.

37. Provisional Army Council minutes, February–October 1975, Brendan Duddy Papers, POL 35/64, National University of Ireland Galway (hereafter cited as NUIG).

38. Provisional Army Council minutes, April 2, 17, and 23, and May 7, 1975, NUIG; Brendan Duddy Papers, POL 35/64; Craig, *Crisis of Confidence*, 182–83.

39. Bew et al., *Talking to Terrorists*, 58.

40. Powell, *Great Hatred, Little Room*, 72; interview with Dermot Nally, Dublin, January 13, 2009.

41. Telephone conversation with Dermot Nally, Dublin, October 22, 2009.

42. Interview with Dermot Nally, Dublin, January 13, 2009; Nicholas Henderson, *Mandarin: The Diaries of Nicholas Henderson* (London: Weidenfeld & Nicolson, 1994), 272–73, June 16, 1979.

43. Interview with Lord Armstrong, London, December 3, 2009; Sir Robert Wade-Gery interview, February 13, 2000, British Diplomatic Oral History Project, CCCA; telephone conversation with Dermot Nally, Dublin, October 22, 2009. Nally's *Daily Telegraph* obituary, January 11, 2010, records that Mrs. Thatcher came to trust him.

44. See examples of extreme redaction in 2008/151/55, "Ulster Protestant Militant Groups" and 2008/151/2, "Cathal Goulding," National Archives of Ireland.

45. The final report of the Smithwick Tribunal of Inquiry is available at http://opac.oire achtas.ie/AWData/Library3/smithwickFinal03122013_171046.pdf.

46. Eunan O'Halpin, *Spying on Ireland: British Intelligence and Irish Neutrality during the Second World War* (Oxford: Oxford University Press, 2008), 297–99.

47. See the comments of RUC inspector general Sir Charles Wickham in 1941 and 1944 in O'Halpin, *Spying on Ireland*, 109–10, 164, and 261.

48. *Report of the Commission of Investigation into the Dublin and Monaghan Bombings of 1974* [MacEntee Report] (Dublin, 2007), 73.

49. Ibid., 72.

50. Ibid., 217.

51. Author's interviews with four former attorneys general, 2008–10, who wished to remain unnamed; various conversations with Dr. Garret FitzGerald, 1991–2011 (Dr. Fitz-Gerald frequently attended my weekly Research Seminar in Contemporary Irish History, 2001–11); interview with Professor James Dooge, Dublin, October 4, 2004; note by Mr. Bruton on my letter to him of May 5, 2009, read out to me by his personal assistant in Washington, DC; conversation with the late Col. John "Jack" Duggan, Dublin, October 4, 2007. Some significant Garda briefing documents have, however, come to light: See Craig, *Crisis of Confidence*, 186–7, regarding correspondence from the Garda commissioner on PIRA strategy in 1975.

52. Sir Robert Wade-Gery interview, February 13, 2000, British Diplomatic Oral History Project, CCCA; interview with Lord Armstrong, London, December 3, 2009.

53. British embassy, Dublin, draft assessment of Irish security, October 28, 1976, TNA, FCO 87/536.

54. Ambassador, Dublin, to State Department, October 1, 1974, State Department RG84, National Archives and Records Administration (hereafter NARA), accessed at http:// aad.archives.gov/aad/createpdf?rid = 221521&dt = 2474&dl = 1345, August 8, 2013; minutes of prime minister's meeting at Army Headquarters, Lisburn, April 18, 1974, TNA, PREM 16/145.

55. Ambassador, Dublin, to State Department, July 6, 1976, State Department RG84, NARA, accessed via http://aad.archivesgov/aad/createpdf?rid = 157545&dt = 2082&dl = 1345, August 8, 2013.

56. Eunan O'Halpin, ed., *MI5 and Ireland, 1939–1945: The Official History* (Dublin: Irish Academic Press, 2003); O'Halpin, *Spying on Ireland*, 297–98.

57. Guy Liddell diary, October 4, 1951, TNA, KV 4/273; interviews with Brigadier Magan, Kilkenny, August 22, 2001, and August 29, 2002.

58. Eunan O'Halpin, "'A Greek Authoritarian Phase'? The Irish Army and the Irish Crisis, 1969–70," *Irish Political Studies* 23, no. 4 (2008): 475–90. For a contrasting assessment, see Justin O'Brien, *The Arms Trial* (Dublin: Gill & Macmillan, 2000). The "arms crisis" was a scandal that erupted in the Republic of Ireland in 1970, when Irish police uncovered evidence that two ministers in the Irish government, Charles Haughey (minister of finance) and Neil Blaney (minister for agriculture), together with three accomplices, had conspired to smuggle arms to republicans in Northern Ireland. The taoiseach, Jack Lynch, dismissed Haughey and Blaney from the government. All five men were prosecuted, though the charges against Blaney were later dropped. The remaining four men were tried and acquitted of the charges.

59. Journal entry for October 4, 1975, Merlyn Rees Papers 1/9, LSE; British embassy, Dublin, draft assessment of Irish security, October 28, 1976, TNA, FCO 87/536.

60. Presentation by Col. Joseph O'Sullivan, Research Seminar in Contemporary Irish History, Trinity College Dublin, October 19, 2011.

61. Interview with Dermot Nally, Dublin, January 13, 2009; Report of Group (Nally Report) established by the minister for justice, equality, and law reform to examine matters arising from the "Report Raising Concerns of the Activity of An Garda Síochána Officers during 1998," dated March 22, 2002, prepared by the police ombudsman for Northern Ireland for the minister for foreign affairs, June 2003, available at http://www.justice.ie/en/JELR/NallyReportFinal.pdf/Files/NallyReportFinal.pdf, 13–14.

62. MacEntee report, 217; off-the-record comments on an earlier draft of this chapter, Dublin, July 23, 2013.

63. Thus no consideration is given to the role of Irish government agencies in Bradley W. C. Bamford, "The Role and Effectiveness of Intelligence in Northern Ireland," *Intelligence and National Security* 20, no. 4 (2005): 581–607.

64. Legal Attaché, London, to FBI headquarters, August 21, 1964, FBI records 61–7606, Section 22, and FBI headquarters to Legal Attaché, London, March 26, 1974, FBI records 61–7606, Section 27, NARA.

65. FBI records 60–7606, Section 22, NARA. Alec Douglas Home MP was prime minister from 1963 to 1964.

66. Interview with Dr. Cleveland Cram, Washington, DC, May 13, 1998.

67. Helms to Rennie, January 14, 1969, and Trend to Helms, April 26, 1971, boxes 7/22/398 and 8/14/423, Richard Helms Papers, Georgetown University Library; interview with Brian Stewart CMG, Dublin, October 8, 2011.

68. Peter Jay interview, February 24, 2006, British Diplomatic Oral History Project, CCCA.

69. "DCI [Director of Central Intelligence]'s schedule," March 5 and May 12, 1981, CIA RDPB00443R0011003830205–3 and CIA RDP88B00443R001003830165–8, CREST, NARA.

70. CIA "Worldwide Report: Terrorism," June 28, 1982, CIA RDP82–0085R000500070064–9, CREST, NARA.

71. Legal Attaché, London, to FBI headquarters, August 21, 1964, and FBI headquarters to Legal Attaché, London, March 26, 1974, FBI records 61–7606, Section 22 and Section 27, FBI records 61–7606, NARA.

72. Sonnenfeldt to Kissinger, and Kissinger to Fagan (Dept. of Commerce), November 15 and 29, 1969, and memorandum for General Haig, as requested for the president, July 28, 1972, Country Files Europe box 694, Nixon National Security Council Papers, NARA. These records have since been moved to the Richard M. Nixon Presidential Library.

73. FBI Chicago to headquarters and reply, October 21 and November 22, 1974, and headquarters to Chicago, January 31, 1975, FBI records 61–7606, Section 28, NARA.

74. Folder "IRA MISC 17," November 20, 1973, State Department records, box 3, RG59 150 73 16 Entry 5573, NARA.

75. Ambassador, Dublin, to State Department, April 14, 1976, State Department RG84, NARA, accessed at http://aad.archives.gov/aad/createpdf?rid = 26890&dt = 2082&dl = 1345, August 8, 2013.

76. Reagan to Thatcher, October 12, 1984, NSA Head of State file (box 36), Ronald Reagan Presidential Library, accessed via http://www.margaretthatcher.org/archive/display document.asp?docid = 109351, August 17, 2009.

77. Telephone conversation with Dermot Nally, Dublin, October 22, 2009, and interview with Lord Armstrong, London, December 3, 2009.

Israeli Intelligence Threat Perceptions of Palestinian Terrorist Organizations, 1948–2008

TAMIR LIBEL AND SHLOMO SHPIRO

THROUGHOUT THE SIX DECADES since it gained its independence, the State of Israel has been a target of terrorist activities and violent attacks. Israel's intelligence services have had to devote extensive efforts to containing the terrorist threat, preventing attacks, and providing information for decision makers in support of peace initiatives. Over time, intelligence has become the frontline weapon against terrorism, both by providing immediate warning of impending attacks and by enabling Israel to follow and try to understand social and political changes within the Palestinian population.

Perceptions of the enemy are important not only because they provide the prism through which intelligence assessments are made but also because they are often catalysts for structural changes, intelligence division of labor, and collection-and-analysis priorities. They also affect the interaction between intelligence and decision makers. Changes in the intensity and types of threats may not necessarily be followed by equal changes in perceptions, since perceptions are longer lasting and depend on a set of personal, institutional, and political factors, not only on facts. Perceptions are used to frame facts. Studying intelligence perceptions is crucial for understanding the development of a country's intelligence services, systems, and roles.

This chapter analyzes the perceptions of the Israeli intelligence community toward Palestinian terrorism, how these perceptions have changed over time, and how perceptions have influenced intelligence assessments and structural changes in the intelligence community. The chapter begins by examining the early development of perceptions of terrorism during the period of cross-border terrorist raids in the 1950s. It then goes on to examine perceptions of terrorism and intelligence division of labor between the Six-Day War of June 1967 and the outbreak of the Palestinian First Intifada in December 1987 and the intelligence perceptions of terrorism during the crucial decade of the Oslo peace process and early years of the Second Intifada. The chapter concludes with an analysis of the importance of intelligence perceptions in the Israeli context and how these perceptions have affected counterterrorism capabilities and intelligence support to policy.

The chapter argues that throughout Israel's history, terrorism has been perceived as an existential threat. Alongside the threat of conventional interstate war, it has played a crucial role in the incremental development of Israel's national security strategy. At times, state-supported terrorism has been perceived as little different from the continuation of conventional interstate war by other means. Israel's civilian intelligence services, the Mossad and the Shabak, have seen their principal duty as the prevention of terrorist attacks. As a result, they have developed formidable counterterrorism capabilities and prevented hundreds, possibly thousands, of deadly terrorist attacks. However, by concentrating on the operational aspects of prevention, the intelligence services paid less attention to the political dimensions of Palestinian terrorism. The unclear and often excessive division of responsibility between the various intelligence services persistently damaged their political opportunity analysis and their intelligence support to the peace processes. While the Israeli intelligence services were able to provide good warnings of impending terrorist attacks, they were not as good at monitoring and analyzing Palestinian terrorism as a phenomenon that has reflected changes in Palestinian society.

Throughout this chapter, the term "strategic assessment" is used to denote all-source assessment of the multiple dimensions of a given issue (e.g., political, military, social, economic). In contrast, "operational assessment" is defined as narrower analysis usually confined to the direct security implications of a situation, such as plans or capabilities of a particular terrorist group. While these definitions are somewhat different from the traditional military distinctions among tactical, operational, and strategic issues, they were the ones used by the Israeli intelligence community during most of the period under discussion.[1] This chapter focuses on Palestinian terrorist activities within and on the borders of Israel but docs not examine terrorist threats emanating from outside Israel, such as those presented by the Lebanese Hezbollah organization or from global jihadist terrorist groups.

The methodology adopted for the present research was dictated by the particular limitations of intelligence research in Israel. Intelligence assessments are classified as secret and are almost never published or made available for research, even after the statutory limitation on government documents has expired.[2] Lacking primary assessments, the authors relied on a range of secondary sources, mainly material written by senior intelligence officials who themselves were involved in the assessment process. Among these sources are studies on the structure, evolution, and challenges of the Israeli intelligence community, autobiographies and autobiographical accounts of former intelligence and military officials, and official publications of the Israeli intelligence services and the intelligence veterans' association, which enjoys close cooperation with the community. Perceptions are time-sensitive, and the later recollection of perceptions is inevitably marred by new knowledge and hindsight gained in the time that has passed. Personal interviews with former intelligence officials conducted for the present research proved of little value, since people generally tended to judge their perceptions according to later developments. In addition, much effort was made to collect and analyze media items contemporary to the events discussed. Thus it was possible to reconstruct both an accurate historical account of events and the threat perceptions within the intelligence community. However, the present analysis is focused on the collective perceptions of the intelligence services and not limited to specific assessments or to case studies of intelligence failures. Without access to primary archival sources and to intelligence assessments themselves, which is denied in Israel, such studies are almost impossible.

Israeli Intelligence: Organizations and Responsibilities

The structure of Israel's intelligence community was created in the early 1950s and has changed little in the following six decades. These structures draw their origins from preindependence underground organizations formed in the 1930s and 1940s to defend the Jewish community in Palestine from Arab attacks. Israel's intelligence community comprises three main organizations: an internal security service, the Shabak; a foreign intelligence service, the Mossad; and a military intelligence service, the Military Intelligence Directorate (MID), which is also often also known by its Hebrew acronym "AMAN" and forms an integral part of the Israel Defense Forces (IDF).

Israel's internal security service, the General Security Service, was founded in June 1948. Over the years, the service was commonly known by its Hebrew acronyms Shabak or Shin Bet and more recently as the Israeli Security Agency. Until 1967, the Shabak was mainly tasked with traditional counterespionage activities and with monitoring extreme right- and left-wing political activities inside Israel. Following the Six-Day War and Israel's occupation of the West Bank and Gaza, the Shabak became progressively more occupied with countering Palestinian terrorism, combating Palestinian terrorist groups inside Israel and in the West Bank and the Gaza Strip. The Shabak is traditionally divided into three operational divisions: the Arab Affairs Division, responsible for counterterrorism; the Non-Arab Division, responsible for counterespionage and political subversion; and the Protective Security Division, responsible for dignitary protection and the security of key government facilities.[3]

Israel's foreign intelligence service, the Mossad (the Hebrew abbreviation of "Institute for Intelligence and Special Duties"), was founded in December 1949. Traditionally its role was conducting human intelligence (HUMINT) activities outside Israel. In recent years, the Mossad has concentrated its activities in the fields of global counterterrorism, nuclear weapon proliferation, and threats presented to Israel by Hezbollah and by Iran. The Mossad is traditionally divided into several divisions, including a Collection Division, responsible for human intelligence operations abroad; a Foreign Liaison Division, responsible for the Mossad's extensive cooperation with the intelligence services of other countries; a small Research Division, producing analysis; and a Special Operations Unit, separate from mainstream Mossad, responsible for sabotage and assassinations. Both the Shabak and the Mossad are under the direct authority of the prime minister.

Israel's third intelligence service, perhaps the least known but by far the largest and politically also the most important of the three, is the MID. Unlike the Shabak and the Mossad, the MID is not an independent service but an integral part of the IDF. Its main field of activities is signals intelligence, but it also operates a small HUMINT section running agents in Arab countries bordering Israel. Unit 8200 of the MID is the central collection unit, responsible for communications interception.[4] Other units deal with satellite intelligence, other forms of electronic intelligence gathering, and open-source collection. Its Analysis Branch is the central unit for intelligence analysis, assessment, and prediction. The MID is answerable to the chief of the IDF's General Staff and to the minister of defense.[5]

Israel's national security strategy is based on the assumption that, as a small country both in terms of size and population, Israel will always be at a military numerical disadvantage when attacked by its Arab neighbors. Unable to afford a large permanent army, Israel relies for its defense on a small army of conscripts stationed along its borders, backed by much larger reserve units, and a large air force. The key to stopping a large-scale military attack is a quick and efficient mobilization, arming and bringing to the front combat units made up of civilian reservists. The principal role of Israel's intelligence services, therefore, is to provide early warning of an impending attack, which will provide time for mobilization.[6] Every other intelligence activity is secondary to this key role in ensuring national survival. The legacy of Israel's wars with its Arab neighbors, and especially of the intelligence failure to provide sufficient warning before the October 1973 war, is the constant need to question assumptions and key concepts in intelligence assessments in order to prevent prejudices and institutional bias from tainting the validity of intelligence analysis and recommendations.[7]

Early Perceptions of Terrorism and the "Destiny of Israel"

The State of Israel has been the target of terrorism throughout its six decades of independence. In the early 1950s, small terrorist cells were formed by Egyptian intelligence among Palestinian refugees in the Gaza Strip. The aim of the Egyptian government and high command was to continue the war against Israel, which had ended with the Israeli-Arab armistice of July 1949, by means that would not provoke another all-out war. Young Palestinians, unemployed and bitter, were recruited and paid to carry out terrorist attacks on people and infrastructure targets inside Israel. These volunteers came to be known as fedayeen, from the Arabic for "redeemers," referring to their perceived role as the redeemers of lost *Palestinian* lands. The unfenced and sparsely patrolled border between Israel and its neighboring states provided ample opportunities to enter Israel secretly and ambush civilian vehicles on lonely roads, blow up water pipes, and destroy agricultural and transport facilities. In the years 1951–55, over a thousand Israeli citizens were killed in terrorist attacks and thousands of others were injured.

Intelligence analysis of the fedayeen threat was hampered from the outset by diffused lines of authority between various security and intelligence organizations and by different threat perceptions on both the political and the intelligence levels. Early assessments of the threat of fedayeen terrorism concentrated on the role of Egypt in the operational organization of the attacks and downplayed the Palestinian political aspects of these developments. There were also disagreements over who would be responsible for countering these terrorist attacks: Prime Minister David Ben-Gurion wanted the police to be responsible for what he perceived as criminal activities, while the influential finance minister, Levy Eshkol, argued that this was a military problem and as such should be dealt with by the IDF. The resulting compromise was the establishment, in 1953, of a military-type police force, the Border Guards, which was nominally part of the Israeli national police force but was equipped with military weapons and vehicles.[8] Border Guards units were stationed on Israel's southern and eastern borders but lacked an independent intelligence collection-and-analysis capability. Instead they had to rely on information provided by the MID and by the miniscule civilian police intelligence capability in the region bordering Gaza.

The fedayeen terrorist attacks caused public anxiety in Israel, and their economic cost was high, especially in the destruction of infrastructure targets. The Israeli population felt an increasing sense of insecurity and threat.[9] By 1954, MID assessments of the fedayeen problem began stressing its strategic and political nature. Its analysts perceived fedayeen attacks as a possible vanguard of wider violence that could result in the loss of territory by Israel. IDF units were ordered to open fire on Palestinians crossing the border into Israel. The higher echelons at the MID and the IDF felt that the fedayeen threat could be resolved only through significant political developments.

The pace of fedayeen attacks accelerated in 1955 and the early months of 1956. On April 29, 1956, Lt. Roi Rothberg, a twenty-one-year-old IDF officer serving at a kibbutz on the Gaza border, was ambushed and killed by terrorists while riding his horse. His body was dragged across the border into Egypt and mutilated, and his remains were only returned to Israel through United Nations (UN) mediation.[10] At Rothberg's funeral, the IDF chief of staff, Gen. Moshe Dayan, made a public speech that became perhaps the most memorable eulogy in Israel's history. Generally considered a cold and emotionless person, Dayan passionately said:

> Not from the Arabs in Gaza but from ourselves we shall ask Roi's blood. How did we close our eyes from looking straight at our destiny, from seeing the destiny of our generation in its full cruelty? Did we forget this group of youngsters, sitting in Nachal Oz, carrying on its shoulders the heavy gates of Gaza, gates beyond which are crowded hundreds of thousands of eyes and hands praying for our weakness, so that they can tear us to pieces—did we forget this? We know that, for their hope to destroy us to die, we must be, day and night, armed and ready. . . . We should not back away from seeing the hatred that accompanies and fills the life of hundreds of thousands of Arabs, sitting around us and waiting for the moment they can spill our blood. . . . This is the destiny of our generation, the choice of our lives. Be prepared and armed, strong and tough, for if the sword falls from our fist, our lives will be lost.[11]

In his uncompromising speech, Dayan emphasized two key issues. The first was that political violence, in the form of terrorism, was an existential threat to Israel; the second was that terrorism, based on hatred, was a permanent feature of the Arab-Israeli conflict and would last for generations. Dayan perceived terrorism as a major threat with an infinite lifespan. As such, it required the best efforts of the nation to prevent, or limit, the effects of terrorism.

Dayan's speech shocked the young nation, already accustomed to numerous deadly cross-border terrorist raids. Dayan made clear that, in his opinion, the terrorist threat was permanent and represented the popular will of a majority of Palestinian refugees. The speech had a profound effect on both public and intelligence perceptions of the terrorist threat facing Israel. It affected the thinking and perceptions of generations of Israelis and stood for decades as a fundamental definition of the terrorist threat by one of Israel's most respected generals. In terms of its impact on the formation of Israeli identity, this eulogy was rated by some researchers as one of the most important formative texts in modern Jewish history.[12] In his influential article about the evolution of cognitive militarism in Israel, noted Israeli sociologist Baruch Kimmerling attributed a major significance to Dayan's eulogy. He argued that Dayan's words reflected and symbolized the eternity of the Arab-Israeli conflict and the necessity of collective mobilization in face of such threats.[13]

In the years of the fedayeen terrorist threat, Israel became probably the most mobilized democratic country in the world. The security and intelligence establishments were elevated to a very prominent place in political, economic, and even social decision making, a place they have retained ever since. Military conscription at the age of eighteen was extended to include almost all citizens, both men and women, who had to serve several years in the armed forces. Even after being released from military service, a citizen remained in practice "a soldier on an eleven-month leave" who had to serve a month of reserve duty in the IDF until the age of about forty-five. Not only citizens were mobilized: Defense considerations affected much of the state's construction, infrastructure, and energy policies. Ordinary road bridges had to be built high enough to allow the passage of tanks on their heavy carriers. New settlements were established in strategic positions along the borders. The civilian infrastructure, including roads, hospitals, train lines, fuel depots, and water pipes, was constructed along defense requirements. The IDF mobilization times were calculated in hours, not days or weeks.[14] The entire country was geared toward repelling an enemy attack, whether from a neighboring state or a terrorist organization. The fedayeen threat all but disappeared in the aftermath of the October 1956 Suez War, but Israel's society remained mobilized for decades to come.

Terror Perceptions and Intelligence Analysis after 1967

Between the establishment of the Palestine Liberation Organization (PLO) in 1964 and the Six-Day War of 1967, relatively few terrorist attacks were launched against Israel. The major turning point in the way the Israeli intelligence community dealt with terrorism came with the increased Palestinian terrorist activity following Israel's occupation of the West Bank and Gaza Strip in the Six-Day War. The territories captured by Israel during the war contained over a million and a half Palestinians. Israeli decision makers were concerned about the potential for a new wave of terrorist attacks emanating from refugee camps in Gaza and the West Bank. In response to the new threat, the Shabak was expanded and moved swiftly to recruit and train new personnel, to gain familiarity with the terrain and population, and to recruit new sources and agents.[15] However, Israeli counterterrorist activity in the late 1960s was undermined by the fact that responsibility for collecting and analyzing intelligence on Palestinian organizations and on political developments inside the Occupied Territories was shared by a number of intelligence components, resulting in duplications and redundancy in several areas, especially focusing on military capabilities of terrorist groups, the location of arms caches, and so forth, while other issues received little attention.[16]

Before the 1967 war, the intelligence apparatus responsible for analysis of Palestinian issues was Section 2 of the MID's Analysis Department (later renamed Analysis Branch), which dealt with Jordan. Following the post-1967 increase in Palestinian terrorist activity, the Analysis Department established Section 4 as a unit dedicated to the analysis of "Hostile Terror Activity and the Inter-Arab System," as well as the diplomatic dimensions of the Palestinian national movement's activities. By the mid-1970s, the prevailing perceptions inside Section 4 toward the terrorist threat had undergone a significant change. The section's analysts came to believe that there was a clear distinction between the PLO, which had begun to institutionalize and act as a national movement with clearly defined political aims, and other Palestinian organizations, which focused almost exclusively on terrorism.[17] This analysis could have had major implications for Israeli policy toward the Palestinians but was generally ignored by the government of the day.

Despite these structural changes, the Israeli intelligence community failed to predict the outbreak of the First Intifada in December 1987. On its eve, both the Shabak and the MID had only partial responsibility for intelligence collection and analysis on the Palestinian issue. While the Shabak was responsible for the prevention of terrorism and political subversion, the MID had overall responsibility for the national intelligence estimates on the subject. To make matters even more convoluted, the IDF assigned intelligence officers to the regional brigades in the West Bank, and these reported directly to the commander of IDF Central Command, exacerbating the lack of coordination between so many different intelligence actors. As a result of the Agranat Commission, which investigated the intelligence failure of the 1973 Yom Kippur War, both the Mossad and the Shabak, predominantly collection agencies, developed small analysis units. These units composed intelligence estimates on Palestinian matters, but both organizations lacked the political clout to compete with the MID, and their analysis was given much less attention than the estimates produced by the MID's Section 4.[18]

While most of the intelligence community's analysis units dealt one way or another with Palestinian matters, almost all of this effort focused on terrorism and mainly tactical issues it raised, such as the activities of small terrorist cells in the Gaza Strip or the West Bank, their acquisition of arms or explosives, and their immediate plans for carrying out attacks. In practice, little attention was given to the diplomatic dimensions of Palestinian activities abroad. One exception was the involvement of the MID's Analysis Branch in the Israeli diplomatic struggle surrounding PLO chairman Yasir Arafat's historic speech at the UN

General Assembly in November 1974. The MID is divided into "arenas," or spheres of operation, each covering a specific region or topic. The head of Section 4 suggested establishing a new arena comprising two adjacent units as a way to improve analysis: One would be dedicated to Palestinian diplomatic aspects and the other to terrorism. Such an organizational structure would have enabled a constant integration between collection and analysis of intelligence on both diplomatic activities and terrorism. However, this proposal was rejected, and in 1974–75 Section 4 was dismantled. Instead a new section dedicated to "Palestinian and International Terrorism" was established, reflecting the growing perception that international terrorist organizations that supported Palestinian terrorism, such as the German Baader-Meinhof Group and the Italian Red Brigades, were becoming a significant threat. The new section also included a small team to analyze intelligence on diplomatic and inter-Arab affairs.[19] After Section 4 was dismantled, the integration of analysis on the various dimensions of the Palestinian problem was achieved only at the level of the head of the Analysis Branch, which often resulted in fragmentation or diffusion of efforts.

Almost a decade later, after the 1982 Lebanon War, the idea of a unified Palestinian arena at the MID was revived. In 1985 the MID established a new "Terrorism and Palestinians Arena." But the new arena had to contend with structural problems and internal rivalries, with responsibility for Palestinian issues at times taken from it and rotated between the "Terrorism Arena," which worked mainly on Palestinian organizations outside the Occupied Territories, and the "Central Arena," which focused mainly on Jordan.[20] At that time, the MID Analysis Branch concluded that the military struggle of the PLO had, in practice, failed.[21] Former head of the West Bank Civil Administration and experienced intelligence officer Gadi Zohar argues that the Terrorism Arena predicted in 1985 that by mid-1987 a major change would take place in Palestinian politics and activities—a change unlike anything that had so far occurred inside the Occupied Territories. The heads of the MID and of the Analysis Branch rejected this assessment on several grounds and argued that military intelligence could not deal with, and was not responsible for, studying the Palestinians in the Occupied Territories.[22] Zohar believes that their decision to ignore those warnings reflected a cultural bias on the Palestinian issue. This was reflected in the fact that the Palestinian problem was given a low priority in the Key Intelligence Topics (KIT), the annual document setting out Israel's national intelligence requirements.[23] Developments in the Occupied Territories were not even included in Israel's annual National Intelligence Estimate, traditionally prepared by the MID, until the outbreak of the First Intifada. This was a clear indication of how small a threat the IDF regarded Palestinian terrorism as being.[24] By the late 1980s, Israeli intelligence perceptions of terrorism were split. The civilian intelligence services perceived terrorism as a substantial security problem but restricted mostly to the Occupied Territories and thus containable if enough efforts were devoted to detecting and intercepting individual terrorist cells and groups. Although Israeli public perceptions of the Palestinians continued to reflect Dayan's ideological legacy, the IDF nevertheless regarded terrorism as a low priority.

The Shabak also gave a low priority to Palestinian political issues. The agency maintained that it had only partial responsibility for collecting and analyzing political and social intelligence on the Occupied Territories. The situation began to change when the coordinator of government activities in the Occupied Territories (CGA-OT), Maj. Gen. Rehavia Vardi, protested in 1983 to Minister of Defense Moshe Arens that no intelligence agency had provided him with warning of impending mass disorder and public demonstrations. His protest came after a dramatic increase in the number and scale of disorders and riots in the West Bank. Minister Arens succeeded in convincing Prime Minister Yitzhak Shamir in 1983 to assign the principal responsibility for issuing such warnings to the Shabak, despite the protests of its director.[25]

However, the Shabak interpreted its new responsibilities narrowly, providing only tactical warnings of impending public disorder rather than wider analysis of their political and social significance.[26] The Shabak hardly considered social processes and their influence on Palestinian society.[27] As a result, the main burden of analysis of developments and trends in Palestinian society fell on two government units hardly suited for such analysis: the CGA-OT and the Advisor for Arab Affairs at the Occupied Territories' civilian administration.[28] These two offices, neither of which had been established with any intelligence function in mind, became the de facto agencies for open-source analysis on Palestinian affairs in the crucial period before the outbreak of the First Intifada in December 1987.[29] The surveys these offices prepared and disseminated within the government included political and social studies, sometimes written with the assistance of civilian experts.[30] However, their voices were too weak to carry real political weight with Israel's political decision makers, most of whom were convinced that the Palestinians would be content with slow, incremental economic development and would not resort to large-scale violence in the foreseeable future.

These hopes and wishful thinking changed dramatically in December 1987 as thousands of Palestinians marched and rioted in the streets, breaking down Israel's tight control of the Occupied Territories. The situation was especially critical in the Gaza region, where refugee camps became almost "no-go areas" for Israeli forces. The popular uprising was accompanied by sporadic terrorist attacks, as waves of violence flooded Palestinian towns and villages. Once the Intifada broke out, any warning was too late. The Israeli intelligence community failed at first to understand fully the nature and implications of the First Intifada, but within a few weeks it began to adapt to the new challenge. In January 1988 the head of the MID Analysis Branch, Lt. Gen. Dani Rothschild, told the weekly IDF General Staff forum, and later the government, in plain language that a general solution to the Palestinian violence was not and could not be achieved by military means alone. This assessment, very extraordinary and unpopular at the time, almost cost him his job.[31] Two weeks after the outbreak of the First Intifada, it had already become clear to intelligence analysts and to the Consultants for Arab Affairs that the uprising had not been, as first suspected, stage-managed by the PLO from its headquarters in Tunis but was the spontaneous result of local frustrations, neglect, and oppression.[32]

The escalating Intifada created an urgent need for a clear and logical division of responsibilities within the intelligence community over the Occupied Territories. On January 14, 1988, Israel's intelligence chiefs met at their periodic "Varash" meeting to decide on a division of labor and of responsibilities, a topic they had studiously avoided for years.[33] The meeting included the head of the Shabak, Yaacov Peri; the head of the MID, Gen. Amnon Lipkin-Shahak; and the head of the Mossad, Shabtai Shavit. Their decisions were later formally approved by Minister of Defense Yitzhak Rabin and had profound implications for budgets, manpower, and resource allocations, as well as for the future political roles of the intelligence services. The following decisions were made:

1. The Shabak would have overall responsibility for intelligence assessment on the Palestinians.
2. The Shabak would develop the research-and-analysis capabilities required for strategic intelligence assessments, including political and social issues, as a complementary activity to its operational counterterrorism analysis, carried out daily in the field, of the activities and capabilities of individual terrorist cells and groups.
3. The Shabak would hold twice-daily national intelligence coordination meetings, with the participation of representatives from the Shabak, the Mossad, and the MID, to liaise and coordinate intelligence activities and information.
4. The Shabak would establish a permanent high-level working group including representatives of the Shabak, the Mossad, and the MID. The group's job would be to direct the collection of intelligence and the sharing of operational information on everything related to the Occupied Territories.

As a result of the Varash decision, the Shabak was assigned the overall responsibility for the Occupied Territories. Its research unit was expanded and upgraded.[34] This greatly increased the political importance of the Shabak, which until 1988 had been considered the least politically important of Israel's three intelligence services. Now it moved to lead the group and became the main source of analysis and advice for politicians and generals alike.

Intelligence Perceptions and the Oslo Peace Process

The assessments of Israel's intelligence services concerning the peace process in the period between October 1991 and early 1995 were quite similar. The MID predicted correctly the willingness of all sides to resume the diplomatic process in the aftermath of the 1991 Gulf War (Operation Desert Storm). It also predicted quite accurately the Palestinian, Syrian, and Lebanese attitudes toward the peace process. However, the MID's estimates were affected by the fact that even Israel's decision makers kept much of the negotiations with the Palestinians secret and did not provide the intelligence analysts with critical information on proposals and possible compromises on the table.

In the second half of 1992, the MID developed a research model of the Palestinian "red lines"—those issues on which the Palestinian leadership would not compromise, which proved to be quite accurate. The MID identified the central long-term goal of the Palestinians as an independent state with Jerusalem as its capital. It assumed that the Palestinian leadership would be willing to accept interim agreements in the short term so as to pursue their long-term objective and would postpone reaching agreement on the most divisive issues to a later stage. The MID assessed that for the PLO, negotiations with Israel would be crucial to its survival and that the Palestinians would therefore be prepared to reach some form of agreement even without progress in peace negotiations between Israel and the Arab states.[35]

In spite of early successes in the Oslo process, the Israeli intelligence community failed to adapt appropriately to the new reality of the Palestinian Authority (PA) in the Occupied Territories. This was vividly demonstrated by its failure in 1996 to predict the Palestinians' violent reaction to the opening of the Hasmonean Tunnel, examined later in the chapter. In June 1996, a new government was elected in Israel. It was headed by Benyamin Netanyahu and comprised mainly right-wing and national religious parties. Netanyahu's government was presented with assessments on the state of the peace process with the Palestinians prepared by the MID, the Shabak, and the civilian administration in the Occupied Territories. Their view was that the process was about to collapse. The assessment of all three agencies was that the difficult economic situation in the Occupied Territories, the frustration of the Palestinian supporters of the peace process at the lack of progress it was making, and the growing opposition of Islamic factions would result in violence breaking out. The head of the Shabak, Ami Ayalon, said in October 1996 to the members of the Foreign and Security Affairs Committee of the Israeli Parliament: "I told the political leadership that the [peace] process would collapse and that I wouldn't be able to predict the exact date when it happens. We don't have such a delicate sensor. But we warned that it would happen and that something should be done in advance." At the end of July 1996, the prime minister's counterterrorism advisers conducted several war games to try out possible scenarios. Their conclusion was that two scenarios were the most probable:

1. The Palestinian Authority loses control over "the street." The Islamic opposition becomes the dominant force and provokes the masses to demonstrations and massive disorders. Simultaneously, the armed cells of these organizations conduct attacks within the 1967 borders and against Jewish settlers in the Occupied Territories.
2. There is tacit cooperation between the PA and the opposition forces in support of the Oslo process. Parallel cooperation exists "in the field." The assessment was that the outbreak of violence would not be similar to the First Intifada but worse.[36]

Ayalon told the committee members, without being asked, that at that time neither he nor his staff predicted that events might take a third course: The PA might initiate intentionally a violent conflict with Israel. The Shabak also failed to predict that Palestinian policemen would use their weapons against IDF soldiers, even on joint patrols. He added: "The fact [that we didn't predict] such a development should be analyzed and be clarified for understanding why we were wrong in the assessment."[37] The failure to predict the PA's decision for open conflict with Israel had several reasons: a genuine belief among some analysts, especially at the MID, that Palestinian president Yasir Arafat had abandoned violence in a quest for peace; the fact that there had been no structural changes or reassignment of responsibilities to adapt to the new situation created by the establishment of the PA; and an overestimation of the Palestinian leadership's control of their own militias.

Between 1994 and 1998, the division of labor among the MID, the Mossad, and the Shabak on Palestinian issues was laid down in an agreement called "Magna Carta 2" (this had been preceded by "Magna Carta 1," an agreement between the MID and the Mossad). This agreement, concluded after long and protracted negotiations and approved by the Israeli government, was based on the assumption that the PA was not a "target state"—that is, an enemy state to be the target of intelligence collection but rather a partner of growing importance, similar to Jordan or Egypt.[38] The agreement was signed by the then heads of the three intelligence organizations: Maj. Gen. Amos Malka (MID), Ephraim Halevy (Mossad), and Maj. Gen. (Ret.) Ami Ayalon (Shabak). The document laid down the responsibilities not only of each agency but also of every main unit in each of them. It gave primacy in the areas of collection and analysis on the Palestinian issue to the MID, while the Shabak was assigned the responsibility for the prevention of terrorist attacks.[39] The MID did its best to prepare as best it could for its new responsibilities. In the summer of 1994, it diverted much attention and many resources to developing the collection-and-analysis capabilities it needed. It directed its activities at both the PA and Palestinian opposition organizations such as Hamas and Islamic Jihad.[40]

The Hasmonean Tunnel Crisis

By late 1996 both the MID and the Shabak correctly predicted that negotiations between Israel and the PA would fail and that the prospects for a renewal of violent conflict would increase. However, it failed to predict the crisis over the opening of the Hasmonean Tunnel or its grave implications. This crisis became the worst calamity in Palestinian-Israeli relations and led to a complete breakdown of trust between the two sides.

The Hasmonean Tunnel is part of a large web of tunnels under and adjacent to the Wailing Wall in Jerusalem's Old City. For many years the Hasmonean Tunnel was not open to visitors since its northern side was blocked and it was impossible to have large numbers of people turn back and return to the southern exit inside such a narrow confine. Archaeologists recommended that a small opening be dug in the tunnel's northern end leading to an open street near the Via Dolorosa in the Old City's Muslim Quarter. This, they argued, would enable large numbers of tourists to visit the tunnels and exit safely. But, beyond the issue of crowd safety, the tunnel had a deep nationalistic meaning for both Jews and Muslims: For many Jews it symbolized their historic heritage in the Old City, while for Muslims it touched the sanctity of the Temple Mount and its mosques. For many years, Israeli governments considered opening an exit at the northern end of the tunnel, but concern over Palestinian reactions kept the idea on the shelf. In September 1996, Prime Minister Netanyahu decided to authorize the digging of the new exit at the tunnel's northern end.

Although provided with assessments stating that violent crisis was likely if he did open the tunnel, Netanyahu did not consult the intelligence community before making his decision. This was in contrast with a tradition of consulting with elements such as the head of the MID, the commander of the IDF Central Command (CENTCOM), and the Israeli Police before taking such a step in Jerusalem.[41] Shortly before the tunnel's opening, several senior security officials predicted in a meeting of the Committee for Jerusalem Affairs that the measure would provoke a furious Palestinian reaction.[42]

On September 22, 1996, the eve of Yom Kippur, the holiest Jewish holiday, Shabak head Ayalon was informed of the coming opening of the tunnel. He ordered his agency to be prepared and to analyze the reactions of the Palestinian street and the PA. On September 23, 1996, Netanyahu called Defense Minister Yizhak Mordechai to discuss other matters. During the conversation he briefly mentioned that the tunnel would be opened later that night. Five minutes after the conversation was over, Mordechai called his military secretary, Lt. Gen. Yaacov Amidror, and ordered him to inform the chief of the General Staff and the head of the MID immediately. He ordered that the IDF be prepared for imminent hostilities with the Palestinians and that the MID prepare an analysis of the situation.

From the early morning of September 24, the head of the Shabak began to receive reports on the PA's preparations for massive disorder. He traveled to Jerusalem and observed the situation personally. By noon he understood the scale of the planned demonstrations. He sent warnings to all the relevant parties. Mordechai called an emergency meeting of security and intelligence officials in his office. In the short time left, the IDF did its best to prepare for riots and to contact its Palestinian counterparts in an unsuccessful attempt to prevent violence.[43]

In a televised speech on the evening of September 24, Arafat called for the Palestinian people to respond with violence to the opening of the tunnel. On the following morning, violent demonstrations broke out in the West Bank and the Gaza Strip. As Israeli forces arrived on the scene, they were fired upon by Palestinian police and militiamen. Soon many demonstrations escalated to exchanges of heavy fire between IDF soldiers and PA police officers. Demonstrations and violence spread to all the main Palestinian cities of the West Bank and Gaza Strip. Israeli soldiers on joint Israeli-Palestinian patrols were attacked by their Palestinian counterparts. On September 26 the violence reached its zenith, with eleven IDF soldiers and sixty-nine Palestinians dead. US president Bill Clinton called an emergency summit with Arafat, Netanyahu, and King Hussein of Jordan in Washington. The summit a week afterward resulted in the end of violence and a new agreement between Israel and the PLO.

Senior security officials reported, on September 30, that the IDF had not predicted the intensity of the conflict. They argued that for a day and a half after the outbreak of violence, the IDF did not even begin to assess the situation. Indeed, the IDF assessed that demonstrations might take place in the cities near Jerusalem but did not predict that Palestinian policemen might open fire on IDF soldiers.[44] Other sources indicated that only on September 25 were intelligence warnings received suggesting that the PA had encouraged the intensification of conflict in the Occupied Territories.[45] The lack of early warning over a possible complete breakdown of security cooperation with the PA indicated a severe intelligence failure in Israel to understand Arafat's political strategy and his willingness to risk an open confrontation with Israel to advance his vision of a future Palestinian state. The near obsession of some senior Israeli intelligence officials with understanding Arafat's intentions led to almost a complete neglect of the wider PLO and PA leadership. It is perhaps unsurprising that once Arafat disappeared from the Palestinian political scene upon his death in 2004, these officials were quick to underestimate his successor, the new PA president Mahmoud Abbas.

Wars of the Generals

The intelligence failure to warn of the PA's involvement in direct violence against Israel during the Hasmonean Tunnel crisis resulted in recrimination and prolonged exchanges of blame between the heads of the different intelligence services, as well as between the prime minister and the intelligence community. These recriminations soured relations between Netanyahu and his intelligence chiefs and caused a rift between the MID and the Shabak.

Gen. Moshe Yaalon, the head of the MID from 1995 to 1998, blamed the Shabak for presenting tainted assessments regarding the crisis. According to Yaalon, he had strong disagreements over assessments with Shabak head Ami Ayalon during the tunnel crisis. In his opinion, Ayalon consistently interpreted the PA's actions in a way that supported his personal position that the PA was committed to the peace process and not interested in conflict with Israel. Ayalon maintained that the tunnel crisis violence had not been ordered by Arafat but rather resulted from Arafat's loss of control over the situation, an approach Yaalon found inconsistent with actual events or with the intelligence picture at the tactical level.[46]

In the aftermath of the Hasmonean Tunnel crisis, an effort was made by the Israeli government to divert the responsibility for its controversial decision to the Shabak. Colleagues of Netanyahu claimed that the Shabak had recommended to the prime minister that he open the tunnel. The result of these leaks was a serious crisis of confidence and souring of working relations between decision makers and the Shabak (and to a lesser degree with the intelligence community in general), with accusations exchanged both ways. At the height of this crisis, some politicians even threatened to take the unprecedented step of publishing secret transcripts of Ayalon-Netanyahu meetings. Security officials said they could not tolerate such a threat and suggested that the heads of the intelligence services might begin to keep their own records of these key policy meetings. A source close to the Shabak was quoted as saying that "there is a lot of anger among intelligence officials. The concern is that the next round of accusations will lead to resignations in the service." In response, officials of the Prime Minister's Office claimed that no threats had been made to release the highly confidential meeting records. They further maintained that elements within the Shabak were simply trying to embarrass the new government, presumably for political reasons.[47]

The tunnel crisis proved to be a watershed in the attitudes of the intelligence community toward the Palestinian issue and in the division of responsibilities among the intelligence services. Concerns over the outdated division of labor were further intensified in 1998 when a potential Palestinian unilateral declaration of independence initiated preparations on both sides toward a renewed conflict. The MID leadership concluded that the Magna Carta 2 agreement did not provide an adequate answer to Israel's evolving intelligence needs and demanded its renegotiation. One of its main arguments was that the Shabak lacked the required collection-and-analysis capabilities for an overall strategic assessment, since its collection efforts were directed mostly at preventing terrorist attacks and its strategic analysis capabilities were minimal. Such capabilities were to be found at the MID's Analysis Branch. The Shabak, in turn, agreed that the responsibility for strategic assessments on the Palestinian issue would be assigned to the MID but that on other issues there would be a "parallel intelligence responsibility."

In spite of making this minor concession, the Shabak did claim sole responsibility for operational intelligence collection and analysis for the prevention of Palestinian terrorist attacks. Reflecting the fundamental importance of early warning to the role of the intelligence services in Israel, the Shabak still reserved the right to provide, alongside the MID, warnings about impending armed conflict or popular massive demonstrations within the Occupied Territories.

While strategic analysis is the exclusive domain of the MID, the IDF routinely had to rely on information from the Shabak for the daily prevention of terrorist attacks. Only in 2005 did the MID overcome the Shabak's opposition and begin to develop its own operational counterterrorism collection-and-analysis capabilities.[48] However, despite these improvements, there still were significant "blind spots" in the Analysis Branch's assessments of the Palestinian arena. A major drawback was the lack of suitable collection capabilities on social trends and developments within that arena. As a result, the role of Arafat in controlling political developments was overemphasized, while insufficient attention was given to the influence of the Palestinian public and opposition to his rule. In addition, some blind spots were the result of methodological failures. One of the main tools used by the Analysis Branch in trying to follow trends in Palestinian society was public opinion polls. Former senior MID official Col. Ephraim Lavi argued that the branch lacked understanding of the limitations of such a tool in a society such as that of the Palestinians. The undemocratic nature of the PA and its restrictions on freedom of speech have limited the validity of such public opinion polls.[49] A later effort to replace the quantitative tools with qualitative ones failed too because of a similarly poor methodological understanding.[50]

Lavi stated that the MID provided continuous estimations for the diplomatic negotiations between Israel and the Palestinians between September 1999 and January 2001.[51] He maintains that there were two competing assessments within the Analysis Branch on the reasons for Israel's failure to achieve a political agreement with the Palestinians and for the outbreak of the Second Intifada. The first was the assessment produced by many analysts at the Analysis Branch that the Intifada was an expression of growing frustration within Palestinian society at the PA's domestic policy and at the lack of progress in the peace process.

Furthermore, it concluded that Arafat had used the increasing violence as means to silence domestic protests, force concessions from Israel, and pursue the internationalization of the conflict as an alternative to direct negotiations with Israel.

The second assessment was that of the head of the Analysis Branch, Lt. Gen. Amos Gilad, and the head of the MID, Maj. Gen. Aharon Zeevi-Farkash. They believed that Arafat had rejected the Israeli proposals put forward during the negotiations, instead opting to plan and initiate an armed conflict with Israel. They believed this was part of a strategy aimed to defeat Israel by forcing it to accept the return of Palestinian refugees and thus achieving an Arab numerical demographic majority within Israel's 1967 borders. Ephraim Lavi suggested that the heads of the MID and its Analysis Branch not only held this view, which opposed that of most of their analysts, but also actively involved the intelligence apparatus in Israel's public diplomacy efforts to gain acceptance of their version of the assessment. As a result, the MID Revision Department (RD), also known as the "Devil's Advocate Department" and responsible for raising alternative interpretations based on the same intelligence sources as a means of testing assessments, warned that this was a dangerous step and the principle of separation between intelligence and public diplomacy should be maintained.[52]

In February 2006 Hamas won a landslide victory in the elections to the PA held in the Occupied Territories. In 2008, the head of the MID, Maj. Gen. Amos Yadlin, ordered the Analysis Branch to conduct an internal investigation of how well it had performed in relation to these elections. The investigation concluded that the branch had not predicted Hamas's victory. Nor had it warned that Hamas would take over the Gaza Strip by force following Israel's unilateral withdrawal or foreseen the intensity of Palestinian rocket attacks on nearby Israeli settlements. The investigation found that the branch had adjusted its assessments to suit the inclinations of the political leadership. Alongside professional failures, the report concluded that a practice of dual assessments had developed: Written assessments were intended for internal inspections and investigation committees, while oral assessments—the really influential ones— were given to the political leadership, the media, and the public.

The investigation's report pointed out structural and professional problems that had contributed to poor assessments of the Palestinian arena in general and Hamas in particular. This was a result of the organizational culture of the Analysis Branch. As a rule, much of the routine work was done by relatively young and inexperienced officers and NCOs (Noncommissioned Officers). While they were among the best and brightest of Israel's youth, they were familiar mostly with current events and lacked the experience and sometimes the familiarity with Arab culture and history required to make broad judgments about long-term trends.

By contrast, the head of the Analysis Branch, Lt. Gen. Yossi Kuperwasser, argued that the Analysis Branch dismissed any prospect of Fatah winning and forwarded two main possibilities. One was equilibrium and the other an impressive victory on the part of Hamas and its takeover of power in the Gaza Strip. He argued that the branch had consistently warned decision makers about Hamas's upcoming victory and had failed to persuade them to prevent its participation in the elections.[53] Kuperwasser admitted that, on the eve of the Second Intifada, the amount of attention given to socioeconomic affairs by the MID had been insufficient and there had been a lack of coordination between the teams working on Palestinian issues and on social research. He argued that in 2003–4, reforms were undertaken in the MID to solve these problems. These unprofessional practices led Lavi to send the head of the MID, General Zeevi-Farkash, a bulletin titled "Failures in the Intelligence Work on the Palestinian Issue." Lavi was greatly bothered by the duality of assessments—written and oral ones:

> This is a fundamental and ethical problem. The situation gave the Head of the MID and Head of the Analysis Branch the ability to say "we told you" and be "covered" regarding any direction in which reality develops: towards that contained in the Branch's analytical products or toward that presented orally to the political leadership. . . . This situation created a bad feeling among analysts that the written intelligence products were without any real influence and were intended mainly for future commissions of investigation. This way, the expensive collection work and the professional analysis work of dozens of officers and NCOs were getting lost.[54]

Zeevi-Farkash wrote to him in response: "There is no need for us to check the reliability of your arguments, as we believe that you wrote them—although with a subjective perspective—with honesty and clarity, and this is indeed your perception of the events."[55] Perceptions, rather than reality, were again a crucial influence on intelligence analysis, the way it was distributed, and its resulting political impact.

Conclusions: Brilliant Answers to Wrong Questions

Until the 1990s, Israel's national security policy lacked a clear distinction between high-intensity conflict, principally interstate war, and low-intensity conflict, including terrorism and guerrilla warfare. Until well into the Oslo process, Israel's security policy was focused on symmetrical threats posed by the regular armed forces of its Arab neighbors. The threat of terrorism was considered secondary, though serious, and classified with other threats under "Current Security." Since the founding of the IDF, its main mission has been to counter threats defined by Israeli security terminology as "Basic Security"—in practical terms, conventional war. The emphasis was on defending the state from an attack by regular Arab forces across the borders. Nevertheless, the Israeli security doctrine recognized the existence of a wider range of threats and military activities that did not constitute conventional warfare. It classified them all under the category of Current Security. The security doctrine lacked a differentiation and specific responses to the different types of low-intensity threats.[56] The importance of conventional military threats in Israel's security doctrine is not surprising given the country's vulnerability to a surprise attack, owing to the small size of Israel's territory within the 1967 borders and its long, difficult-to-defend borders. Israel's main military strength lay in the IDF's reserve units. Any mobilization to discourage or repel a conventional attack is dependent on early warning provided by the intelligence community. This provides the crucial time to mobilize hundreds of thousands of civilian reservists and get them to the front.

In its work on Palestinian terrorism, the Israeli intelligence community mostly concentrated on the violent operational aspects of terrorism, perceiving the threat as emanating from Palestinian terrorist organizations in almost quantifiable terms of actual attacks, loss of life, and economic damage to the country. Analysis and assessments focused on immediate prevention of planned or impending attacks, rather than on the long-term understanding of political and social trends. The intelligence services attached less importance to the social and political sources of Palestinian terrorism and thus were rarely involved in proposals or efforts to alleviate these causes by "winning hearts and minds." As a result, intelligence analysis units were directed to focus on the operational prevention of terrorism, with only minimal attention given to other dimensions of Palestinian hostile activities. Unsurprisingly, most intelligence assessments did not cover these dimensions, even in the periods leading up to the two Palestinian uprisings. The Palestinian population in the Occupied Territories was regarded as passive and inherently hostile, and little effort was made to diminish its hostility to Israel through economic development or political reforms. The lack of a single, unified office for all-source analysis of both the violent and the political dimensions of Palestinian terrorism delayed a proper understanding of the PLO's political potential until the late 1980s.

Intelligence analysis is not carried out in a vacuum, and analysts are often influenced by public opinions, popular perceptions, and biases. Until 2004 the main political representative organization of the Palestinian people, the PLO, was located in foreign countries, first in Jordan, later in Lebanon, and after 1982 in Tunisia. Covert intelligence collection, both human and technological, could easily be focused on the limited number of targets it presented, including headquarters facilities and training camps. But such a concentration missed wider developments within the Palestinian population. Perceiving the PLO as a terrorist organization meant that Israel's prevention-focused intelligence-collection efforts targeted the PLO's operational leaders and elements, with less attention being dedicated to its political activities and the level of public support it enjoyed inside the Occupied Territories.[57] This was clearly illustrated by the insistence of the Israeli government, led by Prime Minister Yitzhak Shamir, that no PLO representatives be allowed to participate in the crucial 1991 Madrid Peace Conference meeting since "the PLO is a terrorist organization" and should not be negotiated with.[58] The 1994 Oslo Accords meant that Israel had to recognize the PLO's political status but did not completely alter the decades-long intelligence perception that the PLO was Israel's archenemy.

When examining the difficulty of all-source analysis and making sense of wider issues, Michael Herman notes a differentiation between secrets and mysteries.[59] He quotes former director of Central Intelligence Robert Gates, who defined secrets as things that are potentially answerable, while in mysteries there are no clear-cut answers since decisions or actions over them have yet to take place. The case of Israel corresponds well with Herman's assumptions. In its analysis of the Palestinian terrorist organizations, Israeli intelligence has consistently been able to provide their secrets but has been markedly less successful at predicting, or even spotting, mysteries. While this is partially an inherent and general limitation of intelligence, it is also a result of diffused all-source responsibilities, the marginalization of open-source intelligence, the constantly changing Israeli political attitudes toward the Palestinians and their national aspirations, and the intelligence community's deference to the country's political leaders.

In his ground-breaking treatise on intelligence assessment, Ernest May focuses on the two components of assessments: capabilities and proclivities.[60] May examines how accurate were the intelligence assessments of the major European powers before the two world wars in both assessing the enemy's capabilities, often in quantitative terms, and in understanding and predicting the enemy's proclivities. May argues that the governments of the 1930s were less capable of appraising potential enemies and forming net assessments than the governments before 1914. Consequently, he argues, the governments of today are even less capable of performing them than those of the Second World War. He also finds little correlation between perceptiveness concerning proclivities and investment in collection and analysis.

The case of Israel and Palestinian terrorism vindicates May's assumptions. The Israeli intelligence community was able very effectively to analyze the capabilities of Palestinian terrorist organizations and provide the IDF and police with the intelligence needed to prevent numerous attacks, arrest terrorist leaders and activists, uncover arms caches, and break up terrorist financing. But on questions of proclivities, the Israeli record is weaker. Israeli intelligence failed to understand and alert decision makers to the social and political developments inside the Palestinian areas that led to the outbreak of the First Intifada in 1987. It viewed suspiciously the incremental development of the Oslo peace process between 1994 and 2000 and could not conclusively answer the question about

Arafat's direction of terrorism in the period after the Oslo Accords. Nor did it estimate the level of violence that would erupt following the opening of the Hasmonean Tunnel in 1996. Much of the assessment effort before 1994 focused on the wrong questions but answered those brilliantly.

May argues that organizational continuity, rather than organizational change, is one key to successful assessment.[61] Israel's intelligence community has changed remarkably little since its inception more than six decades ago, despite huge changes in Israel's strategic environment and the threats it faces. On the one hand, this is an indication of the flexibility and professionalism of the existing agencies and their ability to expand or contract collection efforts with relative ease. This continuity, coupled with effective "organizational memories," enabled effective prevention of terrorist attacks and prevented terrorism, for most of the period examined, from exerting an overwhelming influence on policymaking. On the other hand, vested interests in the existing intelligence services ensured that new players, or those outside the traditional confines of the intelligence community but with access to information and the ability to assess it, were marginalized or even ignored. May admits that intelligence services in general perform poorly in making long-term projections and are generally better at short-term predictions, including warning intelligence. The case of Israel certainly confirms this observation, but since short-term predictions provide for effective terrorism prevention, this inherent weakness did not diminish the value of intelligence in the eyes of Israeli decision makers. As long as intelligence and the military could keep terrorist attacks and casualties at a manageable level, politicians could get on with pursuing their policies without too much public pressure for major change.

Intelligence analysis of Palestinian terrorism was often diffused and fragmented by the lack of clear lines of responsibility and by intelligence turf wars. It was never made the sole responsibility of one service. Instead all of Israel's intelligence services were involved in both the collection efforts and in the analysis of the terrorism problem. While this came about partially owing to the increasingly internationalized nature of Palestinian terrorism in the 1970s and 1980s, it hampered unified assessments and the maximization of resources. It also brought about the risk of politicization of assessments, especially during the Oslo period between 1994 and 2000, as the intelligence services were called upon to cooperate with their former bitter enemies in the PLO and the PA.

The Israeli intelligence community has generally ignored open-source information that could have been used to evaluate social and economic trends within Palestinian society. Potential analysis mechanisms that collected such information, such as the CGA-OT, were marginalized and frequently ignored within the intelligence community. The military-centered collection and analysis of the intelligence community resulted in minimal attention paid within the analysis units to open-source economic and social data and their long-term meaning.

Traditionally the MID Analysis Branch arenas have been designated along geographical lines, with each arena comprising a political (i.e., civilian) section and a military one. The political sections rely heavily on daily translations of open-source material, mainly media reports. In contrast, the military sections emphasize the use of clandestine intelligence collection sources, both human and technological, assumed to be critical for providing early warning of a surprise attack. Assessments of military dimensions of threats based on clandestine sources were judged both inside the intelligence community and the political echelon as more significant and reliable. The low status and priority given in the past to open-source material, and thus indirectly also to the work of the Analysis Branch's political sections, contributed to a continual failure to develop effective methodologies to make use of open-source tools, such as public opinion polls, socioeconomic international indexes, and data-mining tools, in the wider analysis process.

The few institutional mechanisms that collected and analyzed open-source data on the Palestinians before the 1987 outbreak of the First Intifada, such as the CGA-OT, were excluded from intelligence and policy discussions through their designation as "nonintelligence organs." Their reports were marginalized or even trivialized by the larger intelligence services, and they were deprived of skilled manpower in the areas of the Arabic language and data analysis. The fact that a small number of poorly funded CGA-OT intelligence officers carried out such valuable work of analysis and warned repeatedly of the deteriorating social and economic conditions of the Palestinians and their growing anger toward Israel is a tribute to their professionalism and dedication. It is also an indication that regarding terrorism and insurgencies, the most relevant assessments may sometimes be found outside the traditional and prestigious analysis departments of the intelligence community.

Richard Betts argues that governments should expect to be surprised no matter how good their intelligence capabilities are because the ability of intelligence services to understand and interpret other people's politics is always limited.[62] Confident in its military capabilities, most Israeli governments were aware of but not overly worried about possible surprises from Palestinian terrorist organizations because they considered terrorist attacks to be tactical, not strategic, threats. Only in 2002 did the massive campaign of Palestinian suicide terrorism that resulted in hundreds of Israelis killed alter these perceptions, and terrorism came to be perceived as a strategic threat.

The present analysis of Israeli intelligence perceptions of Palestinian terrorism illustrates the limits of intelligence assessment and prediction. The Israeli intelligence community is highly professional and experienced and is often rated as one of the best in the world. Yet its track record on assessments of Palestinian terrorism is a mixed one. Ironically, the Israeli intelligence services may have become victims of their own success. Since they were able to prevent so many

Palestinian terrorist attacks on the operational level, users of intelligence developed such great expectations from the intelligence community that ultimately could not realistically be met. While in previous decades IDF commanders sometimes complained about outdated intelligence information, in some cases many years old, officers in the January 2009 offensive in Gaza complained about maps that, they claimed, were more than three days old. Perhaps this is an indication that the era of perfect intelligence coverage, if it ever existed, is well and truly over. The complexities of modern low-intensity warfare and the interaction among national interests, violence, international law, media coverage, and morals make assessments of terrorism much more difficult and prone to misconceptions than assessments during the Cold War, when the front lines, both geographical and ideological, were clearly defined.

Israeli intelligence perceptions of terrorism changed after the 1994 Oslo Accords and the commencement of a political peace process with the Palestinians. Threats of conventional war in the Middle East diminished as a result of the end of the Cold War and the 1991 Gulf War. The possibility that terrorist attacks would derail the crucial Oslo process and the declining threat of conventional interstate war changed Israel's traditional intelligence priorities. As the threat of a conventional attack from Israel's Arab neighbors became less probable, threat perceptions shifted toward two types of threats: terrorism and the threat of weapons of mass destruction from countries farther afield, such as Iraq and Iran. As a result, the perception of the terrorist threat was elevated to that of a strategic one. But structural changes to adapt to the new situation, as well as to the creation of the PA and its relations with Israel, were slow and painful.

Over five decades of Palestinian terrorism, the concentration of Israeli intelligence on the detection and prevention of terrorist attacks created an intelligence community with extensive prevention capabilities. However, highly effective efforts at operational prevention of attacks meant that less attention was given to the root causes of terrorism. The resulting concentration on preventative analysis often meant less opportunity analysis in support of political developments and peace.

Notes

1. Operational assessments are most often referred to within the classification of "current security," meaning all security issues other than interstate war ("basic security").

2. Thirty years for the archival release of most government documents, fifty years for IDF documents, and seventy years for sensitive intelligence-related documents.

3. Shlomo Shpiro, "Israel," in *PSI Handbook of Global Security and Intelligence*, ed. Stuart Farson et al. (Westport, CT: Praeger, 2008), 570–72.

4. Ibid.

5. Ian Black and Benny Morris, *Israel's Secret Wars* (London: Hamish Hamilton, 1991), 98–100.

6. Shlomo Gazit, *Between Warning and Surprise: On Shaping National Intelligence Assessment in Israel* (Tel-Aviv: INSS, 2003) (in Hebrew).

7. For more information on the structure of Israel's intelligence community, see Ephraim Kahana, "Reorganizing Israel's Intelligence Community," *International Journal of Intelligence and CounterIntelligence* 15, no. 3 (Fall 2002): 415–28, and Uri Bar-Joseph, "A Bull in a China Shop: Netanyahu and Israel's Intelligence Community," *International Journal of Intelligence and CounterIntelligence* 11, no. 2 (Summer 1998): 154–74. On Israel's intelligence collection, see Uri Bar-Joseph, *The Watchmen Fell Asleep: The Surprise of Yom Kippur and Its Sources* (New York: State University of New York Press, 2005). See also Ephraim Kahana, "Humint vs Terrorism: The Israeli Case," paper presented at the Forty-Seventh Annual Intelligence Studies Association Convention, San Diego, March 22–25, 2006, http:// citation.allacademic.com/meta/p_mla_apa_research_citation/0/9/8/0/6/pages98061/p98061 -1.php.

8. The uniforms of the Border Guards units are green, more similar to the IDF than to the ordinary civilian police force, and its members are equipped with military-type assault rifles, military jeeps, etc.

9. Black and Morris, *Israel's Secret Wars*, 44–50, 122–24.

10. During the November 1956 war, several of the terrorists who participated in the attack were arrested and tried in Israel. On the attack and its perpetrators see Meir Uziel, "The Father, the Son and the Israeli Spirit—and the Kibbutz Memory," *HaKibbutz*, May 11, 2006, http://www.kibbutz.org.il/itonut/2006/haver/060511_rotenberg.htm (in Hebrew).

11. The original text, dated April 30, 1956, is kept at the IDF Archive. It was reproduced in Anonymous, "The Destiny of Our Generation: Chief of Staff Moshe Dayan Eulogizes Lieutenant Roi Rothberg," *Maariv*, May 9, 2011, http://www.nrg.co.il/online/1/ART2/239/ 021.html (in Hebrew).

12. Alon Gan, "Exposed in the Turret and Warriors Dialogue as Diverging Axis of Identity," *Israel* 13 (2008): 267. A Google search of Dayan's eulogy yielded 230,000 references, December 23, 2011 (in Hebrew).

13. Baruch Kimmerling, "Patterns of Militarism in Israel," *European Journal of Sociology* 34 (November 1993): 208–9.

14. Dov Tamari, *The Armed Nation* (Ben-Shemen, Israel: Modan, 2012), 184–87 (in Hebrew).

15. Ephraim Lapid and Doris Liling, "An Interview: From Anti-Terrorism Fighter into the Supreme Firefighter: Rav Tafsar Shimon Romach the Primary Firefighter Commissioner, Former Deputy Head of Shin Bet's Division," *Mabat Malam* 43 (December 2005): 12 (in Hebrew).

16. Zeev Schiff and Ehud Yaari, *Intifada* (Jerusalem: Schoken, 1990), 33 (in Hebrew). In the early 1970s, the PLO extended its terrorist attacks abroad, especially to Europe. The Black September faction in the PLO launched deadly attacks against Israeli and Jewish targets in Europe, hijacked aircraft, and attacked the Israeli team at the 1972 Munich Olympic Games. For Israeli intelligence operations against Black September, see Daniel Byman, *A High Price: The Triumphs and Failures of Israeli Counterterrorism* (New York: Oxford University Press, 2011), 29–57.

17. Gadi Zohar, "Dealing with Structural Problems in Israeli Defense Intelligence in the Palestinian Arena," in *Masterpiece: An Inside Look at Sixty Years of Israeli Intelligence*, ed. Amos Gilboa and Ephraim Lapid (Tel Aviv: Yediot Acharonot, 2008), 116–17 (in Hebrew).

18. Yochi Erlich, "For Whom the Bell Tolls? Intelligence and the First Intifada 1987: Was It Possible to Predict a Spontaneous Uprising?," *Mabat Malam* 51 (February 2008): 30 (in Hebrew).

19. Zohar, "Dealing with Structural Problems," 117.

20. Shlomo Gazit, *Trapped Fools: Thirty Years of Israeli Policy in the Territories* (Tel Aviv: Zmora Beitan, 1998), 118 (in Hebrew). It is mentioned also in Schiff and Yaari, *Intifada*, 33.

21. Ibid., 33.

22. Gazit, *Trapped Fools*, 33.

23. Zohar, "Dealing with Structural Problems," 119.

24. Schiff and Yaari, *Intifada*, 33.

25. Yochi, "For Whom the Bell Tolls?," 31.

26. Gazit, *Trapped Fools*, 55n4.

27. Schiff and Yaari, *Intifada*, 36–37.

28. Gazit, *Trapped Fools*, 55n4.

29. Ibid., 55n3.

30. Schiff and Yaari, *Intifada*, 39.

31. Erlich, "For Whom the Bell Tolls?," 30.

32. Schiff and Yaari, *Intifada*, 11.

33. The Varash committee is a semiformal coordination forum between the heads of the Mossad, the MID, and the Shabak, with the military secretary to the prime minister participating as an observer. Traditionally Varash meetings are convened at the office of the head of the Mossad.

34. Erlich, "For Whom the Bell Tolls?," 31–32.

35. Shmuel (Colonel), "Intelligence Research in the Middle East Peace Process (from the Madrid Conference to the Peace Treaty with Jordan)," in *Intelligence for Peace: The Role of Intelligence in Times of Peace*, ed. Hesi Carmel (London: Frank Cass, 1999), 119–27.

36. The First Intifada was mainly a civilian protest campaign. There were relatively few armed attacks.

37. Ron Ben-Ishai, "The Secret Maneuvers Pressures to Open the Hasmonean Tunnel," in Shabat Supplement, *Yediot Acharonot*, October 4, 1996, 8–9 (in Hebrew).

38. Ephraim Lavie, "Intelligence Challenges in the Palestinian Arena," in Gilboa and Lapid, *Masterpiece*, 102–3.

39. Kahana, "Reorganizing Israel's Intelligence Community," 422.

40. Lavie, "Intelligence Challenges in the Palestinian Arena," 102.

41. Anonymous, "Netanyahu Consulted Only with Several of the Intelligence Community's Senior Officials," *Haaretz*, September 26, 1996 (in Hebrew). The IDF is divided into four territorial commands: Central, Northern, Southern, and Home.

42. Ben-Ishai, "The Secret Maneuvers," 11.

43. Ibid.

44. Shimon Shiffer, Alex Fishman, and Nitzan Ramon, "Mordechai: I Was Told Five Minutes before the Opening of the Tunnel," *Yediot Acharonot*, October 1, 1996 (in Hebrew).

45. Alex Fishman, "The After-Action Review of Joseph Tomb: Weakness of the Command Echelon," *Yediot Acharonot*, October 3, 1996 (in Hebrew).

46. Moshe Yaalon, *The Longer Shorter Way* (Tel-Aviv: Miskal, 2008), 84 (in Hebrew).

47. Steve Rodman, "Shabak Threatens to Record Meeting with Government," *Jerusalem Post*, December 23, 1996, 12.

48. Lavie, "Intelligence Challenges," 109n2.

49. Amir Kulick, "Action, Not Words: Principal Trends in Palestinian Public Opinion of 2007," *Strategic Assessments* 10, no. 4 (February 2008).

50. Lavie, "Intelligence Challenges," 105–9 and n. 9–11.

51. Ibid.

52. Ibid., 102–7. Established in 1974 owing to lessons learned from the Yom Kippur War, the MID Revision Department is a unique feature of Israeli military intelligence. It is a small unit tasked with thinking "outside the box" and challenging perceptions held by intelligence analysts on important issues. Its work is not limited to military matters but also covers political issues and questions relating to the peace process. On the establishment, functions, and products of the RD unit, see Shmuel Even, "The Revision Process in the Intelligence," in Gilboa and Lapid, *Masterpiece*, 309–15.

53. Akiva Eldar, "Cast Lead: Military Intelligence Directorate Did Not Predict the Hamas 2006 Electoral Victory, and It's Taking Over on Gaza Strip; Intelligence Failure? Not Necessarily," *Haaretz*, November 9, 2009.

54. Ibid.

55. Ibid.

56. Tamir Libel, "David's Shield? The Decline and Partial Rise of the IDF Command and General Staff College," *Baltic Security and Defense Review* 12, no. 2 (2010): 51.

57. In a poll conducted by the Al Najah University in Nablus in September 1986, over 93 percent of the Palestinians expressed the belief that the PLO was the only legitimate representative of the Palestinian people. Over 78 percent of those who participated justified terrorist attacks against Israel. Meron Benvenisti, *The West Bank Data Base Project: 1987 Report* (Jerusalem: West Bank Data Base Project, 1987), 45.

58. For the background and developments leading to the Madrid peace conference, see Moshe Shemesh, "The PLO Road to Oslo," *Iyunim Betkumat Yisrael* 9 (1999): 186–245 (in Hebrew).

59. Michael Herman, *Intelligence Power in Peace and War* (Cambridge: Cambridge University Press, 1996): 103–4.

60. Ernest May, "Conclusions: Capabilities and Proclivities," in *Knowing One's Enemies: Intelligence Assessment before the Two World Wars*, ed. Ernest May (Princeton, NJ: Princeton University Press, 1986), 503–42.

61. Ibid., 533.

62. Richard Betts, "Analysis, War and Decisions: Why Intelligence Failures Are Inevitable," *World Politics* 31, no. 1 (October 1978): 61–89.

7

Pakistani Intelligence and India

JULIAN RICHARDS

MANY SCHOLARS AND ANALYSTS have described the security standoff between India and Pakistan as the classic enduring rivalry. Confrontation between the two states commenced almost from the first day of independence in 1947 and has continued to varying degrees ever since. Since the 1970s, this confrontation has unfolded under the shadow of nuclear weapons, which have had a shaping effect on the confrontation without, as I will discuss, freezing it completely. For Pakistan the question of India has been the single most defining issue of national security. Even the question of Afghanistan is sometimes described in terms of the need for "strategic depth" against India, a notion inherited from the former colonial power Great Britain.[1] The key focus has been the continuing dispute over the region of Kashmir, which was left unacceptably unresolved (in the view of the Pakistanis) at the time of the partition of British India. On several occasions since, adventures in Kashmir have taken on a galvanizing nationalistic focus for Pakistan, especially during periods of military rule, even if the results have always been less than satisfactory.

This chapter explores the development of Pakistan's intelligence capability and the manner in which it has focused so comprehensively on the question of India. I will examine a set of structural weaknesses that have meant that intelligence has not always served defense decision making and policy very effectively in Pakistan, leaving a sense of frustration that the question of Kashmir in particular has remained the oldest unresolved item on the United Nations' agenda.[2] Many of the problems are addressed in Ernest May's five "injunctions" to governments faced with the task of "knowing one's enemies."[3] In particular, the question of "who are 'they' and who are 'we'" in security and intelligence planning has been a question that has, perhaps, not been examined carefully enough in senior defense and intelligence circles in Pakistan and has been muddied by a bellicose prevailing wisdom about India and its supposedly nefarious intentions. As I will discuss, the foundational myth that has taken root is that India has been determined to see the dismemberment and collapse of Pakistan from the beginning and will take every opportunity to make this happen. This has shaped every plan and action. Consequently May's injunction to "look hard at all presumptions" is a particularly prescient one for Pakistani defense planners.[4]

Aside from analytical problems, the organization of intelligence in Pakistan, and particularly the role of the military within the national intelligence machinery, has led to problems that have adversely affected Pakistan's intelligence assessments of its neighbor. To a large degree, intelligence has been just one area of national life that has been shaped by tumultuous civilian-military relations that have characterized Pakistan's development since independence. Much as has been the case with the governance of the country for most of the time (notwithstanding the unprecedented current period of parliamentary democracy), the intelligence community (IC) in Pakistan has been completely dominated since independence by the military. This has persisted from the initial period in which the Directorate for Military Intelligence (MI) was the primary actor in the IC, through the creation and rise to prominence of the Inter-Services Intelligence Directorate (ISI), whose senior staff members are military personnel.[5]

As David Thomas notes, "military intelligence" is often dismissed as an oxymoron by senior civilian policymakers and intelligence officers.[6] Military predilections can be overly infected with "hubris or inattention," which can lead military commanders to "discard, misunderstand, or fail to act" on important intelligence.[7] Michael Herman noted similar issues in his experience of military intelligence and recalled that many consider the military mindset to be "incompatible with open-mindedness."[8]

In his study of pre–World War II France, Peter Jackson considered that tensions between the civilian policymakers and the military (the latter dominating the IC in France at the time) led to disagreements and inertia in the intelligence assessment process regarding German intentions during the 1930s.[9] Johnson observed similar issues in contemporary Pakistan, noting that the political culture has been such that the ISI regards civilian politicians "with suspicion if not contempt."[10] Significantly, this has led the ISI to consider that the job of ensuring national security is beyond the capability of politicians and lawyers.[11] It can be assumed that such a political culture has a great bearing on intelligence assessments, considering the military's dominance of the IC in Pakistan.

These factors are also important in terms of cultural attitudes toward "the enemy." Returning to prewar Europe, Jackson noted the tendency of military intelligence officials in France to expect the worst of the "warrior spirit of the German race," a view that had been prevalent in French military circles since the First World War.[12] In Pakistan, senior military and intelligence officials have often spoken about the "Hindu mentality" and its approach toward confrontation between the two states, although in this case the assessment is generally not that the enemy is warlike and possessing of a "Teutonic efficiency"[13] but rather that it is weak and likely to crumble under a "couple of hard blows," as the first military ruler of Pakistan, Gen. Ayub Khan, once proclaimed.[14] Experience has shown in Pakistan that such a fixed military mindset toward the cultural characteristics of the enemy and the failure of civilian or other points of view to moderate this mindset within the intelligence process have usually led to strategic failures in confrontations with India.

Investigating Pakistan's intelligence structures and performance is not as straightforward as it might be in the case of other countries. While a national archive does exist in Pakistan, it focuses on the Pakistan Movement in the years immediately before independence from colonial British India and does not generally include declassified papers of security or intelligence interest in later periods. The intelligence agencies in Pakistan do not publish assessments or papers in the manner of the American IC's National Intelligence Estimates, for example, and much of the internal mechanism for processing intelligence through government channels remains unknown to all but those immediately involved.[15] Occasional reports about the activities of the intelligence services will emerge in the press in Pakistan, and the memoirs of former military officers and leaders such as General Khan remain a valuable secondary source of information on how intelligence has performed, particularly during periods of military conflict with India. It should be noted that the intelligence agencies do not have a good relationship with the press in Pakistan and have been implicated in a number of cases recently of violent intimidation of journalists who have written unfavorable reports about their activities.[16] Part of the problem is that the intelligence agencies in Pakistan are not on any statutory footing, which means that oversight and accountability of their activities remains very limited. The highly controversial Hamood-ur Rehman Commission report of 1974, for example, which was extremely critical of the performance of the Pakistani military in the conflict with India in 1971, was made public only in 2000 by Gen. Pervez Musharraf after details of the report had been leaked to the media.[17] This lack of accountability contributes to weaknesses in the efficiency and performance of Pakistan's intelligence services in the face of complex problems.

Major conflicts between Pakistan and India occurred in 1947, 1965, 1971, and 1999. While the last of these conflicts was more limited in scope than the earlier episodes, it was no less worrying as both states had tested nuclear weapons the year before. In many ways, the conflict in 1971 over East Pakistan was the most traumatic, resulting as it did in the humiliating defeat and surrender of the Pakistani forces to India and the dismemberment of the two wings of Pakistan to create Bangladesh from the eastern part of the country. There is much evidence that this series of defeats on the battlefield led to a change of policy from the 1980s onward to "bleed India" through low-intensity conflict in Kashmir rather than taking it on directly on the battlefield, although the 1999 conflict was something of an anomaly in this regard.

In all of these cases, Pakistani intelligence failures abounded and were both tactical, relating to miscalculations on the battlefield, and strategic, relating to flawed estimations of India's intentions and likely responses to attacks. Miscalculations were also made in assessments of how key international allies such as the United States and China would react to conflict with India. The result has been one of ongoing frustration for Pakistan in that the Kashmir dispute has still not been resolved and shows little sign of catching the serious attention of the international community at large. I will examine issues of intelligence failure in these episodes of confrontation with India, but it is worth initially examining the nature of Pakistan's IC.

Intelligence Machinery

The current intelligence community in Pakistan is centered on three main agencies: the Intelligence Bureau (IB), MI, and the ISI. These agencies are organized in such a way that they report up to the prime minister by different routes, with no coordinating body at the top.[18] The IB, which is primarily a police agency concerned with counterespionage, organized crime, and some elements of domestic counterterrorism, reports directly to the prime minister. The ISI, which is responsible for a wide range of intelligence activities at home and abroad, reports, in theory, simultaneously to the defense minister, the prime minister, and the president. This allows it to operate semi-independently of both civilian and military structures, although, as discussed, it is essentially a creature of the military. MI, coordinated in Joint Staff headquarters, represents the intelligence-gathering functions of the armed forces on the ground, including tactical signals intelligence (SIGINT) and human intelligence (HUMINT) activities. In the early military confrontations with India, MI was the dominant intelligence actor. During Gen. Mohammad Zia ul-Haq's regime between 1977 and 1988 and the war against the Soviets in Afghanistan, the ISI rose to prominence as the most powerful element of Pakistan's intelligence community and has remained in this position ever since.

During the 1970s, under Zulfikar Ali Bhutto's government, an additional security agency was created called the Federal Security Force (FSF), which acted in parallel to the regular police as a form of private army and which was subsequently implicated in a number of cases of alleged human rights abuses of political opponents.[19] The agency was subsequently disbanded by General Zia after his military coup in 1977. In 2009 Pakistan announced the imminent formation of a new national counterterrorism agency, the National Counter Terrorism

Authority (NACTA), which would cooperate with overseas intelligence agencies on international terrorism cases. It was reported that the agency "would not be an operational unit . . . but more of a research wing collating and analyzing intelligence."[20] At the time of writing, the new agency has not yet come fully into operational being, despite the NACTA Act being finally passed in parliament under Nawaz Sharif's civilian administration in late 2013. Early signs of frustration were evidenced by the fact that the agency's first chairman, Tariq Pervaiz, resigned after one year after no progress had been made in activating the agency.[21] The key issue is almost certainly one of turf battles with the other intelligence agencies and particularly the ISI, on whose turf it will mostly be treading.

In terms of strategic intelligence, Pakistan found itself slightly better off than India for intelligence capability following the partition, since the northwest of British India was considered a key frontier, looking westward toward the Soviet Union, Persia, and Afghanistan. An Indian army commander in 1947, L. P. Sen, notes that Pakistan initially fared much better than India on the intelligence front, as the director of the IB in British India had transferred on independence to Pakistan, taking with him, as it transpired, a wealth of information and equipment.[22]

As far as agencies were concerned, however, the only real institution in place was the IB (or remnants thereof left in what became Pakistan), which was largely a police agency focusing on domestic security issues. The first conflict with India, just months after independence in 1947, revealed the IB to be totally inadequate in the provision of tactical military intelligence and assessment, and this led to the creation of the ISI in 1948.

There is some evidence that a growing preoccupation with domestic affairs led to a damaging lack of resources allocated to military intelligence during the 1965 war with India.[23] Over the ensuing years, the ISI continued to flourish under both civilian and military regimes and became very much the predominant intelligence actor in Pakistan. It involved itself increasingly in gathering intelligence on internal insurrections in Balochistan and the North-West Frontier Province (now Khyber-Pakhtunkhwa Province), in orchestrating military and logistical assistance to proxy forces in Afghanistan and Kashmir, in helping to nurture the Taliban as a strategic force in Afghanistan, in establishing a network of spies and intelligence activities throughout India, and in interfering in domestic elections within Pakistan, notably in 1990 when the situation was looking unfavorable to the military-bureaucratic center of power. By the turn of the twenty-first century, the ISI had again become a strategic partner for the United States in the so-called war on terrorism, resuming its role of the 1980s, albeit one built on sometimes shaky levels of trust. The size of this agency is difficult to establish at the time of writing. Official figures suggest it comprises twenty-five thousand personnel, including agents.[24] Of this total, ten thousand are permanent staff, of which twenty-five hundred are "core officers."[25]

The ISI is purportedly organized into eight divisions. Among these, Joint Intelligence X (known as JIX) serves as an overarching secretariat to the agency, providing administrative support and preparing intelligence estimates and threat assessments for senior policymakers.[26] Joint Intelligence–North (JIN) is focused solely on Kashmir operations and monitoring Indian troop movements in the region. The Joint Signal Intelligence Bureau gathers data from a range of SIGINT stations, the great majority of them arrayed along the border with India.

As Shaun Gregory points out, the ISI is unlike many models of intelligence agency in Western countries—at least those in the English-speaking ones—in that it has both internal and external intelligence remits.[27] It also has no direct rivals in what it does (the IB and MI tend to have different responsibilities and are much smaller), so it avoids the turf wars seen between the FBI and the CIA, for example.[28] As well as covering internal and external intelligence, the ISI also brings together a gamut of capabilities in one agency, comprising SIGINT and HUMINT collection and running covert operations.[29]

SIGINT operations in Pakistan have a long history, dating back to the British era when signals intercept stations were located in what is now Pakistan to gather intercepts from the Far East and from British India's Persian and Afghan neighbors.[30] Muslims were heavily overrepresented in intelligence activities generally in British India, and the Indian Army's Intelligence Corps was headquartered in Karachi.[31] Following independence, tactical military SIGINT units were established, primarily along the border with Kashmir, focusing mostly on Indian military radio signals. In the 1971 conflict, a SIGINT station in Dacca in East Pakistan was also used to monitor political radio traffic, notably that of the leader of the secessionist Awami Party, Sheikh Mujibur Rehman.[32]

The strategic considerations of the Cold War led to the establishment of a very large US SIGINT station at Bada Bier, near Peshawar in the northwest of Pakistan, in the period between 1958 and 1970. This facility was also an important base for U-2 imagery aircraft flights. The reestablishment of the station in the 1980s also allowed the ISI in Pakistan to receive substantial SIGINT assistance from the United States in monitoring the war in Afghanistan, in the shape of access to tactical radio interception and direction-finding equipment.[33] More recent experience suggests that cooperation between the CIA and the ISI has been effectively frozen following the arrest of the CIA contractor Raymond Davis in Lahore in January 2011.[34] This is underlined by the manner in which US special operations forces undertook the raid on Osama bin Laden's compound in May 2011. How far this will have affected technical cooperation between the two agencies is uncertain, but it is bound to be having an impact. It is certainly the case that the ISI and Pakistani intelligence community in general have not come favorably out of the official inquiry into the failure to discover Bin Laden's whereabouts, which bemoaned the collective "incompetence and negligence" of the agencies.[35]

Ashley J. Tellis notes that SIGINT assets are "disproportionately oriented towards targeting India," despite the recent counterterrorism activity on Pakistan's western flank.[36] Retired major general Yashwant Deva of the Indian army suggests that India has, by contrast, made slower progress toward technical intelligence gathering, preferring to focus for too long on a "sprawling network of spies and human analysts."[37] However, occasional breakthroughs have revealed capabilities. Ramesh Vinayak refers to an Indian success in 1998 in intercepting covert radio transmissions from a militant cell in Srinagar.[38] The discovery (if true) was an important one for understanding how Kashmiri militants communicate with their controllers, but it also shows how Pakistan's intelligence and security war with India has been spearheaded since the 1971 war by use of proxy militant forces undertaking "covert action." At the time of the Srinagar discovery in 1998, Vinayak, quoting Indian security agency sources, claimed there were four hundred covert militant radio calling stations operating in the Kashmir Valley alone.[39]

Tactical and Strategic Intelligence Failure

The first military conflict with India happened just two months after independence in August 1947, during the period when the ruling maharaja of the Princely State of Jammu and Kashmir was vacillating over whether to accede to India or to Pakistan. The Pakistani military determined that he should be helped in his decision by a military incursion. On October 23, a force of two thousand militant Pashtun tribesmen from what was then the North-West Frontier Province in Pakistan entered Jammu and Kashmir, led by Khurshid Anwar, a former Indian army officer and commander of the Muslim League National Guards.[40] The idea was that "the Kashmir Valley would be Pakistan's before India realized what had happened."[41] In the event, the plan backfired, as the maharaja decided three days later formally to accede to India, and the Indian forces that came to his aid were able to repel the attack. By December 1948, hostilities had settled around a Line of Control (LOC), which still broadly forms the de facto border between India and Pakistan in the area. The intelligence situation was rather unusual during this conflict, since both sides had effectively been part of the same Indian army just a few months before. This meant that both sides knew the area well and knew each other's capabilities. It became apparent during the conflict that both sides were using the same field radios and were able to tune in to each other's broadcasts with ease; this, in turn, allowed deception to be undertaken on the battlefield.[42]

Despite these advantages, there was much evidence of crucial intelligence miscalculations on the Pakistani side, notably in predicting how the Indians would react to the incursion. The commander of the Pakistani forces, Col.

Akbar Khan (who would later become chief of national security under Zulfikar Ali Bhutto) believed that India "was not militarily strong enough" to widen the 1947 conflict into a more general attack against Pakistan, assessing that its army was only twice the size of Pakistan's. It is not clear on what he based this notion, but it proved to be a great underestimate.[43] It was also apparent at this time that there was much disagreement between the military and the executive over how to run the conflict. On the question of whether to launch a more aggressive incursion backed by the full Pakistani military, most were of the opinion that this would be too risky.[44] Col. Akbar Khan, on the other hand, was all for escalating the operation, in part because of his miscalculations described above. The general analysis, certainly from those close to the military, is that such disagreement and vacillation allowed the Indians to regroup and repel the poorly organized militants with relative ease.[45] As discussed, such schisms between civilian and military decision making on defense issues have been damaging to Pakistan on several occasions.

The next major episode of conflict was in 1965, when a further Pakistan-backed incursion of militants called Operation Gibraltar was launched by the first military ruler of Pakistan, Gen. Ayub Khan. Islamic symbolism was important: Gibraltar, derived from the original Moorish term *Jabal Tariq* (mountain of Tariq) was the place from which the Umayyad general Tariq established a beachhead in Iberia for the main force invasion into Europe in AD 711.

The 1965 plan was similar in essence to that of 1947 in that an initial invading force of tribal militants would enter the province from Pakistan and team up with local insurgents to provoke a wider rebellion against India. On the issue of popular support in Kashmir for the operation, far from welcoming the incursions with open arms, however, there were incidents in which locals actually turned in to the Indian authorities the thinly disguised Pakistani military personnel posing as popular militants. Within three weeks the Indians had effectively halted the operations of the infiltrators.[46] On the ground, no gains were made by Pakistan.

The run-up to the 1965 conflict involved a number of strategic intelligence calculations and miscalculations on both sides of the border. In 1962 India had become embroiled in a military confrontation with China over disputed territories in the Ladakh region, in the far northeast of Kashmir. In late November, China made a substantial military incursion into India's North-East Frontier Agency (NEFA) territory, which revealed Indian forces to be ill-equipped to fight in the high-altitude conditions. After this incursion, China successfully gained agreement on a cease-fire to consolidate its gains. Recriminations raged in India over its strategic failure. Onlookers drew two interesting conclusions. First, many in the military hierarchy in Pakistan saw their prevailing wisdom confirmed that India's military was weak under pressure.[47] It was also not well equipped to fight in cold and high-altitude conditions (a calculation that became important in 1999 when Pakistan decided to attack India in the lofty Kargil Heights area). The wider world, meanwhile, was worried about the possibilities of a communist invasion southward from China, and this meant that Western allies such as the United States became keen to bolster India's military capability. A number of younger generals in the Pakistani army at the time assessed that a "window of opportunity" to strike India in Kashmir was closing.[48]

In 1965 a small military skirmish between India and Pakistan in the thinly populated and territorially disputed Rann of Kutch region, on the southeastern border of Pakistan, revealed India to be poorly organized and lacking in tactical intelligence capability. Pakistan's robust rebuff of an Indian incursion into the territory further confirmed Pakistani military views of the weakness of Indian military capabilities. Gen. Ayub Khan was bellicose in his assessment of the situation, pledging that "smaller though we are than India, we shall hurt India beyond repair."[49] By this stage, many in the region assessed wider war between the two countries to be "inevitable."[50]

Plans for Operation Gibraltar in 1965 appear to have been drawn up within a newly established "Kashmir Cell" at the top of government, which comprised the foreign and defense secretaries, the director of the IB, the chief of the General Staff (CGS), and the army's director of military operations. The relatively new ISI also participated in discussions, although it appears not to have played a leading role.[51] Plans emerged for a two-pronged operation, starting with a militant incursion as had happened in 1947, followed by a full Pakistani military operation dubbed Grand Slam by the bridge-playing Gen. Akhtar Malik, to consolidate gains.[52] There is a suggestion that Gen. Ayub Khan questioned the thinking of the Kashmir Cell in drawing up its plans but eventually accepted their proposals.[53]

In the event, the military campaign was hampered by much confusion and a breakdown in communications. Many analysts in both India and Pakistan assess that a key moment was when the army chief, General Mohammed Musa, replaced General Malik with Gen. Yahya Khan during the heat of the battle when Musa lost contact temporarily with Malik.[54] This led to a brief hiatus in operations while Gen. Yahya Khan consulted his commanders about the best course of action. This, in turn, allowed India to regain the military initiative. From the point of view of tactical intelligence, Indian plans to launch a major counteroffensive into Pakistani territory toward the end of the conflict seemed to be a surprise when they should not have been, although some of the detailed intelligence about Indian troop movements toward the border were only obtained by the chance capture of an Indian dispatch rider who was carrying documents for the Indian First Armored Division.[55]

One of the critical intelligence failings in this episode was exposed by General Malik, writing some years later in the Pakistani newspaper *The News* about what had gone wrong.[56] Malik recalled that the information gleaned from the captured dispatch rider had been forwarded to General Headquarters (GHQ) immediately, owing to its intelligence significance. However, it transpired later that the staff at GHQ had dismissed the intelligence as fake because of the amount of deception that was being spread around the battlefield by both sides. It appeared, noted Malik, that "people had read too much military history and considered this to be a plant by the enemy."[57]

Here we can see two classic aspects of intelligence failure within the Pakistani system at the time. First, prevailing wisdom about the likelihood of deception meant that a piece of incoming intelligence was fitted into a particular hypothesis and dismissed, much as had been the case in the early stages of the Cuban Missile Crisis with incoming HUMINT reporting.[58] Second, the policymakers, in this case the GHQ, were placing their own interpretation on the intelligence and deciding to ignore it, when others in the intelligence system considered it significant. Recalling Ernest May's observations about prewar Europe, the story is therefore as much about intelligence users as about intelligence producers.[59] It is also about the mechanisms in place in government to process intelligence up through the system to the top decision makers.

A few years later, in 1971, Pakistan endured the most grievous episode in its conflicts with India, when a campaign to suppress a secessionist rebellion in East Pakistan ended in military defeat and the dismemberment of the country. With evidence growing of Indian support for the emergent resistance movement in East Pakistan (the Mukhtar Bahini force, which was assisted by India's Research and Analysis Wing [RAW][60]), Pakistan made the bold and ultimately disastrous move to launch a preemptive strike on Indian air bases across northern India in December 1971 and widen the front in the conflict. This, coupled with the growing issue of large refugee movements westward from East Pakistan into West Bengal, forced India to respond with a declaration of war on Pakistan. It did so with overwhelming military superiority and very quickly took control of the region. Less than two weeks after the commencement of the war, Lt. Gen. A. A. K. Niazi of the Pakistani army formally surrendered to the Indian forces at Ramna Race Course in Dhaka on December 16, and the independent state of Bangladesh was born.

A major contributing factor in this disastrous episode in Pakistan's history was the manner in which power was concentrated in the hands of a small number of key figures in the military. M. Asghar Khan recalls from his personal experience of the period that the head of MI, Gen. Yahya Khan, had fed to ailing President Ayub Khan selective and misleading intelligence that by 1969 suggested the rebellion in East Pakistan had reached such a serious stage that a military response was required.[61] Once the president agreed to this course of action, he was further persuaded by Yahya Khan that martial law ought to be imposed in the East and that Yahya Khan should take over as chief martial law administrator.[62]

A further structural problem within the intelligence machinery was that different agencies sometimes disagreed significantly on their assessments of the situation. Of course, this is not unusual or necessarily a problem, unless the intelligence machinery does not exist to clarify and resolve such differing assessments for the policymakers. By June 1971, when the rebellion and subsequent crackdown by Pakistani forces was well under way, the question arose as to whether and how India might intervene militarily in the situation. The ISI issued a report in senior circles that "hinted at the possibility of war" but suggested it could be avoided if care was taken.[63] MI concluded in its report that "India is unlikely to resort to all-out war with Pakistan." The CGS, Gul Hassan, however, assessed the situation to be very close to what actually transpired in the end—namely, that with the Pakistani forces bogged down in suppressing a rebellion, the Indian army could strike at the right moment and easily overrun the country. For his part, Gen. Yahya Khan and his immediate coterie refused to take note of the warning signals, preferring to believe their own story that everything was under control and that it would be too costly for the Indians to intervene.[64]

It can be seen in this instance that a concentration of power and military decision making in the hands of a forceful and charismatic military leader, as was the case with Yahya Khan, can distort the process of properly assessing intelligence and making it heard in the right circles. A dictator can run the risk of becoming isolated from the true situation on the ground, and many of those immediately around him may be too afraid to disagree. As noted below, Ayub Khan established a National Security Council (NSC) in 1968, but his successor, Yahya Khan, was not particularly interested in this layer of bureaucracy and preferred to receive only the news he wanted to hear.[65] The existence of an NSC alone is not enough, therefore, if it is subverted by the political system.

We can also see throughout this period much evidence of the cultural problems arising from a military-dominated intelligence structure. Herman recalled a telling observation once made by the director-general (DG) of intelligence at Britain's Ministry of Defense, Vice Adm. Sir Louis Le Bailly, that his job had been to tell "all those who won't listen all the things they don't want to know."[66] Such a refusal to listen is common among senior military staff in many countries and was certainly a considerable problem for Pakistan in its first major conflicts with India.

The trauma of the 1971 episode meant that open conflict with India was not considered again for some time afterward. Civilian rule was reestablished under Z. A. Bhutto's Pakistan People's Party (PPP) while the military returned to their barracks to lick their wounds (a situation that lasted only until 1977, when the military seized power again under General Zia). The late 1970s saw a new regional preoccupation emerging for Pakistan as the Soviets invaded Afghanistan and the ISI was called in to help coordinate and supply the mujahideen resistance movement. In Kashmir a growing use of proxy Islamist militant groups, as opposed to direct military confrontation with India, accelerated under

General Zia in the 1980s. Lawrence Sáez notes that following the Zia period "it is undeniable that several radical pan-Islamic insurgent groups operating in Kashmir have their operational roots in Pakistan."[67]

Many of the mujahideen veterans of the conflict with the Soviets sought new channels for their jihadist agenda in the 1990s and found the answer in armed insurrection in Kashmir against the "infidel Hindu." Since 1989, when the militant group Hizb-ul Mujahideen (HM; Party of Holy Warriors) was formed under the aegis of the Islamist Pakistani political party Jamaat-i Islami, a policy of low-level proxy war in Kashmir through organized militant groups has been the main feature of the conflict. HM, which has now been proscribed as a terrorist organization in the European Union (EU) and the United States, was clearly aided by the ISI in its early years, as were other militant groups in the region.[68] The shift in policy toward covert support for such groups is generally seen as a conscious strategic policy shift on the part of the Pakistani military establishment.[69]

The militant fight in Kashmir was soon joined by newer, more brutal militant groups. These were spearheaded by Lashkar-e Toiba (LeT; The Army of the Righteous), formed in 1991 as the militant wing of the extreme Ahl-e Hadith sect in Pakistan, and later by Jaish-e Mohamed (JEM; The Army of Mohammed). While it is a matter of great conjecture and fiercely denied by Pakistan, the orthodox view is that both LeT and JEM have clearly been supported in their endeavors by the ISI as a strategic proxy force fighting the Indians, although more recently they may have become largely autonomous groups, and many of the official ties may now have been severed.[70]

While General Zia had refrained from major operations in Kashmir, General Musharraf (who was the army's chief of staff at the time) launched a new military offensive in Kashmir in 1999. It has been suggested that Indian intelligence had become accustomed to small-scale infiltrations and covert operations by militant groups and was caught somewhat off guard by a larger-scale military intrusion, the like of which had not been seen for some years.[71]

The plan for the operation was broadly that the Pakistani military would catch the Indians by surprise immediately before winter set in, by seizing some of the checkpoints in the very high-altitude Kargil Heights area in the far northeast of the LOC in Kashmir. India, it was suggested, would have to wait until spring to launch a major counteroffensive, by which time the strategic gains could have been consolidated by Pakistan.[72] It appears that the operation had been the subject of extensive war-gaming and scenario planning that the military had undertaken over many years. Former prime minister Benazir Bhutto recalled receiving a presentation during her second term in office (1993–96) by the DG of military operations and future president, General Musharraf, about scenario planning that the military had been conducting over a military offensive in Kashmir and the likely Indian response.[73] The recollection was interesting, not only because of Bhutto's claim that she was always being accused by the military of being "soft on India"[74] (a significant charge for a prime minister to receive from the military) but also because it reveals the fact that the Pakistani military and intelligence structure appears to be fairly continuously engaged in thinking about how to redraw the map with India.

At the same time, the political analyst Shuja Nawaz also cites a conversation with an unnamed senior officer in the Joint Chiefs' staff, who had been alarmed at the bellicose suggestions being made in the run-up to the Kargil operation.[75] This officer had conducted a "staff check" with some of his colleagues (a "red teaming" exercise) that had suggested the assumptions were flawed. He felt unable to challenge the generals leading the operation, however, since the planning seemed to have developed an unstoppable momentum and the politicians were acquiescing in the military's offensive plan.[76] Such a situation is reminiscent of the infamous Downing Street memo, written by the chief of the Secret Intelligence Service in Britain after a visit to Washington in the run-up to the Iraq War in 2003, which claimed that preparations for war seemed to have developed a momentum of their own and that "the intelligence and facts were being fixed around the policy."[77]

The intelligence miscalculations by Pakistan in this case were intricately connected with the nuclearization of the subcontinent, following successful nuclear tests by both Pakistan and India in 1998. S. P. Kapur argues that the 1999 conflict represents an interesting challenge to the "stability/instability paradox," which suggests that strategic stability achieved through the threat of nuclear escalation normally reduces the risk of conventional war between adversaries.[78] During the Cold War in Europe, the logic of mutually assured destruction ensured that both sides were wary of provoking conventional conflict in Europe lest it escalate. There is clear evidence that one of Pakistan's strategic calculations was that, having shown India that it had a viable nuclear deterrent, India would be wary of undertaking a robust conventional counterattack to a Pakistani incursion, and gains made by Pakistan on the ground could be consolidated.[79] Furthermore, as Benazir Bhutto recalled from her discussions with senior military planners at the time, there was also a thought that the risk of nuclear escalation would bring international attention to Kashmir (particularly from the United States and China) if a low-level conflict were initiated with India and that a renewed drive would be made by the international community to resolve the situation once and for all.[80] In this way, establishing a nuclear deterrent actually made Pakistan more confident in confronting India in a conventional conflict.

In actual fact, however, after the initial surprise in Delhi over the Kargil incursion and doubts about the effect of a robust conventional response, Kapur concludes that India decided that Pakistan's actions and veiled threats of nuclear escalation were little more than "bluff and bluster," since to provoke a nuclear conflict could ultimately prove the end of Pakistan altogether.[81] Having decided this, India did respond robustly to the incursion, launching airstrikes and extended infantry operations against the Pakistani positions and regaining the military initiative. Pakistan was partly right to the extent that the conflict did rattle the international community and led the United States in particular to undertake energetic diplomatic efforts to resolve the dispute, although one of Pakistan's key military allies, China, did not apply the pressure on India that Pakistan had wanted, and the ultimate result was diplomatic isolation for Pakistan.[82] What the episode did show is that the stability/instability paradox seems to work differently in South Asia than it had in Europe during the Cold War: Nuclearization of adversaries may have actually increased the likelihood of low-level and conventional conflict as each side tried to call the other's bluff and draw the attention of the international community.

The Kargil confrontation aside, there is no doubt that Pakistan's strategic view of India has been that a low-level insurgency, backed up by a nuclear deterrent, is the best way to mitigate the asymmetry of the two states' respective military capabilities. Former DG of the ISI Lt. Gen. Javed Nasir displayed this strategic mindset in a 1999 article on the military confrontation with India in Kashmir. "Counter-insurgency operations," he wrote, "are a bottomless bucket, a super-sucker of more and more troops."[83] The effects of sustaining an extended low-level counterinsurgency operation are both physical and psychological: "These operations sap energies and resources with such rapidity that even the strongest economies and the best of soldiers start wilting under it very quickly."[84] Whether this can be said to be borne out by experience in Kashmir is a moot point. While Pakistan has not made substantive gains, there is no doubt that a counterinsurgency operation of this nature has been a more effective way of striking India than direct military confrontation.

Outside Kashmir, there is some evidence that Pakistani intelligence has supported covert militant operations across India for many years. Some commentators in India feel that the ISI has an almost ubiquitous presence in the country, with active or "sleeper" agents in every Indian city.[85] The truth of this is hard to establish, but there is no doubt that the ISI has become increasingly adept at running clandestine operations in parts of India. Throughout the 1960s, Pakistan and the ISI exploited the Cold War by supporting destabilizing and secessionist movements in India, such as the Sikhs' "Khalistan" movement in the Punjab, receiving patronage in doing so from the CIA in the light of India's political leanings toward the Soviet Union.[86] Meanwhile, in the far northeast of India, a collection of revolutionary and separatist groups under the umbrella of the United Liberation Front of Seven Sisters (one of the main elements of which is the ULFA—the United Liberation Front of Assam) is purportedly receiving training and assistance from the ISI.[87] In some cases the training is conducted locally in the border area close to Bangladesh, while in others it is suggested that ULFA militants have trained in Islamist militant camps in Afghanistan (which, if true, reflects the logic of "strategic depth" to Pakistan's west).[88]

Operations against India may not be confined to Kashmir or to India itself. Former Afghan president Hamid Karzai frequently expressed suspicion of the ISI's continuing meddling in his country, not least following an assassination attempt in April 2008 and the suicide bombing of the Indian embassy in Kabul in July 2008, which killed forty-one people.[89] The CIA has backed up these claims, pointing out to former Pakistani prime minister Yusuf Raza Gilani during a visit to the United States in July 2008 that it had solid evidence of the ISI's role in the Indian embassy bombing.[90] As regards Afghanistan, Pakistan does not want a state on its western flanks to pursue a pro-Indian policy. Obtaining strategic depth in Afghanistan will be frustrated if Kabul becomes a key ally of Delhi and thus effectively helps India to encircle Pakistan and prevent it from concentrating its forces on its eastern border. The policy analyst Farhana Ali claims that an unknown actor is funding and supplying the Pakistani Taliban and that Pakistanis naturally suspect India.[91]

In the meantime, Pakistan continues to accuse India of undertaking destabilizing covert action in return. In early November 2009, Pakistan's information minister and a senior military spokesman announced in a press conference that "concrete evidence of India's involvement in militancy in South Waziristan" had been found, in the shape of Indian literature, arms, ammunition, and other equipment uncovered in military raids in the region.[92] The interior minister, Rehman Malik, had gone further a week before by accusing India of involvement in "almost every terrorist activity in Pakistan" and making a thinly veiled threat of nuclear retaliation.[93]

This may be a fine example of "mirror-imaging" within the intelligence community in Pakistan. As Peter Gill describes it, this is one of the "structural problems" that befall many intelligence agencies from East to West, and it was noted most recently in the failure of the Western allies to make the right intelligence calculations about Saddam Hussein's weapons of mass destruction (WMDs) in Iraq.[94] In a South Asian context, Loch K. Johnson sees the same factor at work in the CIA's failure to predict the Indian nuclear test in 1998, as it assumed Indian claims that this would happen were merely empty electoral rhetoric, as would happen in the United States.[95] Vikash Yadav and Conrad Barwa argue that the RAW, one of India's intelligence agencies, which is often invoked in Pakistan's claims of destabilizing activity, simply does not have the resources to be able to undertake an extended operation of covert destabilization in such places as Balochistan.[96] If there is any truth to this claim, it may mean either that accusations are made about Indian behind-the-scenes activity merely for populist political purposes or that, as May commented about the prewar situation in Europe, "analysts and decision-makers alike ascribed to their potential enemies a high order of rationality, cunning and skill." In Europe, ultimately, this predisposition "was a source of error."[97]

Problems with Intelligence: Civilian-Military Structures and Relations

It is likely that intelligence assessments in Pakistan make their way directly to senior policymakers, mostly at the top of the military, with little intervention from other departments. In 2002, when General Musharraf's regime found itself at the forefront of the newly invigorated war on terrorism, he expressed a desire to reform the intelligence sector in Pakistan. He announced that he was working to end the infiltration of militant groups over the border into Kashmir. He formally banned the two militant groups, LeT and JEM—an announcement met with deep skepticism by India. He also made sweeping changes to the structure and personnel of the ISI in an attempt to bring it back under greater central control, including placing it formally under the scrutiny of MI.[98] In 2008 the government announced that the "political wing" of the ISI, whose main preoccupation had been interference in domestic Pakistani politics and the monitoring of internal political targets, had been disbanded in favor of a shift of emphasis toward counterterrorism.[99]

The general was speaking in the aftermath of the 9/11 attacks in the United States, which many had felt were a substantial intelligence failure, not only on the part of the Americans but also in the Afghanistan/Pakistan region.[100] There was evidence that recommendations that Pakistan establish an intelligence coordination body similar to the United Kingdom's Joint Intelligence Committee (JIC),[101] which were rejected during General Zia's rule in the 1980s, were being made again.[102] There is no outward evidence that such a body has been established yet, suggesting that the ISI and other agencies continue to relay intelligence directly to senior policymakers with little input from other departments in government. There is also evidence, arising from the official Pakistani inquiry into the failed hunt for Bin Laden after 9/11, that the degree of coordination between Pakistani intelligence agencies has remained lamentable.[103]

As discussed, Pakistan has made various generally short-lived attempts to establish an NSC at stages in its history. As Thomas C. Bruneau, F. C. Matei, and Sak Sakoda observe, NSCs can be a critical element of civilian-military relations in democratic societies and generally aim to perform some or all coordination, information, policy-formation, and oversight functions, particularly focused on the activities of intelligence and security agencies.[104] In Pakistan the first NSC was established, ironically, under the first military regime of Gen. Ayub Khan in 1968, following the failure of Pakistan's conflict with India in 1965. The general, as president at the time, was the chair, and the ministers of home and Kashmir affairs the vice chairs. While, as Nawaz notes, this was "a potentially useful forum for assessing intelligence and giving direction to the various intelligence agencies," General Yahya Khan, who took over from Ayub Khan in 1969, was "generally allergic to this formal decision-making apparatus" and left its deliberations largely in the hands of his aide, Maj. Gen. Ghulam Umar.[105] Yahya Khan's style of leadership was such that he "only got news that he wanted to hear."[106] Such a flawed structure for speaking truth to power within the Pakistani establishment almost certainly contributed to the defeat and breakup of the country in December 1971.

The civilian regime of Zulfikar Ali Bhutto that followed disbanded the NSC on the ground that its membership, which included the three chiefs of the armed forces alongside civilian government ministers, meant that the military continued to hold an unusually powerful position in national security decision making. Under General Zia's rule, an NSC was reestablished in 1985 but promptly disbanded again within weeks.[107] The caretaker government that followed the dismissal of Benazir Bhutto's second government in 1997 established a Committee for Defense and National Security, to be chaired by the president, but this was also disbanded by the Nawaz Sharif government that followed on the ground that its membership had been handpicked by the caretaker government.[108] The civilian government of Asif Ali Zardari that followed Musharraf's rule remained uncertain about whether to reestablish an NSC. There is a parliamentary National Security Committee that provides some sort of reporting mechanism on the activities of the intelligence agencies, although its degree of autonomy and influence should probably not be overstated.

The problem for Pakistan is that the NSC, unlike the equivalent in the United Kingdom, for example, which is chaired by the prime minister, has always included chiefs of the armed forces at a level equivalent to the prime minister. It has also habitually been chaired by the president, who, for most of Pakistan's existence, has been a senior army officer. This means that the military has always retained the preeminent decision-making role on issues of national security, including the governance of intelligence agencies and the interpretation of their intelligence reporting. Such issues lie at the heart of the civilian-military struggle within Pakistan's administration and mean that intelligence continues to be dominated by the military mindset. Conditions are far from suitable for the establishment of an objective and autonomous intelligence assessment body, such as the JIC, which would be able to coordinate intelligence assessments for government.

Indeed, the military has shown that it fundamentally distrusts the civilian government's ability to make sensible decisions on matters of national security. Smruti S. Pattanaik notes that during Benazir Bhutto's tenure as prime minister many senior personnel in the military and intelligence, especially Lt. Gen. Hamid Gul (the DG of the ISI who was eventually removed by Bhutto), believed that Bhutto's family had direct and secret links with the Indian leadership.[109] Such was the distrust that the ISI covertly recorded a discussion between Bhutto and Indian prime minister Rajiv Gandhi and played it to her political opponents to win their support and ensure that she was deposed.[110]

Like many intelligence agencies across the world, the ISI and Pakistan's other intelligence agencies appear to operate with little or no formal legal oversight. As former DG of both the ISI and MI Lt. Gen. Asad Durrani has said, intelligence agencies "have to use unconventional means. And, to neutralize similar methods by the other side, they will be seriously handicapped if they were to strictly operate under the law."[111] During the 1994 "Mehrangate" financial fraud trial in Pakistan, it was alleged that Durrani, who was DG of the ISI during the controversial 1990 elections, had himself covertly used money from Mehran Bank to pay political rivals of the PPP and ensure the latter's defeat in the elections.[112] Such a culture at the top of the IC is very different from that in a country such as the United Kingdom in the post–Cold War era, for example, where, in the words of former intelligence and security coordinator David Omand, "it is difficult to overstate the overall impact in recent years of . . . legislation on the ethos of the UK agencies in creating a disciplined culture within the agencies, while enabling them to carry out a full range of intelligence-gathering operations for authorized purposes."[113]

When civilian government returned in 2008, the ruling PPP attempted to reopen dialogue about placing the activities of the intelligence agencies on a proper statutory footing.[114] Discussions included passing a law to govern telephone tapping and removing the power of arrest from the federal IB, confining it to intelligence gathering on behalf of the police. There was also a bizarre episode in which a decision to place the ISI under the Interior Ministry was publicly reversed within twenty-four hours, presumably following a robust protest from the military.[115] No visible progress has been made on these discussions, and the brief attempt to subordinate the ISI to civilian governance shows that the military hierarchy still very much holds the reins in the intelligence sector.

Difficult questions of human rights abuses by Pakistani intelligence agencies, such as those exposed by the Commission of Inquiry on Missing Persons (CIMP),[116] and evidence of the severe intimidation of journalists,[117] merely reflect the degree to which the intelligence agencies feel they can operate with autonomy and impunity. While these are serious questions in themselves, they are also signs that a culture of accountability for decision making within the Pakistani IC is fundamentally lacking. This is likely to contribute to failed assumptions about enemies and targets as much as it affects domestic affairs.

The National Security Psyche

The manner in which India has loomed so large in Pakistan's security outlook reflects national construction and mythmaking in Pakistan and the acrimonious circumstances in which the country was formed out of what many had assumed previously would be a unified India. These experiences have led to what Stephen

P. Cohen describes as an "institutional distrust" of India within the Pakistani army.[118] In 1966 former foreign minister and later prime minister Zulfikar Ali Bhutto struck a chord with many in the country by asserting that "India cannot tolerate the existence of Pakistan" and that the destruction of Pakistan was a "sublime dream" for its larger neighbor.[119]

Much has been written about Pakistan's particular issues of nationhood and state identity, which have shaped its security picture from the outset. One of the first prime ministers of Pakistan, Chaudhry Muhammad Ali, described some years after independence that the general feeling in the Pakistani leadership after 1947 was that Jawaharlal Nehru had finally agreed to partition, having opposed it all along, in the belief that Pakistan would be unviable and quickly collapse.[120] Among others, Mahatma Gandhi himself is purported to have said on the day of independence that a time would come when the division between India and Pakistan would be reversed.[121]

These perspectives on history have influenced the Pakistani national security psyche. There is a constant belief in "hidden hands" operating secretly and trying to destabilize the country. As noted, the Indian intelligence agency RAW is frequently accused in Pakistani media and government statements of orchestrating such activities, whether it is the ongoing secessionist insurgency in Balochistan,[122] the Taliban insurgency in Waziristan and neighboring districts, or the creation of militant groups within Pakistan, such as the Muhajir Qaumi Mahaz (MQM; Muhajir Qaumi Movement) in Karachi.[123] As discussed, such a belief may represent mirror-imaging, since there is adequate evidence of Pakistan itself funding and supporting militant groups within India for its own strategic political purposes. It should also be said that such conspiracy theories are common in the region at all levels of debate.

The blow delivered to the national psyche of Pakistan with the dismemberment of the country in 1971 and the humiliation and determination for revenge felt by the Pakistani military establishment thereafter can hardly be overstated.[124] More importantly, the episode fed into the historical narrative that India was indeed intent on dismantling the state of Pakistan and ensuring that it ultimately failed. Sarwar Khan describes Pakistan's foreign policy at the time as "an obsession with the question of its very survival after the separation of East Pakistan."[125] He argues that this, in turn, strengthened the attitude in Pakistan that a nuclear deterrent was needed following India's first successful testing of its atomic capability just a few years after the Bangladesh episode, in 1974. Pakistan felt it needed a "minimum credible deterrence against the security threat from India."[126]

The founder of Pakistan and first prime minister, Mohammed Ali Jinnah, was always disappointed that the Pakistani state was riven with disputes over which areas should be in and which out. Nowhere was this more the case than with respect to the territory of Jammu and Kashmir. As Rajesh Basrur outlines in his analysis of Pakistan's foreign policy toward India, domestic politics are central to Pakistan's antagonism with India over Kashmir.[127] Rather like the "Malvinas effect" in Argentinian politics, railing against Indian oppression in Kashmir is often invoked when there is a need to tap into deep nationalist sentiment in Pakistan and gain support from the public. Successive regimes in Pakistan, and particularly military ones, have made conflict with India over Kashmir central to their national security policy.

Part of the underlying psychology in the conflictual stance with India involves a mobilization around religious and cultural differences—the rationale, after all, for Kashmir to be part of Pakistan rather than of India was that it is a Muslim-majority area. At times of conflict, the religious dimension becomes apparent. On the eve of Gen. Yahya Khan's ill-fated decision to widen the Bangladesh conflict of 1971 to India's western front with what was then West Pakistan, the general started to speak of the "mujahids" (Muslim holy warriors) ranged against India, who were "imbued with the love of God and the holy Prophet."[128] Such rhetoric mirrors a traditional "martial race" view of many in the Pakistani military. As Hafeez Malik describes it, the unequal outcome of partition for the new states of India and Pakistan was "unacceptable to the psyche of the Pakistani elites who wanted the past glory of the Muslim rule over India to miraculously repeat itself."[129] It is indicative that the Pakistanis have called their medium-range "Hatf-V" ballistic missile ("Hatf" signifies the lance purportedly carried by the Prophet Muhammad) the "Ghauri," after the Afghan dynasty that con-solidated Muslim rule across northern India in the twelfth century, having defeated the Hindu maharajas.[130]

As Pattanaik describes, the Pakistani elite will often prefix any reference to India with the word "Hindu,"[131] showing a psychological conception of the two states as being separate religious identities and cultures and attaching a sense of otherness to Pakistan's larger neighbor.[132] As we have seen, Gen. Ayub Khan had reportedly claimed that "as a general rule, the Hindu morale would not stand more than a couple of hard blows at the right time and place."[133] In 1999 Lt. Gen. Javed Nasir, who had been DG of the ISI in the early 1990s, noted that he "knew the Hindu mentality" in wanting to hold on to the Siachen Glacier but that Pakistan would have a "tremendous psychological ascendancy" in its efforts to recover the territory.[134] Such a misplaced view of the enemy proved to be a miscalculation in the 1965 and 1999 conflicts and may reflect a fundamental groupthink in Pakistani military circles about the military capability of the Indi-ans that has contributed to the poor quality of intelligence assessments over the years. Again we are reminded of Ernest May's injunction to think carefully of how one defines oneself and how one defines one's enemies.[135]

It appears that General Nasir brought a particularly Islamist strand to the outlook of Pakistan's premier intelligence agency during his tenure as DG of the ISI in 1992–93. Nasir had previously been implicated in providing covert material support to Muslim militants in Bosnia, among other activities.[136] He was himself closely affiliated with the Salafi group Tablighi Jamaat (Evangelizing Party), and he undoubtedly brought this culture to the ISI. On taking office, his successor as DG, Lt. Gen. Javed Ashraf Qazi, purportedly found a much less military and more religious culture in the corridors of the ISI than had prevailed before, in which long beards and Islamic dress were much more on display, and the business day was more punctuated by prayer times.[137] Perhaps more important, the agency had become much more preoccupied with coordinating and managing militant operations in the field than gathering and assessing intelligence.[138] Such a change in emphasis was probably inevitable given the frontline role the ISI had played in Afghanistan during the 1990s, but the seeds of a particular strand of Islamist thinking in culture and staffing may well have been sown in this period within the ISI and led to some of the difficulties that it had in cooperating with the United States in the war on terrorism.

The upshot, as Gregory argues, is that military decision making in Pakistan is inevitably shaped by both personal and national psychological postures, which "have in the past included complex ethno-religious-cultural elements of face-saving, fatalism, 'honour,' obduracy, over-confidence, risk-taking and victimhood."[139] While Gregory acknowledges that such issues are "difficult to evidence,"[140] there is no doubt that they can affect intelligence perspectives to a dangerous degree if the system for processing intelligence is such that individual personalities and institutional mindsets are allowed to have a disproportionate influence on decision making. The risk is one of groupthink and "prevailing wisdom" about the adversary, an institutional pitfall originally described by the psychologist Irving Janis and highlighted by Lord Butler in his review of intelligence on WMDs in the period prior to the Iraq War of 2003.[141] In this way, as discussed, the contemporary Pakistani IC shows some similarities with the French IC in the 1930s in that a "relatively homogenous" group (in both cases dominated by the military) can lead to "serious miscalculations" in intelligence assessments of the identified enemy.[142]

Conclusions

The seemingly perpetual confrontation between Pakistan and India is a clear example of T. V. Paul's notion of an enduring conflict.[143] A complex interplay with domestic politics in both countries adds further endurance to the confrontation.[144] As Sheen Rajmaira argues, the foreign policy behaviors of both South Asian countries are "long-memoried," and several decades after independence, the "equilibrium level of behaviour has been characterized by high levels of sustained hostility punctuated by an intense ideological, religious and political rivalry."[145] As Ramesh Thakur described it in 1992, "official relations [between

India and Pakistan] are based on a permanent state of paranoia and zero-sum mentality."[146]

The combination of a military groupthink mindset about the will and effectiveness of India in responding to Pakistani aggression, and the fact that the military has been firmly in control of national security strategizing and decision making since independence and even during the infrequent periods of civilian rule, has meant that a perceived need for "perpetual confrontation" with India has strongly influenced intelligence and security in Pakistan.[147] A deep-seated national belief that India is determined to bring about the disintegration of Pakistan and thereby right the wrongs of partition has had a profound influence on the perspective of the intelligence services. This has become apparent in mistakes made in several military conflicts with India. It also manifests itself in the belief that RAW is instigating covert destabilization across Pakistan. Often these factors have meant that Pakistan's intelligence has performed poorly on both the tactical and strategic levels and confrontations with India have usually ended badly for Islamabad.

Personal and institutional psyches have not been enough in themselves, however, to cause Pakistan to underperform in intelligence capabilities against India. We have seen how a number of organizational factors are also very significant. The military's dominance of the defense and security infrastructure has meant that civilian governments have so far failed to take control of intelligence processes and to ensure that holistic and objective intelligence assessment is built into the system. (Whether this will change with the new civilian government of Nawaz Sharif remains to be seen.) Military leaders such as Ayub Khan, Yahya Khan, and Mohammad Zia-ul Haq all experimented with the establishment of NSCs at the top of their security decision making, but they all ensured either that the defense chiefs were always at least on a par with the prime minister or, in the case of Yahya Khan, that the whole NSC machinery was largely ignored in favor of personal decision making based on what the leader wanted to hear rather than objective intelligence. This has meant that civilian governments have been reluctant to reestablish an NSC in its previous form but are not yet able to win the battle of wills with the military. The brief attempt to subordinate the ISI to the Interior Ministry in 2008, which was hastily ended, shows that the army still has the last word on intelligence governance. This is probably the reason why no assessment body working across the IC in Pakistan, in the style of the JIC in Britain, has yet been created. The lack of such a unit may have led to the problems highlighted by the recent inquiry into the Bin Laden affair.

The intelligence structure in Pakistan also suffers from there being no legal framework governing the intelligence community and providing accountability and oversight. While this has been suggested by successive civilian governments, the experience of the CIMP and the flagrant intimidation of some journalists who have written critically about Pakistan's intelligence agencies show that the latter believe themselves to be above the law; they are not interested in the creation of a statutory framework governing their activities. While this may appear to offer operational flexibility and autonomy in the eyes of some senior intelligence officers, it perpetuates the incompetence and lack of objectivity of the IC as a whole and ensures that it is not processing intelligence in a way that allows for the fresh air of challenge and all-source perspectives to be breathed into the process. Nor, indeed, will the IC be able to learn easily from its mistakes.

In considering prospects for the reform of Pakistan's intelligence sector with the advent of a new period of parliamentary democracy in 2008, Frédéric Grare makes a comparison with the situation in Indonesia and in Chile, which have both recently entered a period of civilian government after military rule. This has entailed substantial restructuring and curtailment of previously very strong intelligence sectors (the Badan Intelijen Strategis [Strategic Intelligence Agency] and Dirección de Inteligencia Nacional [National Intelligence Directorate], respectively, being the main agencies in question).[148] Slowly but surely, progress is being made in those cases. It is too early to say whether Pakistan has definitively entered a period of civilian government, but it bodes well that in 2013 one civilian government handed power over to another after an election and a full term in office, for the first time in Pakistan's history.

The missing persons inquiry marks a significant step in potential reform of the agencies in Pakistan. It is hard to imagine such a case being brought at the height of the military regimes in Indonesia and Chile. Indeed, despite fearful intimidation (to the point, in some cases, of murder), Pakistani journalists have increasingly published stories not only criticizing the intelligence agencies for being above the law,[149] but also suggesting that they have been responsible for grave strategic errors in Pakistan's foreign policy.[150] The embarrassment of US forces' killing of Bin Laden under the noses of the Pakistani military in May 2011 has added to this chorus of criticism, and the publication in July 2013 of a damning official inquiry into the affair and the intelligence failings that led up to it further strengthens a sense of renewed openness, even if there is still a long way to travel.[151]

As Woodrow Kuhns has noted, intelligence failure has become the most widely studied aspect of intelligence since the 9/11 attacks in the United States.[152] There are many historical examples of strategic surprise occurring owing to poor intelligence or unwillingness on the part of policymakers to accept good intelligence. The two world wars provide many examples, such as the "Maginot Line of the mind" among senior French military planners in the 1930s,[153] which repeated a mistaken belief made in the First World War that the Germans would not advance through the Low Countries.[154] As Robert J. Young points out, in the case of the Maginot Line the problem was not so much faulty or lacking intelligence (as it might have been twenty-five years earlier) as the stubborn and closed mindset of senior policymakers who wished not to be contradicted in their beliefs.[155] The failures of Pakistani military ventures against India reflect a similarly chauvinistic and embittered attitude toward the enemy among senior military officials and a failure to process and assess incoming intelligence objectively. Indeed, at least one Pakistani analyst has likened a preoccupation with a threat from India as Pakistan's very own Maginot Line.[156]

Notes

1 Aparna Pande, *Explaining Pakistan's Foreign Policy: Escaping India* (Abingdon, UK: Routledge, 2011), 61.

2. Benazir Bhutto, cited in S. P. Kapur, "India and Pakistan's Unstable Peace: Why Nuclear South Asia Is Not like Cold War Europe," *International Security* 30, no. 2 (2005): 143.

3. Ernest May, "Conclusion: Capabilities and Proclivities," in *Knowing One's Enemies: Intelligence Assessment before the Two World Wars*, ed. Ernest May (Princeton, NJ: Princeton University Press, 1986), 541–42.

4. Ibid., 542.

5. Johnson notes that the director-general of the ISI is always a serving officer at the rank of lieutenant general, as are the three deputy directors-general. Robert Johnson, "Uncertain Loyalties: Pakistan's Inter-Services Intelligence (ISI) and Its Relationship with Western Intelligence Agencies," in *Spooked: Britain, Empire and Intelligence since 1945*, ed. Patrick Major and Christopher R. Moran (Newcastle upon Tyne, UK: Cambridge Scholars Publishing, 2009), 123.

6. David Thomas, "US Military Intelligence Analysis: Old and New Challenges," *Analyzing Intelligence: Origins, Obstacles, and Innovations*, ed. Roger Z. George and James B. Bruce (Washington, DC: Georgetown University Press, 2008), 142.

7. Ibid., 147.

8. Michael Herman, *Intelligence Power in Peace and War* (Cambridge: Cambridge University Press, 2008), 250.

9. Peter Jackson, *France and the Nazi Menace: Intelligence and Policy-Making, 1933–1939* (Oxford: Oxford University Press, 2000), 11.

10. Johnson, "Uncertain Loyalties," 122.

11. Ibid., 123.

12. Peter Jackson, "French Intelligence and Hitler's Rise to Power," *Historical Journal* 41, no. 3 (1998): 811.

13. Jackson, *France and the Nazi Menace*, 14.

14. Shuja Nawaz, *Crossed Swords: Pakistan, Its Army, and the Wars Within* (Karachi: Oxford University Press, 2008), 209.

15. Johnson notes that the "difficulty of accessing archival material on the ISI does not enable any analyst to make a final definitive judgement" about the activities of the preeminent Pakistani intelligence agency. See Johnson, "Uncertain Loyalties," 119.

16. Despite this situation, one of the successes of the Pakistani state has been the enduring courage and independence of the press since independence. The Dawn Group of newspapers, which is the largest and oldest media group in Pakistan, remains a crucial source of

information relating to the IC in Pakistan. Reports in *Dawn* are drawn upon extensively in this chapter.

17. Vikash Yadav and Conrad Barwa, "Relational Control: India's Grand Strategy in Afghanistan and Pakistan," *India Review* 10, no. 2 (2011): 98.

18. Pakistan Institute of Legislative Development and Transparency, *Peace and Conflict in Pakistan: The Structure and Role of Intelligence Agencies* (Islamabad: PILDAT, Dialogue Group on Civil-Military Relations, background paper, August 2007).

19. Iftikhar Haider Malik, *State and Civil Society in Pakistan: Politics of Authority, Ideology and Ethnicity* (New York: St. Martin's, 1997), 75.

20. Jeremy Page, "British Personnel Seconded to Pakistan Terror Agency to Combat Al-Qaeda," *Times* (London), October 6, 2009, http://www.timesonline.co.uk/tol/news/world/asia/article6863700.ece.

21. "Counter-Terrorism Authority Dormant," *Dawn*, May 25, 2011, http://www.dawn-.com/2011/05/25/counter-terrorism-authority-dormant.html.

22. Lt. Gen. L. P. Sen, *Slender Was the Thread: Kashmir Confrontation 1947–48* (New Delhi: Orient Longman, 1994), 19.

23. Bindanda M. Chengappa, "The ISI Role in Pakistan's Politics," *Strategic Analysis* 23, no. 11 (2000): 1863.

24. "Overview of Intelligence Services," *PakistanDefense.com*, http://www.pakistanidefence.com/Info/Intelligence.html.

25. "The ISI," *New Internationalist*, July 1, 2007, http://www.newint.org/columns/worldbeaters/2007/07/01/isi/.

26. Frédéric Grare, *Reforming the Intelligence Agencies in Pakistan's Transitional Democracy* (Washington, DC: Carnegie Endowment for International Peace, 2009), 15.

27. Shaun Gregory, "The ISI and the War on Terrorism," *Studies in Conflict and Terrorism* 30, no. 12 (2007): 1014.

28. Ibid.

29. Ashley J. Tellis, *Pakistan and the War on Terror: Conflicted Goals, Compromised Performance* (Washington, DC: Carnegie Endowment for International Peace, 2008), 25.

30. For an excellent and unique description of Pakistan's SIGINT capabilities, see Desmond Ball, *Signals Intelligence (SIGINT) in South Asia: India, Pakistan, Sri Lanka (Ceylon)* (Canberra: Australian National University, Papers on Strategy and Defense, no. 117, 1996).

31. Ibid., 45.

32. Siddiq Salik, *Witness to Surrender* (Karachi: Oxford University Press, 1977), 43.

33. Mohammad Yousaf and Mark Adkin, *The Bear Trap: Afghanistan's Untold Story* (London: Leo Cooper, 1992), 94.

34. "US-Pakistan Intelligence Operations Frozen: Official," *Dawn*, April 10, 2011, http://www.dawn.com/news/619688/us-pakistan-intelligence-operations-frozen-official.

35. Jon Boone, "Bin Laden Killing: Official Report Criticizes Pakistan and US," *Guardian*, July 9, 2013.

36. Tellis, *Pakistan and the War on Terror*, 25.

37. Maj. Gen. Yashwant Deva, *Of Tapes and Tapping: Technical Intelligence Scores over Human Intelligence* (New Delhi: Institute of Peace and Conflict Studies, paper no. 21, July 2, 1992).

38. Ramesh Vinayak, "Wireless Wars," *Nation*, September 14, 1998, http://www.india-today.com/itoday/14091998/war.html.

39. Ibid.

40. Nawaz, *Crossed Swords*, 48.

41. Sen, *Slender Was the Thread*, 17.

42. Nawaz, *Crossed Swords*, 71.

43. Ibid., 51.

44. Ibid., 67.

45. Ibid.

46. Maj. (Ret.) Argha Humayun Amin, "Grand Slam: A Battle of Lost Opportunities," *Defense Notes* (2000), http://www.defencejournal.com/2000/sept/grand-slam.htm.

47. Nawaz, *Crossed Swords*, 194.

48. Ibid., 201.

49. Gen. Ayub Khan, cited in *Dawn*, July 20, 1965.

50. Peter Wilson Prabhakar, *Wars, Proxy Wars, and Terrorism: Post-Independent India* (Delhi: Mittal Publications, 2003), 79.

51. Nawaz, *Crossed Swords*, 205–6.

52. Ibid., 217n39.

53. Ibid., 206.

54. Victoria Schofield, *Kashmir in Conflict: India, Pakistan and the Unending War* (London: I. B. Tauris, 2000), 109.

55. Nawaz, *Crossed Swords*, 222.

56. Ibid.

57. Ibid.

58. Julian Richards, *The Art and Science of Intelligence Analysis* (Oxford: Oxford University Press, 2010), 102–3.

59. Ernest May, "Introduction," in May, *Knowing One's Enemies*, 5.

60. Bhashyam Kasturi and Pankaj Mehra, "Geo-Politics of South Asian Covert Action: India's Experience and Need for Action against Pakistan," *South Asia Terrorism Portal*, IDR 16, no. 2 (2001).

61. M. Ashgar Khan, *We've Learnt Nothing from History: Pakistan: Politics and Military Power* (Karachi: Oxford University Press, 2005), 22.

62. Ibid., 22.

63. Nawaz, *Crossed Swords*, 286.

64. Ibid.

65. Ibid.

66. Herman, *Intelligence Power*, 251.

67. Lawrence Sáez, "The Political Economy of the India-Pakistan Nuclear Standoff," in *South Asia's Nuclear Security Dilemma*, ed. Lowell Dittmer (Armonk, NY: M. E. Sharpe, 2004), 13.

68. Zahid Hussain, *Frontline Pakistan: The Struggle with Militant Islam* (London: I. B. Tauris, 2007), 25.

69. Poonam Mann, "Fighting Terrorism: India and Central Asia," *Strategic Analysis* 24, no. 11 (2001): 2037.

70. Hussain, *Frontline Pakistan*, 53.

71. Bhashyam Kasturi, "The Intelligence Process and Kargil," *South Asia Terrorism Portal*, IDR 15, no. 3 (2001).

72. Nawaz, *Crossed Swords*, 508.

73. Interview with Benazir Bhutto, cited in Nawaz, *Crossed Swords*, 511.

74. Nawaz, *Crossed Swords*, 508.

75. Ibid., 514.

76. Ibid.

77. Cited in Richards, *Art and Science of Intelligence Analysis*, 76.

78. Kapur, "India and Pakistan's Unstable Peace," 127–28.

79. Ibid., 143.

80. Ibid.

81. Ibid., 147.

82. Ibid., 146.

83. Lt. Gen. (Ret.) Javed Nasir, "Calling the Indian Army Chief's Bluff," *Defense Notes* (February–March 1999), 2.

84. Ibid .

85. W. John, "ISI Fangs," *Pioneer*, June 30, 1999.

86. Gregory, "The ISI and the War on Terrorism," 1014.

87. Jaideep Saikia, "The ISI Reaches East: Anatomy of a Conspiracy," *Studies in Conflict and Terrorism* 25, no. 3 (2002): 190.

88. Boobli George Verghese, *India's Northeast Resurgent* (New Delhi: Konark Publishers, 1996), 60.

89. Jyoti Thottam, "Afghan Bombing Fuels Regional Furore," *Time*, July 7, 2008.

90. "Spy Games: Pakistan's Elusive ISI," *Jane's Intelligence Digest*, August 12, 2008.

91. Cited in "Pakistan in Peril: Pakistan Country Briefing," part 1, *Jane's Defence Weekly*, November 10, 2008.

92. "Proof of India's Involvement in Militancy Found," *Dawn*, November 2, 2009.

93. "India behind Most Terrorist Attacks, Says Malik," *Dawn*, October 21, 2009.

94. Peter Gill, "Securing the Globe," in *Secret Intelligence: A Reader*, ed. Richard J. Aldrich, Christopher Andrew, and Wesley K. Wark (Abingdon, UK: Routledge, 2009), 485.

95. Loch K. Johnson, "Introduction," in *Handbook of Intelligence Studies*, ed. Loch K. Johnson (Abingdon, UK: Routledge, 2009), 7.

96. Yadav and Barwa, "Relational Control," 117.

97. May, "Conclusion: Capabilities and Proclivities," 538.

98. Gregory, "The ISI and the War on Terrorism," 1022.

99. "Deactivating ISI's Political Wing," *Dawn*, May 24, 2008.

100. "Pakistan to Reorganize Intelligence Services," *Jane's Defence Weekly*, April 3, 2002.

101. The JIC is a panel of key intelligence stakeholders—including but not limited to the intelligence agencies—chaired by the Cabinet Office rather than by any of the agencies. Its remit is to assess available intelligence objectively, independently of departmental influences. It aims thus to mitigate any excessive influence that any one agency might have on the interpretation of its output. See Michael S. Goodman, *The Official History of the Joint Intelligence Committee*, vol. 1 (Abingdon, UK: Routledge, 2014).

102. "Pakistan to Reorganize Intelligence Services."

103. Boone, "Bin Laden Killing."

104. Thomas C. Bruneau, F. C. Matei, and Sak Sakoda, "National Security Councils: Their Potential Functions in Democratic Civil-Military Relations," *Defense and Security Analysis* 25, no. 3 (2009): 257–58.

105. Nawaz, *Crossed Swords*, 313.

106. Ibid.

107. Smruti S. Pattanaik, "Civil-Military Coordination and Defense Decision-Making in Pakistan," *Strategic Analysis*, 24, no. 5 (2000): 953–54. Zia also, in 1985, passed the critical

Eighth Amendment to the Constitution of Pakistan, which gave the president additional powers, including the right to dissolve the National Assembly when he considered it necessary for national security reasons. This was repealed in 1997 but partially restored again with the Seventeenth Amendment under General Musharraf.

108. Pattanaik, "Civil-Military Coordination," 954.

109. Ibid., 957.

110. Ibid.

111. Quoted in Pakistan Institute of Legislative Development and Transparency, *Peace and Conflict in Pakistan*, 9.

112. Johnson, "Uncertain Loyalties," 132.

113. David Omand, *Securing the State* (London: C. Hurst, 2010), 284.

114. Umer Farooq, "Herald Exclusive: Revealing the Secret," accessed 10 March 2015, http://www.dawn.com/news/601181/revealing-the-secret.

115. Ibid.

116. Shakeel Anjum, "Missing Persons Report Submitted to Govt," *News* (Islamabad), January 14, 2011. The commission began its work in 2010.

117. In June 2011 a Pakistani journalist, Saleem Shahzad, was abducted and his dead body dumped on a roadside near Islamabad. Mr. Shahzad had claimed to have received death threats from the ISI on at least three occasions after he had published articles critical of it. His last warning had come after an article critical of the military's handling of a siege at the Mehran naval base. See "APNS President Rejects ISI Charge," *Dawn*, June 3, 2011. Another journalist, Najam Sethi, has claimed that he has been abducted, threatened, and beaten on more than one occasion by ISI officers following critical articles and that torture "was an interrogation technique long favored by Pakistan's police and intelligence agencies." See Omar Waraich, "Risky Business: When Pakistani Journalists Take On the ISI," *Time*, July 5, 2011.

118. Stephen P. Cohen, "India, Pakistan and Kashmir," *Journal of Strategic Studies* 25, no.4 (2002): 39.

119. Pande, *Explaining Pakistan's Foreign Policy*, 59.

120. Chaudhry Muhammad Ali, *The Emergence of Pakistan* (New York: Columbia University Press, 1967), 122.

121. Henry Salomon, Leon Polak, Henry Noël Brailsford, and Lord Pethick-Lawrence, *Mahatma Gandhi* (London: Oldham's Press, 1948), 295.

122. Muhammad Bilal, "India Behind Unrest in Balochistan: Malik," *Daily Times*, April 23, 2009.

123. Reply statement filed by the government of Pakistan and the government of Sindh on June 5, 1995, petition number 46/94, in case brought by the MQM, 72, http://www.scribd.com/doc/4929754/MQM-VS-Government-reply-by-Government.

124. Samina Yasmeen, "Pakistan's Kashmir Policy: Voices of Moderation?," *Contemporary South Asia* 12, no. 2 (2003): 191.

125. Adnan Sarwar Khan, "Pakistan's Foreign Policy in the Changing International Scenario," *Muslim World* 19, no. 2 (2006): 238.

126. Ibid.

127. Rajesh Basrur, *Domestic Politics and Systemic Constraints in Pakistan's India Policy*, Pakistan Security Research Unit (PSRU) Brief Number 60 (Durham: University of Durham, 2010): 6, available at https://www.dur.ac.uk/resources/psru/briefings/archive/Brief60.pdf.

128. Nawaz, *Crossed Swords*, 298.

129. Hafeez Malik, *US Relations with Afghanistan and Pakistan: The Imperial Dimension* (Karachi: Oxford University Press, 2008), 110.

130. The Indian missile program is somewhat less nationalistic, naming missiles after Sanskrit names for the elements, such as *prithvi* (earth) and *agni* (fire).

131. Pattanaik, "Civil-Military Coordination," 951.

132. Such a notion is paradoxical since more Muslims live in India than in the whole of Pakistan.

133. Nawaz, *Crossed Swords*, 209.

134. Nasir, "Calling the Indian Army Chief's Bluff," 3.

135. May, "Conclusion: Capabilities and Proclivities," 538–39.

136. "Ex-ISI Chief Reveals Secret Missile Shipments to Bosnia Defying UN Embargo," *South Asia Tribune*, no. 22, December 23–29, 2002.

137. Nawaz, *Crossed Swords*, 467.

138. Ibid., 468.

139. Shaun Gregory, "Nuclear Command and Control in Pakistan," *Defense and Security Analysis* 23, no. 3 (2007): 318.

140. Ibid.

141. House of Commons, *Review of Intelligence on Weapons of Mass Destruction*, report of a Committee of Privy Councillors, chairman Rt. Hon. Lord Butler of Brockwell (London, TSO, July 14, 2004), 16.

142. Jackson, *France and the Nazi Menace*, 14.

143. Basrur, *Domestic Politics*, 3.

144. Ibid.

145. Sheen Rajmaira, "Indo-Pakistani Relations: Reciprocity in Long-Term Perspective," *International Studies Quarterly* 41, no. 3 (1997): 549.

146. Ramesh Thakur, "India after Nonalignment," *Foreign Affairs* 71, no. 2 (1992): 168.

147. Pattanaik, "Civil-Military Coordination," 940.

148. See Grare, *Reforming the Intelligence Agencies*.

149. "Hope Is All They Have," *Dawn*, January 11, 2011.

150. Irfan Hussain, "Pakistan's Maginot Line," *Dawn*, January 19, 2008, http://www.dawn.com/news/1073465.

151. Government of Pakistan, *Abbottabad Commission Report* (Islamabad: Government of Pakistan, Ministry of Law, Justice and Parliamentary Affairs, 2013).

152. Woodrow Kuhns, "Intelligence Failures: Forecasting and the Lessons of Epistemology," in *Paradoxes of Strategic Intelligence,* ed. Thomas G. Mahnken and Richard K. Betts (London: Frank Cass, 2003), 80.

153. Robert J. Young, "French Military Intelligence and Nazi Germany, 1938–1939," in May, *Knowing One's Enemies*, 309.

154. Jan Karl Tanenbaum, "French Estimates of Germany's Operational War Plans," in May, *Knowing One's Enemies*, 171.

155. Young, "French Military Intelligence," 309.

156. Hussain, "Pakistan's Maginot Line."

American Intelligence Assessments of the Jihadists, 1989–2011

MARK STOUT

RECONSTRUCTING THE PICTURE of the enemy held by intelligence analysts is a problematic endeavor for historians, even laying aside the difficulties of researching the secret world of intelligence. First, there may not be a single picture; analysts may disagree among themselves as to the fundamental nature of the enemy and the threat he poses. This is most starkly the case when some intelligence analysts perceive the existence of an enemy and others do not. Second, the true nature of the enemy is likely to change over time, presumably leading to changes in the image of the enemy. This was a problem even in assessing the Soviet Union, a country renowned for its ossified nature. It can be a much greater problem when the enemy is a flexible networked entity, orders of magnitude smaller than the Soviet Union, and largely unencumbered by bureaucracy. The problem grows again when the enemy is under stress and obliged to evolve rapidly.

It is important, then, to examine the processes by which images of the enemy change. How do enemies come to be perceived as such in the face of analytical opposition, and how do changes in an established image of the enemy take place? What role does the arrival of new information, often out of chronological order, play? Above all, what is the role of contingency?

American intelligence assessments of the jihadist threat illustrate these issues. The terrorist attacks of September 11, 2001, will be remembered as one of the great intelligence failures of American history. However, the failure to stop the

248

attacks obscures a success story, one that has much more to do with the real world of intelligence than does the prediction of specific events. This success was the emergence in the face of great opposition of a coherent and compelling picture of a Salafi jihadist enemy, an enemy capable of doing great physical harm to American interests but also an enemy who violated numerous presumptions.[1] Notable among these presumptions was that terrorism was not a vitally important national security issue and that to the extent it was important, the primary threat came from state-sponsored terrorists. This picture of the jihadist enemy also violated the presumption that religion was not a factor to be considered in national security.

Any discussion of the evolution of intelligence analyses of the jihadist threat must acknowledge the fact that the analysis took place in the recent past as did the events that were analyzed. True, historians are helped by the fact that the US government has declassified a great deal of very sensitive intelligence information about Al-Qaeda. However, these declassifications are very unevenly spread across the period 1989 to 2011. In addition, in many cases they have been summaries of raw reporting or finished analyses rather than the original documents themselves. Inevitably distortions creep into any summary, not least when they come out of the partisan environment of the US Congress. In short, this discussion can only be very preliminary in its findings.

Nevertheless, a great deal has been written about the struggle against Al-Qaeda in the decade leading up to the attacks of September 11, 2001. Most of this literature has either studied policy actions undertaken against Al-Qaeda and its affiliates or has consisted of narrative reconstructions of the 9/11 plot; it has not concerned the assessments made by intelligence analysts during that period, although it usually contains a great deal of information about assessments. There have been major accounts of the struggle against Al-Qaeda during the decade after September 2001, but again their focus has been on the fight against terrorism rather than on intelligence assessments per se.[2] The only post-9/11 period that has engendered sizable studies of intelligence analyses has been September 2001 to March 2003 when the United States and a handful of allies invaded Iraq. Analyses of the existence and extent of Iraq's ties with Al-Qaeda during this time were the subject of significant investigation as Congress probed the decision making of George W. Bush's administration pertaining to the war with Iraq. These investigations brought about the declassification of a great deal of intelligence material dated up to 2003. The US government has declassified very little information about Al-Qaeda since then, so a subsequent narrative about intelligence analyses must necessarily be less detailed and resulting conclusions less certain.

While histories of assessments of other major intelligence topics, such as the Soviet Union or China, can use National Intelligence Estimates (NIEs), the most authoritative assessments of the US intelligence community (IC), to illustrate the evolution of analyses, this is impossible when writing about assessments of Al-Qaeda. There were literally hundreds of NIEs on the Soviet Union, for instance, but information about only four NIEs dealing with Al-Qaeda was available in the writing of this chapter, and only one of those had the group as its central topic. While some relevant NIEs produced since September 2001 may have gone publicly unreported, we know with certainty that only two were written before September 11, 2001.[3]

This need not be a problem. One scholar has observed that "an NIE is a safe estimate, an unimaginative document, which is generally unremarkable for providing a fresh, creative understanding of international affairs."[4] This suggests that NIEs should be lagging indicators of emerging threats. One reason that NIEs are seldom bold in their conclusions is that they are lowest-common-denominator analyses. Though agencies can take dissents in NIEs, this is rare, and the nature of the NIE process does not readily accommodate truly fundamental disagreements. As a practical matter and as a matter of formal process, all agencies come to a consensus on NIEs; agencies never take their names off of them. Within agencies there is supposed to be a similar consensus on NIEs. This creates a false impression of unanimity. The lack of NIEs and their bland nature motivate us to look at other forms of analysis that contain more flavor and that, taken collectively, convey more of the cut and thrust that characterizes American intelligence analysis on important issues.

The US Intelligence Community

Many art forms fall under the rubric of "intelligence assessment," including NIEs, assessments by single agencies, assessments by offices within agencies, and the work of individual analysts. Sometimes these assessments are polished written products, other times briefings, personal letters, or oral responses to questions. Any assessment beyond the orally expressed ideas of individual analysts have to go through a coordination process meant to ensure that it reflects the agreed view of the organization publishing it. That said, it is often possible to define the subject at hand in such a way as to exclude from the coordination process people or organizations whose views might be contrary or otherwise problematic.

The IC that produces these assessments is large and complex. However, during most of the period in question, it had a stable structure. The IC included several agencies that produced assessments of the jihadist threat or influenced them. In theory, the director of Central Intelligence (DCI) oversaw these agencies, but his powers over the IC were actually modest. Nevertheless, the National Intelligence Council, the body responsible for preparing NIEs, reported directly to him. As director of the Central Intelligence Agency (CIA), he had control over the Directorate of Operations (DO) and the Directorate of Intelligence (DI), the former responsible for clandestine collection of human intelligence, the latter responsible for all-source intelligence analysis. The DI produced a variety of analytical papers, briefings, and other products that were substantively coordinated only within the CIA, usually only within the DI itself. Its flagship product was the President's Daily Brief (PDB), which it took to the president and a tiny handful of senior officials every day. The DI also prepared the Senior Executive Intelligence Brief (SEIB), which went every day to the second tier of government officials. While this publication was nominally a product of the entire IC, in fact CIA analysts drafted all the articles in it, and CIA officials edited the publication.

Within the CIA, responsibility for terrorism analysis resided primarily within the Counterterrorism Center (CTC). This organization was part of the DO, but unusually for a DO office it contained a small cadre of analysts from the DI. Immediately after 9/11 this cadre expanded substantially with the creation of the DI's Office of Terrorism Analysis (OTA), still within the CTC.

In addition, the Defense Intelligence Agency (DIA) and the State Department's Bureau of Intelligence (INR) were home to substantial numbers of all-source analysts. Meanwhile, the National Security Agency (NSA) was responsible for intercepting communications that the all-source analysts used as inputs in their work. The NSA, though primarily a collection agency, participated alongside the others in the preparation of NIEs.

One agency that was very active in counterterrorism but that did little to contribute to the IC's overall understanding and that usually did not produce analytical products prior to 2002 was the Federal Bureau of Investigation (FBI), the United States' national police agency and home of the country's domestic intelligence function. Prior to 9/11, the FBI was reluctant to share the product of its work with policymakers or intelligence agencies, believing that there were legal restrictions on doing so and that such sharing could contaminate the law enforcement process. For their part, other agencies were happy to use the "wall" between the IC and the FBI as an excuse not to share with the bureau, thereby protecting their sources and operations and further limiting the extent to which the bureau could contribute to the overall understanding of the jihadists.[5]

While there was substantial continuity in the structure of the IC during the period, there was some change as well. The Intelligence Reform and Terrorism Prevention Act of 2004 (IRTPA) abolished the position of the DCI in favor of a director of National Intelligence (DNI) who actually had only modestly enhanced powers and was not the director of the CIA but who nominally sat above him. The IRTPA also led to the creation of the National Counterterrorism Center (NCTC), which reported directly to the DNI.

Preconceptions: Religion and Nation-States

Military historian John Keegan has noted that "intelligence officers work at a subordinate level . . . they have to convince the decision-makers . . . of the reliability of their submissions."[6] This is a challenge, especially when intelligence analysts try to convey unpalatable messages. Because strategic preconceptions can hinder the reception of intelligence assessments, the dialogues between analysts and policymakers are especially difficult when the two do not share a common set of preconceptions about the world.[7]

Among the preconceptions that were at play in the intelligence and policy communities was the idea that nation-states were almost the only important actors when it came to American national security. A related notion held that religion was nearly irrelevant to national security. In such an environment, terrorism—let alone religiously motivated terrorism—was not a high priority. Furthermore, terrorism had "fizzled" and, anyway, seemed to be an Israel-centric issue.[8] Hence, working on terrorism was not considered a stepping-stone to bigger and better things, so the CTC was a "backwater."[9] Winston Wiley, who became the deputy director of the CTC in the early 1990s, remembers colleagues asking him why he wanted to take on a "dead account."[10]

The result was that there were few analysts working on the Salafi jihadist problem, and there was no preexisting body of analysis, or "theory," to build on. Analysts, particularly those in the CTC, were laboring alongside the collectors, "driving collection," struggling to find individual facts, often referring to themselves as "detectives."[11] Ironically, the CTC's analysts had potential allies elsewhere in the CIA, but they seldom forged coalitions with them for various reasons including internal politics, different office cultures, and routine personnel transfers. For instance, a few regional analysts continued to study the Sunni extremists in Egypt, the religious nationalists from whose ranks Anwar Sadat's assassins had come.[12] In addition, a November 1990 special issue of the *Near East and South Asia Review* prepared by the CIA's Office of Near Eastern and South Asian Analysis was devoted to Islamic fundamentalism. It enunciated a typology of Sunni fundamentalists similar to those that would circulate in the years following 9/11. On the other hand, the articles in this issue tended to lump Sunni and Shia "fundamentalism" into a single "movement" despite the fact that the fundamentalists in question would not have perceived such a commonality. Nor did they mention Osama Bin Laden or Afghanistan, and the concept of Salafi jihadism did not exist yet in the IC. In any event, the analysts who did this work did not stay with the agency.[13]

For all these reasons, the small cadre of intelligence analysts devoted to the problem felt themselves to be in a game of catch-up with the jihadists right from the Soviet withdrawal from Afghanistan in 1989. Though Al-Qaeda was founded in 1988, the IC did not discover that fact until 1996, though it had unwittingly been tracking the group for some time at that point. Indeed, during the 1990s, the CTC's analysts generally considered themselves "ten years behind."[14]

Painting a Picture: 1989 to 2001

By 1991 a few CIA analysts knew enough about Osama bin Laden that they fought to include mention of him and his associates in the assessments that were being written about the repercussions of the coming war with Iraq. Some analysts of Saudi Arabia who had been following the Islamic Awakening in that country lent their support, but they were unsuccessful.[15] These analysts were on the right track. The presence of Christian military forces in the Arabian Peninsula was contrary to the mandates of Islamic scripture as Bin Laden understood them, and this complaint would become one of Al-Qaeda's most prominent indictments of the United States. So too would the United Nations sanctions that followed the war.

The 1993 bombing of the World Trade Center by Ramzi Yousef and his coconspirators, the initial effort to topple the Twin Towers, was the first occasion on which the IC's analysts began to focus seriously on jihadists as a threat to the United States. In the wake of the "WTC 93" attack, a few analysts sensed that a new type of terrorism was emerging, different from that of the radical leftist and ethnic or nationalist groups that had carried out most previous attacks.[16] This perception led to new lines of analysis. During the war in Afghanistan, there had been little interest in studying Islamic nongovernmental organizations (NGOs) because these groups were implicitly America's allies in the struggle against the Soviets. However, this changed after WTC 93. The bombing engendered some of the early analyses on jihadist NGOs, notably the Maktab al-Khidmat, the group that evolved into Al-Qaeda.[17]

Analysts now focused on the Sunni jihadists who were looking for their next battlegrounds after the expulsion of the Soviets from Afghanistan. Gina Bennett, an analyst at INR, wrote a penetrating paper in August 1993 titled "The Wandering Mujahidin: Armed and Dangerous." In it she warned of an exodus from Afghanistan as "eager Arab youths" who had flocked to jihad against the Soviets started to look for new battlefields. Among the leading personalities in this "fluid" network was Osama bin Laden, whose money "has enabled hundreds of Arab veterans to return to safehavens and bases in Yemen and Sudan, where they are training new fighters." Buoyed by their victory over the Soviets, these fighters were inspired to continue their jihad against Middle Eastern regimes, Israel, and the United States. The paper specifically mentioned the Egyptian Islamic Group (EIG) as well as groups in Yemen and Algeria. It highlighted the wars in Bosnia, Tajikistan, and Kashmir as particularly attractive to the jihadists and mentioned spots as far-flung as the Philippines, Somalia, and New York City as other venues to which jihadists had traveled from the Afghan battlefields.[18]

Whatever the merits of her analysis, Bennett worked in INR, a bureau that had never had much clout in the State Department or the IC. There is no evidence that this work or parallel analyses coming from Bennett's colleagues in the CTC made much of a splash. However, she started to build a coalition of like-minded individuals across the IC. In July 1995 many of Bennett's ideas found their way into a rare NIE that noted that a "new breed" of terrorist had emerged.[19] It pointed to the radical Islamist network formed in the Soviet war in Afghanistan and warned that it was increasing its abilities to operate in the United States, speculating that civil aviation, the White House, the Capitol, and "symbols of US capitalism such as Wall Street" might be particularly attractive targets.[20]

Like most NIEs, this estimate made little impact on the government, but by late 1995 Bennett and her allies had another success that demonstrated the growing influence of their thinking.[21] They formed a working group to share their thoughts and analyses on what they saw as an emerging threat. On November 13, 1995, the day of their first meeting, a car bomb destroyed the headquarters of an American training mission in Saudi Arabia. Seven people died, sixty were injured. Subsequent information from the Saudi government indicated that three of the four perpetrators were veterans of the "jihads" in Afghanistan, Bosnia, and Chechnya who had been influenced by Bin Laden.[22] The next year saw a substantial increase in awareness in the IC.[23] The year 1996 was also when the CIA identified Al-Qaeda by name and determined that Bin Laden was its leader. Putting together the fragments they had, the coalition of revisionist analysts now realized that Al-Qaeda maintained links with groups such as the EIG and the Egyptian Islamic Jihad (EIJ).[24]

The number of analysts devoted to the problem started to grow, and each individual analyst added to the coalition was a significant percentage increase to the cadre of believers. Most of them were female. Veteran CIA analyst Susan Hasler, who joined the CTC about a year before 9/11, offered a typical explanation: "We have patience, perseverance, and we're not always looking for the sexy payoff immediately."[25] The phenomenon may also have been a result of gender inequality in the CIA under which for many years women were given lower-status jobs.[26] Generally terrorism was a low-status account among both operators and analysts. In addition, within the CIA, operators looked down on analysts and vice versa. One female participant recalled that "guys didn't want to listen to women, especially on the DO side. And not only were they women, but they were women who came from the DI."[27]

In any event, among the leaders of the revisionist movement were Bennett at INR, Cynthia Storer in the CTC, an analyst at the NSA, and an analyst at the

DIA. There were also a few analysts around the IC who were starting to take another look at the Egyptian groups.[28] In addition, in January 1996 the CTC created an experimental "virtual station" to track Bin Laden and his associates. The station started with about sixteen CIA officers, not all of them analysts, and eventually grew to about forty from across the IC.[29] Its first chief was Michael Scheuer, a former analyst who became noted for his simultaneous respect and loathing for Bin Laden.[30] The initial name of this station was "Terrorist Financial Links." It then became the "Bin Laden Issue Station" before adopting the name "Alec," after Scheuer's son.[31] Alec Station became another organizational base for proselytizing the threat posed by Bin Laden and Al-Qaeda.

On the other hand, in fact, it was extremely difficult to spread the idea that the jihadists posed a serious threat. Sometimes when analysts in one agency were unable to get a new idea published, they would help colleagues in another agency publish it.[32] In addition, the passion of the analysts in Alec Station made others uncomfortable; some CIA officers took to calling Scheuer and his largely female team of analysts "the Manson Family." Indeed, other elements of the DO "hated" Alec Station. Inside the group people were so driven, Scheuer recalled, that "we had marriages break up, we had people who delayed operations they needed. People were working sixteen, seventeen hours a day, some of them seven days a week for years." The ridicule merely stoked an us-versus-them mentality in the station that probably made the analysts hold all the more firmly to their views and probably also made it more difficult to reach out to other analysts and add them to the coalition.[33]

There were also actual or potential setbacks in the coalition-building process. Three times before 9/11, Storer came close to giving up the portfolio in frustration. Each time, however, she stayed because she received what she interpreted as messages from God.[34] Late in the 1990s, Julie Sirrs, at the DIA, became upset that the IC was paying insufficient attention to the link between Bin Laden and the Taliban. Sirrs's account was Iran, but she began to work terrorism and Afghanistan "because no one really especially cared about the issue." On her own time and with her own money, she twice traveled to Afghanistan to investigate the question, making contact there with Northern Alliance warlord Ahmad Shah Masoud and interviewing Taliban prisoners held by his forces. Accounts vary on how she ran afoul of American authorities, but in any event she ended up losing her security clearance and left the IC.[35]

Despite the low collection priority of the topic and the relative marginality of the analysts who carved out time to follow the jihadist problem, these analysts had succeeded in putting together scraps of information to form a fairly complete conceptual skeleton of Al-Qaeda. In 1996 they saw their analyses validated. In the spring of that year, a member of Al-Qaeda defected after embezzling money from the group. The defector, Jamal al-Fadl, had been present at the founding of Al-Qaeda and had worked at Bin Laden's headquarters

in Sudan. In his head, he brought a blueprint of Al-Qaeda, its worldwide operations, and its connections to other groups. For the first time, intelligence analysts
could flesh out their understanding of Al-Qaeda and confirm their assessments
from the inside. Al-Qaeda, it now appeared, was a sophisticated entity with a
command-and-control structure and a presence in some fifty countries. It even
had ambitions to acquire weapons of mass destruction (WMDs). Finally, it was
at the center of a constellation of Salafi jihadist groups; Al-Qaeda was not the
entirety of the problem.[36] In 1997 the IC published a short update to the 1995
NIE. It underlined the threat posed by Bin Laden and explicitly mentioned his
intention to strike inside the United States.[37]

George Tenet became DCI on July 31, 1997. He was aware of Bin Laden
but initially was not particularly concerned about him or the jihadists, being
more focused on instability in Russia, the Chinese threat, and rogue states Iran,
North Korea, and Iraq.[38] Over time, however, the issue became more and more
prominent in his perceptions. He later recalled that "you simply could not sit
where I did and read what passed across my desk on a daily basis and be anything other than scared to death about what it portended."[39]

It was the surprise of the August 7, 1998, embassy bombings in Kenya and
Tanzania that took Bin Laden to the top of the agenda for Tenet. The CTC
had reported in 1997 and early 1998 that Al-Qaeda was planning a major attack
against American interests. These analyses had also said that Al-Qaeda had a
fatwa (an Islamic legal opinion) justifying suicide bombings, that it was present
in Africa, that it had a pattern of conducting multiple simultaneous attacks, and
that it could conduct car bombings. Al-Qaeda had issued a statement in February warning of an attack, and the analysts' knowledge of the group's interpretation of the tenets of Islamic law pertaining to warnings and truces allowed them
to conclude that the attack would come after May.[40] After the attack, Tenet
found himself confronted by an angry, sobbing CIA operations officer who
told him, "You are responsible for those deaths because you didn't act on the
information we had, when we could have gotten [Bin Laden]."[41] In the White
House, however, National Security Adviser Sandy Berger and President Bill
Clinton had already begun to devote some attention to the Bin Laden problem
and had considered preparations to snatch Bin Laden out of Afghanistan.[42] The
embassy bombings motivated the administration to launch cruise missile strikes
that hit Al-Qaeda–associated facilities in Afghanistan, as well as a factory in
Sudan that US intelligence thought was linked to Bin Laden.[43]

After the 1998 embassy bombings, analytical production on the Salafi jihadists accelerated substantially. The Manson Family—Bennett, Storer, and their
allies—were carrying the day. Analysts published papers on Bin Laden's political
philosophy, the evolving goals of the jihadist movement, the operational style of
Al-Qaeda, and the way Bin Laden exerted his influence over the movement.
PDBs, SEIBs, and other intelligence publications ran literally hundreds of articles on the jihadism problem.[44] Despite this flurry of productivity, the IC did

not provide an authoritative depiction of the scale of the threat that the group posed to the United States. Nor did it assess Al-Qaeda's relationships with governments.[45]

The IC's failure to address this question would come back to haunt it in 2002 and 2003 when suddenly the meaning and contradictions inherent in a huge mass of raw reporting would have to be discussed and coordinated among analysts in mere months instead of at leisure as it trickled in over the years. On the other hand, the fact that analysts did not deem it necessary to address the possibility that Al-Qaeda might be linked with state sponsors was itself a sign of the erosion of the dominant state-centric model of national security threats.

As all this was taking place, DCI Tenet joined the ranks of those who were viscerally dedicated to the problem. When the nature of the perpetrators of the embassy bombings became clear, he "declared war" on Bin Laden and Al-Qaeda. In a December 1998 memorandum to his senior subordinates, Tenet wrote, "We must now enter a new phase in our effort against Bin Ladin. . . . We are at war. . . . I want no resources or people spared in this effort, either inside the CIA or the Community."[46] However much these words may have rung through the halls of the CTC, they found little echo elsewhere in the bureaucracy where resource decisions were made, and Tenet made little effort to push it.[47]

However, concerned that formal analyses were not having sufficient impact, Tenet began writing personal letters to senior Clinton administration officials to persuade them to pay attention to the threat, a practice he continued into the Bush era. "My intention," he recalled, "was not to cry wolf, and certainly not to scare the recipients out of their wits, although a careful reading of the letters would certainly have accomplished that." He wrote the first letter on 18 December 1998. It said, in part: "I am greatly concerned by recent intelligence reporting indicating that Usama Bin Ladin is planning to conduct another attack against US personnel or facilities soon . . . possibly over the next few days." He wrote two more such letters in the remaining thirteen days of 1998 and then another one on January 14, 1999. Four more would follow later.[48]

Into this environment came the "millennium plots." As Tenet recalled it, "throughout the fall of 1999, the threat situation was bad and then it got worse." Reporting indicated that Al-Qaeda had entered the "execution phase" of perhaps five to fifteen attacks around the world timed to coincide with the millennium. Though the CTC's staffers were "tired and frustrated," they coordinated a flurry of operational activity by the CIA and partner agencies, both American and foreign. In a possible sign of the still incomplete acceptance of the revisionist analysts' vision of Al-Qaeda, these operations included engineering the arrest of forty-five Hezbollah operatives in the Far East and running a disruption operation against the Iranian Ministry of Intelligence and Security, Hezbollah's main backer. In the end, no attacks happened, and several plots were clearly broken up.[49]

There was little post-millennium relief. In the summer of 2000 the threat reporting picked up again. Then, on October 12, 2000, Al-Qaeda attacked the USS *Cole*, a destroyer on a port call in Aden, killing seventeen sailors. However, though Al-Qaeda operatives were known to have been involved, the intelligence was not then available to prove that Bin Laden or his deputies had personally controlled the attack, and this fact thwarted retaliation.

Then came the summer of 2001 when, as Tenet famously put it, "the system was blinking red."[50] Looking back on that time, Storer commented, "People say, 'Why didn't you connect the dots?' Well, because the whole page is black."[51] Bits and pieces of intelligence poured in from every quarter, maddeningly short of details, but all suggesting that everyone in the jihadist community was holding their breath waiting for something big. Reports in May hinted at attacks in the United States, but then reports in June and July pointed to attacks in the Middle East or Rome.[52] On July 3 reporting indicated that Bin Laden had promised his associates that an attack was near. Among the reports pointing to a major impending attack was a great deal of signals intelligence, but while it indicated that many Salafi jihadists were expecting a major attack—a "Hiroshima" even—there was no specificity. On June 28 and July 10, the IC issued formal warnings that terrorist attacks could be expected to "have dramatic consequences on governments or cause major casualties" and that the "attack will occur with little or no warning."[53]

Post-9/11 Debates: WMDs, State Sponsorship, and Islam

After the 9/11 attacks, there was no further need to build the coalition of analysts who perceived a threat; the threat was evident to all. Terrorism analysts had wide latitude to "determine which terrorism stories we should tell" in their analyses and to "develop our own storylines," as Phil Mudd, the deputy director of the OTA recalled.[54] The threat that emerged was far more expansive than the one that Bennett, Storer, and Scheuer had argued for. In the eyes of many in the IC, Al-Qaeda not only was the foremost challenge, but it also seemed linked to numerous other adversaries—not just the other Salafi jihadist groups engaged in their own local struggles but even rogue states and adversaries on literally every inhabited continent. Al-Qaeda was even present in the United States. In addition, after the attacks religion was thrust front and center on the national security agenda. This was a major break with tradition. One career intelligence officer observed that "at least after 9/11 we could start saying the words 'Islam' and 'religion' out loud."[55]

Tenet finally put the CIA and the IC on a genuine war footing. One officer recalls that the 9/11 attacks "fundamentally alter[ed] . . . how the Agency perceived its mission."[56] One result was that very soon the networked structure of the Salafi jihadist community changed as the American military and intelligence services, aided overtly, covertly, and tacitly by allies and partners around the world, demolished every link and node of that network that they could find. The changed CIA mission also manifested itself in how the agency allocated its billets. After the attacks, CIA analysts covering other hotspots were reassigned to the CTC, and many more from all over the DI volunteered for duty in the center.[57]

The new perception of mission also showed up in the surging emotions of the time. On September 16, Tenet wrote a memo to his senior subordinates declaring war again.[58] As for the CTC's analysts, there was "a lot of emotion running around," one veteran recalled. "We all were literally insane." Another analyst has commented that "people do not understand how goddamn dangerous we thought it was [after September 11]. The absence of solid information on additional threats was terrifying."[59] Even in this highly charged environment, there was a range of opinion about the extent of the threat. The CTC was slightly less sweeping in its assessments than the administration, while the regional analytical offices and the old-timers in CTC were even less sweeping and more nuanced in their understanding of the severity of the threat.[60]

The perception of an imminent devastating threat fed itself, making the enemy seem omnipresent and endlessly resourceful. In an effort to avoid missing any clues to the next attack, intelligence collectors "lowered their reporting thresholds," passing on to analysts doubtful or ambiguous information that they might previously have kept back as being of no value. The result was that the flow of information became, in Mudd's words, "voluminous and dominating."[61] The CIA also began publishing the "Threat Matrix," a document put together under Tenet's personal supervision that went to the president every morning with the PDB. The matrix was more a project of intelligence compilation than intelligence analysis. In part because the IC was stung by the charge that it had been guilty of a "failure of imagination" before 9/11, it contained all the new threats that had emerged over the past day, no matter how vague.[62] Everyone knew that most of them were probably bogus—some were laughable on their face—but nobody knew which might turn out to be real.[63] Exposure to the Threat Matrix made it difficult for its readers and presumably its writers to view the world in the same way again.[64] The very volume of reporting, generated in large part by the lowering of the reporting threshold, seemed to underline the seriousness of the threat.[65] The December arrest of Al-Qaeda member Richard Reid just as he was about to explode his footwear on a transatlantic flight reinforced the feeling that the enemy might be anywhere doing anything.[66] One customer recalled that reading the Threat Matrix every day was "like being stuck in a room listening to loud Led Zeppelin music"—it induced "sensory overload" and "paranoia."[67] The Threat Matrix continued going to the president until approximately 2004.[68]

Weapons of Mass Destruction

Though there had been hints before 9/11 that Al-Qaeda was interested in WMDs, the consensus view outside of the Bin Laden analysts had been that this was not a serious possibility. Now the possibility seemed all too real, and the IC became acutely alert to the potential for WMD attacks. The OTA established a group to track these threats, and other agencies covered them as well. The group within the OTA was led by Rolf Mowatt-Larssen, who entered the job expecting to find that Al-Qaeda's WMD capabilities and intentions were minimal. Over time he and his subordinates became more and more alarmed. Many of their colleagues looked on their fears as overblown threat-hyping, but Mowatt-Larssen cultivated an us-versus-the-world culture anchored in the view that even a 1 percent chance of a WMD event needed to be tracked down.[69]

As early as September 14, 2001, the CIA briefed the president about the possibility of such attacks in the United States.[70] Soon records captured in Afghanistan seemed to confirm that Al-Qaeda had indeed been making serious efforts in this direction. In November the IC began to receive reports suggesting that Al-Qaeda might be close to acquiring a nuclear or radiological weapon. This captured the president's attention, particularly when reports started to come in that a nuclear device of some type had been smuggled into the United States and would be taken to New York City. Though such threats ebbed and flowed over time, there was a constant drumbeat of them for years. Often Al-Qaeda was reported to be negotiating with the Russian mafia for nuclear materials or even actual nuclear weapons, though a far more serious and persistent concern was the group's contacts with nuclear scientists in Pakistan.[71]

Chemical and biological weapons in the hands of these terrorists were also a major concern. Anthrax was a particular concern, and it became clear that Al-Qaeda had done work on this agent in Afghanistan. Though the invasion of Afghanistan clearly disrupted this and similar work, a great deal of analytical effort went into determining whether any of the lethal agents had survived and where Al-Qaeda's scientists had fled to.[72] A January 2003 CIA paper was open to the possibility of WMD cooperation between Iraq and Al-Qaeda, stating that "the general pattern that emerges is of Al-Qaeda's enduring interest in acquiring CBW [chemical/biological weapon] expertise from Iraq." This paper leaned heavily on information from interrogations of Ibn al-Shaykh al-Libi, a senior Al-Qaeda operational planner who had told a foreign intelligence service that in 2000 Iraq had agreed to provide chemical or biological weapons training for two Al-Qaeda figures.[73] The al-Libi information also made its way into a January 2003 NIE, "Nontraditional Threats to the US Homeland through 2007." However, DIA was more skeptical about the reporting and repeatedly published analyses making that clear. DIA was eventually vindicated when al-Libi recanted, saying that he had made the story up under torture by the foreign intelligence service.[74] The concern about WMDs in the hands of Al-Qaeda persisted over a course of years. However, over time the IC saw the terrorists as preferring progressively less sophisticated delivery devices as the "war on terrorism" eroded their ability to mount sophisticated plots.[75]

The understanding of the enemy began to change in another way too, as the IC came to see the jihadist problem as having a substantial domestic component. This was not an entirely new topic, but now the presence of terrorists or their support personnel in the United States seemed much more widespread and threatening.[76] Time and again foreign terrorists turned out to have relatives, business associates, or other acquaintances in the United States. There were suspicions that Bin Laden must already have posted "sleeper cells" in the United States to launch a second wave of attacks.[77] The concerns seemed validated when in early 2002 a group of Yemeni Americans in Lackawanna, New York, who had received training at an Al-Qaeda facility in Afghanistan before 9/11 came to the attention of the federal government. The FBI and the CIA kept President Bush regularly briefed on the "Lackawanna Six" until their arrest in September 2002. They eventually pled guilty to terrorism-related charges.[78] The May 2002 arrest of American citizen Jose Padilla in Chicago on charges (of which he was never convicted) of involvement in a "dirty bomb" plot on behalf of Al-Qaeda contributed to the perception of a domestic threat.

State Sponsorship

The question of state sponsorship of Al-Qaeda occasioned a great deal of controversy between the administration and the IC and within the IC itself. To some degree this was simply an expression of the enduring presumption that states were the entities that mattered in the international community.

In the 1980s and 1990s, state-sponsored terrorism was the predominant mode of terrorism in the estimation of the intelligence and policy communities. Iran was perceived as the most active and capable state sponsor, and Hezbollah was its primary terrorist client.[79] The idea that Hezbollah was the greatest non-state terrorist threat to American interests was persistent. For instance, even after Bin Laden's declarations of war on the United States in 1996 and 1998 and several attacks on American interests by terrorists in Bin Laden's orbit, the CTC's immediate inclination after the 1998 African embassy bombings was to suspect Hezbollah, a Shia terrorist group. A similar view about the importance of Iran and Hezbollah persisted in much of the US military, the Central Command excepted, until 9/11. This fixation obscured the growing importance of the Sunni extremists and created competition for scarce analytical resources.[80] One of the reasons that it was difficult for many intelligence analysts to take Sunni extremists seriously before 2001 was that Sunnis from different countries (unlike the Shia) were thought to be incapable of working together.[81]

After 9/11 there was general agreement that Iran, though initially cooperative with American operations against the Taliban in Afghanistan, was insufficiently helpful in detaining Al-Qaeda members who had sought refuge there. However, Iraq's links with Al-Qaeda and its allies were a more contentious issue.[82] Many Bush administration officials even suspected that Iraq had conspired with Al-Qaeda to mount the 9/11 attacks. In fact, there were stray bits of reporting indicating a relationship between Bin Laden and the Saddam Hussein regime.[83] Early on the administration's suspicions seemed to be confirmed when the Czech intelligence service told the CIA that it had information that an Iraqi intelligence officer had met with Mohammed Atta, the leader of the 9/11 operation, in Prague in April 2001. However, by mid-2002 the FBI and the CIA had cast grave doubt on this report.[84]

In September 2001 the CIA prepared a short paper for PDB recipients about the possible relationship between Iraq and the 9/11 attacks. At the request of a PDB recipient, the agency prepared another in October 2001 looking at Iraq's relationship with terrorism. Neither of these papers has been released or publicly described in detail, but in mid-2002 the CIA produced a paper called "Iraq and al-Qaeda: Interpreting a Murky Relationship" that became a cause célèbre. Here the previous lack of attention to Al-Qaeda's connections (or lack thereof) to state sponsors came back to haunt the agency. Having not hashed out their collective views at leisure during peacetime, the analysts were forced to do so in the pressure cooker of wartime. The results were time-consuming and vitriolic battles among analysts and accusations (ultimately unsubstantiated) of politicization.

The paper hinted at these tensions, saying that "our [analytical] approach is purposely aggressive in seeking to draw connections, on the assumption that any indication of a relationship between these two hostile elements could carry great dangers to the United States." The Iraq experts from the Office of Near East and South Asian Analysis (NESA) tended to believe that ideological differences would keep Saddam and Bin Laden from cooperating. The terrorism analysts from the CTC, however, while noting the ideological differences, tended to credit reporting that suggested that there had been some sort of relationship in the past. Both sides agreed that no conclusive answer was possible, but even after eight months of coordination they could get no closer than that. Eventually the CTC published the paper over NESA's objections.[85]

Next the CIA wrote a paper that it coordinated with the DIA called "Iraqi Support for Terrorism." This paper used some extremely sensitive sources and methods and went to only a very few senior officials. In January 2003, however, the CIA, in an effort to broaden dissemination of the findings, produced a new version, which left out the most sensitive materials but also included updated information. With regard to the Iraq–Al-Qaeda relationship, the updated version said that "reporting from sources of varying reliability points to a number of contacts, incidents of training, and discussions of an Iraqi safehaven for Usama bin Ladin and his organization dating from the early 1990s."[86] Overall, however, the paper concluded that the relationship between Iraq and Al-Qaeda most closely "resembles that of two organizations trying to feel out or exploit each other."[87]

Islam: Threat or Opportunity?

As previously noted, during the early post–Cold War period the US government was disinclined to consider religion in a national security context.[88] There are several reasons for this. First, many national security practitioners view religion as inherently subjective and not a worthy subject for consideration in what they believe should be the business of making hard-headed decisions or realpolitik based on objective factors. Others see religion as being purely a matter of inner life. Religion, these people believe, is about the soul, not the world. Taking religion explicitly into account also comes with risks to the reputations of analysts, to the government, and to American standing in the world. Finally, and most obviously, American political culture and political structures take extremely seriously the separation between church and state.[89]

As a result, policymakers were predisposed not to consider religiously based terrorism to be a matter of fundamental strategic importance. For instance, a 1989 Department of State cable from Cairo expressed the bemusement felt by American diplomats when Cairenes told them that the United States of America must certainly have an "official policy toward Islam."[90] This prejudice against religion manifested itself in the IC no less than in the rest of the government. Lt. Gen. James Clapper, who led the DIA from 1991 to 1995, recalls no senior-level discussions of religion whatsoever during that time.[91] For its part, the CIA "veered toward 'hard fact' reporting" (names, dates, places, and the like), creating an environment in which consideration of the divine did not fit comfortably.[92] The result was that analysts tended to address terrorism either through ethnic or national lenses (despite the fact that this enemy explicitly denigrated such distinctions) or simply focused on the tactical mechanics of the problem. In essence, the IC projected its self-image onto the enemy, ignoring Sun Tzu's mandate to know the enemy and instead imagining the Salafi jihadists in a way that seemed convenient and comfortable.

Ironically, the jihadists themselves had no doubt about the importance of religion to their cause. Sayyid Qutb (1906–66), a prominent member of the Muslim Brotherhood, enunciated the fundamental principles of Salafi jihadism in the early 1960s. He argued that true Islam was extinct from the world. Jihad was, he maintained, the central component of the solution to this problem. Qutb was unshakeable in his characterization of the fundamentally religious nature of the struggle, warning that infidels "may wish to change this struggle into an economic or political or racial struggle, so that the Believers become confused . . . and the flame of belief in their hearts becomes extinguished. The Believers must not be deceived, and must understand that this is a trick."[93]

Even when individual intelligence analysts did recognize the importance of religion, external constraints kept them from expressing these views. Terrorism analysts at the CIA during the 1990s found that discussions of theology were effectively forbidden.[94] Similarly in 2000, when preparing an unclassified NIE assessing the principal drivers of international politics, the National Intelligence Council consciously avoided naming religion as one of those drivers so as not to give offense to the global public to whom the document would be released.[95]

In the first years after the 2001 attacks, there was an increased realization among many people in the intelligence business of the importance of religion as a factor in national security and as the animating spirit of Al-Qaeda and its allies and affiliates. A conference sponsored by the CIA's Center for the Study of Intelligence found that "intelligence must radically revise the perspectives and procedures that served it well in the . . . Cold War." Religion was a part of this. However, the attendees found that addressing the religious factor of terrorist movements "poses particular difficulties for both the policy and intelligence communities. . . . We are both unfamiliar and uncomfortable dealing with religion as a driver of violence and hostility."[96]

With religion newly on the table, a current of thought surfaced within the IC that the problem was Islam itself. This perspective was particularly strong within the military and may have had a few adherents in the CTC. Analysts at the NSA, State/INR, and the regional offices at the CIA subscribed minimally, if at all, to the view.[97] Some people made this argument from an explicitly Christian perspective. For instance, Lt. Gen. William G. Boykin, the deputy undersecretary of defense for intelligence, spoke for many evangelical Christians in the military in 2003 when he publicly characterized the war on terrorism as a war between the forces of Jesus and Satan.[98] Others argued that the traditional American disinclination to consider religion in a national security context had to change as the United States faced an adversary that was fighting a religious war. One wrote that the United States was "disarmed in the war of ideas."[99] Another warned that "this [intellectual] journey will be profoundly uncomfortable."[100]

In any event, the DIA began to pay more attention to Islam than it had during the 1990s, looking at the role that theology played in defining Al-Qaeda and its goals.[101] For instance, in April 2005 the Joint Military Intelligence College published a deeply researched monograph titled *The Sources of Islamic Revolutionary Conduct*, by a former student, Maj. Stephen Lambert. In self-conscious emulation of George F. Kennan's work, Lambert used the pseudonym "Y." Lambert tried to determine "why the religion of peace seems to perpetually produce passionate warriors for Allah." He concluded that the answer lay in

Islam itself, that the Islamic revolutionaries of Al-Qaeda and other groups "have not hijacked their religion. . . . Instead, they are Islamic purists."[102] Similarly in 2006, William Gawthrop, a former army officer and a senior official in the Defense Department's Counterintelligence Field Activity, wrote in a professional journal that "the United States, and an increasing number of other governments, are beleaguered by an expanding array of states, groups and individuals whose goals, actions and norms are animated by Islamic values." These violent values were inextricable from Islam. The implication was clear: The United States and its partners were "in the unenviable position of having to fight, at the strategic level, against an idea," namely, Islam.[103]

The most prominent of these critics was Maj. Stephen Coughlin, an army intelligence officer who became a controversial adviser to the Pentagon on the subject of Islamic law. He argued that official Americans must understand key Islamic ideas, particularly the idea of jihad. Urging the application of the military doctrine of "intelligence preparation of the battlefield" to the war on terrorism, he maintained that existing approaches were intellectually and strategically untenable. He argued that the "Current Approach" assumed that Islamic-based extremism was "aberrant" and that its practitioners had "hijacked" the religion. The implication of this assumption, he warned, would be that "true" Islam would be unjustifiably "excluded from analytical processes."[104]

The analysts at the CIA did not tend to support these views, and in about 2004 some of them started to fight back, expressing ideas some of which had been bubbling below the surface for years. They agreed with Coughlin and others that Islam was relevant, and they acknowledged the power and coherence of Al-Qaeda's ideas and its genuine links to the rest of Islam, but they also emphasized the marginality of the Salafi jihadists in the Muslim community. Perhaps, they suggested, Al-Qaeda was not merely a "network" but also an idea or even a sputtering social movement. DCI Tenet laid out much of this thinking in 2004 testimony before Congress when he said that Al-Qaeda's "leadership structure" had been seriously damaged, "but as we continue the battle . . . we must overcome . . . a global movement infected by Al-Qaeda's radical agenda." In the years following 9/11, the term "Al-Qaeda" had come to refer in various contexts to various things. First, it referred to "Al-Qaeda Central," the conspiratorial group led by Osama Bin Laden. Second, it referred to Al-Qaeda Central plus the groups allied and affiliated with it, many of which had taken the Al-Qaeda name. These included many groups of greater or lesser longevity, such as Al-Qaeda in the Islamic Maghreb, Al-Qaeda in the Arabian Peninsula, Al-Qaeda in Iraq, the Afghan Taliban, Jemaah Islamiyah, the Caucasus Emirate, and others. Third, it referred to all of those plus the very idea of Salafi jihadism and everyone down to the disconnected cells and "lone wolves" inspired by it.[105]

In approximately 2005, Cynthia Storer and her colleagues, including Gina Bennett, received a request from a consumer to put the Al-Qaeda phenomenon into a "holistic context." These analysts found that the question quickly answered itself. The result was the "Ziggurat of Zealotry," a graphic model of the Islamist community that situated the jihadists in a meaningful Islamic context. The ziggurat itself was a stepped pyramid (see figure 8.1) on which each level portrayed a jump in radicalism. At the bottom of the ziggurat was the enormous population of peaceful Muslims simply seeking to lead pious lives. At the very apex of the pyramid was the tiny community of violent radicals such as the members of Al-Qaeda who sought to destroy or at least neutralize the West and the present nation-state system and used violence around the globe to bring about this result.[106]

The CTC quickly disseminated the "Ziggurat of Zealotry" in a paper inside the government. It was an instant hit with the policy community, and CIA analysts briefed it widely.[107] Policymakers uncomfortable with considering religion as a national security issue but also unable to avoid the question found in the ziggurat a way of acknowledging the religious component of the war on terrorism while avoiding the proposition that Islam itself was the enemy.

Then in April 2006 a new NIE continued this trend toward seeing a more diffuse, ideologically based threat characterized at least as well by the word

FIGURE 8.1   The Ziggurat of Zealotry

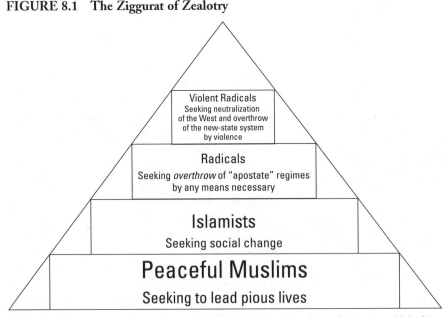

Note: This is the author's interpretation of the Ziggurat of Zealotry based on a description published in Jonathan Shainen, "The Ziggurat of Zealotry," *New York Times Magazine,* December 10, 2006. The original US government version has not been released to the public.

"movement" as by the word "network." One of its key findings was that the global jihadist movement was decentralized, had no coherent overall strategy, and was spreading itself broadly over the globe even though it remained numerically small. Indeed, it found, terrorist cells might even be "self-radicalized." Importantly, it added that the jihadists' desired ultimate objective was unpopular among the vast majority of Muslims around the world and that some major Muslim clerics had recently come out against the jihadists, perhaps enabling the establishment of Islamically informed, peaceful political activism.[108]

By now the analysts had made clear the weakness of the link between the Salafi jihadists and the broader Islamic world. It became obvious to the nation's leadership that this was a point of strategic weakness for the jihadists. This weakness could not be exploited through violent or "kinetic" military means. Accordingly, the phrase "war on terrorism" became less and less satisfactory because it seemed to imply the application of only kinetic measures. When the Obama administration came to power in 2009, it decided that it would increase the relative emphasis on nonviolent measures to break the jihadists' link to other Muslims and then widen the resulting gap. The primary goal of "countering violent extremism" was to stop the process of radicalization through noncoercive measures, including social programs, counterideology initiatives, and the delegitimization of Al-Qaeda's narrative.[109] The administration enshrined this idea in its 2011 *National Strategy for Counterterrorism*, which said that Al-Qaeda preyed on local grievances, propagating a "self-serving" narrative and drawing on a "distorted interpretation of Islam." "Countering this ideology—which has been rejected repeatedly and unequivocally by people of all faiths around the world—is," it said, "an essential element of our strategy."[110]

Coda

On May 1, 2011, a team of US Navy SEALs operating under the command of CIA director Leon Panetta killed Osama Bin Laden at his home in Abbottabad, Pakistan.[111] Analysts exploiting the materials captured there found that he had continued to plot attacks against the United States but that he was frustrated that Al-Qaeda's message was not catching on among Muslims. He speculated that perhaps Al-Qaeda needed a more explicitly Islamic name (it means only "The Base" in Arabic), and he lamented that Al-Qaeda's regional affiliates were still not in a position to make even preliminary steps toward establishing the caliphate. He and his subordinates were also concerned about the group's financial problems and the damage being done to the group, particularly by American drone strikes.[112]

In July 2011, Secretary of Defense Leon Panetta, who had moved to his new job only days before, told reporters that he believed that the "strategic defeat" of

Al-Qaeda was "within reach."[113] Some officials said that Bin Laden's death was important not only because he kept the network focused on the "far enemy," the United States, but also because his charisma was inextricable from the Al-Qaeda brand that had inspired the creation of affiliates across the Muslim world. Not all intelligence personnel were sanguine about the future, however. Recently retired director of the NCTC Michael Leiter and other US officials warned that even if Al-Qaeda Central—the clandestine organization headed by Osama Bin Laden and then Ayman al-Zawahiri—were to be defeated, Al-Qaeda's affiliates were far from vanquished. Leiter also maintained that the threat to the American homeland was much changed from the early 2000s, having evolved from a threat of large-scale attack to one of small-scale attack.[114]

Assessing the Assessments

Intelligence analysis is not a dry intellectual process conducted by like-minded and disinterested analysts. It does not inevitably produce any particular answer, let alone the right one. It is a social process in which ideas come and go for reasons relating to the real world and the real nature of the enemy but also for reasons relating to bureaucratic processes and politics, personality, emotion, and numerous contingent factors. In addition, of course, the real nature of the enemy may change as well in response to policy actions of the observing country. The image of the enemy painted by intelligence services will hopefully change as a result. Because intelligence assessments are an input to policy and operations that can then affect the nature of the enemy, the image of the enemy can carry the seeds of its own destruction.

The birth and evolution of an image of the enemy goes in fits and starts. Contingency is everywhere one looks in the present story. Indeed, one might plausibly hypothesize that this is particularly true for intelligence problems that are being worked on by small numbers of analysts and receive a relatively small amount of raw intelligence collection. It is plausible to speculate that the emerging image of the enemy might have been colored in faster if not for the "Manson Family" slur against the analysts in Alec Station. Analytical progress might have gone more slowly if the initial handful of analysts seized of the problem had disliked each other and been disinclined to collaborate. It might also have gone more slowly if Cynthia Storer had quit the first time she was tempted to do so. Perhaps it would have gone somewhat faster if Julie Sirrs had not been so crusading that she lost her job. On the other hand, while we have little data, we can reasonably speculate that after September 2001 petty rivalries and the comings and goings of individuals probably played much less of a role in shaping assessments as the number of people working the problem exploded.

Also during the pre–September 2001 period, if George Tenet, who ascended to the DCI position in 1997, had been less receptive to the emerging analyses about Osama Bin Laden, there probably would have been fewer collection resources to provide the raw information needed for analysts to analyze. Tenet used the bully pulpit of his position to bring the subject forcefully to the attention of the Clinton and Bush administrations. Had he not done this, the level of policy interest would have been less and there would have been less policy feedback to influence the direction of analysis.

The enemy's actions also played a role in shaping the image of it in the early years when analysts were struggling to sell their message and fighting to get each scrap of reporting. For instance, the WTC 93 bombing led to early studies on Islamic NGOs and gave a boost of credibility to the few analysts who were trying to sound an alarm. Had Jamal al-Fadl not embezzled money from Al-Qaeda and then sought refuge with the Americans to avoid punishment, the analytical case that Al-Qaeda was a far-flung, well-organized, and deadly threat would have been much thinner.

Finally, it is interesting to speculate what the IC's analyses would have looked like if the Bush administration had not been fixated on Iraq. We shall never know the opportunity cost of the work that went into investigating the ultimately inconsequential links between Saddam Hussein and Al-Qaeda. The issue of torture may also have played a role in shaping the image of the enemy. Some people have argued that the US government's willingness to engage in what it called "enhanced interrogation techniques" led to great intelligence windfalls.[115] Other people say that this "torture" has produced a great deal of bad information.[116] For all their heartfelt disagreements, the two sides seem to agree that US policy on interrogations influenced the extent and veracity of raw information that was collected. It is likely that in some ways, great or small, this affected the understanding of the enemy.

The Scorecard

In *Knowing One's Enemies*, Ernest May offers five maxims for intelligence analysis: Expect intelligence to be more useful for tactical warning and forecasting "short-term developments than for long-term projections"; "be cautious about changing organizational structure and pay more attention to procedures and routines as vehicles for achieving coordination"; "assume that in any estimates of how 'the other fellow' sees things prudence is likely . . . to lead to overestimation of his capabilities," cunning, and knowledge; know your enemy, know yourself; and carefully scrutinize all presumptions, particularly those that would disrupt current policies and programs.[117]

To what extent did the IC measure up to May's maxims in assessing the jihadist enemy? The first two of May's maxims have only glancing relevance to analyses of the jihadist problem. In suggesting that intelligence is better at providing short-term projections and warning than long-term projections, May is on solid but narrow ground. In particular, he neglects other important functions of intelligence: educating policymakers, framing problems, and providing expertise.[118] This is where the picture of the enemy is drawn and colored in. Without a deep understanding of the enemy, it may be possible to undertake effective counterterrorist actions at the tactical level but only accidentally will the government be able to craft effective counterterrorist strategies. It must also be said that the reform of the IC that took place in 2004 in response to the 9/11 attacks was largely irrelevant to the big-picture understanding of the jihadist enemy.

In fact, an understanding of the jihadists was not to be found in specific data points about things such as names, times, and locations. Rather it was in understanding the ideology, the culture, the goals, the capabilities, and the modes of operation of this new enemy. In other words, a sound understanding lay in gauging—as May has elsewhere recommended—the jihadists' "capabilities" and "proclivities" and asking questions that might "be useful guides to action."[119] Before 9/11 a small group of analysts were reasonably successful at doing just that despite the obstacles in their path. Over time the analysts developed a reasonable strategic understanding of the enemy as well, though the enemy was not static and there were spirited debates along the way.

Before 9/11 most of the IC was focused on topics other than terrorism and, to the extent that it considered terrorism at all, it was largely in the context of sponsorship by national governments that were thought to be pursuing fundamentally secular interests. (This thinking even applied to Iran, despite its theocratic form of government.) In some sense, this represents an implicit judgment by the IC in general that the jihadists' capabilities were negligible. However, the analysts concerned argued vociferously that the "wandering mujahidin" represented a new and severe threat that should be given a much higher priority. Taking into account the information deficit from which these analysts started and the institutional bias against the consideration of religion, their assessments of the Salafi jihadists' "proclivities" must be rated highly. It is clear that their assessments of the jihadists' capabilities were somewhat short of the mark: They thought the jihadists could inflict severe pain on the United States, but few expected such a devastating strike within the United States itself.

After 9/11 the IC gave too much credit to the jihadists' capabilities and cunning, at least initially. In retrospect it is clear that many specific threats, particularly those pertaining to WMDs, were taken too seriously. In this period the number of intelligence analysts working on the jihadist problem expanded rapidly. The new analysts were reasonably accurate in assessing the proclivities of Al-Qaeda and its affiliates. They came to understand the violently Manichean theology that drove the jihadists, though some thought that it was more widely spread among Muslims than it really was. They deserve credit for situating the Salafi jihadists almost entirely outside the context of the nation-state system in the "Murky Relationship" paper and even more so in the January 2003 CIA paper despite what senior members of the Bush administration wanted to believe. Furthermore, many analysts asked important questions about the relationship between Salafi jihadism and Islam and the general Muslim population. In so doing, they enabled the development of strategies that sought not merely to slay the jihadists but to pry them apart from the communities within which they sought sanctuary and to which they tried to spread their message. These included the efforts that fell under the rubric of "countering violent extremism."[120]

May also suggests that the willingness to challenge presumptions, particularly those that are tied to existing policies and programs, is a characteristic of good analysis. The record here is mixed. With regard to formal intelligence assessments—papers, briefings, the IC's daily publications—the record was good. Analysts swam against the tide first in the 1990s when the presumptions were that terrorism was primarily state-sponsored, that it was not a particularly serious problem, and that religion was irrelevant to national security. The record is less good, though still positive, in the post-9/11 period when analysts seriously questioned the connection that the Bush administration believed existed between Al-Qaeda and Saddam's Iraq.

In true Sun Tzuvian form, May advises analysts not only to understand their enemy but also to understand their own country. Some analysts understood America's thoroughly secular approach to the world because they butted up against it every day before 9/11, and they understood the other bureaucratic and cultural obstacles to their message that existed within the IC and the rest of the government. Where they fell short in understanding the United States was in failing to foresee the emotional impact that a major attack in this country would have and the sweeping response that a new Pearl Harbor would engender.

In the future, how well can the US IC expect to do in understanding jihadist threats? Of course, a lag between reality and its comprehension by intelligence analysts is unavoidable. There are grounds for thinking that future analyses of the jihadists will generally be better and that the lag will be shorter than it has been at least in the 1990s. Many of the factors that hobbled good analysis in that period are gone: the relegation of intelligence against terrorism to a back burner, the emphasis on state sponsors, and the disinclination to discuss religion. Furthermore, the analytical overreactions of the early post-9/11 period are over and will probably return only if there is a new attack on the United States rivaling or exceeding the attack on the Pentagon and the Twin Towers.

With regard to May's questions about "proclivities," "capabilities," and intelligence that can guide action, the prognosis is mixed. The proclivities of the

Salafi jihadists are well understood. The reason for this is simple. Islam, like Christianity, sees itself as having universal applicability. In particular, Salafi jihadists seek to spread their understanding of the faith, with its intrinsic call to action, to all the Muslims in the world. Thus, most of the important aspects of their thinking are freely available on the Internet and other open sources. Accurately assessing capabilities is rather more challenging. In part this is a question of numbers, and while counting members of Al-Qaeda Central may be difficult, it is easy to determine whether and to what extent Salafi jihadist ideas are catching on around the world or in any particular country. The terrorist intentions and capabilities of Salafi jihadists are easy to discern in outline and can often be determined in detail through secret methods. When the jihadists are involved in insurgencies or civil wars as in Afghanistan, Somalia, and Chechnya at the present time, a sound assessment of their capabilities entails consideration of a wide range of military, political, social, cultural, economic, and other factors. In some cases it may be easy to collect raw intelligence on these factors; in others it may be difficult. Then taking proper account of them in intelligence assessments is a separate problem.

The big analytical wild card is the assessment of the WMD capabilities of the jihadists. The immense destructive properties of WMDs take what would otherwise be a subsidiary detail, precisely what weapons are in the enemy's arsenal, and make it strategic. Unfortunately, plans for the acquisition of such weapons are among those pieces of information that jihadists would keep most deeply secret and not broadcast to the world. As recent history makes all too clear, it is easy to misjudge the WMD capabilities and intentions even of a nation-state. How much easier it must be to misjudge—or simply to miss—these matters among a small group of conspirators. In sum then, it is in the possibility of the use in the United States of a WMD that the greatest potential exists for a serious misunderstanding of the jihadist enemy.

Notes

Thanks to Shawna Cuan, Muhammad Haniff Hassan, Stephanie Kaplan, Paul Maddrell, Thomas Quiggin, and William Van Heuvelen. I would also like to thank certain veterans of the intelligence community who shall remain anonymous. Not all agreed with my conclusions but all helped immensely. This chapter has undergone a security review by the Publication Review Board of the Central Intelligence Agency.

1. For an explanation of the Salafi jihadist theological construct by a former graduate fellow of the CIA's Counterterrorism Center, see Jarret M. Brachman, *Global Jihadism: Theory and Practice* (New York: Routledge, 2009), especially chap. 2.

2. Peter Bergen, *The Longest War: The Enduring Conflict between America and al-Qaeda* (New York: Free Press, 2011); Eric Schmitt and Thom Shanker, *Counterstrike: The Untold Story of America's Secret Campaign against al Qaeda* (New York: Times Books, 2011); Garrett

M. Graf, *The Threat Matrix: The FBI at War in the Age of Global Terror* (New York: Little, Brown, 2011).

3. National Commission on Terrorist Attacks upon the United States, *The 9/11 Commission Report: Final Report of the National Commission on Terrorist Attacks upon the United States* (New York: Norton, 2004), 343.

4. Sulmaan Wasif Khan, "The Aesthetic of Analysis: National Intelligence Estimates and Other American Appraisals of the Cold War Triangular Relationship," *Diplomatic History* 32, no. 5 (2008): 896.

5. See, for instance, the 9/11 Commission interview with Mark Steinitz, September 25, 2003, http://cryptome.org/nara/state/state-03-0925.pdf. Also, see Daniel Benjamin and Steven Simon, *The Age of Sacred Terror: Radical Islam's War against America* (New York: Random House, 2002), 226–27, 296–98; *9/11 Commission Report*, 74, 77; Garrett M. Graf, *Threat Matrix*, 168–69 and 281–82; and Richard A. Clarke, *Against All Enemies: Inside America's War on Terror* (New York: Free Press, 2004), 15–18.

6. John Keegan, *Intelligence in War: Knowledge of the Enemy from Napoleon to Al-Qaeda* (New York: Knopf, 2003), 5.

7. Richard K. Betts, *Enemies of Intelligence* (New York: Columbia University Press, 2007), 22. See also Richards J. Heuer Jr., *Psychology of Intelligence Analysis* (Washington, DC: Center for the Study of Intelligence, 1999), 10; Ernest R. May, "Introduction," in *Knowing One's Enemies*, ed. Ernest R. May (Princeton, NJ: Princeton University Press, 1984), 4; Michael I. Handel, "Intelligence and the Problem of Strategic Surprise," in *Paradoxes of Strategic Intelligence: Essays in Honor of Michael I. Handel*, eds. Richard K. Betts and Thomas G. Mahnken (London: Frank Cass, 2003), 22–24; and James J. Wirtz, *The Tet Offensive: Intelligence Failure in War* (Cornell University Press, 1991), 9–10.

8. Interview with anonymous source, August 17, 2011.

9. Glenn L. Carle, *The Interrogator: An Education* (New York: Nation Books, 2011), 301.

10. 9/11 Commission interview with Winston Wiley, November 25, 2003, http://cryptome.org/nara/cia/cia-03-1125.pdf.

11. Interview with anonymous source, July 31, 2009; e-mail from anonymous source, November 11, 2009; Bruce O. Riedel, *The Search for Al Qaeda: Its Leadership, Ideology and Future* (Washington, DC: Brookings Institution Press, 2010), 45.

12. Interview with anonymous source, June 30, 2009.

13. Central Intelligence Agency, Office of Near Eastern and South Asian Analysis, "Islamic Fundamentalism: An Ideology for the 1990s," *Near East and South Asia Review: Special Issue: Islamic Fundamentalists and the Gulf Crisis*, November 30, 1990, 4, http://www.foia.cia.gov/sites/default/files/document_conversions/89801/DOC_0000258785.pdf; e-mail from anonymous source, September 11, 2009; e-mail from anonymous source, November 11, 2009.

14. Interview with anonymous source, July 31, 2009; Riedel, *Search for Al Qaeda*, 45.

15. Cynthia Storer, "Analytical Challenges on al-Qaeda before 9/11" (paper presented at conference "Ten Years Later: Insights on al-Qaeda's Past and Future through Captured Records," Washington, DC, September 13, 2011), 2.

16. *Joint Inquiry into Intelligence Community Activities before and after the Terrorist Attacks of September 11, 2001*, Report of the US Senate Select Committee on Intelligence and US House Permanent Select Committee on Intelligence, 107th Cong., 2nd sess. December 2002, 4.

17. Interview with anonymous source, July 31, 2009; Paul R. Pillar, "Metaphors and Mantras: A Comment on Shultz and Vogt's Discussion of Terrorism, Intelligence, and War," *Terrorism and Political Violence* 15, no. 2 (2003): 143; Steve Coll, *Ghost Wars: The Secret History of the CIA, Afghanistan, and Bin Laden from the Soviet Invasion to September 10, 2001* (New York: Penguin, 2005), 251–52, 257–58.

18. Department of State, Bureau of Intelligence and Research, "The Wandering Mujahidin: Armed and Dangerous, *Weekend Edition*, August 21–22, 1993," posted March 11, 2008, on Harvard Blogs, http://blogs.law.harvard.edu/mesh/files/2008/03/wandering_mujahidin .pdf.

19. *Joint Inquiry*, 4.

20. Paul R. Pillar, "Good Literature and Bad History: The 9/11 Commission's Tale of Strategic Intelligence," *Intelligence and National Security* 21, no. 6 (2006): 1029. On the 1995 estimate, see also George Tenet with Bill Harlow, *At the Center of the Storm: My Years at the CIA* (New York: HarperCollins, 2007), 104.

21. Pillar, "Good Literature and Bad History," 1029; Mark M. Lowenthal, "He Blames the Israel Lobby: But the Job Wasn't Worth It," *Washington Post*, March 15, 2009, B2.

22. Gina M. Bennett, *National Security Mom: Why "Going Soft" Will Make America Strong* (Deadwood, OR: Wyatt-MacKenzie, 2008), 20; Riedel, *Search for Al Qaeda*, 50–51.

23. *Joint Inquiry*, 4.

24. Central Intelligence Agency, "Usama Bin Laden: Islamic Extremist Financier," February 23, 1996, Digital National Security Archive, TE01108.

25. *Manhunt*, HBO, May 1, 2013.

26. Valerie Plame, "The Women of the CIA," *Daily Beast*, January 24, 2010, http:// www.thedailybeast.com/articles/2010/01/24/the-women-of-the-cia.html.

27. Interview with anonymous source, June 30, 2009.

28. Schmitt and Shanker, *Counterstrike*, 18; interview with anonymous source, June 30, 2009.

29. *Joint Inquiry*, 4.

30. Interview with anonymous source, June 30, 2009.

31. Tenet, *At the Center of the Storm*, 99–100.

32. Interview with anonymous source, September 14, 2011.

33. 9/11 Commission interview with David Cohen, June 21, 2004, http://cryptome.org/ nara/cia/cia-04-0621.pdf; Philip Shenon, *The Commission: The Uncensored History of the 9/11 Investigation* (New York: Twelve, 2008), 190; "Book Discussion on *Intelligence: A Novel of the CIA*," *C-SPAN Video Library*, November 20, 2010, http://www.c-spanvideo.org/pro gram/296686-7.

34. "In the Counterterrorism Center on 9/11: One Analyst's Story," *International Spy Museum*, September 9, 2011, http://www.spymuseum.org/multimedia/spycast/episode/in -the-counterterrorism-center-on-911-one-analysts-story/.

35. "Julie Sirrs, Former Defense Intelligence Agency Analyst, Talks about How US Officials Ignored Her Information about Bin Laden's Link to Taliban," ABC News, February 18, 2002, http://s3.amazonaws.com/911timeline/2002/abcnews021802b.html; Rep. Dana Rohrabacher, "9/11 Represented a Dramatic Failure of Policy and People," *Congressman Dana Rohrabacher*, June 21, 2004, http://rohrabacher.house.gov/News/DocumentSingle.aspx?Docu mentID = 17093.

36. Clarke, *Against All Enemies*, 148; 9/11 Commission, "The Performance of the Intelligence Community," Staff Statement No. 11, http://govinfo.library.unt.edu/911/staff

_statements/staff_statement_11.pdf; 9/11 Commission, "Diplomacy," Staff Statement No. 5, http://govinfo.library.unt.edu/911/staff_statements/staff_statement_5.pdf; United States District Court, Southern District of New York, "United States of America vs. Usama Bin Laden, et al.," February 6, 2001.

37. Pillar, "Good Literature and Bad History," 1030. See also Tenet, *At the Center of the Storm*, 104; 9/11 Commision, "Performance of the Intelligence Community." For a more negative view of the 1997 estimate, see Shenon, *Commission*, 314.

38. Coll, *Ghost Wars*, 366–67.

39. Tenet, *At the Center of the Storm*, 99.

40. Storer, "Analytical Challenges on al-Qaeda before 9/11," 3.

41. Coll, *Ghost Wars*, 405; e-mail from anonymous source, November 11, 2009.

42. See, e.g., Coll, *Ghost Wars*, chap. 27.

43. Ibid., 407–12.

44. 9/11 Commission, "Performance of the Intelligence Community."

45. Ibid.

46. Quoted in *Joint Inquiry*, 5–6.

47. Amy Zegart, *Spying Blind: The CIA, the FBI and the Origins of 9/11* (Princeton, NJ: Princeton University Press, 2007), 81–82; 9/11 Commission interview with NSA official [name redacted], November 6, 2003, http://cryptome.org/nara/nsa/nsa-03-1106-2.pdf; 9/11 Commission interview with Mark Steinitz.

48. Tenet, *At the Center of the Storm*, 122–23.

49. Ibid., 124–26; Bennett, *National Security Mom*, 22.

50. *9/11 Commission Report*, 259.

51. *Manhunt*, HBO, May 1, 2013.

52. Betts, *Enemies of Intelligence*, 106–7.

53. Tenet, *At the Center of the Storm*, 149–50.

54. Philip Mudd, *Takedown: Inside the Hunt for Al Qaeda* (Philadelphia: University of Pennsylvania Press, 2013), 31.

55. Liora Dana and Alice E. Hunt, "How Did the U.S. Government Look at Islam after 9/11?," in *The Impact of 9/11 on Religion and Philosophy: The Day That Changed Everything?*, ed. Matthew J. Morgan (New York: Palgrave Macmillan, 2009), 52.

56. Melissa Boyle Mahle, *Denial and Deception: An Insider's View of the CIA* (New York: Nation Books, 2004), 335.

57. Central Intelligence Agency, Office of Public Affairs, *Devotion to Duty: Responding to the Terrorist Attacks of September 11*, December 2010, 29–30, https://www.cia.gov/library/publications/resources/devotion-to-duty/15601-pub-FINAL-web.pdf.

58. DCI Tenet, "We're at War," Central Intelligence Agency, September 16, 2001, http://www.foia.cia.gov/sites/default/files/document_conversions/89801/DOC_0001260492.pdf.

59. Interview with anonymous source, June 30, 2009; Tenet, *At the Center of the Storm*, 342.

60. Carle, *Interrogator*, 293–94; interview with anonymous source, August 31, 2011.

61. Mudd, *Takedown*, 33.

62. Ibid., 54.

63. Graf, *Threat Matrix*, 344; 9/11 Commission interview with Maj. Gen. Ronald Burgess, November 10, 2003, http://cryptome.org/nara/dod/dod-03-1110.pdf.

64. Graf, *Threat Matrix*, 19.

65. Carle, *Interrogator*, 274, 294–95.

66. Tenet, *At the Center of the Storm*, 231–32; Bob Woodward, *Plan of Attack: The Definitive Account of the Decision to Invade Iraq* (New York: Simon & Schuster, 2004), 52–53.

67. Jack L. Goldsmith, *The Terror Presidency: Law and Judgment inside the Bush Administration* (New York: Norton, 2007), 72.

68. Graf, *Threat Matrix*, 426.

69. Mudd, *Takedown*, 68–69; Sasha Talcott, "Spotlight with Rolf Mowatt-Larssen," Belfer Center for Science and International Affairs, John F. Kennedy School of Government, Harvard University, Spring 2010, http://belfercenter.ksg.harvard.edu/publication/19964/spotlight_with_rolf_mowattlarssen.html.

70. George W. Bush, *Decision Points* (New York: Crown, 2010), 144.

71. Tenet, *At the Center of the Storm*, 259–80; Woodward, *Plan of Attack*, 46–47; George Tenet, "DCI Threat Testimony: Converging Dangers in a Post-9/11 World," *News and Testimony*, February 6, 2002, https://www.cia.gov/news-information/speeches-testimony/2002/senate_select_hearing_03192002.html; Schmitt and Shanker, *Counterstrike*, 27; Mudd, *Takedown*, 66.

72. Mudd, *Takedown*, 64.

73. Senate Select Committee on Intelligence, *Postwar Findings about Iraq's WMD Programs and Links to Terrorism and How They Compare with Prewar Assessments*, 109th Cong., September 8, 2006, 75–76, 82.

74. Senate Select Committee on Intelligence, *Postwar Findings about Iraq's WMD Programs*, 76–82.

75. Mudd, *Takedown*, 65.

76. For an example of a pre-9/11 SEIB article pertaining to Al-Qaeda support networks in the United States, see *Joint Inquiry*, 171.

77. Tenet, *At the Center of the Storm*, 239.

78. Ibid., 244; Dina Temple-Raston, *The Jihad Next Door: The Lackawanna Six and Rough Justice in an Age of Terror* (New York: PublicAffairs, 2007), 3.

79. 9/11 Commission interview with Mark Steinitz, September 25, 2003.

80. Gary Berntsen, *Jawbreaker: The Attack on Bin Laden and Al Qaeda; A Personal Account by the CIA's Key Field Commander* (New York: Crown, 2005), 7; interview with anonymous source, June 30, 2009; George Tenet, "DCI Testimony before the Joint Inquiry into Terrorist Attacks against the United States," Central Intelligence Agency, June 18, 2002, https://www.cia.gov/news-information/speeches-testimony/2002/dci_testimony_06182002.html; Bootie Cosgrove-Mather, "FTN—5/11/03," *Face the Nation*, May 11, 2003, http://www.cbsnews.com/stories/2003/05/12/ftn/main553425.shtml.

81. Storer, "Analytical Challenges on al-Qaeda before 9/11," 5.

82. Tenet, "DCI Threat Testimony"; George Tenet, "The Worldwide Threat Testimony in 2003: Evolving Dangers in a Complex World," *News and Information*, February 11, 2003, https://www.cia.gov/news-information/speeches-testimony/2003/dci_speech_02112003.html. See Donald Rumsfeld, *Known and Unknown: A Memoir* (New York: Sentinel, 2011), 374, with regard to Deputy Secretary of Defense Paul Wolfowitz.

83. See, e.g., *9/11 Commission Report*, 61, 66.

84. *9/11 Commission Report*, 228–29. After the invasion of Iraq, American forces captured the Iraqi intelligence officer. He denied having met with Atta, and the Czechs also backed off from the story. James Risen, "Iraqi Agent Denies He Met 9/11 Hijacker in Prague before Attacks on the U.S.," *New York Times*, December 13, 2003.

85. Tenet, *At the Center of the Storm*, 344–45; Senate Select Committee on Intelligence, *Report on the U.S. Intelligence Community's Prewar Intelligence Assessments on Iraq*, 108th Cong., 2nd sess., July 9, 2004, 304–7. Sen. Carl Levin has released a copy of the "Murky Relationship" paper, heavily redacted by the CIA: Central Intelligence Agency, "Iraq and al-Qaeda: Interpreting a Murky Relationship," June 21, 2002, https://web.archive.org/web/20050427004036/http://levin.senate.gov/newsroom/supporting/2005/CIAreport.062102.pdf.

86. Senate Select Committee on Intelligence, *Report on the U.S. Intelligence Community's Prewar Intelligence Assessments on Iraq*, 313–14.

87. Department of Defense, Inspector General, *Review of the Pre-Iraqi War Activities of the Office of the Under Secretary of Defense for Policy*, February 9, 2007, 11, https://web.archive.org/web/20070601004502/http://levin.senate.gov/newsroom/supporting/2007/SASC.DODIGFeithreport.040507.pdf.

88. Madeleine Albright with Bill Woodward, *The Mighty and the Almighty: Reflections on America, God, and World Affairs* (New York: HarperCollins, 2006); Edward Luttwak, "The Missing Dimension," in *Religion: The Missing Dimension of Statecraft*, ed. Douglas Johnston and Cynthia Sampson (New York: Oxford University Press, 1995), 8–19; Thomas F. Farr, *World of Faith and Freedom: Why International Religious Liberty Is Vital to American National Security* (New York: Oxford University Press, 2008), 31–32 and 247–48; Stephen P. Lambert, *Y: The Sources of Islamic Revolutionary Conduct* (Washington, DC: Joint Military Intelligence College, 2005), part 1.

89. Jonathan E. Shaw, *The Role of Religion in National Security Policy since September 11, 2001* (Carlisle, PA: US Army War College, Strategic Studies Institute, 2011), 1; Pauletta Otis, "Religion and War in the Twenty-First Century," in *Religion and Security: The New Nexus in International Relations*, ed. Robert A. Seiple and Dennis R. Hoover (Lanham, MD: Rowman & Littlefield, 2004), 13–14.

90. US Embassy Cairo (1989) 05506, *IntelWire*, http://intelfiles.egoplex.com/1989-03-08-gamaat-guide.pdf.

91. Liora Danan and Alice Hunt, *Mixed Blessings: U.S. Government Engagement with Religion in Conflict-Prone Settings* (Washington, DC: Center for Strategic and International Security, August 2007), 24; Farr, *World of Faith and Freedom*, 31–32 and 247–48; John D. Stempel, Patterson School of Diplomacy and International Commerce, "The Impact of Religion on Intelligence" (paper prepared for the International Studies Association conference, Montreal, March 15, 2004).

92. Reuel Marc Gerecht, "Mirror-Imaging the Mullahs: Our Islamic Interlocutors," *World Affairs* 170, no. 3 (2008): 93.

93. Sayyid Qutb, *Milestones*, 112, https://web.archive.org/web/20121222082712/http://bandung2.co.uk/books/Files/Politics/Milestones.pdf.

94. Interview with anonymous source, July 31, 2009. See also Gerecht, "Mirror-Imaging the Mullahs," 93.

95. Ellen Laipson, "While America Slept: Understanding Terrorism and Counterterrorism," *Foreign Affairs* 82, no. 1 (2003): 147.

96. Center for the Study of Intelligence Conference Report, *Intelligence for a New Era in American Foreign Policy*, Charlottesville, VA, September 10–11, 2003, 1, http://www.fas.org/irp/cia/product/newera.pdf.

97. E-mail from anonymous source, July 21, 2011; interview with anonymous source, August 17, 2011; interview with anonymous source, August 18, 2011.

98. "US Is Battling Satan, Says General," *BBC News*, October 17, 2003, http://news.bbc .co.uk/2/hi/americas/3199212.stm.

99. Stephen C. Coughlin, *To Our Great Detriment: Ignoring What Extremists Say about Jihad* (Washington, DC: National Defense Intelligence College, July 2007), 224.

100. Lambert, *Y*, xvi.

101. Dana and Hunt, *Mixed Blessings*, 24.

102. Lambert, *Y*, xv–xvi, 130.

103. William Gawthrop, "The Sources and Patterns of Terrorism in Islamic Law," *The Vanguard: The Journal of the Military Intelligence Corps Association* 11, no. 4 (2006): 9–10.

104. Coughlin, *To Our Great Detriment*, 18.

105. George Tenet, "The Worldwide Threat 2004: Challenges in a Changing Global Context," *News and Information*, February 24, 2004, https://www.cia.gov/news-information/ speeches-testimony/2004/dci_speech_02142004.html.

106. Jonathan Shainen, "The Ziggurat of Zealotry," *New York Times Magazine*, December 10, 2006.

107. Interview with anonymous source, June 30, 2009.

108. National Intelligence Council, "Declassified Key Judgments of the National Intelligence Estimate 'Trends in Global Terrorism: Implications for the United States' dated April 2006," *Federation of American Scientists*, http://www.fas.org/irp/dni/trends.pdf.

109. Daniel Benjamin, "Testimony before the Emerging Threats and Capabilities Subcommittee of the Senate Armed Services Committee," Washington, DC, March 10, 2010, *US Department of State*, https://web.archive.org/web/20100313132152/http://www.state .gov/s/ct/rls/rm/2010/138175.htm.

110. President Barack Obama, *National Strategy for Counterterrorism*, White House, June 2011, 3.

111. "CIA Chief Panetta: Obama Made 'Gutsy' Decision on Bin Laden Raid," *PBS Newshour*, May 3, 2011, http://www.pbs.org/newshour/bb/terrorism/jan-june11/panetta_05-03 .html.

112. Greg Miller, "Bin Laden Document Trove Reveals Strain on al-Qaeda," *Washington Post*, July 1, 2011.

113. Mathieu Rabechault, "Strategic Defeat of al Qaeda 'within Reach': Panetta," AFP, July 9, 2011, https://sg.news.yahoo.com/us-defense-chief-panetta-surprise-visit-kabul-afp -002235112.html.

114. "ASF 2011 Counterterrorism: Past, Present, and Future with Michael Leiter," Aspen Institute, http://www.aspeninstitute.org/video/counterterrorism-past-present-future-mich ael-leiter.

115. Massimo Calabresi, "Ex-CIA Counterterror Chief: 'Enhanced Interrogation Led US to Bin Laden," *Time*, May 4, 2011; Richard Miniter, *Mastermind: The Many Faces of 9/11 Architect Khalid Shaikh Mohammed* (New York: Sentinel, 2011), 176–80.

116. Carle, *Interrogator*, 297–98.

117. May, *Knowing One's Enemies*, 541–42.

118. Mark M. Lowenthal, *Intelligence: From Secrets to Policy*, 4th ed. (Washington, DC: CQ Press, 2009), 3.

119. May, *Knowing One's Enemies*, 503–4.

120. For instance, see Schmitt and Shanker, *Counterstrike*, chaps. 6 and 10.

Conclusion

Intelligence and Policy

PAUL MADDRELL

THIS COLLECTION DEMONSTRATES that during the Cold War, intelligence was only one influence on policy among many. More is known about its influence in the West than in the East, but the evidence presented in this book is that in the West, more than in the East, intelligence was a significant factor in making policymakers less prone to exaggeration and misjudgment. Decision makers established the policy framework in which intelligence operated; intelligence won influence by providing good answers to questions raised by this set of policies.[1] Intelligence sustained, rather than undermined, the policy framework; it did not call for radical policy change in either East or West. The most important mindset of all shared by policymakers and intelligence analysts was that the Cold War had to be waged.[2] Michael Herman has rightly called for realistic expectations of intelligence during the Cold War, arguing that the importance of intelligence, as a force multiplier, is greatest in war.[3] The Cold War between the superpowers never became a real war between them, so the main task of intelligence from 1945 to 1990 was to prepare armed forces for a war that, mercifully, they did not have to fight.

How much influence intelligence had depended on the character of the government it served. The PGU and HVA departments "analyzing" foreign intelligence in the Soviet Union and East Germany, respectively, were principally news services; their main task was to summarize and distribute information. The lesson of the volume is that the more intelligence tries to satisfy the wishes of policymakers, the less genuine influence it has over policy. It merely becomes ammunition for a policy debate, supporting particular positions already held by policymakers.[4] Consequently, intelligence had no influence over the Soviet regime's understanding of the United States. Quite the opposite: Ideological hostility toward the United States was so strong that intelligence had to provide evidence to justify it. This affected both the collection and assessment of intelligence. Its influence over Soviet foreign policy initiatives was small. It often seems to have had influence

279

not because it moderated but because it reinforced Soviet leaders' existing outlook. For instance, in 1962 Nikita Khrushchev was fearful of American aggression; false intelligence reports about American preparations for a nuclear first strike on the USSR heightened his fear and encouraged him to order the deployment of medium- and intermediate-range nuclear missiles to Cuba.[5] The Communist Party's general secretaries were so powerful that they could disregard intelligence.

Intelligence on the outside world seems to have had little influence on the policy of the East German communist regime. It had some, though. One example is the intelligence obtained by the HVA on Willy Brandt's eastern policy from one of the chancellor's assistants, Günter Guillaume. It diminished the GDR leadership's suspicion of Brandt and his overtures toward them. Much of this suspicion derived from ideological misunderstanding and simple wishful thinking; Erich Honecker interpreted Brandt's first overtures toward the GDR as subversive and as reflecting a capitalist crisis in West Germany.[6] Guillaume's information helped to persuade the East German leaders that, while better relations with West Germany involved the risk of destabilizing their regime, Brandt was genuinely offering a measure of cooperation that would also strengthen it.[7]

Encouraged by the gravity of the threats facing Israel, the country's intelligence agencies have a culture of professionalism and independence of mind that has saved them from the obsequiousness of their communist counterparts. Nevertheless, aggressive political leaders in Israel have tried to bully their intelligence services into supplying analyses supportive of their policies.[8] It is unlikely that such an aggressive, Indophobic policy actor as Pakistan's Inter-Services Intelligence Directorate supplies its government with objective intelligence. Indeed, it has subordinated intelligence collection and analysis to organizing guerrilla warfare. In West Germany during the Cold War, as Matthias Uhl shows, the BND had a very poor relationship with its government; the government was skeptical of its analyses. Uhl does not show any influence on policy; it is unlikely that the service's intelligence had much. Its primary task was, anyway, to give warning of attack.

Intelligence's record of influencing policy is better in the United States than elsewhere. Richard Kerr's assessment has been referred to in the introduction to this volume. During the Cold War, the US intelligence community tried harder than its communist counterparts to educate policymakers and challenge their thinking. Ben Fischer maintains that National Intelligence Estimates had no effect on policy. They reflected, rather than initiated, changes in official thinking in Washington. NIEs reflected policy in the 1970s in arguing that détente would enable the United States to influence the USSR's international conduct; they also did so in the late 1980s in overestimating Gorbachev's staying power. (By contrast, the analyses of the CIA's Office of Soviet Analysis [SOVA] made the George H. W. Bush administration fully aware of the deterioration in Gorbachev's political position in the years 1989–91 and of his vulnerability to a coup. When the coup came, in August 1991, SOVA rightly maintained that there was a strong chance that it would fail.[9])

While NIEs may have had no influence on US policy in the late Cold War, other forms of intelligence did have an impact. The intelligence obtained from the British agent in the KGB's First Chief Directorate, Oleg Gordievsky, on Soviet fear of an American first strike prompted President Ronald Reagan, from late in 1983, to moderate his aggressive rhetoric about the USSR. Economic intelligence was a valuable influence on him as well. It persuaded him, in the mid-1980s, that Gorbachev's economic reforms were aggravating, rather than alleviating, the Soviet Union's economic difficulties; that the Soviet leader needed arms control; and that arms control negotiations were therefore worth pursuing.[10]

Intelligence may well have more influence on counterterrorism policy. American leaders were encouraged to trust their own judgment in determining Cold War policy by the lack of intelligence on Soviet leaders' intentions. American presidents also met their Soviet counterparts, which further encouraged them to trust their judgment. They do not meet terrorist leaders; such contacts are therefore no longer a rival influence to intelligence. Terrorism, as a hidden threat, is one which intelligence is particularly well suited to explaining to policymakers. Mark Stout demonstrates that intelligence on jihadism has influenced US policy, making clear to policymakers that jihadists are a small minority and that most Muslim opinion does not favor this course. This has encouraged the US government to take nonviolent measures to prevent radicalization.

Notes

1. Lawrence D. Freedman, *US Intelligence and the Soviet Strategic Threat*, 2nd ed. (Basingstoke, UK: Macmillan, 1986), 190.

2. See Raymond Garthoff, "Foreign Intelligence and the Historiography of the Cold War," *Journal of Cold War Studies* 6, no. 2 (Spring 2004): 40–41.

3. Michael Herman, "Intelligence Effects on the Cold War: Some Reflections," in *Did Intelligence Matter in the Cold War?*, ed. Michael Herman, J. Kenneth McDonald, and Vojtech Mastny (Oslo, Norway: Institutt for Forsvarsstudier, no. 1 [2006]), 38–41.

4. See Freedman, *US Intelligence and the Soviet Strategic Threat*, 192–94.

5. Christopher M. Andrew and Vasili Mitrokhin, *The Mitrokhin Archive: The KGB in Europe and the West* (London: Allen Lane / Penguin, 1999), 722.

6. Hermann Wentker, *Außenpolitik in engen Grenzen: Die DDR im internationalen System 1949–1989* (Munich: Oldenbourg Verlag, 2007), 322.

7. Markus Wolf, *Spionagechef im geheimen Krieg* (Munich: List Verlag, 1997), 267–68.

8. Uri Bar-Joseph, "A Bull in a China Shop: Netanyahu and Israel's Intelligence Community," *International Journal of Intelligence and CounterIntelligence* 11, no. 2 (Summer 1998): 154–74.

9. Christopher M. Andrew, *For the President's Eyes Only: Secret Intelligence and the American Presidency from Washington to Bush* (London: HarperCollins, 1995), 505–7, 510–11, 518, 526–30.

10. Ibid., 475–77, 494–95.

CONTRIBUTORS

Benjamin B. Fischer served in the Central Intelligence Agency for more than thirty years and retired as chief historian.

Raymond L. Garthoff has been a close observer of Soviet policy since 1945, first as a student at Princeton and Yale, then in the 1950s as an analyst at RAND and the Central Intelligence Agency. In the 1960s and 1970s, he served as a US Department of State Foreign Service officer and ambassador, and since 1980 he has been a diplomatic historian of the Cold War as a senior fellow at the Brookings Institution and in retirement. He is the author of numerous books, articles, and other contributions on Soviet affairs.

Tamir Libel is a postdoctoral teaching fellow in the Intelligence and National Security Studies Program at the University of Texas.

Paul Maddrell is a lecturer in modern history and international relations at Loughborough University in the United Kingdom. His most recent book is *Spying on Science: Western Intelligence in Divided Germany, 1945–1961* (Oxford University Press, 2006).

Eunan O'Halpin is professor of contemporary Irish history at Trinity College Dublin. His most recent book is *Spying on Ireland: British Intelligence and Irish Neutrality during the Second World War* (Oxford University Press, 2008).

Julian Richards is senior lecturer in security studies at Buckingham University in the United Kingdom and codirector of the university's Centre for Security and Intelligence Studies. He has written three books on intelligence analysis and national security. Before joining Buckingham, he worked for the British intelligence community.

Shlomo Shpiro is professor and head of the Political Studies Department at Bar-Ilan University in Israel and chairman of the International Intelligence History Association.

Mark Stout is the director of the MA in Global Security Studies and the Graduate Certificate in Intelligence programs at Johns Hopkins University's Krieger School of Arts and Sciences in Washington, DC. He has worked at the Central Intelligence Agency and the Bureau of Intelligence and Research at the US Department of State. His doctorate is from the University of Leeds.

Matthias Uhl is a well-known German historian who has published extensively on the history of the Cold War and the history of intelligence. Since July 2005 he has been a senior researcher at the German Historical Institute in Moscow.

INDEX